W9-APM-385

CONTEMPORARY SCHOOL ADMINISTRATION

AN INTRODUCTION

THEODORE J. KOWALSKI
Ball State University

ULRICH C. REITZUG
University of Wisconsin—Milwaukee

Longman
New York & London

Contemporary School Administration

Longman, 10 Bank Street, White Plains, N.Y. 10606

Associated companies:
Longman Group Ltd., London
Longman Cheshire Pty., Melbourne
Longman Paul Pty., Auckland
Copp Clark Pitman, Toronto

Acquisitions editor: Laura McKenna
Development editor: Virginia Blanford
Production editor: Dee Amir Josephson
Cover design: David Levy
Production supervisor: Joanne Jay

Library of Congress Cataloging-in-Publication Data

Kowalski, Theodore J.
    Contemporary school administration : an introduction / by Theodore
J. Kowalski and Ulrich C. Reitzug.
        p.   cm.
    Includes index.
    ISBN 0-8013-0832-1
    1. School management and organization—United States.
    2. Leadership.   3. Education—Social aspects—United States.
    I. Reitzug, Ulrich C.,   II. Title.
    LB2805.K635   1992
371.2'00973—dc20   92-27033
                                                                        CIP

1 2 3 4 5 6 7 8 9 10-HA-9594939291

Contents

Alternate Table of Contents

Illustrations

Preface

Ever since 1983, educators have been bombarded with recommendations for change. The products have been uncertainty and promise. On the one hand, teachers and school administrators fear the unknown. The traditional frameworks that they experienced as students, and continue to experience as practitioners, provide substantial security. Transformation is a threat to safe and familiar beliefs, values, and practices that give meaning to their world of work. On the other hand, education has a rare opportunity to become a true profession—to move from a highly regulated occupation to one in which professional knowledge will be respected and rewarded. Thus, envisagements of empowered schools, environments in which teachers are treated as professionals and students receive instruction based on individual needs, are both intimidating and alluring.

School administrators will play a central role in transforming schools. They must be leaders who bring together teachers, parents, students, and others to create new instructional environments to meet needs that will extend into the twenty-first century. Predicated on this challenge, this book is an introduction to the study of administration in the context of school transformation.

Many individuals contributed to this effort. Diana Meyer, Vicki Villarreal, Roberta Cunningham, and Rick Bothel provided valuable assistance with the technical dimensions of the book. We are especially grateful to four professional colleagues for their insights and constructive criticisms: Professor Carvin Brown, University of Georgia; Professor John Daresh, University of Northern Colorado; Professor Lawrence Giandomenico, State University of New York, Plattsburgh; James Guthrie, University of California, Berkeley. Finally, we wish to thank our families—Mary Anne, Catherine, Christopher, Timothy, and Thomas Kowalski; and Mary, Ben, and Rebecca Reitzug—for their patience and support.

Introduction

In many respects, the future of public education is in doubt. National groups (e.g., New American Schools Development Corporation) are calling for "mold-breaking" concepts to reshape public schools; state-level initiatives are encouraging alternatives to traditional schools (e.g., Minnesota is permitting the creation of *charter schools,* schools that can be operated by licensed teachers under special charter from the state); and public schools in many parts of the country are facing increasing competition from private ventures because of concepts such as *choice* and the creation of *for-profit schools.* Although dissatisfaction, criticism, and reform initiatives are not novel to American education, efforts to transform elementary and secondary education that commenced in the early 1980s appear to be more than just another cycle of "education bashing." School reform has become a national issue, and the transformation of public education now appears to be a distinct possibility.

Two major purposes of this book are to (1) acquaint you with issues and trends that are likely to shape tomorrow's schools and (2) exhibit how these issues and trends affect the practice of school administration. This information provides a foundation for academic study in school administration and enhances your ability to make informed decisions regarding your professional career.

The attention given to career-related topics is one of the features that make this book truly unique. Students taking an introductory course in school administration frequently do so without fully knowing whether they want to enter this challenging area of education. A decision to continue studies in school administration should not be impulsive, nor should it be based on your experiences in a single course. Rather, your decision should be predicated on three critical pieces of information: (1) a complete understanding of yourself, (2) knowledge of school administration as a profession, and (3) knowledge of schools as a workplace.

Another unique feature of this book is the discussion of contemporary topics that are redirecting the preparation of school administrators and role expectations for practitioners. Examples include national initiatives to reform graduate study; licensing; demographic realities relating to society, women, and minorities; teacher empowerment; private education; and the infusion of ethics and morality into administration.

Core information commonly addressed in the introductory study of school administration also is included. Examples of this coverage include a history of public education and administration, the organizational context of schooling, leadership, and a review of the various jobs included in school administration. The depth of presentation is sufficient to prepare you to continue your studies in more narrowly focused courses.

There are five parts to the book. The first provides an overview of educational leadership as a field of study and a specialization within a profession. Topics such as the nature of administrative work, professional preparation, licensure, and job opportunities are covered. The next part focuses on the work environments of administrators. Here topics such as the origins and control of public education and the relationship of schools to society are discussed. The third part looks at leadership challenges and responsibilities in educational settings. A special focus is given to leadership styles. Part IV explores contemporary issues that affect schooling and the practice of school administration. Transitions in society, issues surrounding women and minorities in school administration, and school reform are topics addressed in this portion of the book. The final section examines career decisions and commitments.

Each chapter concludes with a section titled "Implications for Practice." This material is designed to engage you in introspection—to prompt you to consider how the chapter content relates to your personal needs and interests. To do this, you need to identify your personal frame of reference—your values, beliefs, needs, experiences, motivations, wants, and so forth. Relating the information provided here to your personal frame of reference spawns the process of reflection. A major intention of this book is not to have you consume and memorize information; rather, it is to make you think about information in the context of schooling, society, and yourself.

PART I
An Overview

CHAPTER 1

A Perspective of Educational Administration

Chapter Content

Defining Leadership, Management, and Administration

The Organizational Context of Schools

The Evolution of School Administration

Contemporary Conditions

Implications for Practice

> *The greatest mistake you can make in life is to be continually fearing you will make one.*
>
> —*Elbert Hubbard*

In every organization there are leaders. Many are individuals who possess and exercise authority by virtue of the positions they hold. But there are others who have claim to neither title nor legitimate power yet still exert influence over the behaviors of peers and even supervisors. When we think about leadership, however, we usually envision only those individuals who occupy high-level management or supervisory positions.

Increasingly, men and women who lead major organizations exhibit differing philosophies, priorities, and administrative styles. This condition produces variant approaches to administration that interact with organizational dynamics and specific tasks to produce a range of subordinate behaviors. Often it is quite difficult to isolate the precise influence of a leader's behavior on organizational outcomes; nevertheless, informal observations and research findings are providing a growing body of knowledge that helps us to understand this relationship. The more we learn about leadership, the less likely we are to accept stereotypical perceptions that suggest philosophical and behavioral uniformity among these individuals.

This book is an introduction to the study of administration in educational systems and individual schools. The content explores the meanings of leadership and management, the environment of contemporary schools, the range of practice, and careers in school administration. In many chapters, contrasts are made between past practices and contemporary conditions. These comparisons are especially cogent given the continuing efforts to reform elementary and secondary education. Also, unceasing efforts to restructure schools has placed the practice of school administration at a critical juncture. Debates persist with regard to professional preparation, entry into the profession, and the nature of practice.

Educational administration has matured as a specialization over the past seventy years. Academically, this field of study and practice has evolved in stages. Early years were marked by a preoccupation with management practices deemed to be responsible for the advancement of American industry. More recently, subjects such as ethics, human behavior, policy analysis, and organizational theory have taken their place in the curriculum.

As you read this book, you will come to understand challenges, opportunities, and complexities inherent in the practice of school administration. You will be exposed to evolutionary elements of public education in America as well as contemporary demands placed on principals and superintendents. This first chapter provides definitions and traces developmental changes that have occurred from the first days of school administration to present conditions.

DEFINING LEADERSHIP, MANAGEMENT, AND ADMINISTRATION

One of the difficulties you are likely to confront in reading books and journals focusing on educational administration is the varying uses of the terms *leadership, management,* and *administration.* The problem stems from disparate meanings given to these three words. Although some authors refer to them loosely as if all shared a common definition, others go to great lengths to distinguish among them (Hanson, 1985). Context does not ensure clarification. Take for example the meanings of *leadership.* In describing the practice of school administration, some writers use the term broadly to include both administrators and those who hold no formal position but influence the behavior of others (e.g., influential teachers); others use the word as if it were synonymous with management; and researchers tend to define it according to their individual perspective and the aspect of the phenomenon that most interests them (Yukl, 1989). In view of the multiple meanings given to *leadership, administration,* and *management,* a review of definitions is provided.

First, let us examine several definitions of leadership. Some focus on achieving improved organizational performance:

> The essence of leadership is found in a person's ability to move an organization from state A to state B, that is to a higher level of performance. (Hitt, 1988, p. 6)

Some emphasize both the process of directing the human element of an organization and the actualization of organizational goals:

> Leadership is influencing people to follow in the achievement of a common goal. (Koontz & O'Donnell, 1959, p. 435)

> Leadership is the activity of influencing people to strive willingly for group objectives. (Terry, 1960, p. 493)

And still others include the formulation of organizational goals, motivation of individuals to achieve those goals, and influence over the prevailing values and beliefs commonly held by those in the organization:

> . . . leadership is defined broadly to include influence processes involving determination of the group's or organization's objectives, motivating task behavior in pursuit of these objectives, and influencing group maintenance and culture. (Yukl, 1989, p. 5)

Despite differences, there are recurring themes in these definitions. These common elements suggest that leadership involves a social influence process in which a person steers members of a group or organization toward a specific goal (Bryman, 1986). The concept of leadership used in this book incorporates an emphasis on the development goals, that is, providing leadership in determining the direction(s) for the organization. Thus, *leadership* is defined here as a process that: (1) results in the determination of organizational objectives and strategies, (2) entails building consensus for meeting those objectives, and (3) involves influencing others to work toward those objectives.

In research studies and other writings, authors often separate management and leadership. Yukl (1989) pointed out:

> It is obvious that a person can be a leader without being a manager, and a person can be a manager without leading. Indeed, some managers do not even have subordinates (e.g., a manager of financial accounts). (p. 4)

Management typically encompasses worker supervision, supervision of resources, and resolving conflicts that interfere with the efficient achievement of goals (Orlosky, McCleary, Shapiro, & Webb, 1984). It does not necessarily include activities associated with long-range planning, setting goals and objectives, and setting organizational priorities. Here *management* is defined as the process of implementing strategies and controlling resources in an effort to achieve organizational objectives.

Distinctions between managers and leaders are not always made on the basis of formal roles or job descriptions. A person's orientation toward the world, people, and work also has been examined. Zaleznik (1989), for example, contends that managers and leaders differ in their perceptions regarding the value of others and the degree to which they concentrate on their own accomplishments. He wrote:

> Career-oriented managers are more likely to exhibit the effects of narcissism than leaders. While busily adapting to their environment, managers are narrowly engaged in maintaining their identity and self-esteem through others, whereas leaders have self-confidence growing out of the awareness of who they are and the visions that drive them to achieve. (p. 6)

Such observations suggest that leaders possess certain values, beliefs, and personality traits that distinguish them from career-oriented managers.

A number of administrative theorists also distinguish leadership from administration (e.g., Sergiovanni, 1991b). When such differentiations are made, administration is usually perceived as a management activity; that is, the distinctions between administration and leadership are essentially the same as those made between management and leadership. In this book, school administration is viewed broadly to include both leadership and management. This conceptualization is evident in the following definition of school administration:

> . . . a specialized set of organizational functions whose primary purposes are to insure the efficient and effective delivery of relevant educational services as well as implementation of legislative policies through planning, decision making, and leadership behavior that keeps the organization focused on predetermined objectives, provides for optimum allocation and most prudent care of resources to insure their most productive uses, stimulates and coordinates professional and other personnel to produce a coherent social system and desirable organizational climate, and facilitates determination of essential changes to satisfy future and emerging needs of students and society. (Knezevich, 1984, p. 9)

This definition includes key words associated with leadership (e.g., *planning, decision making*) as well as management (e.g., *optimum allocation, care of resources*). The following description of school administrators also addresses both leadership and management:

> School administrators must be both managers and leaders. As managers they must ensure that fiscal and human resources are used effectively in accomplishing organizational goals. As leaders they must display the vision and skills necessary to create and maintain a suitable teaching and learning environment, to develop goals, and to inspire others to achieve these goals. (Guthrie & Reed, 1986, p. 199)

In this book, *administration* is defined as a process that encompasses both leadership and management responsibilities.

THE ORGANIZATIONAL CONTEXT OF SCHOOLS

Bob and Mary are products of the same graduate program in school administration. Both are now elementary school principals, but in very different communities. Bob works for a large urban school system, whereas Mary is employed in a small farming community. The degree to which they involve teachers in decision making differs markedly. Bob's behavior in this area is influenced by a union contract that stipulates precisely when teachers must be involved; Mary's faculty is not unionized. Bob's district has forty-five elementary schools; Mary's has only two. Mary approaches teacher involvement on a case-by-case basis, Bob involves teachers only when the union contract so stipulates. Even though the two principals were exposed to the same educational experiences in preparing to be administrators, their actual work behavior differs substantially. In part, these differences may be due to personal values and beliefs. But their behaviors are also influenced by the organizational environments in which they work.

In studying school administration, you should always remember that it occurs in an organizational context. Here, the term *organization* is used in a simple yet formal manner to mean a link between structures. As such, organization is defined as an integrated system of independent structures known as groups, and each of these groups consists of individuals (Berrien, 1976). Organizationally, schools and school districts are viewed as networks of groups (e.g., teachers, staff members, departments). These groups may be formal (i.e., they are recognized as a unit of the organization) or informal (i.e., groups not recognized within the formal structure of the organization).

You also should understand that the evolution of schools in American society played a major role in shaping school administration. The context in which an administrator must execute responsibilities helps to shape both theoretical and actual roles. In this regard, both leadership theory and organizational theory are critical to studying educational leadership. Both bodies of theory become inextricably linked in practice. Because of their importance, both leadership and organizations are discussed in detail in subsequent chapters. At this point, however, it is advantageous to understand how schools and school administration evolved.

THE EVOLUTION OF SCHOOL ADMINISTRATION

One-room schoolhouses were the norm in colonial America. The simple environments mirrored values and resources of those times. As the population increased, the country became more demographically heterogeneous. Population growth induced more and larger schools; and in urban areas, high concentrations of population encouraged the creation of school districts and the separation of grammar and high schools. As schools became larger, they required multiple faculty. This condition led to the practice of designating one of the instructors as "head" teacher—a teacher who has some authority over other faculty. This position of head teacher eventually became known as the *principal* and was the first office in American schools with administrative and supervisory duties (Brubacher, 1966). There was, however, little professional development of the principalship prior to the nineteenth century. Those who occupied the post relied on common sense and innate abilities to perform largely management-related tasks. In comparison to modern educational organizations, schools in colonial America were small and their programs narrow. Tasks such as curriculum coordination, faculty evaluations, and staff development were virtually non-existent. Administrative duties were rather simple and confined to managing resources—and often a portion of these tasks were performed by community volunteers rather than school personnel (Grieder, Pierce, & Jordan, 1969). For example, a group of citizens may have assumed responsibility for making needed repairs to the schoolhouse. During this era, communities were uncomplicated settlements of families; as a central agency in community life, schools enjoyed a rather high level of citizen support and involvement.

Corresponding with the development of cities was the creation of school districts. These larger, more complex organizational structures quickly developed needs to coordinate educational programs among individual schools and to manage resources systematically and efficiently. These novel duties resulted in one person assuming overall responsibility for the school system. The person appointed to this position became known as the superintendent of schools.

Larger city school systems possessed several characteristics not commonly found in rural schools, and these assets gave them educational advantages. For instance, larger student enrollments permitted greater specialization in instruction and a more diversified curriculum; social and cultural conditions of cities resulted in a greater emphasis on education; and a greater concentration of economic and cultural resources provided more material support for program development. School districts in the largest cities, such as Boston, New York, and Chicago, became lighthouses for public education. Superintendents in these urban systems emerged as prototypes for educational management, and their behaviors were admired and adopted by many principals and superintendents throughout the United States (Callahan, 1962).

By the 1920s, discussion of educational administration as a field of practice became common in textbooks and journal articles. Cubberley (1922), for example, enthusiastically described the opportunity in this emerging field of practice:

> School supervision represents a new profession, and one which in time will play a very important part in the development of American life. The opportunities offered in this new profession to men of strong character, broad sympathies, high purpose, fine culture, courage, exact training, and executive skill, and who are willing to take the time and spend the energy necessary to prepare themselves for large service, are to-day not excelled in any of the professions, learned or otherwise. (pp. 130–131)

The emergence of school administration as a specialization abetted the movement toward creating work environments in which clear divisions were made between management and teaching. This separation of responsibilities resulted in administrators having higher salaries and status than teachers. It also produced troublesome professional questions about the relationships of administrators and teachers that continue to be debated in contemporary reform initiatives.

Many early school administrators lacked specific training in their field, and few had completed graduate degrees. Those who found themselves in these positions relied on instinct, political savvy, experience, and a limited knowledge about peer practices. That era stands in sharp contrast to present-day conditions in which some reformers are advocating that all principals and superintendents possess a doctorate as a condition of licensure (National Policy Board for Educational Administration, 1989). Then, only men were considered fit to occupy superintendencies; today, many graduate programs in school administration enroll more women than men. Then, our largest city school systems were models of good practice; today, educational improvement is most challenging in urban schools plagued by poverty and a deterioration of community.

Many social, political, economic, and intellectual factors contribute to the current conditions of public education. Some of the more influential, such as inequities in state funding formulas, movement to a global economy, discriminatory practices, and the empowerment of teachers, are examined throughout this book. These same forces played essential roles in shaping contemporary administrative practice. But more precisely, the present state of school administration is the product of evolutionary stages in three interacting elements: academic study, certification, and practice.

Academic Study

Shortly after 1900, a period when American society was undergoing an industrial revolution, public schools became targets of extensive criticism. In particular, administrators were chastised for lacking management skills and scientific knowledge in their assigned duties. For the most part, those who were placed in managerial posts were teachers. Criteria used for selecting these individuals varied. Some were elevated to administration because they were perceived by school trustees, or others legally in control of the school, as possessing the qualities of a leader; some were selected because they were effective teachers; others were advanced because of political connections; and still others were promoted simply because they were men. School management in this era was a male-dominated occupation. (Virtually all women in administrative posts were elementary school principals.)

The adoption of scientific management by American private industry had a profound influence on the practice of educational administration. In the early twentieth century, a select number of education professors sought to establish school administration as a truly separate profession. These advocates believed that the acquisition of status and respect, similar to that accorded to other learned professions (e.g., law and medicine), would be an essential element of their quest. It was in this context that they focused on what were then highly publicized accomplishments of business management.

Captains of industry had gained public respect for creating massive industries, jobs, and profits largely by using techniques of organizational efficiency. Those who championed the movement of school administration made invidious comparisons and concluded that the same knowledge and techniques used in public education would produce more functional schools, lower-cost schools, and improved public perceptions. Ultimately, these gains would result in higher status for administrators (Callahan, 1962).

Prior to 1900, there were very few administration courses offered in schools and departments of education. The first two doctorates in this specialization were awarded by Columbia University in 1905 (Cooper & Boyd, 1987). Yet six years after conferring these inaugural degrees, the Teachers College of Columbia University offered only two courses in school administration—a practicum and a seminar. But starting in 1914, pressures to utilize management techniques to broaden the education of school executives forced Teachers College to give more attention to business methods, finance, and efficiency techniques. By 1917, offerings in educational administration at Columbia increased to eight courses. By 1927, the catalogue of this institution described the superintendent of schools as the general manager of the entire school system and claimed that the job compared with the best of older professions in business and industry (Callahan, 1962).

Following 1920, graduate school degrees and professional degrees in educational administration became more prominent. Although the Master of Arts (M.A.) and Doctor of Philosophy (Ph.D.) degrees had been offered by the graduate schools of established universities, such degrees were considered appropriate for those preparing to be professors and researchers. The establishment of schools of education encouraged the creation of professional degrees—degrees geared toward the needs of practitioners. Degrees such as the Master of Education (M.Ed.), Education Specialist (Ed.S.), and Doctor of Education (Ed.D.) emerged during this period.

During the 1940s, the study of educational administration in universities continued to grow. An increasing number of institutions during that decade started offering degrees in this specialization. Simultaneously, elementary and secondary schools were becoming more complex social organizations. Prominent figures in school administration at that time recognized two specific needs: (1) to provide graduate education for all who aspired to administrative positions at the school and school district levels and (2) to broaden the academic study of school administration through the infusion of theoretical content. The latter realization was particularly cogent since the preoccupation with management roles and skills prior to 1940 was a force that retarded the study of so taxing and demanding a subject as theory (Grieder, Pierce, & Jordan, 1969).

The incorporation of leadership and organizational theories into the curricula for degrees in school administration spawned arguments that continue even today. Observers of educational administration often characterize the field as having two divisions: one consisting of those who see practice as largely an art in which practical experiences are a prime source of practitioner knowledge, and the other composed of those who view practice as science requiring mastery of basic and theoretical knowledge. Interestingly, one criticism of educational administration, especially in its formative years, was a perceived preoccupation with practical matters and the application of management techniques developed in other disciplines. In this respect, the evolution of curricula in schools and colleges of education differ from most other professional schools. Medical schools, for instance, often were criticized for placing too much emphasis on scientific research while providing insufficient instruction related to the needs of common practice (Schon, 1987). The fact that professional schools have moved to incorporate both elements transmits a vital message about professional practice as a combination of art and science.

Today, professors of educational administration continue to consider potential improvements to professional studies. These considerations are prompted by new societal needs as well as unresolved issues of practice (e.g., the appropriate relationship between principals and teachers). Should graduate study emphasize managerial skills or problem-solving skills? Should programs produce practitioners or scholars?

Central to reform in professional preparation are lingering arguments as to whether school administration is science, an art, or a craft (Blumberg, 1989). The continuing existence of these queries is reflected in the less-than-uniform approach used by the approximately 500 institutions of higher education offering programs in school administration. Some institutions maintain an orientation toward preparing practitioners; others, especially elite research universities, continue to focus on the preparation of professors; and a small number of universities are attempting to provide both types of programs. Texas A&M University, for example, recently created an alternative to its traditional doctoral program—one designed to address the needs and interests of would-be practitioners (Hoyle, 1990). Similarly, Saint Louis University offers two separate doctorates with specialization in school administration. An Ed.D. program was added in the mid-1970s to provide an alternative for aspiring practitioners who did not want to pursue the more traditional Ph.D. program.

Even though preparation programs in educational administration have changed with regard to content and balancing theory-practice relationships (Miklos, 1983), these modifications have not totally resolved essential questions. Reformers continue to point out that in the real world of school administration, practitioners benefit from both theory and *craft knowledge* (knowledge and skills that evolve from practitioner experiences within a given profession). The key curricular challenge is not choosing between the two sources of knowledge; rather, it entails squarely joining them. In the past three decades, many scholars have advocated a professional school curriculum that appropriately integrates craft knowledge, theory, and practical experiences—particularly for the vast majority of students who eventually will become practitioners. Balancing professional studies in educational administration requires equalization along three continua:

$$\text{craft knowledge} \longrightarrow \text{theory}$$
$$\text{experiential training} \longrightarrow \text{classroom learning}$$
$$\text{management} \longrightarrow \text{leadership}$$

Departments of educational leadership often find it especially difficult to provide greater practical and experiential training without sacrificing academic study (Allison, 1989). This is evidenced by the fact that practitioners often complain that their advanced graduate studies were abstract and unrelated to problems faced in the real world. Murphy and Hallinger (1987) described this concern:

> Practitioners have become disillusioned by the failure of university programs to ground training procedures in the realities of the workplace and by their reluctance to treat content viewed useful by administrators. (p. 252)

Since many administration students are working in schools at the same time they are pursuing graduate studies, they often seek instruction that has applicability to their current work assignments. They prefer to study theory in an integrative fashion—one that links theory to practice.

Interests of students in professional programs do not always coincide with concerns raised by those who seek to transform public education. Whereas administration students tend to focus on current work-related problems, many of which are managerial in nature, reformers are more interested in recasting the role of practitioners. In this regard, the latter group repeatedly voices concern about the degree to which administration students are adequately prepared to be organizational leaders, especially in the realms of curriculum and instruction. A number of noted professors of school administration also note deficiencies in the academic preparation of practitioners, ranging from the lack of emphasis on study in curriculum and instruction (e.g., Murphy & Hallinger, 1987) to inadequate preparation in performance and program evaluation (e.g., Gerritz, Koppich, & Guthrie, 1984).

Goodlad (1990) noted that socialization as well as education is a powerful contributor to the enculturation of members to a profession. Thus, those who attempt to reform the preparation of school administrators do not restrict their attention to courses and teaching methods. They also explore values and beliefs of educational administration faculty and institutions, the social climate created by student interactions among themselves and with professors, and other issues that contribute to or detract from creating professionalism. These issues are visible in the following criticisms raised by Clark (1989):

- There are hundreds of institutions preparing administrators and the quality in these universities varies markedly.

- Few students pursue professional studies on a full-time basis. As a result, many of the benefits of traditional residency programs have been lost (e.g., creation of a cohort group, interaction with faculty).

- Many institutions have low admission standards and weak instructional programs—a condition that does not exist in prestigious professions.

In recent years, there has been a mounting interest in creating more rigorous standards for the study of school administration (e.g., higher admission standards, two-year residence programs). Such actions would make standards in school administration more like those in other professions. But efforts to seek higher levels of professionalization are not universally cheered. Sergiovanni (1991a), for one, warned that the escalation of degree requirements has a potential dark side. He contended that increasing requirements for professional preparation, especially if those requirements focus largely on managerial responsibilities, may further separate administrators from teachers by emphasizing their differences rather than their common interests and abilities.

What are the motives for suggesting that all principals possess a doctorate? If all principals are required to have a doctorate, what will be the content and scope of graduate study? These are particularly pressing questions given that the exact role of the next generation of school administrators remains uncertain. Consider two possible scenarios:

Scenario A: School administrators become more specialized in instructional practices and group decision making. Teachers gain stature and are given greater freedom to make critical instructional decisions. Faculty view the principal as a source of professional knowledge. The relationship between the principal and faculty is one of professional peers, not superior-subordinates. Yet, the principal continues to oversee managerial tasks, but much of this work is now completed by support staff or technology.

Scenario B: Reformed schools divide responsibilities into two major categories: instructional and managerial. Teachers assume much of the responsibility for decisions focusing on curriculum and instruction. Principals assume responsibility for managing physical resources. Principals oversee budgets, facilities, food programs, and the like. Their contacts with teachers are limited to functions where instructional programs require the use of resources.

Which of these scenarios is apt to produce more status and prestige for administrators? Which is more likely to evolve as political forces reshape American public education?

Within the arena of school reform, most concerns and criticisms of public education receive attention. Ideas calling for reordering authority and decision-making processes, such as school-site management, are already impacting curricula at some institutions. Yet, there remain many skeptics who believe that schools and the roles of administrators will remain essentially unchanged. These individuals resist attempts to revamp radically the academic preparation of the next generation of school administrators. In this environment of divided visions, the degree to which programs turn away from technical management and organizational studies toward curriculum, instruction, and evaluation is yet to be determined.

Certification

Certification of school administrators played a pivotal role in the evolution of preparation programs. During the 1920s, certification was advocated for two primary reasons: (1) many superintendents of that period had not taken a single college course in school administration, and (2) certification was perceived as one avenue for achieving professionalization. Certification is a responsibility of individual states, one usually assigned to state departments of education. By 1932, nearly half of the states had already adopted certification standards for administrators (Callahan, 1962).

As states adopted and refined certification requisites for the principalship and superintendency, the mandated quantity of graduate study was increased.

State certification standards gradually became more specific, even to the extent that individual courses were stipulated. The establishment of certification standards was central to the enhancement of educational administration as a specialized area of study within universities. By restricting practice to those who held proper certificates, state departments of education assured universities that students would enroll in their courses. In this regard, schools of education had a captive audience.

During the 1980s, certification of teachers and administrators became a popular target for state-level reformers. By 1985, twenty eight states had revised portions of professional certification and another sixteen states were considering such modifications (Stellar, 1985). Actual and recommended changes to certification standards did not flow in one direction. Although some states expanded licensing requirements, others tinkered with alternative certification (i.e., allowing individuals to enter practice without having completed a professional program of study). Alternative certification is not a popular concept among educators who see the process as yet another affirmation of society's indifference toward education as a profession. Those who seek nontraditional paths to entering the practice of school administrators usually cite one or more of the following three reasons:

1. There is a perceived or real shortage in the number of licensed professionals in a given state, and the problem can be solved most easily by allowing access to individuals who have not pursued traditional preparation.
2. School administration programs largely stress managerial tasks that many not prepared in education have mastered (e.g., persons holding an M.B.A. degree).
3. School administration programs simply are not necessary.

In New Jersey, for instance, an alternative certification plan for principals was largely based on a judgment that there was a need to reconceptualize the work principals ought to do (Jacobson, 1990).

To fully appreciate the importance of certification standards, one need only look at the association between such standards and the curricula of preparation programs. A late 1980s study reaffirmed that strong ties still exist between the two. For instance, continued emphasis on management skills in certification standards is paralleled by similar standards in degree requirements (Peterson & Finn, 1988). State universities are especially conscious of providing students with courses they will need to acquire licensing.

During the twentieth century, there has been an increase in degree requirements to enter the education profession. As will be discussed later in the book, some states now require the completion of an advanced graduate degree beyond the master's degree to be a school superintendent; and as already noted, some reform proposals even call for the doctorate to be required of all principals and superintendents. Historically, there have been those who have recommended higher degree levels (e.g., requiring a master's degree to become a teacher) as a means of either increasing professional status or decreasing the number of persons admitted to practice (e.g., Stinnett & Henson, 1982). Individual states are less than uniform on the issue of degree requirements. Added coursework and additional degrees are viewed as inputs, and many reformers believe that licensing should be based on outputs. For this reason, certification examinations and internships are receiving greater attention from state legislators and state boards of education than is the issue of increased degree requirements.

Practice

Pioneering practitioners in the early part of this century were expected to be effective managers and individuals of unquestionable character. Often we read about restrictions that were placed on female schoolteachers sixty years ago (e.g., not being able to wear lipstick or not being able to marry); however, we know much less about the expectations that existed for the men who occupied the top administrative position. Cubberley (1922) developed a lengthy list of characteristics that represented popular thought of what was necessary to become a superintendent in his day. He noted that this chief executive must:

- be clean and temperate
- be able to look men straight in the eye
- possess a sense of honor
- possess good manners
- not be prone to bragging
- avoid oracularism
- possess the solemnity and dignity of an owl
- possess a sense of humor
- be alert
- understand common human nature
- know when to keep silent
- be able to accept success without vainglory
- possess political skills
- be clever
- avoid being a "grouch"
- possess a level head
- know when to take the public into his confidence
- avoid falling victim to political tricks and the discoveries of wild-eyed reformers
- know how to accept defeat without being embittered.

Many contemporary administrators sarcastically comment that the public still seeks these qualities because they cling to a mythical image of an educational leader without fault.

Education historians (e.g., Butts & Cremin, 1953) noted that creating a professional orientation to the superintendency was not an easy task. State superintendents circa 1900, for example, were often considered political appointees, and this fact coupled with relatively short terms of office and low pay discouraged the best school leaders from pursuing these posts. The development of graduate study and the imposition of certification standards helped to create more positive public perceptions of school administrators. Gradually, the prestige and salaries of school superintendents increased. Large city systems often took pride in employing individuals who possessed the doctorate. In many urban systems, the superintendent was an individual who was respected—a father figure who had great influence in the community.

Following World War II, a number of significant demographic changes occurred in the United States. Suburbs started to develop, and this necessitated more schools. Often new schools and school districts were shaped by the belief that "bigger was better." School consolidation, which forced many small districts to merge into larger entities, reflected this philosophy. In 1962, Knezevich wrote:

> Only in extreme cases can districts with fewer than 1,000 enrolled pupils be justified. There is evidence to show that effective district structure is an important step toward the improvement of quality in education; there is a definite relationship between pupil achievement and school size; and there is considerable variability in the size of enrollments and geographic area of school districts in the United States. (p. 149)

The consolidation movement was extremely controversial because it pitted local control against efficiency and program expansion. In many parts of the United States, scars of forced consolidation are still evident. In addition to growth in urban and suburban areas and school consolidation, a third significant demographic variable was a rapidly rising birth rate. The "baby boomers" born in the years following World War II created an unprecedented need for more schools, more teachers, and more administrators. In the period from 1930 to 1980, approximately 90 percent of the local school districts in the United States were eliminated—yet, school enrollments almost doubled and the number of teachers increased by 250 percent (Knezevich, 1984).

As school districts became larger, an increasing number of them found it necessary to create centralized administrative positions to serve on the staff of the district superintendent. A model for this type of administrative structure existed in very large urban school systems (centralized administrative staffs existed in some of these urban districts as early as the start of the twentieth century). Large school systems also were heavily influenced by industrial developments in their environment; and as such, many embraced tenets of bureaucracy in designing administrative structures (Callahan, 1962). Thus, the creation of centralized administrative structures, both in large urban systems and in school districts that modeled them, was directed by a quest for efficiency (e.g., larger organizational units) and the subsequent adoption of bureaucratic ideals (Campbell, Cunningham, Nystrand, & Usdan, 1990). The traditional model became one where there was a division of labor with the division heads being considered specialists in the functions placed under their direct supervision. Finance and instruction/curriculum became the most common divisions, but others included buildings and grounds, pupil services, transportation services, and food services.

Individual schools, especially secondary schools, also were increasing in size following World War II. James B. Conant (1959) declared that any high school with fewer than 100 students in the graduating class was too small to provide a sufficiently diverse curriculum. Again, the message was, "bigger is better." Assistant principal positions became more common as administrative needs of larger schools made leadership more demanding.

During the movement toward larger organizational units, the managerial emphasis of school administration remained essentially intact. Values and beliefs adopted from private industry in the early 1900s often were viewed as even more critical as schools and school districts became increasingly complex. Over time, however, observers noted that administrative behavior was becoming more political and advocative. Their role was broadened to include that of spokesperson for children and public education. Often this additional responsibility of advocate was necessary to garner necessary levels of fiscal support. The dual role of organizational manager and political advocate made the practice of school administration more stressful (Hess, 1983).

CONTEMPORARY CONDITIONS

Administrators are expected to work toward common organizational goals and to preserve and propagate the values and beliefs of the organization. This latter task is accomplished through the enforcement of policy and the development of rules and regulations. Both general responsibilities, to provide direction and to assure implementation of goals, require the ability to affect worker behavior. They also require knowledge and skills in using resources, conducting planning, and completing evaluations. For the vast majority of school administrators, these charges must be carried out in the context of a public organization, a condition that makes practice in education substantially different from management in profit-seeking companies.

Traditionally, many school administrators relied on power inherent in their positions to control the behavior of subordinates. That is, a title carried with it an understood level of authority. School administrators rarely were challenged when they exercised position-related power prior to the 1960s; but the proliferation of teacher unions and collective bargaining changed that condition significantly. Today, educational leaders work under intricate conditions where initiatives and decisions are not only questioned by teachers and the general public, they often are overtly opposed.

In the first three or four decades of the twentieth century, policy, goals, and objectives typically were formulated by trustees or other influential citizens without benefit of professional direction. As already noted, administrators were viewed as managers, whose sole responsibility was to implement policy. Today, school officials are expected to be experts in management and leadership. They are presumed to be skilled in working with people and to possess planning skills. National reform reports have been especially harsh in noting that administrators have not provided adequate direction for reshaping schools to meet emerging needs of society.

In an unstable environment (an environment experiencing modifications), administrators are expected to personally support change, and they are expected to inspire others to become change agents. Bennis and Nanus (1985) alluded to this reality when they wrote:

> The new leader is one who commits people to action, who converts followers into leaders, and who may convert leaders into agents of change. (p. 3)

Initiatives such as teacher empowerment and school-based management are indicative of concepts that are modifying role expectations for all professional educators. There are growing expectations that administrators will possess the necessary knowledge and skills to lead our schools through a massive restructuring.

Conditions of modern practice have been affected by a myriad of influences that extend beyond academic study, craft knowledge, and certification. Consider these that are among the more cogent:

- As previously noted, employee collective bargaining dramatically altered the authority of administrators and the relationships between teachers and administrators in many school districts.

- The increasing tendency for state and federal courts to review and perhaps reverse decisions made by local school district officials has made administrators more aware of the legal dimensions of their behavior.

- Governmental agencies, unions, pressure groups, and even students demand to participate in policy decisions. Schools are less insulated from the general environment than they were forty or fifty years ago.

- Women have entered school administration preparation programs in large numbers during the 1980s. Major professional organizations, such as the American Association of School Administrators, already have created special committees to address the needs and interests of female administrators.

- The fastest growing segments of school-age population in America are among minority children. Despite this reality, the number of Afro Americans and Hispanics preparing to be professional educators is declining. (Chapter 14 of this book is devoted entirely to issues related to women and minorities in school administration.)

- Demands for reforming America's public school system have included recommendations to reshape the preparation of teachers. In particular, teacher empowerment has been a focal point of curricular revisions in teachers' colleges. This movement is designed to give teachers greater authority and responsibility over what occurs in the classroom (Conley,

1990). Acceptance of greater autonomy for teachers necessarily includes a reconceptualization of the relationship between teachers and administrators.

- Large numbers of administrators will retire during the 1990s. The demand for educational leaders, especially individuals prepared to assume leadership roles in reformed schools, is apt to increase markedly.

- Reform efforts have included attempts to reshape the governance systems of schools. One prominent example is school-site management. This concept attempts to decentralize policy decisions to the local school building. Additionally, democratic decision processes— especially those that advance the participation of parents, students, and teachers—are rapidly becoming the norm in the governance of public education.

- Curricula of schools are apt to change significantly during the 1990s. A global economy, the infusion of technology, and concerns for the environment exemplify stimuli spawning modification efforts.

Unquestionably, the practice of school administration is more demanding now than it was in the past. As a result, administrators need greater knowledge and skills prior to entering practice, and they need to continually enhance and expand their knowledge and skills through continuing education while in practice. These needs are visible in efforts to improve both preservice and in-service education. The National Policy Board for Educational Administration (1989), a group funded by the Danforth Foundation and dedicated to improving educational administration, advocates a broadening of graduate study and a strengthening of degree requirements. The National Association of Elementary School Principals also has developed positions on professional preparation put forth in its publication, *Principals for 21st Century Schools* (1989). The Principals' Center directed by Roland Barth at Harvard University is an excellent example of contemporary efforts to meet in-service needs of practitioners. In such centers, participants learn from each other and have access to university faculty to share in discussions and problem solving. The popularity and utility of these centers also stem from the fact that they are capable of addressing both the professional and personal needs of practitioners (Levine, Barth, & Haskins, 1987), a quality viewed positively by practitioners who realize that it is often impossible for them to neatly divide their professional and private lives.

IMPLICATIONS FOR PRACTICE

The study of school administration focuses largely on formal leadership roles. For this reason, it is critical that you understand differences in the common understandings of leadership, management, and administration. In reviewing the evolution of school administration in American society, the importance of these terms should be clear. As you continue with this book, it is helpful for you to weigh this information with your existing perceptions about schools and those who occupy administrative positions in them. Doing so will help provide a clearer understanding of your beliefs, values, perceptions, and so forth.

Introductory study to school administration appropriately includes a review of the past, an understanding of the present, and the study of alternative futures. Modifications in society, in schools, and in the education profession create new needs and challenges. There is little doubt that reform efforts that commenced in the early 1980s will have lasting implications for both the preparation of school leaders and conditions of practice. Neither the organizational structures of schools nor the traditional roles of school administrators are likely to pass through the 1990s unscathed.

Presently, there are various visions of the future. Will ideas such as choice and site-based management change the structure of schooling? If teachers gain professional power and independence, will principals become more like hospital managers? Or will they emerge as professional coordinators and leaders of professional efforts? If technology radically changes the way instruction is conducted, will principals be managers of things, or will they be the sources of special knowledge that facilitate teacher use of technology? Because these questions remain largely unanswered, proposals for reform and conditions that spawn them are discussed throughout this book.

A host of factors are converging to create new expectations and demands on administrative roles. These include not only reform efforts, but also changing demographics, technology, changing philosophies of education, and other conditions that stem largely from the environments (communities) in which schools function. You should be cognizant of these influences; but more importantly, you should comprehend that these pressures helped to shape expectations for those who enter the practice of school administration.

The contemporary principal or superintendent is expected to be both a leader and a manager. He or she must be capable of leading professionals in a change process, and at the same time, be skillful enough to manage millions of public dollars. As you progress through the book, continually reflect on your image of an ideal school administrator. What is that person like? What does this person know? To what extent do ethical and moral considerations affect decisions made by this ideal administrator? Most importantly, you should seek to identify traits, knowledge, skills, and other factors that contribute to your image of an ideal practitioner.

FOR FURTHER DISCUSSION

1. Do you think the emphasis on management tasks for the very first school principals has had a lasting effect on public expectations? Why or why not?
2. Identify the ways in which certification requirements affect curricula in graduate programs in school administration.
3. Obtain a job description for a school principal. Identify those elements of the job description that address management and those that address leadership.
4. List the behaviors of a principal you admire. Are these behaviors largely related to management or leadership?

5. What are the advantages and disadvantages of removing certification requirements for school administrators?
6. What conditions in American society may be responsible for a growing number of women pursuing careers in school administration?
7. Do you believe that the public's view of the stature of school administrators has increased or decreased since 1970? What factors lead you to your conclusion?
8. What are the common motivators that lead individuals to become administrators? Do these motivators apply to you?
9. Can you identify persons with whom you have had contact in education who did not hold administrative positions—yet were leaders? What attributes or power did they possess?
10. In what ways did school consolidation affect the demand for school administrators?
11. Do the terms *licensure* and *certification* mean the same thing?

OTHER SUGGESTED ACTIVITIES

1. Interview a person who currently is a principal or superintendent. Determine what his or her perception is of school administration.
2. If some students in your class have already completed a course in the history of education, see if they can share information pertinent to the evolution of school administration as a field of practice.
3. Identify components of several recent reform reports that urge administrators to devote more time to leading and less time to managing.
4. Trace the development of certification requirements for school administrators in your state and identify when requirements were either increased or decreased with regard to the principalship or superintendency.
5. Imagine that your governor has introduced a bill to permit school administrators to be academically prepared in schools of business. Develop an argument for or against this proposed legislation.

REFERENCES

Allison, D. J. (1989). *Toward the fifth age: The continuing evolution of academic educational administration.* (ERIC Document Reproduction Service No. ED 306 662.)
Bennis, W. G., & Nanus, B. (1985). *Leaders: The strategies for taking charge.* New York: Harper & Row.
Berrien, F. K. (1976). A general systems approach to organizations. In M. Dunnette (Ed.), *Handbook of industrial and organizational psychology* (pp. 41–62). Chicago: Rand McNally.
Blumberg, A. (1989). *School administration as a craft: Foundations of practice.* Boston: Allyn and Bacon.
Brubacher, J. S. (1966). *A history of the problems of education* (2nd ed.). New York: McGraw-Hill.
Bryman, A. (1986). *Leadership and organizations.* Boston: Routledge & Kegan Paul.
Butts, R. F., & Cremin, L. A. (1953). *A history of education in American culture.* New York: Henry Holt and Company.

Callahan, R. E. (1962). *Education and the cult of efficiency.* Chicago: University of Chicago Press.

Campbell, R. E., Cunningham, L. L., Nystrand, R. O., & Usdan, M. D. (1990). *The organization and control of American schools* (6th ed.). Columbus, OH: Merrill.

Clark, D. L. (1989). Time to say enough! *Newsletter of the National Policy Board for Educational Administration,* 1 (1), 1, 4.

Conant, J. B. (1959). *The American high school today.* New York: McGraw-Hill.

Conley, S. C. (1990). A metaphor for teaching: Beyond the bureaucratic-professional dichotomy. In S. Bacharach (Ed.), *Education reform: Making sense of it all* (pp. 313–324). Boston: Allyn and Bacon.

Cooper, B. S., & Boyd, W. L. (1987). The evolution of training for school administrators. In J. Murphy & P. Hallinger (Eds.), *Approaches to administrative training in education* (pp. 3–27). Albany: State University of New York Press.

Cubberley, E. P. (1922). *Public school administration.* Boston: Houghton-Mifflin.

Gerritz, W., Koppich, J., & Guthrie, J. (1984). *Preparing California school leaders: An analysis of supply, demand, and training.* (ERIC Document Reproduction Service No. ED 270 872)

Goodlad, J. I. (1990). *Teachers for our nation's schools.* San Francisco: Jossey-Bass.

Grieder, C., Pierce, T. M., & Jordan, K. F. (1969). *Public school administration* (3rd ed.). New York: Ronald Press.

Guthrie, J. W., & Reed, R. J. (1986). *Educational administration and policy.* Englewood Cliffs, NJ: Prentice-Hall.

Hanson, E. M. (1985). *Educational administration and organizational behavior* (2nd ed.). Boston: Allyn and Bacon.

Hess, F. (1983). Evolution in practice. *Educational Administration Quarterly,* 19 (3), 223–248.

Hitt, W. D. (1988). *The leader-manager.* Columbus, OH: Battelle Press.

Hoyle, J. R. (1990). Future of education administration: Knowledge and faith. *Record in Educational Administration and Supervision,* 11 (1), 33–39.

Jacobson, S. L. (1990). Future educational leaders: From where will they come? In S. Jacobson and J. Conway (Eds.), *Educational leadership in an age of reform* (pp. 160–80). New York: Longman.

Knezevich, S. J. (1962). *Administration of public education.* New York: Harper & Row.

———. (1984). *Administration of public education* (4th ed.). New York: Harper & Row.

Koontz, H., & O'Donnell, C. (1959). *Principles of management* (2nd ed.). New York: McGraw-Hill.

Levine, S. L., Barth, R. S., & Haskins, K. W. (1987). The Harvard Principals' Center: School leaders as adult learners. In J. Murphy and P. Hallinger (Eds.), *Approaches to administrative training in education* (pp. 150–163). Albany: State University of New York Press.

Miklos, E. (1983). Evolution in administrator preparation programs. *Educational Administration Quarterly,* 19 (3), 153–177.

Murphy, J., & Hallinger, P. (1987). New directions in the professional development of school administrators: A synthesis and suggestions for improvement. In J. Murphy and P. Hallinger (Eds.), *Approaches to administrative training in education* (pp. 245–283). Albany: State University of New York Press.

National Association of Elementary School Principals (1989). *Principals for 21st Century Schools.* Arlington, VA: Author.

National Policy Board for Educational Administration (1989). *Improving the preparation of school administrators: An agenda for reform.* Charlottesville, VA: Author.

Orlosky, D. E., McCleary, L. E., Shapiro, A., & Webb, L. D. (1984). *Educational administration today.* Columbus, OH: Charles E. Merrill.

Peterson, K., & Finn, C. (1988). Principals, superintendents, and the administrator's art. In D. Griffiths, R. Stout, & P. Forsyth (Eds.), *Leaders for America's schools: Final report and papers of the National Commission on Excellence in Educational Administration* (pp. 89–107). Berkeley, CA: McCutchan.

Schon, D. A. (1987). *Educating the reflective practitioner.* San Francisco: Jossey-Bass.

Sergiovanni, T. J. (1991a). The dark side of professionalism in educational administration. *Phi Delta Kappan, 72*(7), 521–526.

———. (1991b). *The principalship* (2nd ed.). Boston: Allyn and Bacon.

Stellar, A. W. (1985). Implications for programmatic excellence and equity. In V. Mueller and M. McKeown (Eds.), *The fiscal, legal, and political aspects of state reform of elementary and secondary education* (pp. 65–120). Cambridge, MA: Ballinger.

Stinnett, T. M., & Henson, K. T. (1982). *America's public schools in transition.* New York: Teachers College Press.

Terry, G. (1960). *Principles of management* (3rd ed.). Homewood, IL: Irwin.

Yukl, G. A. (1989). *Leadership in organizations* (2nd ed.). Englewood Cliffs, NJ: Prentice-Hall.

Zaleznik, A. (1989). *The managerial mystique.* New York: Harper & Row.

CHAPTER **2**

Administration Roles in Professional Education

Chapter Content

Much like other professions, education contains distinguishable specializations. For example, there are counselors, speech therapists, reading specialists, and psychologists as well as teachers and administrators working in elementary and secondary schools. School administration, a field of study as well as an area of practice, is considered a specialization within the education profession. As a field of study, common components include research, theory, and craft knowledge developed in schools of education and practice as well as subject matter in disciplines typically housed in arts and sciences and professional schools of business. Examples include management science, public administration, and the behavioral sciences. As an area of professional practice, there are numerous subdivisions of school administration relating either to levels of professional application (e.g., principalship, central office administration) or to the nature of work assignments (e.g., business manager, director of curriculum).

As you begin your study of school administration, several critical questions are likely to emerge. This chapter contains information designed to help you answer three of the most likely queries:

1. Is school administration a profession?
2. What exactly do school administrators do?
3. What are the various jobs available in school administration?

These questions are central to the study and practice of school administration.

SCHOOL ADMINISTRATION AS A PROFESSION

What is a profession? Does school administration meet the same standards as other professions, for example, law or medicine? Some argue that education, and more specifically educational administration, is not a profession because practitioners do not control specific practices, salaries, or working conditions. Neither do school administrators, at least the vast majority who are practitioners, have control over who enters practice. Given the power and authority of the American Bar Association (ABA) and the American Medical Association (AMA) in their respective professions, it is understandable why one who uses these organizations as points of reference might not consider school administration to be a profession. Control and power, however, are not the sole criteria for classifying an occupation as a profession.

Justification of Professional Status

Spring (1990), writing about teachers, notes that certain conditions justify educators' being classified as professionals:

- the requirement of specialized knowledge
- the justification of a monopoly of services
- obtaining a college degree to enter practice
- the issuance of licenses and certificates
- the growing use of state examinations to enter practice.

These criteria are equally applicable to school administration. But there are additional measures that need to be considered. Professionals are expected to engage in lifelong learning to ensure currency in their practice. Professions utilize special knowledge and skills, and to remain effective, a practitioner is expected to continue learning while in practice. Educators, via graduate work, special seminars, and in-service education, also meet this test of professionalism. In some states, practitioners are now required to engage in continuing education as a licensing requirement. Research is another characteristic commonly used to identify professions. Research is evident in building and refining theories and in the practice of school administration. Practitioners often use applied research to address problems they encounter in educational and managerial realms. In this regard, practitioners approach problems in a scientific manner.

The actualization of a profession often lies in a linkage between standards and effectiveness in practice. That is, practitioners who utilize professional knowledge and skills are likely to excel in performing their responsibilities. Recent research conducted for the American Association of School Administrators by the University of Texas-Austin revealed two significant findings that fortify the existence of such a linkage among school administrators. In observing school superintendents, it was found that (1) the most effective practitioners complete more graduate work and hold more advanced certification than their peers, and (2) the most effective superintendents are more likely to be involved in professional activities such as conferences and workshops (Burnham, 1989).

Professional Organizations

Professions are also marked by the existence of state and national organizations that support needs and interests of practitioners. There are multiple organizations that perform this service for school administrators. In fact, many administrators hold membership in several professional organizations at the same time. Usually, individuals choose to join professional organizations in education on the basis of their job, their interests, or the urgings of their employers. Table 2–1 displays information about some of the major administrative organizations and lists the types of administrators (by position classification) most likely to hold membership.

Clearly, the diversity of administrative work is a major factor leading to the existence of multiple organizations. This condition, however, raises several political concerns for members of the profession. For example, no single organization speaks for all school administrators. It is quite possible for administrative organizations to take divergent positions on critical issues. In this respect, the existence of multiple organizations may dilute the political power of administrators.

Historically, most school administrator groups were departments of the National Education Association (NEA). During the late 1960s and early 1970s, virtually all

TABLE 2–1   Examples of Major National Organizations for Administrators

Organization	Most Likely Members*
American Association of School Administrators (AASA)	Superintendents, central office administrators, professors
National Association of Secondary School Principals (NASSP)	High school principals, junior high/middle school principals, assistant principals, directors of secondary education
National Association of Elementary School Principals (NAESP)	Elementary school principals, assistant principals, directors of elementary education
Association of School Business Officials (ASBO)	Business managers, directors of facility management
Association for Supervision and Curriculum Development (ASCD)	Curriculum directors, principals, college professors, subject area coordinators

* This is not intended to an inclusive list of members. For instance, there are principals who belong to AASA and superintendents who belong to NASSP or NAESP.

specialized divisions of the NEA, especially those serving school administrators, disaffiliated due to growing tensions stemming from the increased popularity of collective bargaining (Hessong & Weeks, 1991). This development resulted in the formation of independent national organizations to serve the needs and interests of school administrators. Although many of these groups maintain a close working relationship with each other, they often compete for members (e.g., a high school principal may be pursued by NASSP, ASCD, and AASA).

Lingering Doubts

Many in American society continue to view school administration as a quasi-profession. Educators, in general, are perceived as being of high value to society, but they are also viewed as having low status—a dubious distinction shared with the clergy (Elam, 1990). The work of all educators is controlled largely by laws, policies, and regulations. Due to this condition, teachers and administrators frequently are compared to nurses and social workers—individuals in occupations typically classified as semi-professions. The movement toward unionism and collective bargaining further eroded public perceptions of educators as professionals.

School Reform and Professionalism

Status of professions frequently is linked to the difficulty of entering practice. The more difficult it is to be accepted to professional study and the more rigorous the examinations for licensure, the higher the status accorded by society. For this reason, some reformers have argued that the number of students admitted to the study of school administration should be dramatically reduced. Others have countered that the ill effects of professional birth control outweigh potential benefits. Browder (1990–91) suggested that improving school administration as a profession must be accomplished by enticing more talented individuals to enter graduate study—not by producing fewer graduates. Sergiovanni (1991a) questioned the wisdom of pursuing professionalization by simply increasing academic preparation standards and making licensing more difficult. He feared that such an approach could lead to an even greater emphasis on management functions (i.e., a version of professionalism that distances administrators from teachers). He offered this recommendation:

> that we build a more limited and hierarchically flatter profession of educational administration, one based on shared educational expertise with teachers, limited specialized knowledge in management and organization, and blurred role distinctions that open rather than restrict access to the profession. (p. 526)

This is a thought-provoking suggestion. It is based on the premise that professionalization ought to be erected on a foundation of specialized knowledge and skills possessed by all educators and not on the collective wisdom of organizational managers.

Reformers also have pointed out that professionalism includes a responsibility for lifelong learning. Hallinger and Murphy (1991), for example, noted that true professionals engage in continuous intellectual growth. They recommended that the curriculum of professional preparation needs to be tied to goals for professional development.

These two examples exhibit how potential changes in academic preparation are inextricably linked to moral, ethical, and intellectual dimensions of professionalism. Efforts to create new schools and new roles for teachers and principals offer a golden opportunity to enhance the professional status of educators.

THE NATURE OF ADMINISTRATIVE WORK

Popular images of teachers and administrators are often narrow—and at times inaccurate. These perceptions frequently are drawn from personal experiences as students or images portrayed by the entertainment industry. In reality, practitioners in any profession differ in several notable ways. Some attorneys are people-oriented and others are task-oriented; some physicians have a good bedside manner and others do not. But beyond personal traits, practitioners differ with regard to the work they perform. For example, psychiatrists and pediatricians have quite different roles in providing health care. Such diversity also exists in school administration. Principals and superintendents do not necessarily share a common philosophy; they do not necessarily approach problems in an identical manner; and their work expectations usually are not uniform. Diversity is created by the person, the job, the organization, and the environment in which the organization exists.

The Purposes of Administration

In the preceding chapter, differentiations were made between management and leadership. These distinctions are important to understanding the primary purposes of administration. Within any organization, there are two general tasks that must be performed by those who assume responsibility for providing direction: (1) doing things appropriately, and (2) determining which things must be done. The former is highly related to management, whereas the latter focuses on leadership (Bennis & Nanus, 1985). Although these tasks are quite different, you should not conclude that they must be done by different individuals. In many organizations, including schools, both typically fall on the shoulders of a single administrator. Practitioners differ in the amount of attention they give to these two functions. Their work behavior can be placed on a continuum as exhibited in Figure 2–1. Some principals and superintendents concentrate almost exclusively on managerial tasks; others focus primarily on leadership functions; and still others attempt to do both.

In contemporary practice, responsibilities of administrators are largely related to institutional adaptation (i.e., leading or managing change). Organizations are dynamic entities; and contrary to popular thought, schools do not remain unchanged over time. Carnall (1990) reminded us, "In a changing world, the only constant is change" (p. 1). All organizations experience some degree of modification, but

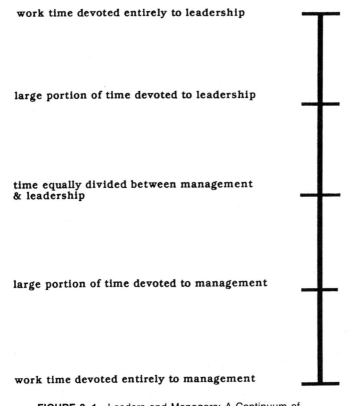

work time devoted entirely to leadership

large portion of time devoted to leadership

time equally divided between management & leadership

large portion of time devoted to management

work time devoted entirely to management

FIGURE 2-1 Leaders and Managers: A Continuum of Administrative Behavior

organizations do not always move in planned or desired directions. Some are led; others simply react to prevailing circumstances in a random fashion. But all organizations experience change. The study of organizations reveals that there are multiple inducements that can actually produce alterations. March (1984) noted that pursuits to comprehend organizations as routine adaptive systems can be divided into six basic models of action:

1. *Evolutionary selection*—action created by the application of standard operating procedures or rules to appropriate situations (e.g., the application of rules is affected by the existing conditions).
2. *Intended rational choice*—action created by attempts to solve problems (e.g., a principal creates a new scheduling paradigm to accommodate space problems).
3. *Trial and error*—action created by past learning (e.g., experience is the basis for action).
4. *Politics and bargaining*—action created by conflict and conflict resolution (e.g., a new policy for corporal punishment results from a conflict between the principal and staff over the old policy).

5. *Diffusion*—action that spreads from one organization to another (e.g., one school district adopts a new policy regarding textbook rentals and other school districts follow the lead and adopt the same policy).
6. *Regeneration*—action caused by a mix of intentions and competencies among humans in the organization (e.g., teachers are given a greater role in decision making).

Because all of these actions occur in organizations, they make change unavoidable.

Although change can be initiated in several ways, it is the selection and management of appropriate techniques that help create the successful organization. Even the purposeful creation of a problem may be a leadership strategy to induce change. An experienced administrator once commented, "The best problems I have are those I create." Planning, implementing, and coping with change are primary functions of leadership in modern organizations (Carnall, 1990). Not all change, however, is generated from within the organization; external forces also can coerce adaptation. The inclusion of air-pollution devices on automobiles demonstrates this point. The passage of legislation requiring catalytic converters forced automobile manufacturers to alter the way they built their products.

Given the inevitableness of change, organizational leaders are faced with the challenge of controlling and directing institutional alterations so that they remain congruent with organizational goals. This responsibility is central to an understanding of one major purpose of administration. *Administrators are expected to provide the leadership necessary to move an organization from its present state to a desired state* (Hitt, 1988). This charge entails influencing group and individual behaviors within the organization, providing direction, conducting periodic assessments, and calibrating procedural components to enhance the probability of long-term goal attainment.

Administration also has more immediate purposes. These relate to supporting operations and augmenting the work of those who perform the primary tasks of producing goods or services. For example, school principals provide managerial supervision for a multitude of functions outside the classroom (transportation, food services, and maintenance, for example). They also strengthen instructional activities by providing assistance to teachers and ensuring that necessary classroom materials and equipment are available. Within any organization, purposes of administration are tied to specific organizational goals. But in general, administration exists to provide direction and support to positive adaptations. Later in the book, leadership styles and organizational change are discussed in greater detail.

The Components of Administration

Before exploring the various positions occupied by school administrators, you need to develop an understanding of the general responsibilities of administrative work. What exactly do superintendents and principals do, and how do they spend their time? These questions can be answered in several ways. For instance, one can describe the social nature of administrative work. Examples of this alternative are found in the works of Walton (1973) and Frase and Hetzel (1990). These researchers described the work of principals by identifying the degree to which they interact with others (teachers, students, parents) during the school day.

A more common method of describing administrative work is to dissect role expectations. The overriding tasks of providing direction and support to organizational activity can be separated into eight general areas of responsibilities that are pervasive in administrative work. These are outlined in Figure 2–2. Keep in mind that although these eight functions are meaningful to all administrators, the relevance of each varies from one work assignment to another. Differences in organizational philosophy, present organizational needs, individual administrator philosophy, and the philosophy of the person supervising the position are responsible for nonuniformity. Each of the eight categories is reviewed separately.

Representing. Administrators are the visible heads of their organizations. In the capacity of chief executive, the superintendent of schools serves as the district's representative to the community and external agencies. Likewise, the principal functions as the official representative of an individual school. The role of representative has both formal and informal elements (Blumberg & Blumberg, 1985). For instance, a superintendent represents his or her school district formally with appearances before state agencies or regulatory commissions. Informally, the superintendent provides visibility for the school district at social functions and other community-based events. The role of official representative is especially important for public school administrators. Often communities expect persons in these roles to maintain a high level of visibility and to be active in civic function.

One indicator of the importance of the representative role is the emphasis many school districts place on candidate image. Personal appearance, communication skills, tact, personality, and warmth are commonly cited by employing officials as desirable characteristics. In larger school systems, the ability of the superintendent to serve in a representative capacity can become the primary attribute sought by the school board.

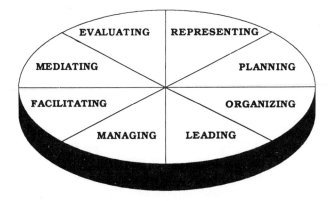

FIGURE 2–2 Components of Administration

The general environment of the school district (the community in which the district is located) often influences the degree of importance placed on personal qualities expected in school leaders. In affluent suburbs, for example, there might be an expectation that administrators possess social skills, appearance, and demeanor commonly associated with corporate executives. By contrast, a small rural school system may seek administrators who are capable of maintaining warm and friendly relationships with the general public. But in all settings, those who assume administrative positions function as representatives of the organizations that employ them.

Planning.   A myriad of factors contribute to an increased emphasis on formal organizational planning. One of the more prominent is the demand for increased accountability. During the past two decades, governors and legislators, responding to public pressures, have required schools to be more answerable for resources at their disposal. Movement to a global economy, the rapid deployment of technology, and the advancement of knowledge in many fields of study exemplify additional factors raising the need for more precise organizational planning.

Planning consists of two essential activities: (1) setting goals and objectives, and (2) developing blueprints and strategies for implementation (Sergiovanni, 1991b). In a good many school districts, planning is centralized. That is, central office personnel develop a system-wide strategic plan that all schools are expected to follow. Such plans typically include needs statements, short- and long-term goals, and suggested procedures for goal attainment. In the last few years, there has been a growing interest in decentralizing the planning process, that is, to have each school develop its own strategic plan. The value of building-level planning is supported by research on effective schools as exemplified by following two notable outcomes: (1) effective schools frequently engage in building-level collaborative planning, and (2) effective schools develop and use clearly stated goals that are produced through a planning process (Purkey & Smith, 1983).

The movement toward decentralized planning increases expectations that principals possess knowledge and skills necessary to lead this process. Even though site-based planning is frequently a team effort involving a broad range of school staff, principals are expected to provide frameworks (paradigms) and appropriate procedures. Leadership in the planning process calls for two sets of abilities: (1) knowledge and skills related to planning as an administrative process, and (2) knowledge and skills related to collaborative decision making.

Organizing.   Although related, planning and organizing are different administrative tasks. Organization includes the arrangement of people, materials, and other resources to ensure proper functioning within a school or school district. At the building level, for example, principals provide organizational structure by developing and administering a daily class schedule and a schedule of extracurricular events. School superintendents perform the task of organization by integrating various elements of the system to assure proper functioning (e.g., creating an organizational chart detailing line and staff relationships). Organization is essential to achieving favorable cost-benefit ratios for human and material resources; and in the eyes of taxpayers, this often is one of the most important tasks of school administration.

Although many different organizational decisions are made by school administrators, perhaps the most important relate to instructional programs, that is, curriculum and instruction. Yet, it is in this area that the greatest gaps between ideal and real roles often are found. For example, a review of relevant research studies indicated that principals typically devote little of their workday to organizational responsibilities focusing on instructional programs (Wimpleberg, 1987).

To many observers, schools appear to be highly standardized: schedules, class periods, and even curricula seem to be relatively constant from one school to another. But similarities in annual calendars or daily schedules does not mean that organizational duties of school administrators are routine. These responsibilities include much more than creating schedules. Often creative ideas, such as satellite lunch programs (where food is prepared in one central area and shipped to schools), save large school districts substantial amounts of money that can be used for instructional purposes. The organization of material resources usually requires special knowledge about functions such as pupil transportation, facility management, and extracurricular programs. In this respect, technical management skills are important. But like all organizational tasks, problem solving, critical thinking, and human relations skills also are critical.

Leading.   Increasingly, educational organizations are placing a higher premium on an administrator's ability to lead—the ability to know what things must be accomplished. In large measure this condition is created by the conviction that significant change is necessary in elementary and secondary education. Rather than being protectors of the status quo, principals and superintendents become the change agents. They are the persons who initiate action, identify alternatives, select appropriate courses of action, and direct individuals and groups to desired levels of functioning so that the organization can reach its goals and objectives.

A reconceptualization of school administration, one that advocates a balance between management and leadership, is evident in a number of the reform reports (e.g., Task Force on Teaching as a Profession, 1986). In practice, however, political barriers may make true leadership extremely difficult. There are school boards that refuse to allow superintendents to be professional leaders—and there are dictatorial superintendents who give principals little latitude to be anything but managers. Nevertheless, momentum toward an increased emphasis on leadership is clearly evident. In large measure, the concept of leadership receives strong support from research outcomes focusing on effective practices. Such studies verify that (1) effective practitioners are able to balance management and leadership, and (2) effective practitioners rely on creative approaches to overcome environmental and organizational barriers that otherwise prevent this balance (Burlingame, 1987).

Leadership requires certain technical skills, but it also entails an artistic component that enhances effective decisions. The more difficult responsibilities of administrators often include one or more of the following three conditions: ambiguity, uniqueness, and value conflict (Schon, 1987). These conditions often frustrate managers who rely largely on technical information. Leadership demands the ability to meet a challenge within the context in which it occurs—both physical and human variables need to be considered. This is why information about society, political behavior, and organizations is so critical to modern practice.

Managing.   By now, it should be abundantly clear that distinctions between leading and managing are consequential. If leaders set institutional directions and influence organizational culture and worker behavior, what is the essence of management? Managing is a process that involves a preoccupation with the here-and-now aspects of goal attainment (Bryman, 1986). It is a process that focuses on the efficient utilization of resources to achieve the purposes of the organization. Sergiovanni, Burlingame, Coombs, and Thurston (1987) note that the professional manager is less concerned with determining major intentions and directions and more concerned with finding out what consumers want from the schools and delivering services accordingly. In essence, management focuses on immediate and specific problems (Yukl, 1989).

Among the more common management tasks found in schools are the following:

- operating school lunch programs
- operating financial procedures (e.g., budgeting, purchasing)
- maintaining the physical plant (e.g., maintenance)
- managing personnel records (students and employees)
- scheduling
- maintaining health and safety
- controlling student behavior
- administering policies.

Although this list is by no means exhaustive, it gives you some idea of the range of responsibilities that are classified as management.

In the past few years, demands for educational improvement have circuitously devalued the importance of management in school administration. In part, this has occurred because management and instructional leadership often are viewed as mutually exclusive choices. This is most unfortunate, because both are essential. Public schools represent massive financial investments, and the public demands that they are operated in an efficient and proper manner. As such, management is an essential component of administration.

Facilitating.   Although the task of educating students falls most directly on the shoulders of classroom teachers, administrators are expected to contribute to the process by being facilitators. How do administrators fulfill this function? To facilitate simply means to make easier. Accordingly, administrators are expected to provide human and material assistance to teachers permitting them to perform their responsibilities more effectively. Facilitation in school administration is both direct and indirect. A principal helping a teacher obtain software is an example of the former, and a superintendent recommending a policy on the acquisition of instructional materials exemplifies the latter.

Another facet of being a facilitator is that of communicator. Administrators serve as an information link between teachers and other parties (e.g., parents, central administration, state agencies). Providing effective and timely communications is one of the most critical elements of school administration. Teachers need accurate data and facts regarding policy changes, new materials, applied research, and grant opportunities to remain effective in the classroom.

The continuing education needs of school district employees also have bearing on the facilitator role. Observing practices in private industry, many school leaders are concluding that reaching organizational objectives in a changing world requires a constant updating of employee knowledge and skills. In education, the achievements of a school or school district are associated with the performance of those who deliver instruction. Accordingly, greater attention is being given to the value of staff development and facilitator roles of school administrators in this process (e.g., identifying individual and organizational needs and preparing programs to meet those needs).

If several popular reform efforts persist, namely site-based management and teacher empowerment, the helping role of school administrators undoubtedly will become more prominent. Enhancement of collegiality and collaboration among professional staff is another facet of facilitation. It is precisely this aspect of leadership, however, that concerns practitioners who fear an erosion of their legitimate authority. Administrators who continue to view their role as largely managerial are especially fearful of sharing power. But again, effective schools research suggests that the establishment of collegial relationships between administrators and teachers not only is possible, but is conducive to productivity. Barth (1987) described the unfortunate condition in many schools where the work of administrators and teachers mirrors "parallel play"—a term used to describe a condition in which children play in opposite ends of a sandbox while largely ignoring each other. He argued that professional environments were both conceivable and preferable:

> . . . somehow most good schools are ones where parallel play and adversarial and competitive relationships among adults have been transformed into cooperative, collegial ones. (p. 251)

A major barrier to collegiality has been the idea that administrators must treat all employees as subordinates. The concept of teacher empowerment directly challenges this long-standing bureaucratic tenet. Nyberg (1990) points out that empowering teachers does not necessarily result in a loss of power for administrators. Through effective facilitation, a principal can actually gain the respect and admiration of teachers; and in so doing, he or she can actually experience an increase of power.

Mediating. In all organizations, conflict is inevitable (Owens, 1991). Disputes between and among groups (e.g., the custodians' union and the school board disagree on paid holidays) or between and among individuals (e.g., two teachers disagree over the use of resources) occur with regularity in public education. Individuals and groups bring to the organization varying beliefs, values, knowledge, and experiences. This fact alone is sufficient to produce periodic conflicts. For instance, primary teachers often hold different views with regard to the best paradigm for the teaching of reading, and middle school teachers frequently are divided over the effectiveness of corporal punishment.

For years, school officials viewed conflict as being unproductive and they went to great lengths to eradicate it (Kowalski, 1982). Even today, many superintendents and principals believe that discord only leads to negative outcomes. These practitioners are likely to choose one of two paths when confronted by conflict: (1) accommodate the source of conflict (give in) so it can be removed, or (2) ignore the source of conflict in an effort to conserve energy (Hanson, 1985). Both choices are likely to produce unforeseen problems. Administrators need to understand the inevitableness of conflict and ways in which conflict can be managed—even to produce positive change. Through the use of mediation, contemporary administrators are expected to build and maintain cooperative working relationships among individuals and groups (Yukl, 1989).

Effective mediation involves more than choosing sides in a dispute. It requires two important elements: (1) an understanding of human and political dimensions within organizations, and (2) knowledge and skill to utilize conflict as a means to produce positive change. Effectiveness in the role of mediator is properly judged by the degree to which the leader is able to build harmony and cooperation among individuals and groups.

Evaluating. There are two primary types of formal evaluation that occur in schools: performance evaluation and program evaluation. The two are often confused even though they are very different processes. The former entails the assessment of employees; the latter assesses the effectiveness of curriculum and instruction. Both forms of evaluation can serve three primary functions: (1) providing a guide for decisions, (2) maintaining accountability, and (3) fostering understandings about organizational behavior (Stufflebeam & Webster, 1988).

Typically, performance evaluation serves a summative function, that is, to determine whether the individual is meeting job expectations. The process also may serve a formative purpose—helping employees to improve job-related performance. For the most part, educators have concentrated on summative processes to respond to legal and political accountability mandates. Historically, the evaluation of teachers has been premised on the assumption that principals know what constitutes good teaching. Increasingly, this judgment is being challenged by teachers, teacher unions, and experts in the field of performance evaluation (Medley, Coker, & Soar, 1984). In contemporary practice, evaluators are expected to defend their actions, and a greater emphasis is being placed on blending formative and summative functions (Natriello, 1990).

Evaluation has both descriptive and judgmental components; but it is the latter that is most difficult to complete (i.e., describing behavior is usually much easier than assessing its worth). Not surprisingly, skepticism about the utility of evaluation is most often directed at the judgmental aspects of the process. This is particularly the case when multiple forms of input are not used—when the only data used to make evaluative decisions are those produced by the supervisor. Employees being evaluated often feel vulnerable, and this insecurity is exacerbated when the teacher views the supervisor to be both inept and biased.

Teachers and administrators do not always agree on the importance or worth of evaluation. A recent study, for example, found that principals saw far more value in this activity than did teachers (Kowalski, Reitzug, McDaniel, & Otto, 1992). In part, administrator perceptions are formed by demands for account-ability and management ideals that advance the notion that summative evaluation is one way the supervisor controls subordinate behavior.

Assessing the performance of other professionals can be a frustrating and destructive feature of school administration (Kimbrough & Burkett, 1990). This is especially the case when evaluation serves only a summative purpose. Despite disagreements regarding the utility of performance evaluation in educational settings and despite apprehensions voiced by those engaged in the process, performance evaluation continues to be a critical component of school improve-ment (Iwanicki, 1990).

Confusion between personnel evaluation and program evaluation is heightened by the fact that it is impossible to entirely exclude the former when completing the latter (Stufflebeam & Webster, 1988). Program evaluation determines whether certain needs or objectives (e.g., school district goals, community needs) are being met by the organization. Some states now mandate public school districts to complete program evaluations on a regular basis. The purpose is to generate outcome data regarding the degree to which the schools are meeting their stated mission and objectives. Beyond state-imposed requirements, the value of program evaluation is being enhanced by a national emphasis on school improvement and research that illuminates the utility of planning and evaluation.

SCHOOL-BASED ADMINISTRATION

Positions in school administration can be broadly classified as either school-based or central office. In the former category, the work is done primarily or entirely in an individual school. Central office administration, by contrast, typically includes district-wide responsibilities and authority. Distinctions between school-based and central office roles are at times difficult in smaller districts where the superintendent's office may be in one of the schools or where a single individual performs the dual roles of superintendent and principal. But in the vast majority of school systems, administrators are identified as either central office or school-based. School-based administrative positions can be divided further by level of schooling. That is, there are elementary, middle grades, and high school administrators.

Elementary School Administration

Over the years, the structure of elementary schools has been altered in several ways. At one time, many included grades kindergarten through eight. With the emergence of junior high schools, circa 1910, this condition was modified as many school districts shifted from an 8-4 (kindergarten not included) organizational pattern to either a 6-3-3 pattern or a 6-2-4 pattern. More recently, acceptance of the middle school concept has further diversified grade organizational patterns in school districts. Today, elementary schools exist with varying grade levels, but the most common organizational formats are K-5 and K-6.

The position of elementary school principal has evolved over time. Initially, management responsibilities were assigned to an individual who was given the title of head teacher. Eventually, full-time administrators became the mode. (A small number of low-enrollment schools still employ individuals as half-time teachers and half-time principals.) One factor responsible for making the elementary principalship a full-time position was increased enrollment. Some elementary schools now enroll over 1000 pupils; however, the common size is in the range of 250 to 500 pupils. Programming complexity also played a part in creating the need for more supervision and management. Table 2–2 briefly outlines examples of conditions that have placed added demands on the elementary school principal. You will note that not all of these factors are caused by school district initiatives. Some are generated by community and societal needs and wants.

TABLE 2–2   Examples of Factors Influencing the Complexity of Elementary School Administration

Factor	Possible Effects
School consolidation	Elementary schools have become larger; there are more sections per grade level
Curricular expansion	Need for more subjects to be taught (e.g., foreign language); greater scheduling pressures
More teacher specialization	Separate classes in art, music, and physical education; departmentalized teaching
Collective bargaining	May affect working relationship with teachers
Modern facilities	Greater need for management
Technology	Need to create added instructional spaces (e.g., computer labs); need to increase staff development efforts
Greater emphasis on home-school relations	Need to involve parents more in the educational programs
Greater demand for accountability	Need to devote more time to planning and evaluation
Demands for reform	New governance approaches (e.g., school-site management) and new instructional strategies (e.g., mastery learning)
Individualized instruction	Greater diversity of special programs (e.g., special education, gifted and talented)
Expanding expectations	Schools are expected to attend to social, psychological and other personal problems

Elementary school administrators are almost always employed on extended contracts (i.e., contracts that go beyond the normal school year). Such extensions may be stipulated in weeks (e.g., six weeks) or months (e.g., one, two, or three months). During these times of additional employment, the principal may oversee a summer school program, engage in planning activities, make schedules for the coming school year, participate in the employment of new teachers and staff, and oversee maintenance activities. In some instances, elementary schools also operate summer recreational programs that require some supervision.

Actual roles assumed by elementary school principals differ significantly from one community to another. In large measure, this multiformity is a product of opposing thoughts as to whether the principal should be a leader or a maintainer (Sergiovanni et al., 1987). What principals really do on the job is a product of several forces such as public perceptions, organizational expectations, socialization, and past practices. Differing orientations for the elementary principalship are clearly visible in analyses of time allocation. Whereas one principal devotes as much as 50 or 60 percent of work time to clinical supervision and curriculum development, another has little or no contact with teachers that directly relates to instruction.

There is little disagreement that the ideal role of the elementary school principal includes both managerial and leadership functions. But on a daily basis, those who occupy these positions face pressures that make it difficult to balance the two responsibilities (Blumberg & Greenfield, 1980). Unfortunately, empirical data regarding the integration of management and leadership among elementary school principals have been limited (Kimbrough & Burkett, 1990). Hopefully, case studies and other forms of applied research can be used to learn more about the practices of model principals.

Assistant principals (either full-time or part-time) often are employed in larger elementary schools. Persons assigned to this role tend to have a designated area(s) of responsibility (e.g., pupil services, managing the facility, instructional programs). Perhaps the greatest benefit to having an assistant principal is that it permits the principal to concentrate on specific activities. In this respect, the presence of an assistant principal appears to be one logical response to the recommendation that principals be both leaders and managers.

The assistant principalship is commonly viewed as an entry-level position in school administration. Most educators who seek this position have aspirations of moving to the principalship at a later time. For this reason, many assistant principals desire to be involved in a wide range of activities as opposed to being assigned a narrow band of managerial tasks.

Middle/Junior High School Administration

The junior high school emerged as a result of studies regarding the vertical organization of public schools. One of the most influential pieces of research was conducted by the Commission on the Reorganization of Secondary Education in 1918. This study concluded that American schools should abandon the 8-4 pattern in favor of a 6-6 organizational plan—six years of elementary education and six years of secondary education (Anderson & Van Dyke, 1963). By 1920, only 55 separate junior high schools existed in the United States; that figure increased to nearly 8000 by 1970 (Wood, Nicholson, & Findley, 1985). Primary purposes of the junior high school, typically containing grades 7–9, were to (1) provide a transition from the self-contained instructional format of the elementary school to the departmentalized organization of the secondary school, and (2) provide an appropriate social setting for children who were reaching puberty and were undergoing a difficult growth period. Over time, concerns emerged about the effectiveness of the junior high school in meeting these missions:

> . . . there is a growing belief that the junior high school is no longer serving its original purpose and is taking on more and more characteristics of a senior high school. Some also believe that American children today are reaching adolescence much earlier than children of many years ago. (Wood, Nicholson, & Findley, 1985, p. 6)

Continuing questions as to whether the junior high school was accomplishing its original mission led to the exploration of alternatives for middle grades education. The middle school, typically containing grades 6–8 or 5–8, emerged in the 1960s and 1970s as an alternative to the traditional junior high school. Researchers note that grade span is not the most critical factor in achieving success at this level of schooling; rather, effectiveness is related to the implementation of philosophy and practices conducive to accommodating the needs of early adolescents (Epstein, 1990).

This brief history of schools in the middle facilitates an understanding of the principalship at this level. Until the emergence of the middle school concept, most junior high school principals were individuals possessing secondary school backgrounds (i.e., former high school teachers and administrators). This employment pattern was largely predicated on licensure requirements since both junior high schools and high school utilize departmentalized teaching, that is, many states issued teaching and administrative licenses that covered grades 7 to 12. Middle schools by contrast typically employ a variety of formats including self-contained, departmentalized, and block teaching. (Block teaching is paradigm in which a teacher may have the same students for several, but not all, subjects, for example, language arts and social studies are blocked together.) The contemporary principal in the middle school may have been an elementary school teacher, a high school teacher, or even a person specially educated and licensed to work at the middle school level. Thus, the career path to the middle school principalship is not as predictable as either the elementary or the high school principalship.

The daily work life of the middle grades principal is likely to be quite different from that of the elementary principal. The curriculum is more complex, services are broader, the school usually has a larger enrollment, and discipline problems demand more attention. Additionally, needs of students at this level often exhibit wide variance because of differing maturation rates, academic achievement levels, and social development. But like all principals, those in middle schools still face the challenge of finding time to provide leadership. Kron (1990) observed:

> Middle level schools are confluent social organizations of human need. The principal's role is multidimensional and by its milieu more reactive than proactive. (p. 259)

Despite environmental demands that require principals to devote a great deal of their time to managerial responsibilities, there are practitioners at this level of schooling who have distinguished themselves as innovators and instructional leaders. The middle school principalship can be exciting and challenging because, in large measure, the parameters for this school are still evolving and the environment abounds with potential (Henson, 1988).

Middle school principals typically receive higher compensation than do elementary school principals—but less than high school principals. Contracts for these positions almost always include two or three months of employment beyond the regular school year. Some educators accept a middle grades principalship largely because they see the assignment eventually leading to a high school principalship. This trend will likely diminish as the middle school grows in prominence and establishes itself as a truly unique level of schooling.

Most middle grades schools have one or more assistant principals. These individuals often have designated areas of responsibility such as student discipline, facilities management, or extracurricular activities. In recent years, the assistant principalship has received added attention. A recent book by Marshall (1992) explores this entry-level position in depth.

Additionally, some middle grades schools may have the following positions classified as administrative:

- dean of boys, girls, students
- director of counseling or student services
- athletic director
- department chairs.

Conditions related to collective-bargaining agreements have been a major factor in the decision to classify department heads as administrators. Such designation usually removes department heads from the teachers' bargaining unit, permitting them to perform supervisory (e.g., evaluation) and managerial (e.g., budget management) functions.

High School Administration

High schools are organized with various grade configurations ranging from 7–12 (combined junior and senior high schools) to 10–12 or even 11–12 schools (commonly called senior high schools). The growing popularity of the middle school has caused a resurgence of the 9–12 organizational format. High schools tend to be larger in enrollment than either elementary or middle grade schools, and a broader curriculum and expanded extracurricular programs create a multitude of managerial responsibilities for the administrative staff.

Hughes and Ubben (1980) divided all the responsibilities of the high school principal into five primary tasks:

school-community relations,
staff personnel development,
pupil personnel development,
educational program development, and
business and building management. (pp. 3–4)

Like all other building-level administrators, high school principals face the challenge of finding sufficient time to be both manager and leader. They, like all administrators, possess what Sergiovanni (1991b) calls "mindscapes"— perceptions of the world, people, and education that determine what principals believe about management and leadership. The presence of one or more assistant principals, however, often makes it possible for the high school principal to decide which responsibilities will receive the greatest amount of personal attention.

In many communities, the high school principalship has a high level of visibility. Morris, Crowson, Porter-Gehrie, and Hurwitz (1984) labeled the modern secondary school as "a true center of community life, not only for the young people who attend it, but for their parents, friends and neighbors" (p. 52). The public role of the principal is an important personal consideration for those who aspire to this administrative post. Communities expect administrators to model ideal behavior for both teachers and students. Rossow (1990) observed:

The behaviors of principals, as authority figures, communicate what is really valued to both teachers and students. Teachers and students tend to imitate the actions, attitudes, and beliefs of those in authority, such as the principal. (p. 34)

Being in the public spotlight is one aspect of the high school principalship that some find bothersome. Yet, there are others who find the public exposure and long hours to be quite satisfying.

The difficulty of the high school principalship is reflected in the fact that the extrinsic rewards usually are higher than for peer positions at lower levels of schooling. These typically include higher salaries, special benefits, and employment contracts that extend over the entire year (i.e., twelve-month contracts). A less recognized benefit relates to career decisions. Studies on career paths of administrators have exhibited that high school principals usually find it easier to move to the superintendency (Miklos, 1988). Perhaps public visibility and the complexity of the assignment contribute to this advantage. School board members may believe that experiences gained through the high school principalship better prepare individuals for the challenges of the superintendency.

Other positions in a high school that may be classified as administrative are the same as those already identified in the previous section on junior high/middle school principals (e.g., assistant principals, student deans, department heads). The assistant principalship remains the primary entry position for career administrators in secondary schools. Although many who become assistant principals have intentions of moving to high level positions in administration, the same is not necessarily true for department heads, guidance directors, or student deans— especially when individuals holding these positions are not required to have a principal's license.

CENTRAL OFFICE ADMINISTRATION

The position of school district superintendent originated in larger cities. By most accounts, the very first were appointed in 1837 in the cities of Buffalo and Louisville (Grieder, Pierce, & Jordan, 1969). As urban systems grew in enrollment, programming and services expanded. Superintendents created their own support staffs by adding positions with titles such as assistant superintendent and director of instruction. Thus, the structure of central administrative services was created. The need for such district-wide leadership and management was the product of a number of environmental and educational considerations. Some of the more cogent are listed in Table 2–3.

Today, virtually every school system has some form of centralized administration. In smaller districts, the staff may include only a superintendent and a handful of secretaries and bookkeepers; but in larger, urban areas, several hundred licensed administrators may be part of central administration.

Superintendency

The most visible position in school administration is that of chief school district administrator, the superintendent of schools. The position is analogous to a company president in the private sector. In its formative years, the superintendency, like the principalship, was viewed largely as a managerial position. Those qualities deemed appropriate for industrial managers were valued by school boards when they appointed individuals to this key post. Clearly, perceptions that the

TABLE 2–3 Major Factors Promoting the Growth of Central Administration

Factor	Consequences
School consolidation	The creation of fewer, but larger, school districts; better transportation programs
Demographic trends	An increasing student population until the early 1970s
Expanded curriculum	The need to provide more specialized assistance in program planning and evaluation
Increase in education laws, curriculum mandates	A greater need for program coordination
Improved educational facilities	The need to provide more sophisticated maintenance
Rising cost of education	Increased attention given to fiscal management
Industrial revolution	Greater emphasis on management, technical efficiency

superintendent is only a manager are being challenged today. Murphy (1991), writing about urban superintendents, noted:

> As power and knowledge become more dispersed, as multiple constituencies demand attention, as schooling becomes more decentralized and professionalized, and as mistrust of government grows, the Terminator approach simply will not work. The image of the steely-eyed, top-down manager who has all the vision and all the answers must be coupled with a gentler, less heroic image. (p. 512)

Compared to twenty or thirty years ago, today's superintendent is apt to spend far more time building consensus, developing and analyzing policy, and executing strategic planning.

Despite the fact that not all needs, problems, and school districts are alike, certain skills and knowledge are considered crucial for all who occupy the superintendency. Among the more prominent are communication skills, public relations, instructional leadership, fiscal management, and political insight. In all superintendencies, there are certain issues that recur as major concerns. A five-year study of new superintendents in Kansas, for instance, revealed that certain problems remain critical year after year. In comparing the results of the Kansas study with national results of studies conducted by the American Association of School Administrators approximately ten and twenty years earlier, it was found that budget formulation and administration remained the top concerns of superintendents (Anderson, 1990).

School district size often affects the actual roles assumed by school superintendents. In districts with fewer than 1500 students—and many remain in the United States—the superintendent personally oversees virtually all operations. In these settings, the superintendent prepares the budget, chairs textbook selection committees, and coordinates facility projects. By contrast, superintendents in large school systems have professional support staff who specialize in various areas of administration, allowing time commitments to be targeted to areas of greatest need or interest. For example, the chief executive of a large district may devote a majority of work time to public relations or strategic planning.

Unlike teachers and principals, the superintendent is not bound to a single school. This permits greater freedom to develop one's personal schedule and to exercise personal judgment in making decisions (Blumberg & Blumberg, 1985). This dimension of the superintendency is not insignificant.

Many of the challenges confronting contemporary superintendents relate to the organizational context of schools, particularly public schools. For decades, comparisons were made between school administrators and private-sector managers. These likenings were misguided because they essentially ignored the effects of organizational environments. In particular, sufficient attention was not given to unique challenges posed to public school administrators because they in essence were answerable to the general public. Take, for instance, the act of evaluating decisions made by the chief executive officer in an organization. Even when a superintendent makes recommendations or decisions that are judged to be professionally sound, he or she always faces the possibility of public dissatisfaction and rejection because the initiatives are politically unpalatable.

Today, communities, schools, and the people who compose these entities are less homogeneous and more demanding, and express a greater range of needs than was true just three or four decades ago. These contemporary conditions are changing the work life of many superintendents. More attention is being given to communications, political analysis, and other functions that help establish healthy interactions between the schools and the community. For example, with fewer taxpayers having a direct contact with public schools and an ever-growing demand for public agencies to produce more services, superintendents are seeking ways to build bridges between the schools and community life.

Superintendents are almost always employed on twelve-month contracts, and some states mandate that the initial employment contract span two to four years. The superintendent usually receives the highest salary in a school district; however, the gap between the superintendent's compensation and the next highest paid employee varies markedly among districts. In one school system this gap may be as high as $25,000 to $30,000, whereas in another district it may be as low as $2000. Actual salaries for this position vary significantly depending on size of district, geographic location, existing problems, economic status of local taxpayers, and similar conditions. Some superintendents in larger school systems earn six-figure annual salaries.

Superintendents may also receive benefits not given to other employees. These may include the use of an automobile, special insurance programs, special retirement provisions, travel allotments, and the payment of professional dues. In some rare instances, superintendents may even be provided with the use of a house and the payment of nonprofessional dues (e.g., Chamber of Commerce, country club). Local standards, economic conditions, past practices, and state laws need to be considered when comparing total compensation packages for school superintendents. The income of administrators, including superintendents, is discussed in greater detail in Chapter 4.

Other Central Office Positions

The most common titles used for central office personnel other than the superintendent are "assistant superintendent," "director," and "coordinator." Although these titles do not have universal meaning, persons holding assistant superintendent positions are usually *line* administrators (they have other professional staff reporting to them) whereas those holding the title of coordinator are often *staff* administrators (individuals primarily serving a support function in the organization). In many states, one must hold a superintendent's license to have a position as an assistant superintendent. Some superintendents prefer to use the title of "assistant to" (e.g., assistant to the superintendent for finance) for some central office personnel. This title may suggest two things: (1) the person holding the position does not possess the appropriate license for being an assistant superintendent, or (2) the position is a staff rather than line position.

Table 2–4 outlines a variety of titles used for central office positions. Keep in mind that variations of the titles are not uncommon. Additionally, titles may not have common definitions from one school district to another. Not all central

TABLE 2–4 Common Titles for Central Office Personnel

Title	Description of Authority/Functions
Deputy Superintendent	Used in very large districts to identify second highest ranking administrator
Associate Superintendent	A high ranking official either serving in the same capacity as a deputy or as the head of a major division in a larger school district (e.g., associate superintendent for instruction, association superintendent for business)
Assistant Superintendent	A high ranking official heading a major division in a school district (e.g., assistant superintendent for instruction, assistant superintendent for business) or the second highest ranking administrator in a smaller school system
Assistant to the Superintendent	Typically, a staff person reporting directly to the superintendent in a designated area (e.g., finance, public relations)
Administrative Assistant	Typically, same designation as assistant to the superintendent
Director	An individual who heads a division or subdivision of the organization (e.g., director of curriculum, director of secondary education, director of special education, director of transportation); person may be either a line or staff administrator depending on the organizational arrangements
Business Manager	Either the chief fiscal officer or a staff administrator responsible for the business functions of the school district
Superintendent of Buildings	The administrator in charge of the maintenance and development of school facilities; the more common title today is director of buildings and grounds
Coordinator	Usually a staff administrator below the director level (e.g., coordinator of music, coordinator of reading, coordinator of food services)

administration positions are occupied by professional educators. Areas such as transportation, food services, and maintenance may be headed by persons who possess special training and experiences in managing specific support services.

Duties of central office administrators typically are divided into divisions. Moderately sized districts may have only two—instruction and business affairs. The larger the district, the more likely that more specificity will be used in establishing divisions. Table 2–5 provides examples of common functions in central administration. These divisions shed light on just how complex school administration has become.

Many times, taxpayers fail to comprehend the magnitude of operations carried out in a school district. For example, it is not uncommon for the public schools to operate the largest food and transportation services in a given community.

Positions in central administration vary in levels of compensation and contract length. Salaries for assistant, associate, and deputy superintendents typically are higher than for building-level principals in the same school system. Positions not occupied by professional educators tend to have the lowest central office salaries. (This is particularly the case if the persons in these jobs do not have a college degree.)

TABLE 2–5 Common Functions in Central Administration

Area of Administration	Examples of Functions
Instructional services	Curriculum development; instructional support; textbook selection; program evaluation; instructional coordination
Business services	Budgeting, purchasing, debt management, payroll
Personnel services	Employment, personnel record keeping, fringe benefit analysis, collective bargaining
Pupil personnel services	Testing programs, health programs, guidance and counseling, social work
Public relations	Newsletters, press releases, media coordination
Governmental relations	Legal issues, state and federal programs, grants, relationships with other governmental units
Special services	Special education, gifted and talented education
Food services	Menu planning, food purchasing, cafeteria recordkeeping
Transportation services	Bus routing, bus purchasing, bus maintenance
Maintenance services	Maintenance and custodial services, purchase of custodial supplies, work coordination

OTHER CAREERS IN SCHOOL ADMINISTRATION

Although most persons who specialize in school administration work for public school districts, a number of other job opportunities exist. This section provides a brief overview of them. One caveat is in order. You should not assume that all of these positions require the same level of experience and academic training. For example, one might enter work in the state department of education with a master's degree in school administration and three years of teaching. By contrast, making a living as an educational consultant may require a doctoral degree and extensive experience in administration.

Government and Special Agencies

Career opportunities for school administrators exist in the federal and state governments and with special agencies that have an interest in education. As expected, the U.S. Department of Education employs a large number of professional educators; but less known is that opportunities also exist in other divisions of the federal government. The Department of Defense, for instance, operates schools around the world for the dependents of military and other governmental personnel, and these institutions employ a relatively large number of principals and a smaller number of administrators in higher-level positions.

State departments of education employ persons with specialized education in school administration in a number of positions. Typically, those holding the highest level positions in state departments of education are school administrators. Other opportunities exist in areas such as facility planning, finance, food services, instructional services, research, accreditation, and so forth.

There are some job opportunities for school administrators with special agencies. Philanthropic foundations, for example, have been exhibiting a greater interest in elementary and secondary education and some employ program officers in these areas. Private clinics and for-profit schools also may seek trained school administrators. The acceleration of staff development activities in private industry also has created some select opportunities for educational specialists. School administrators who have some background in adult education may be especially attractive to businesses investing in human resources development.

Teaching and Research in Higher Education

A limited number of persons who pursue careers in school administration enter teaching or research positions in universities. Employment as a professor in school administration almost always requires an earned doctorate from an accredited university. Salaries and working conditions for these positions are dependent on academic rank as well the type of institution in which the individual is employed. Compared to characteristics of faculty members across the university, professors of educational administration are somewhat different. They tend to enter university work at a later age, largely because many have experience teaching and administering at the elementary and secondary school levels, and they are more likely to receive higher salaries and academic ranks when entering university work (again, largely due to previous experiences) (McCarthy, 1987).

There are some 500 institutions offering courses or degrees in school administration. These institutions represent a variety of philosophies about the purposes of professional education and the roles of professors. In the United States, institutions of higher education have varying standards for tenure and promotion. This results in a wide range of role expectations. Some professors in school administration devote much of their work to research and writing. By contrast, some universities are moving to create clinical professorships for experienced practitioners who devote much of their work to supervising internships and other field-related experiences and providing service to the profession. A majority of the professors of school administration, however, balance their time among the responsibilities of teaching, scholarship, and service.

Educational Consultants

School districts, like most other organizations, occasionally engage the services of professional consultants. Consultants are individuals who possess specialized knowledge or experience, and their service is usually retained for a very specific purpose (e.g., staff development). Some educational consultants function independently (i.e., they are in business for themselves), whereas others work for established firms or perform consulting services on a part-time basis (e.g., professors). Although consulting services may be obtained in virtually any area of operation, the most common in school administration are facility planning, finance, staff development, assessment, instructional improvement, and curriculum development.

Consultants typically serve two primary functions: (1) to provide information based on expert knowledge either because such knowledge is not available in the organization or because an outside opinion is desired, or (2) to serve as facilitators (Roland, 1990). A third function, one that is largely political, often is overlooked. Many times, consultants can objectively address problems that divide school personnel and communities (e.g., the consolidation of two schools).

Although there are no requirements for calling oneself a consultant, the reality is that few individuals in school administration perform this function on a full-time basis. Probably a majority of the consulting work in education is performed by professors or by staff in professional organizations. For those desiring more information about this area, English and Steffy's *Educational Consulting: A Guidebook for Practitioners* (1984) is recommended.

IMPLICATIONS FOR PRACTICE

You may readily identify administrators as professionals. Indeed, most people do. The discussion of professionalism presented here serves two purposes: (1) to create an awareness of similarities and differences between educational administration and other professions, and (2) to create an understanding of the relationship between professionalism and practice. There are at least two visions of professionalism related to school administration that are very much in conflict. One is embedded in management, and the other in education.

Pronouncements that administrators are professionals have not automatically resulted in public acceptance of the claim. Those engaged in the study and practice of school administration must give meaning to this classification. Professionalism is more than income and status. Especially in school administration, it is a topic that also has moral, ethical, and intellectual dimensions—it is a topic that must include the contemporary need to balance management and leadership.

As you contemplate a career as a school administrator, you should establish a foundation of information that permits you to make enlightened choices. You need to know that school administration encompasses many jobs, that each job includes a variety of responsibilities, and that practice occurs in many different types of environments. You should have valid information about the quality of life afforded by a career in school administration, and this includes both extrinsic and intrinsic rewards. In essence, good choices are made possible by complete information about professional practice.

This chapter has provided information about the general functions of administration as well as the application of these functions in various jobs. Too often, educators allow random circumstances in life to dictate their careers. That is, they rely on serendipitous events to carve their career paths. Avoiding this pitfall requires that you think about what you like to do and what you are capable of doing. It necessitates the development of personal and professional goals.

FOR FURTHER DISCUSSION

1. Why do you think school administration has not achieved a status equal to law and medicine in the United States?
2. Has the status of school administrators increased or decreased in the past two decades?
3. Discuss the differences between the average work days of elementary school principals and of high school principals.
4. Should middle school teachers and principals be required to obtain special licenses (i.e., other than elementary or high school licenses)? What forces prevent states from mandating separate licenses?
5. List the advantages of pursuing a career in school administration.
6. What qualities are present in the school administrator you most respect?
7. Do you think that most educators can be successful administrators? Why or why not?
8. At what level of schooling do you think principals are most apt to work closely with teachers in instructional improvement? What factors did you weigh in reaching your answer?
9. Should high school principals make higher salaries than elementary school principals? Why or why not? Should an assistant superintendent make more than a middle school principal? Why or why not?
10. Do you think fewer teachers are planning to go into administration today as compared with ten years ago?
11. Why is the image one holds of school administration as a profession critical to reform recommendations?

OTHER SUGGESTED ACTIVITIES

1. See how many students in your class already have determined what type of position(s) they want to acquire in school administration. Why do some students enter the study of school administration with specific career goals, yet others do not?
2. Discuss the meaning of a profession.
3. Invite several practitioners to address the class on how their jobs have changed in the past decade.
4. Debate the requirement that principals should have at least three years of successful teaching experience at the same level at which they wish to be administrators.
5. Develop a list of goals you would like to accomplish during your study of school administration. What are your expectations of professional preparation?

REFERENCES

Anderson, L., & Van Dyke, L. (1963). *Secondary school administration.* Boston: Houghton Mifflin.

Anderson, R. E. (1990). A five year profile of new-to-site Kansas superintendents and issues encountered. *Record in Educational Administration and Supervision,* 11 (1), 71–75.

Barth, R. S. (1987). The principal and the profession of teaching. In W. Greenfield (Ed.), *Instructional leadership* (pp. 249–270). Boston: Allyn and Bacon.

Bennis, W., & Nanus, B. (1985). *Leaders: The strategies for taking charge.* New York: Harper & Row.

Blumberg, A., & Blumberg, P. (1985). *The school superintendent: Living with conflict.* New York: Teachers College Press.

Blumberg, A., & Greenfield, W. (1980). *The effective principal: Perspectives on school leadership.* Boston: Allyn and Bacon.

Browder, L. H. (1990–91). A critical essay on National Policy Board "Agenda." *National Forum of Educational Administration and Supervision Journal,* 8 (1), 5–40.

Bryman, A. (1986). *Leadership and organizations.* Boston: Routledge & Kegan Paul.

Burlingame, M. (1987). Images of leadership in effective school literature. In W. Greenfield (Ed.), *Instructional leadership* (pp. 3–16). Boston: Allyn and Bacon.

Burnham, J. B. (1989). Superintendents on the fast track. *The School Administrator,* 9 (46), 18–19.

Carnall, C. A. (1990). *Managing change in organizations.* London: Prentice-Hall International.

Elam, S. M. (1990). The 22nd annual Gallup Poll of the public's attitudes toward the public schools. *Phi Delta Kappan,* 72 (1), 41–55.

English, F. W., & Steffy, B. E. (1984). *Educational consulting: A guidebook for practitioners.* Englewood Cliffs, NJ: Educational Technology Publications.

Epstein, J. L. (1990). What matters in the middle grades—Grade span or practices? *Phi Delta Kappan,* 71 (6), 438–444.

Frase, L., & Hetzel, R. (1990). *School management by wandering around.* Lancaster, PA: Technomic.

Grieder, C., Pierce, T. M., & Jordan, K. F. (1969). *Public school administration* (3rd ed.). New York: Ronald Press.

Hallinger, P., & Murphy, J. (1991). Developing leaders for tomorrow's schools. *Phi Delta Kappan,* 72 (7), 514–520.

Hanson, E. M. (1985). *Educational administration and organizational behavior* (2nd ed.). Boston: Allyn and Bacon.

Henson, K. (1988). *Methods and strategies for teaching in secondary and middle schools.* New York: Longman.

Hessong, R. F., & Weeks, T. H. (1991). *Introduction to the foundations of education* (2nd ed.). New York: Macmillan.

Hitt, W. D. (1988). *The leader-manager.* Columbus, OH: Battelle Press.

Hughes, L. W., & Ubben, G. C. (1980). *The secondary principal's handbook.* Boston: Allyn and Bacon.

Iwanicki, E. F. (1990). Teacher evaluation for school improvement. In J. Millman & L. Darling-Hammond (Eds.), *The new handbook of teacher evaluation* (pp. 158–174). Newbury Park, CA: Sage.

Kimbrough, R. B., & Burkett, C. W. (1990). *The principalship: Concepts and practices.* Englewood Cliffs, NJ: Prentice-Hall.

Kowalski, T. J. (1982). Organizational climate, conflict, and collective bargaining. *Contemporary Education,* 54 (1), 27–31.

Kowalski, T., Reitzug, U., McDaniel, P., & Otto, D. (1992). Perceptions of desired skills for principals. *Journal of School Leadership* 2 (3), 299–309.

Kron, J. (1990). The effective middle school principal. In R. Hopstrop (Ed.), *The effective school administrator* (pp. 249–261). Palm Springs, CA: ETC Publications.

McCarthy, M. M. (1987). The professorship in educational administration: A status report. In D. Griffiths, R. Stout, & P. Forsyth (Eds.), *Leaders for America's schools* (pp. 317–331). Berkeley, CA: McCutchan.

March, J. G. (1984). How we talk and how we act: Administrative theory and administrative life. In T. Sergiovanni and J. Corbally (Eds.), *Leadership and organizational culture* (pp. 18–35). Urbana, IL: University of Illinois Press.

Marshall, C. (1992). *The assistant principal: Leadership choices and challenges.* Newberry Park, CA: Corwin Press.

Medley, D. M., Coker, H., & Soar, R. S. (1984). *Measurement-based evaluation of teacher performance.* New York: Longman.

Miklos, E. (1988). Administrator selection, career patterns, succession, and socialization. In N. J. Boyan (Ed.), *Handbook of research on educational administration* (pp. 53–76). New York: Longman.

Morris, V. C., Crowson, R. L., Porter-Gehrie, C., & Hurwitz, E. (1984). *Principals in action: The realities of managing schools.* Columbus, OH: Charles E. Merrill.

Murphy, J. T. (1991). Superintendents as saviors: From the Terminator to Pogo. *Phi Delta Kappan,* 72 (7), 507–513.

Natriello, G. (1990). Intended and unintended consequences: Purposes and effects of teacher evaluation. In J. Millman & L. Darling-Hammond (Eds.), *The new handbook of teacher evaluation* (pp. 35–45). Newbury Park, CA: Sage.

Nyberg, D. A. (1990). Power, empowerment, and educational authority. In S. Jacobson & J. Conway (Eds.), *Educational leadership in an age of reform* (pp. 47–64). New York: Longman.

Owens, R. G. (1991). *Organizational behavior in education* (4th ed.). Englewood Cliffs, NJ: Prentice-Hall.

Purkey, S., & Smith, M. (1983). Effective schools: A review. *Elementary School Journal,* 83, 427–452.

Roland, R. W. (1990). The effective school consultant. In R. Hopstrop (Ed.), *The effective school administrator* (pp. 328–342). Palm Springs, CA: ETC Publications.

Rossow, L. F. (1990). *The principalship: Dimensions in instructional leadership.* Englewood Cliffs, NJ: Prentice-Hall.

Schon, D. A. (1987). *Educating the reflective practitioner: Toward a new design for teaching and learning in the profession.* San Francisco: Jossey-Bass.

Sergiovanni, T. J. (1991a). The dark side of professionalism in educational administration. *Phi Delta Kappan,* 72(7), 521–526.

———. (1991b). *The principalship: A reflective practice perspective* (2nd ed.). Boston: Allyn and Bacon.

Sergiovanni, T. J., Burlingame, M., Coombs, F. S., & Thurston, P. W. (1987). *Educational governance and administration* (2nd ed.). Englewood Cliffs, NJ: Prentice-Hall.

Spring, J. (1990). *The American school: 1642–1990* (2nd ed.). New York: Longman.

Stufflebeam, D., & Webster, W. J. (1988). Evaluation as an administrative function. In N. Boyan (Ed.), *Handbook of research on educational administration* (pp. 569–602). New York: Longman.

Task Force on Teaching as a Profession (1986). *A nation prepared: Teachers for the 21st century.* New York: Carnegie Forum on Education and the Economy.

Walton, H. F. (1973). *The man in the principal's office: An ethnography.* New York: Holt, Rinehart & Winston.

Wimpleberg, R. K. (1987). The dilemma of instructional leadership and a central role for central office. In W. Greenfield (Ed.), *Instructional leadership* (pp. 100–117). Boston: Allyn and Bacon.

Wood, C. I., Nicholson, E. W., & Findley, D. G. (1985). *The secondary school principal* (2nd ed.). Boston: Allyn and Bacon.

Yukl, G. (1989). *Leadership in organizations* (2nd ed.). Englewood Cliffs, NJ: Prentice Hall.

CHAPTER 3

The Study of
School Administration

Chapter Content

Degree Programs

School Administration—An Eclectic Field of Study

Components of Professional Preparation

Critical Considerations

Barriers to Change

Implications for Practice

In the previous chapter, it was noted that school administration as a field of study comprises several basic components. The identification of these components and a discussion of their inclusion in academic studies serves two purposes: (1) they help to answer questions commonly asked by students, and (2) they explain the relevance of certain subject matter that might otherwise not be readily apparent.

Glass (1991) noted that the quality of school executive education received only slight attention during all of the reform discussions of the 1980s. He wrote, "Rarely discussed is why educational administration programs are structured as they are at most post-secondary institutions" (p. 29). Such voids circuitously heighten suspicions (and criticisms) that professional preparation is only remotely associated with contemporary problems. These inquiries do not come only from reform-minded legislators and union officials; a number of scholars also question whether academic study adequately prepares individuals for the real world of practice (e.g., Pitner, 1982). Issues surrounding professional preparation are made even more cogent by the fact that nonuniformity exists among the hundreds of institutions offering degree programs in school administration. In addressing the implications of this diversity, the National Commission on Excellence in Educational Administration, a reform coalition identified in the preceding chapter, concluded that fewer than 200 of the universities now engaged in administrator preparation have the resources and commitments necessary to meet recommended standards for preparing contemporary practitioners (Griffiths, Stout, & Forsyth, 1988).

This chapter begins by examining degree programs in school administration. This is followed by a description of school administration as an eclectic field of study. Much of the chapter is devoted to examining the common components of graduate study. They are presented in six categories of responsibilities, functions, and experiences: (1) management, (2) instructional leadership, (3) organizational leadership, (4) position-specific courses (e.g., the principalship), (5) research, and (6) field-based experiences. The chapter concludes with a discussion of issues related to altering the professional preparation of school administrators.

DEGREE PROGRAMS

Lawyers, dentists, and physicians typically complete professional school (1) while full-time students, (2) during a specified time period (e.g., three to five years), (3) at the same institution, and (4) as part of a cohort group. None of these conditions is generally true for students pursuing careers in school administration. Most likely, graduate study is completed sporadically, at several institutions, and over long time periods (Stout, 1989). Students of school administration often are teachers (or administrators in lower-level positions), employed on a full-time basis, who complete classes at night, by extension, or during the summer months. For many, there is a reluctance to become a full-time student, because doing so would necessitate resigning their current positions. The risk (perhaps giving up a tenured teaching position and taking a substantial reduction in income) often appears greater than the benefit (the opportunity to secure an administrative position). This condition is not true in more highly compensated professions where students often are willing to incur massive debts (sometimes reaching $50,000 to $100,000) in order to complete the academic preparation necessary to enter practice.

Degrees in School Administration

Graduate degrees commonly granted in school administration are broadly categorized as follows: (1) master's degrees, (2) sixth-year degrees, and (3) doctoral degrees. The master's degree is the first level of graduate study. The common titles for degrees at this level are the Master of Science (M.S.), Master of Arts (M.A.), and Master of Arts in Education (M.A.E., or M.A.Ed.). Completion of a master's degree typically requires thirty to forty semester hours of graduate credit. At some universities, completion of a practicum is mandatory. A thesis may be required, especially for the M.A. degree; however, a growing number of universities now offer an alternative to the master's thesis (e.g., internship).

The existence of a graduate degree between the master's and the doctorate is rather unique to the education profession. This degree, commonly called a sixth-year degree, is largely attributable to two factors: (1) requirements for certain licenses may necessitate such a degree, or (2) some institutions with historical missions in professional education, but not granting doctoral degrees, desire to offer a formal degree beyond the master's degree. Some states (e.g., Indiana and Iowa) require that one hold a formal sixth-year degree or doctoral degree to obtain the superintendent's license. Various titles may be used for the sixth-year degree, but the most common are the Educational Specialist (Ed.S.), Certificate of Advanced Graduate Study (C.A.G.S.), and the Certificate of Advanced Study (C.A.S.). Completion of a sixth-year degree usually requires thirty to forty-five semester hours beyond the master's degree. A practicum or internship is almost always required, and a thesis is rather common. A growing number of institutions offer students the option of comprehensive examinations as an alternative to the thesis.

Early in the twentieth century, school administrators possessing an earned doctoral degree were rather rare. This is no longer true. Two doctoral degrees are common among school administrators. The Doctor of Philosophy (Ph.D.) is considered the traditional graduate school doctorate, and the Doctor of Education (Ed.D.) was established as a professional school degree oriented toward practitioners (similar to the J.D., D.D.S., or M.D.). It should be noted that although general distinctions are still drawn between the Ph.D. and the Ed.D. in school administration, universal standards are not adhered to by all institutions. One university's Ed.D. may be another university's Ph.D. (Griffiths et al., 1988). A 1987 study of twenty-seven doctoral programs, for example, found that research and statistical course requirements for the Ed.D. and Ph.D. degrees differed only slightly, except for a somewhat higher expectation for exposure to research methods in Ph.D. programs (Norton & Levan, 1988). Some institutions offer both doctoral degrees, and it is in these universities that the greatest distinctions are likely.

Completion of a doctoral degree typically requires a total of eighty to one hundred semester hours of graduate work. Requirements for the Ph.D. often include successful completion of courses or proficiency examinations for research tools such as foreign languages, computer programming, or statistical analysis. These same requirements may exist for Ed.D. degrees at certain institutions. The completion of a residency—a period of full-time study on campus—remains a standard requirement for many doctoral programs; however, a growing number of institutions either offer alternative residency programs or define residency in a fashion that permits students to continue working on a full-time basis (e.g., simply requiring the completion of twelve semester hours of course work in a given school year). The growing prominence of alternative programs for the doctoral residency is largely attributable to the risk-benefit ratio mentioned earlier. The writing of a dissertation—a scholarly research project—is almost always a requisite for both degrees.

Nondegree Study

Graduate study in school administration is not restricted to students who are pursuing formal degrees. Many practitioners enroll in courses periodically to update personal skills or to meet continuing education requirements associated with licensure or employment. Also, some states mandate that additional work be completed beyond the master's degree to achieve professionalization of a license (e.g., a person may be required to complete thirty semester hours of course work beyond the master's degree as a condition of maintaining a license). Non-degree-seeking students enroll in courses on either a credit or noncredit (auditing) basis. Standards relative to enrolling as a nondegree student are again less than uniform among universities.

SCHOOL ADMINISTRATION—AN ECLECTIC FIELD OF STUDY

School administration is an applied field similar to engineering or medicine, and not a discipline in the sense that chemistry and history are disciplines (Campbell, Corbally, & Nystrand, 1983). Study in this specialization includes knowledge, information, and skills from several academic areas; hence, the overall curriculum is considered to be eclectic. The amalgamation of knowledge and practices from several disciplines and professions is not unique to education. Management and administration in all types of organizations commonly are studied in the context of their application rather than as generic topics. Examples of this format for academic study are found in university-based programs in business administration, hotel and restaurant management, public administration, and hospital administration, to name just a few.

There is no standardized national curriculum for graduate study in school administration, as evidenced by the differences already noted. These variations in professional study are found in (1) the number and types of courses required for specific degrees, (2) the number and types of clinical experiences required, and (3) the titles given to courses of study. In large measure, this multiformity is a product of state licensing standards, each state having its own set of requirements. In this regard, certification standards obstruct the effort to create a national curriculum. This influential factor of certification diversity is explored in detail in the next chapter. Other factors that produce curricular diversity include accreditation standards, the philosophy of faculty, university standards for graduate education, and the needs of students who enroll in the programs. Opposing images of school administrators as professionals, discussed in the previous chapter, is yet another influence.

Concerns for programmatic diversity may appear misplaced, because often the preparation of school administrators is criticized for being too rigid. Reference is made in the literature, for example, to a continuing reliance on the "one best model" (e.g., Cooper & Boyd, 1987). Such connotations address the broad context of entering the profession—not merely academic study. Thus, even though variations exist in graduate school curricula, prescribed paths for entry into professional practice remain rather rigid. The "one best model" is predicated on the fact that three years of teaching experience, a master's degree in school administration, and the completion of specified courses remain the norm for being licensed in the field.

COMPONENTS OF PROFESSIONAL PREPARATION

Although specific courses and course titles vary, the study of school administration includes several common components. Simply to facilitate discussion, these components have been divided into six categories as illustrated in Figure 3–1.

You should realize that the components discussed here are not quantitatively equal. For example, students are likely to complete many more credits in the area of management studies than in field experiences. In addition, balance among the categories varies, in some instances markedly, from one university-based program to another. Again, the purpose of this section is to provide a review of the common components of graduate study in school administration.

Management Studies

Courses included here concentrate on knowledge and skills related to managing human and material resources. Since much of administration entails such functions, this category includes many courses. Two points need to be emphasized. First, content of courses in school administration are never entirely consumed with management issues. Even a course in school facility planning may include the study of planning paradigms and ways that consensus can be obtained in making critical decisions. Courses listed here tend to be heavily oriented toward management functions. Second, varying course titles do not necessarily connote different foci. At one institution, a course labeled "School Budgeting" may have nearly identical content to another institution's course labeled "School Business Management." Because there are so many courses that relate to management responsibilities, they are presented here in subgroups.

Financial Management.   Managing fiscal resources has obvious importance in public education. School finance studies consist of three basic functions: (1) how revenues are generated, (2) how they are distributed, and (3) how they are managed (Guthrie, Garms, & Pierce, 1988). At a number of universities, the study of school finance is spread over two courses. The first focuses on economic dimensions and includes topics such as the value of education, principles of taxation, federal funding, state formulas, equalization, concepts of fiscal neutrality (concepts that address issues of equalized state funding to public school districts), and other topics related to raising and distributing revenues. The second course concentrates on the management of funds. Included are units such as budget planning, budget management, purchasing, insurance programs, and other pertinent tasks. Typically, this course also contains subject matter related to support services such as food services, transportation, and maintenance funding—responsibilities frequently assigned to business managers.

The study of school finance is relevant for both central office and school-based administrators—although implications for the latter group are less obvious. Principals often manage monies in special accounts (e.g., extracurricular fund) and spend appropriations provided by district-wide budgets. Responsibilities

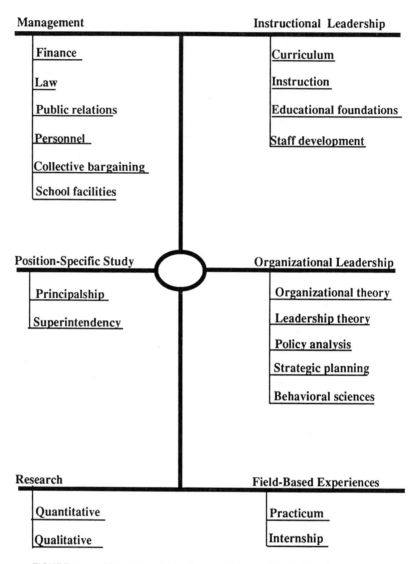

FIGURE 3-1 School Administration: An Eclectic Field of Study

in fiscal management are likely to increase for principals if the movement toward decentralization continues.

School Law. Operating in the public domain, schools are subject to myriad laws and regulations. If these laws were immutable or if they stemmed from a single source, the life of the school administrator would be less complex. But such is not the case. New laws are enacted, and existing laws altered and eradicated, almost continuously. Laws originate from one of three sources: written constitutions, statutes, and judge-made law (Valente, 1980). The first category constitutes the highest form of law. Constitutions provide the basic structure and powers of state and federal governments and their agencies. Statutes, enacted by Congress at the federal level and state legislatures at the state level, are the next highest form of law. Statutes cannot be in conflict with constitutional provisions and are subject to change over time. Judges interpret the meanings of constitutions and statutes; and in so doing, they establish precedents that have a bearing on the enforcement of laws.

Recognizing the dynamic nature of legal issues, school law courses are structured to concentrate on rights, responsibilities, and liabilities of members of the educational community (i.e., administrators, teachers, students, parents, board members). In a society that relies heavily on litigation to resolve disputes, school law is viewed as a very relevant course by most educators. Students examine legal concepts (e.g., *in loco parentis*) and discuss growing responsibilities of practitioners, (e.g., reporting child abuse cases), that permeate the work life of principals and superintendents. One of the major aims of studying school law is to inform future administrators that they cannot develop policy and regulations in an unrestricted manner. Students learn that there are constraints placed on their rule-making prerogatives, and they examine the nature of those constraints (McCarthy & Cambron, 1981).

Public Relations.   Schools, especially public schools, are concerned about relationships with community agencies, private businesses, and other organizations that help form public opinion. In democratic societies, public agencies are expected to be responsive to patrons, because they in essence provide the fiscal resources necessary for operations. Opinions, needs, and frustrations existing in the community at large can significantly alter the operations of a school system. For this reason, administrators do not want public opinion to stem from inaccurate information.

Public relations became a part of school administration as far back as the 1920s. The main objectives were to promote awareness of the importance of schooling, to build confidence and financial support, and to encourage parents to become more involved in their children's education (Holliday, 1990). The study of public relations is designed to provide the practitioner with information necessary to communicate with the public and to establish planned relationships with other agencies. Kindred, Bagin, and Gallagher (1990) defined educational public relations in the following manner:

> Educational public relations is management's systematic, continuous, two-way, honest communication between an educational organization and its publics. (p. 15)

The key words in this definition are *systematic, continuous, two-way,* and *honest.* First, the process of public relations is not helter-skelter; it is the product of planning. Second, the process is not used only when public support is desperately needed (e.g., passing a bond issue). It should be an ongoing effort to inform and enlist support for education. Third, the process exceeds the mere dissemination of information; it includes an obligation to monitor the environment and to gather information. This aspect of public relations is the most neglected. Finally and most importantly, quality public relations is based on honest communication. It should not be a medium for propaganda. Ethical and moral dimensions of practice dictate that administrators provide the public with accurate, candid, and complete pictures of the school system's strengths, needs, and weaknesses to the community (Gorton, 1976).

Management of School Facilities.   School buildings constitute sizable investments and are overt symbols of a community's beliefs and values with regard to education. Seasoned practitioners attest that facilities-related issues often are among the most emotional they encounter. Arguments over the location or size of a new school or disputes regarding which elementary school to close because of declining enrollments exemplify aspects of facility management that can become quite troublesome.

A number of contemporary conditions have made facility planning and management more exacting. Consider the following factors outlined by Kowalski (1989):

- Changing demographic patterns have affected school enrollments in many parts of the country. Some school districts have rapidly declining enrollments; others are building as many as ten to twelve new schools each year.

- Escalating costs for school construction without corresponding changes in funding formulas have made the financing of facility projects more difficult in many states.

- The infusion of high technology into educational environments creates new design needs.

- Concerns about energy sources and environmental pollution have increased demands for more exact planning in areas such as energy efficiency.

- Concerns for health and safety of school facilities have caused the need to alter many existing buildings (e.g., the presence of asbestos, radon).

- Research on the effects of learning environments (colors, lighting) raise expectations that educators will play a more prominent role in specifying the needs of educational environments.

Administrator responsibilities in the area of school facilities are divided into two broad categories: planning and managing. The former is more complicated and requires an understanding of formulating organizational intentions. That is, the planner must be able to employ systemic models that integrate demographic, educational, environmental, and financial data to set goals and objectives. The latter category includes the more common functions addressed by school administrators—the day-to-day care of buildings and grounds.

The importance of school facility management has been illuminated by recent research identifying problems that exist with school buildings. The Education Writers Association (Lewis, 1989) conducted a study of school buildings in the United States and concluded that at least 25 percent of the nation's public school facilities were in poor physical condition and made shoddy places for learning. In large measure, this unfortunate condition stems from decades of neglect during which funds were diverted from maintenance to more politically visible problems (Chick, Smith, & Yeabower, 1987).

In contemporary practice, administrators are much more likely to plan new facility projects in a collaborative mode. Teachers, taxpayers, and even students want to be involved. The days when schools were planned by a few administrators and school board members behind closed doors are rapidly disappearing. Accordingly, administrators need to acquire the knowledge and skills necessary to enlist professional assistance (e.g., retaining architects, attorneys) and to put together planning teams that permit broad-based representation.

Personnel Management.   Courses in personnel administration concentrate on the management and development of human resources, required tasks in every organization. Often educators have a narrow vision of this function, thinking that it only entails employment practices (Rebore, 1991). Actually, it includes a range of responsibilities:

- establishing quantitative and qualitative specifications identifying the organization's needs with regard to employment
- creating recruitment strategies and actual recruitment of personnel
- establishing selection parameters and the actual selection of personnel
- planning placement and induction activities
- planning and organizing staff development
- conducting appraisals of personnel
- fashioning a compensation program (including management of a fringe benefit program) and administering it
- maintaining personnel records (a task made more difficult by a host of legal considerations, such as right-to-privacy laws)
- planning and organizing a program of performance evaluation.

Collective bargaining also is considered a part of personnel management; however, it is addressed as a separate topic in this chapter (and at many universities, it is a separate course).

Although initial employment is not the sole activity in personnel administration, it remains its most visible and critical element. This is particularly true with regard to employing professional staff (teachers and administrators). There are a number of emerging insights into the linkages between school improvement and the effectiveness of employment practices. Kimbrough and Burkett (1990), for example, point out that the way to build a good foundation in the quest for excellence is to locate, recruit, and hire excellent teachers.

All educators have a need to continue to learn, remain current in their profession, and improve as practitioners. Accordingly, the responsibilities of personnel administration do not cease with employment. Forward-thinking school districts systemically connect employment practices, performance evaluation, and staff development.

Collective Bargaining. Since the late 1960s, administrators in virtually all school systems have had to address the challenges growing out of collective bargaining. By the mid-1980s, slightly over two-thirds of the states required school boards to engage in this unbidden practice (Lieberman, 1986). The magnitude of collective bargaining on the lives of school administrators often is not visible to the general public. For instance, taxpayers often do not realize that the school board and the administration have a number of employee groups with which they must negotiate (e.g., custodians, bus drivers). In larger school systems, administrators may have to contend with five or more separate union contracts. Additionally, many patrons only hear about conflicts related to actual bargaining (i.e., the process of reaching an agreement). Yet, the actual demands associated with collective bargaining go well beyond this phase to include a multitude of issues associated with contract administration (Castetter, 1981).

Many departments of school administration now offer a separate course in collective bargaining. Typically, the following issues are included:

- the history of unions in education
- the purposes of collective bargaining
- strategies for the employer in negotiating contracts
- the meaning of associated procedures (arbitration, mediation)
- management of problems stemming from bargaining (strikes, boycotts)
- contract administration
- evaluation of bargaining procedures.

Clearly, the total process of collective bargaining requires more than management. Many of the decisions affect policy and require leadership from the administrators directly engaged. Superintendents and other administrators often recommend, or help forge, school board positions on delicate matters, many of which have direct implications for instructional programming.

Instructional Leadership Studies

Recent research on school improvement exhibits the positive role that can be played by building-level administrators (e.g., Firestone & Wilson, 1985) as well as superintendents and their support staffs (e.g., Pajak & Glickman, 1989) in achieving desired instructional goals. In light of such mounting evidence, it is likely that expectations and methods for measuring the attainment of those expectations will change in the coming years. Smith and Andrews (1987), for instance, have suggested that the performance assessment of school principals ought to be based on both instructional leadership activities (input) and student outcomes (output). Despite such urgings, many hurdles to instructional leadership remain. One of the most menacing is the lingering effects of bureaucratic-like management styles that lead many principals and superintendents to treat teachers not as professionals, but as adversaries—not as colleagues but as subordinates (Liftig, 1990).

Many criticisms of current practice are reinforced by observations of practitioner behavior. Frase and Hetzel (1990), for instance, found that principals spend up to 80 percent of their work time in their offices, and many spend more time away from the school campus than they spend in classrooms. Is this because they are insecure in performing instructional leadership responsibilities, or do they elect not to engage in these functions? Graduate study can prepare you to acquire the knowledge and skills necessary to be an instructional leader; but the actualization of this role also relies on personal and organizational philosophies (values and beliefs about teachers and their capabilities to produce positive outcomes). Crowson and McPherson (1987), in observing principals, wrote:

> Although the experiential, institutional, and political forces influencing principals are often similar, the personal predilections and perceptions of individuals regarding the limits of what can be done appear to vary significantly. (p. 152)

Beyond values and beliefs, administrators, like most workers, tend to avoid those tasks that are threatening or discomforting. In essence, they are drawn to tasks that they believe they can do well. Results of management-centered tasks tend to be more perceptible and immediate than those associated with leadership. Successful management of a cafeteria program, for example, can be determined by visible products such as financial statements or positive feedback from consumers; the outcomes of supervisory interventions in the classroom are far more imperceptible. As teachers know so well, some outcomes of instructional interventions may not be visible for months or even years. Even though there is evidence that many administrators choose not to divide their time between management and leadership, this does not dispel concerns about proper balance between the two functions in academic preparation.

Studies in instructional leadership typically fall into two broad categories, curriculum and instruction. Writers do not consistently differentiate between the two; however, here they are treated as separate topics. Curriculum commonly entails the selection and sequencing of courses of study and related learning experiences. Instruction, by contrast, is process-oriented—it focuses on the application of teaching paradigms, the selection and use of equipment and materials, and similar functions associated with teaching.

Curriculum. The study of curriculum includes a number of domains. Three of the most common are

- curriculum theory (determining what knowledge is of most worth or how knowledge can be structured for desired outcomes)
- curriculum development (deciding what to teach, what materials to use)
- curriculum assessment (evaluating structure and outcomes).

The primary reason that administrators study curriculum is to acquire knowledge and skill relative to planning, organizing, and evaluating learning experiences.

Separate courses in curriculum are found in virtually all institutions that prepare school leaders. The more common include the following:

- Introduction to Curriculum
- Elementary School Curriculum
- Middle Grades Curriculum
- High School Curriculum
- Curriculum Theory
- Curriculum Development
- Program Evaluation.

The number of curriculum courses required by universities varies, but state licensing requirements often are a determining factor. Often, students complete only the minimum number of courses despite observations that it is difficult, if not impossible, to be an effective instructional leader without a thorough grasp of curriculum (Rossow, 1990). The connection between academic study and practice is significant. As Wimpelberg (1987) assessed, one common reason that principals shy away from an active involvement in instructional leadership is that they simply do not have an adequate academic grounding in curriculum and instruction.

The focus and extent of curriculum study often depend on the degree program or license being sought. For example, a person acquiring a master's degree in order to obtain certification as an elementary school principal may take only one course in elementary school curriculum. A candidate seeking a Ph.D. with the intention of obtaining a school superintendent's license may take two or three different courses in curriculum. Some students choose to complete a minor or cognate in curriculum, especially if they desire to work in positions requiring instructional leadership skills (e.g., principal or curriculum director).

Curriculum is not developed solely by school administrators. Communities, school board members, state legislatures, governors, teachers, students, and even publishers of school materials may play critical roles in determining what is taught in our schools (Schubert, 1986). Research on the attainment of instructional excellence, however, exhibits the importance of the principal's being the primary leader in the process (Kimbrough & Burkett, 1990). To fulfill this expectation, the administrator must understand how to plan, organize, and evaluate the content of school programs. In addition, he or she must have the ability to evaluate the social context of schooling, especially with regard to reflectively examining personal beliefs (Liston & Zeichner, 1990). Determining what knowledge is of most worth, organizing that knowledge into instructional segments that meet the tests of vertical and horizontal integration, and evaluating the outcomes are critical responsibilities in the realm of curriculum leadership. Movement toward more decentralized concepts (e.g., school-based management) increases expectations for principals to be well-informed professionals in the area of curriculum.

Instruction. Whereas curriculum focuses on what should be taught and the organizational dimensions of subject matter, instruction concentrates on delivery systems. With regard to school administration, three functions are especially cogent: helping teachers to plan for instruction, helping teachers to present instruction, and helping teachers to evaluate instruction (Oliva, 1989).

The term, *instructional leadership,* much like *leadership,* has multiple meanings in the literature and in practice. Smith and Andrews (1989) created a list of expectations that help describe the role: a provider of human resources, a provider of instructional resources, a communicator, and a visible presence in instructional activities. The most specialized component of instructional leadership is *clinical supervision.* Goldhammer, Anderson, and Krajewski (1980) defined this activity as:

> that phase of instructional supervision which draws its data from first-hand observations of actual teaching events, and involves face-to-face (and other associated) interaction between the supervisor and teacher in the analysis of teaching behavior and activities for instructional improvement. (pp. 19–20)

Clinical supervision is the segment of the instructional leadership role of principals that a number of authors stress. Some authorities go so far as to suggest that the actualization of clinical supervision is the most direct means of making a principal an instructional leader (Smith & Andrews, 1987).

Courses in the area of instruction have an array of titles. Some are broad (e.g., Instructional Theory), whereas others are rather specific (e.g., Development of Middle School Instructional Materials). One of the most common courses completed by school administration students relates to the supervision of instruction. Because instructional supervision entails so many ''hands-on'' and ''face-to-face'' activities, components of this specialization are often learned in practica, internships or through on-the-job experiences. Responsibilities in instructional supervision provide the strongest arguments for the requirement that principals obtain experience as classroom teachers prior to receiving an administrative license.

Social Foundations of Education. In Chapter 1, it was noted that schools are complex organizations that evolved over many decades. Effects of culture, individual learner needs, social trends, popular values and beliefs, and information about learning exemplify factors that have contributed to shaping modern schools. Students preparing to be school administrators acquire knowledge regarding these forces in courses commonly referred to as the ''social foundations of education.'' The most common content includes history, philosophy, and sociology of education.

As mentioned, courses do not fall neatly into any one category of study, and this certainly is true of several foundations courses. Educational psychology, for example, is considered to be part of educational foundations at some universities; others view this area to be part of instructional theory; and still others categorize it as a totally separate entity. The study of multicultural education is treated similarly.

Several institutions structure the study of social foundations into a single course that has direct applicability to the needs and interests of aspiring administrators. Such a course may have a title such as The Social Foundations of School Administration.

Knowledge of history, philosophy, sociology, and educational psychology provides an administrator with insights that enhance leadership responsibilities. Take, for instance, the tasks of curriculum planning and evaluation. Not all the learning experiences in a school are planned or visible in curriculum guides. There is in every school a hidden curriculum composed of unstated, implicit, and sometimes unintentional messages transmitted to students through classes, extracurricular activities, and even social relationships (Bennett & LeCompte, 1990). A solid grounding in the foundations enhances the leader's ability to comprehend these dimensions of schooling; and more to the point, it allows the practitioner to integrate the visible and invisible elements of schooling.

Staff Development.   American industry has learned many lessons in the past fifty years. One of the most cogent relates to improving employee performance. In a global economy, profit-seeking companies continually search for advancements that will give them an edge in manufacturing, marketing, and sales. These betterments could entail acquiring new technology or enhancing employee capabilities to use technology already acquired.

Informed school leaders too are recognizing that purposeful organizational change does not occur easily or naturally. And like their counterparts in business management, they especially realize that planned change is a slow and difficult process for the professional staff (Guskey, 1985). But at the same time, contemporary practitioners face mounting pressures to reshape America's schools. Observations made in private industry indicate that organizational change is enhanced when leaders are able to (1) identify those employees who have an especially high need for change and (2) provide them with growth opportunities (Connor & Lake, 1988). In essence, change is best accomplished with people who are willing to change and when these individuals are properly prepared to engage the process.

The heavy reliance on people to perform the required tasks of education should not be taken lightly; it is this reality that gives staff development both its importance and its urgency (Harris, 1980). Unlike the conditions in highly mechanized factories, school improvement cannot be achieved merely by modernizing equipment or installing robotics. Indeed, computers and other technology can facilitate improved instruction, but it is staff development that permits the cultivation of teacher knowledge and skills, a powerful factor in school improvement (Boyer, 1983).

Exposure to the planning, organization, and management of staff development may occur within courses such as curriculum or personnel administration or in a totally separate course of study. Among the more pressing topics included under the heading of staff development are the following:

- assessing needs
- integrating needs with organizational goals

- organizing effective programs
- principles of successful practice
- principles of adult learning
- assessments of programs.

The cogency of these topics is advanced by the rapid deployment of technology, demands for reform, and new knowledge about learning and teaching methods. But one of the most compelling influences has been the association of staff development to improvements in effective schools (Johnson & Snyder, 1989–90).

The nature of leader responsibilities for staff development is changing. It no longer is a simple matter of a superintendent or principal unilaterally deciding what is important. Basic decisions regarding the planning and organization of staff development increasingly will become collaborative. Glickman (1990) pointed out that administrators need to redefine their responsibilities from all-knowing managers who control the instructional activities of teachers to facilitators who involve teachers in decisions related to self-improvement.

Organizational Leadership

In this book, leadership functions are divided between those that are primarily instructional and those that are primarily organizational. Again, the demarcation between the two is not a bold line, but more like a gray area where one category blends into the other. Whereas instructional leadership is concerned with subject matter largely unique to schools, organizational leadership deals with functions common to all institutions. Broadly, these areas include organizational theory, leadership theory, policy analysis, strategic planning, and the behavioral sciences.

Organizational Theory.   Theory is not a dream or a wish; it is not a supposition or speculation; nor is it a philosophical position indicating the way things should be (Owens, 1991). Rather, theory is briefly described as "a set of systematically related propositions specifying causal relationships among variables" (Black & Champion, 1976, p. 56). Theory is developed through research and serves as a guideline for understanding phenomena. Organizational theory involves the systematic ordering of knowledge within the context of organizational behavior. Included is the study of interactions among a particular organizational structure, individuals, groups, and the general environment (Kowalski, 1988).

Study in organizational theory examines several key concepts. These include:

- organizational climate (policies, management styles, communication techniques and similar functions that create expectations and understandings commonly held by those within the organization)
- organizational development (the conceptual framework of how organizations function; a strategy for helping organizations self-correct and self-renew)

- organizational variance (differences in size, structure, leadership, goals, methods, and so forth among organizations)
- organizational adaptability (how institutional change occurs to meet needs and demands).

The study of these and related concepts reveals the significant differences that exist among schools and school districts. The organizational dimensions of schooling constitute a critical area in school administration and Chapter 6 of this book is devoted to this topic.

Leadership Theory. Although organizational and leadership theories are highly intertwined, they are clearly separate domains of study. Leadership in education almost always occurs in organizations; and as such, the outcome of any decision or behavior is likely to be a mixture of environmental, organizational, and personal conditions. Yukl (1989) aptly pointed out that the study of leadership is in a state of ferment. Although many scholars accept its importance, there remain a number of critics who question leadership effectiveness (i.e., the degree to which administrators really make a difference in organizational outcomes). And even among those who believe that leadership makes a significant difference, there are myriad disagreements about the future roles desired for leaders. Two entire chapters in this book (Nine and Ten) review the challenges of leadership and the varying styles used to address these challenges. Over time, leadership theory has emerged as a central theme in the preparation of school administrators.

Policy Analysis. Although the American public often goes to great lengths to separate politics and education, the truth is that schooling has many political dimensions. This is especially the case with regard to policy formulation. Policies are broad guidelines created to give direction to organizations. In public education, policy is made by the federal government (e.g., laws governing the rights of handicapped), state government (e.g., mandates to teach certain subjects), courts of law (e.g., rulings regarding employee rights and responsibilities), and local school boards. Regulations are formulated by administrators to facilitate the implementation of policy. It should be noted, however, that distinctions between policy and regulations, especially legal distinctions, are neither crisp nor clear.

Public policy making has five distinct components: problem formation/identification, policy formulation, policy adoption, policy implementation, and policy evaluation (Portney, 1986). Nagel (1988) defined policy analysis as:

> the process of determining which of various alternative public or governmental policies will most achieve a given set of goals in light of the relations between the policies and goals (p. 3).

Accordingly, policy analysis in education is a procedure used by practitioners and scholars to weigh alternative paths to goal achievement. For example, there may be several courses of action for creating support for tax increases. Policy analysis provides a mechanism for weighing the advantages and disadvantages of each. Social, political, educational, and financial issues are integrated as the analysis evolves.

The importance of studying policy analysis in schools is largely related to two prevailing conditions in all public organizations. First, public institutions historically have relied on trial and error to test policy. In today's world, technology, demographics, and scarce resources make this alternative far less effective. Second, public organizations are less apt than are private, profit-seeking organizations to have employees who are specialists in policy analysis (Quade, 1989).

Another condition elevating the importance of policy studies in public education is the call for decentralization and deregulation. Rubin (1984) made the following two cogent observations: (1) School improvement is most likely if it is achieved through local policies, and (2) knowing what to do and how to do it are critical skills if policy is to be successfully developed. In essence, reform at the local level requires that school officials possess sufficient skills to formulate and evaluate public policy.

Policy studies constitute one of the more difficult areas of preparation for students in school administration. Research in this field has often been marked by inconsistency and bias; however, such problems are being diminished by improved procedures. Boyd (1988) noted that even though the process was far from perfect, policy analysis maintained an essential value:

> . . . despite all the warts and blemishes, policy analysis has made major and extraordinary contributions to our knowledge about social policy and its implementation and about the nature of organizations and their management. (p. 518)

Policy development is an essential task for organizations, and its usage can be enhanced markedly by integrating the process into a system-wide strategic planning effort (Bell, 1989). Thus, the ascending importance of policy development is related to the increasing emphasis on organizational planning. But not all practitioners are fortunate enough to receive a solid grounding in this area. Practitioners reflecting on their academic preparation often cite policy development and analysis as areas where they feel inadequately prepared (Stout, 1989).

Strategic Planning.   When you hear the term *strategic planning*, you may immediately think of long-range planning (i.e., planning that will project two or more years into the future). Although strategic planning has a future orientation, the process more precisely refers to proposed actions by which administrators systematically evaluate organizational opportunities and the potential impacts of environmental changes in an effort to fulfill the missions of the school district (or school) (Justis, Judd, & Stephens, 1985). The word *strategic* stems from military applications and implies that three elements must be addressed: (1) the recognition of an existing situation, (2) the depiction of a desired future situation, and (3) a strategy for adaptation (Stone, 1987). In other words, it is a procedure by which school leaders identify gaps between what is and what is desired and develop a plan of action to eradicate those gaps.

Modern strategic planning is predicated on the belief that organizations are shaped by forces that are external (communities, courts, legislatures) and internal (school district policies, needs identified by teachers and administrators). Accordingly, planning is viewed as a series of linkages between a school system and its community. Strengths of the school district are interfaced with needs, demands, and potential support in an effort to provide overall organizational directions (Verstegen & Wagoner, 1989).

The study of strategic planning often is integrated into several courses of study; but some preparation programs offer a separate course on this topic. The intention of such a study is to enable practitioners to be analysts and assessors of their situations in terms of politics, markets, and finances. Students learn to use political, social, educational, economic, and demographic data to adjust visions, missions, and procedures (Mauriel, 1989).

Behavioral Sciences. The development of integrated planning models illuminated the information needs of school administrators in disciplines such as psychology, sociology, and political science. Perhaps the best-known integrated paradigm is *systems analysis.* This process serves to create understandings of how each part of an organization is interrelated. A good example can be seen in a midwestern university that decided to close its school of engineering. On the surface the decision appeared only to touch faculty and students specifically enrolled in this school. In reality, the decision had a chain reaction for the entire university (lower overall enrollments, a reduction in tuition income, fewer students enrolling in general studies). Similarly, any decision made within one department or unit of a school district can potentially affect all segments of the organization. Milstein and Belasco (1973) noted that the advances of systems analysis models in public education were a primary factor that led to the inclusion of behavioral sciences in school administration study.

Typically, reference to behavioral studies is directed to the liberal arts. Some contend that they also include courses in the social foundations of education; but here, this latter component already has been referenced as part of instructional leadership studies. Some who advocate the broadening of professional education for school administrators stress the humanities as well as the behavioral sciences as essential components of professional study (e.g., Popper, 1989). It is not uncommon for doctoral students in school administration to complete a cognate in one of the behavioral sciences or humanities. Issues such as ethics, moral behavior, human behavior, social behavior, cultural influences, and social science research can be injected into professional education via the behavioral sciences and humanities.

Position-Specific Studies

Several courses included in the study of educational administration center on a given position rather than specific functions. The two most common courses found in this category are the principalship and the superintendency. To a lesser degree, some universities offer position-specific courses for the business manager or the director of curriculum. Since position-specific courses examine the scope of responsibilities associated with a single assignment, the emphasis is on the application of leadership and management techniques in the context of a given administrative role.

The American public school system is organized largely on a three-tier pattern: elementary, middle grades, high school. The latter two divisions have many commonalities such as departmentalized teaching, extracurricular activities, and segmented instructional periods. Partly for this reason, middle schools (and junior high schools) and high schools are commonly referred to as secondary schools. The study of the principalship often breaks down along these lines; that is, a separate course is offered on the administration of elementary schools and a separate course on the administration of secondary schools. The latter encompasses both middle grades and high school. At some institutions, the principalship, elementary and secondary, is studied generically in a single course.

The principal wears many hats. The leadership role in an individual school is often labeled "middle management," suggesting a position between the central administration and the teachers. The person holding this post has many responsibilities, and as mentioned earlier, expectations for enhanced leadership and calls for decentralization and deregulation are making the list longer.

The superintendency also can be studied in a separate course or seminar. Many specialist and doctoral programs provide such an experience as a capstone to professional preparation. One facet of this course is the examination of the dynamics of school superintendent-school board relationships. Additionally, the course content may contain practical dimensions such as preparing agendas and supporting materials for board meetings, delegating authority, and creating an organizational plan for the central office.

Position-specific courses offer an excellent opportunity to bridge theory with craft knowledge; and in so doing, link academic study more directly to practice. These courses can be used to allow students to apply knowledge to problems and to reflect on the potential consequences of their decisions. This can be done by using simulations, vignettes, and case studies to hone critical thinking skills, decision-making skills, reflective thinking, group leadership skills, and other cognitive and affective processes critical to contemporary leadership (Kowalski, 1991). Position-specific courses also offer an excellent format for interfacing political and ethical considerations.

Research Methods

In professional practice, knowledge is power. This is especially true when the practitioner is able to utilize scientific methods to address current concerns, develop alternative solutions, and evaluate the merits of each of these alternatives. The primary process used to gain such knowledge is research. Kerlinger (1986) defined scientific research as the

> systematic, controlled, empirical, and critical investigation of natural phenomena guided by theory and hypotheses about the presumed relations among such phenomena. (p. 10)

Research may be used by the practitioner in two primary ways: (1) to study problems by applying scientific methods (i.e., collecting data that give clearer focus to the problem) and (2) by using the research findings of others as a source of information (i.e., using research outcomes to help inform decisions).

One fundamental purpose of studying research is to prepare the student to be a consumer of research—a purpose that is most cogent to practitioners. All administrators can profit from keeping abreast of new knowledge reported in journals and books. Students who pursue the doctorate typically are required to complete several advanced courses in quantitative research (e.g., statistics, experimental design) and qualitative research (e.g., ethnography). The advanced study prepares students to conduct research and to critically analyze the work of others.

Field-Based Experiences

Recurring criticisms that preparation programs fail to do an adequate job of bridging theory with practice have led to increased emphasis on field-based experiences. These opportunities can be among the most exciting in your academic studies. Either through practica or internships, you are given the opportunity to put your knowledge and skills to work—and to do so under the guidance of a seasoned practitioner.

The practicum is commonly defined as a course structured to provide opportunities for practical experiences in a given field of study. Often, persons use this term synonymously with *internship.* Anderson (1989), however, distinguished between the two by noting that the practicum usually is a significant project, at least one semester in duration, that permits the student to demonstrate a specific skill (or skills), and it is not typically a full-time assignment. On the other hand, he described the internship as an experience that was usually full time and more generic in orientation. Milstein, Bobroff, and Restine (1991) commented that the internship not only allowed students an opportunity to apply knowledge from coursework, it also permitted them to determine if they possessed the ability and desire to be administrators.

The National Policy Board for Educational Administration (1989) suggested that preparation programs ought to develop long-term formal relationships with school districts in order to provide meaningful clinical study, field residency, and applied research. Such partnerships have the potential of reducing concerns about unstructured experiences or experiences that are artificial (e.g., the student is sheltered from many of the activities of the practitioner). Practitioners who serve as supervisors of these internships may hold status as clinical or adjunct professors.

CRITICAL CONSIDERATIONS

To this point, this chapter has described degrees and courses that comprise the study of school administration. Also cogent to a full understanding of professional preparation is a review of circumstances that suggest that major changes in academic preparation may be in the offing. These factors are broadly categorized here as those that relate to the reform movement and those that are associated with certification, competition, and accreditation.

Calls for Reform

Practices in school districts and curricula in many departments of school administration still reflect a management orientation (Snyder & Anderson, 1986). And despite efforts to diversify graduate school experiences, especially by adding practica and internships, it is noteworthy that practitioners continue to cite deficiencies in their graduate training as a primary concern as they enter practice (Anderson, 1989). Often such dissatisfactions stem from unreasonable expectations that professional school experiences should provide them with all the knowledge and skill they will ever need. Goodlad (1990) noted that programs for professional educators must be conducted in such a way that practitioners accept lifelong learning and continual inquiry as a natural aspect of professional practice. That is, administrators need to recognize that professional study does not constitute a complete and comprehensive "training"; rather, such study provides the tools that permit the practitioner to become increasingly proficient by utilizing experience, continuing education, and reflection.

Professional preparation is clearly not the sole, or in many cases the primary, determinant of practitioner behavior. Hallinger and Murphy (1991) claimed that although graduates of school administration programs can recite the characteristics of effective schools, many remain unconvinced of their applicability. Learning facts does not ensure changes in beliefs. Once employed, practitioners encounter socialization processes that can lead to severe conflicts between what they learned in graduate school and the prevailing philosophy of the organization in which they work. This is but one reason why some reformers believe that professional study and practice need to be more closely aligned.

Emanating from reform initiatives are strongly stated suggestions that the academic preparation of school administrators needs to be reconstructed. The National Policy Board for Educational Administration (1989), for one, recommended that elements of the professional curriculum should contain a common core of knowledge and skills grounded in real problems confronted by practitioners—and many of these real problems are in the realms of instructional and organizational leadership. The board stated that this core should address

- societal and cultural influences on schooling,
- teaching and learning processes and school improvement,
- organizational theory,
- methodologies of organizational studies and policy analysis,
- leadership and management processes and functions,
- policy studies and politics of education,
- moral and ethical dimensions of schooling. (p. 19)

The central question confronting those who must decide whether change is possible is how curricula can be broadened at a time when fewer students are willing or able to become full-time students.

The mounting pressure to revolutionize professional preparation is in many respects a by-product of public dissatisfaction with schools in general (Griffiths, Stout, & Forsyth, 1988). For example, analyses of institutional problems often uncover leadership voids—a condition even more troublesome when considered in the context of effective schools research. Thus initiatives for reforming public education often include direct or indirect urgings that transformed schools need to be led by professionals who possess a broad range of knowledge and skills. It seems most unlikely that preparation programs can escape the implications of these demands for a new breed of school administrators. Consider the following two observations that exhibit how contemporary conditions transmit messages that ought not be ignored by those responsible for professional preparation:

- The necessity for political action (i.e., building coalitions with mayors, governors, and private business) has increased markedly since the mid-1950s. Often superintendents take on added responsibilities such as being a advocate for needy children (Murphy, 1991).
- Research is providing evidence that the principals who are viewed as most effective are those who take an active role in areas such as instructional improvement and the development of conducive teaching/learning environments (Kimbrough & Burkett, 1990).

These two examples illustrate how changing conditions in relationship between school and society are placing novel demands on practitioners.

Certification, Competition, and Accreditation

Largely as outgrowths of the reform movement, three specific forces are pressuring traditional school administration programs to change. The first is state licensure. Historically, administrative licensure in many states has been based on the completion of a prescribed set of courses, largely courses addressing the management areas of administration. Politicians and other reformers have raised two burning questions regarding these long-standing standards: (1) Are the right types of courses being required? (2) Are examinations a better method for issuing licenses?

Second, universities are facing mounting competition. This is especially true with regard to students who are not seeking to complete degrees. Cooperatives forged by practitioners (e.g., principal centers) as well as educational programs offered by organizations and entrepreneurs directly compete with universities in many parts of the country. These programs often focus narrowly on needs that repeatedly have been expressed by practitioners. Experienced practitioners often seek programs that have a high degree of relevance to their current positions (Pitner, 1988).

Accreditation of university-based programs is the third cogent force confronting the professional preparation of administrators. In recent years, there have been a growing number of attempts to tie accreditation to licensure. Some critics of current practices, for example, believe that only graduates of accredited programs should be permitted to obtain administrative certification.

There are two basic types of accreditation: regional and professional. The former is granted by several associations having jurisdiction over set territories. The Southern Association and the North Central Association of Colleges and Schools serve as examples of regional accrediting agencies. These voluntary groups essentially approve entire institutions and specific levels of programs (e.g., accrediting a university at the bachelor's, master's, and doctoral levels). Professional accreditation is more program focused. In education this function is assumed by the National Council for the Accreditation of Teacher Education (NCATE). The NCATE provides accreditation for basic and advanced programs for professional educators. Accreditation signifies that an institution and/or program meets certain standards of quality. Because accreditation is politically important for most institutions and because the process increasingly is being tied to licensure, it can force major changes in professional preparation.

BARRIERS TO CHANGE

Even though demands for changing administrator preparation are strong, there is still substantial doubt as to whether meaningful revisions will occur. One potential reform barrier is certification. Although this factor was just mentioned as a potential force for change, it also constitutes a primary barrier. In some states, the process is being used to encourage universities to reshape academic study; but in other states, inflexibility serves to protect the ststus quo. Clark (1989) described how the latter condition affects the experiences of aspiring administrators:

> Generally the required core consists only of those courses necessary for licensure in the home state. Any concept of sequence is lost. Course content is often irrelevant, outdated, and unchallenging. Essential learnings, such as knowledge of the teaching and learning process, may not be covered at all. Students routinely complete certification requirements with minimal information about the classroom, the school as an organization, or the social context of schooling. (p. 4)

The movement away from a curriculum skewed heavily toward management studies is also hampered by several other conditions. First, local-level criticisms of school administrators tend to be harshest in areas that are largely or exclusively managerial (e.g., finance, facilities). This condition reinforces practitioner beliefs that the general public places instructional issues well behind economic matters.

Second, many students enter graduate study already socialized by people and groups in the schools in which they are or have been working. That is, they may already harbor beliefs that management is far more important than leadership. Principals and superintendents knowingly and unknowingly influence the thoughts of aspiring administrators. Take, for example, the principal who told one of his teachers who was pursuing a degree in school administration, "Don't let those professors fill your head with that theory stuff. Learn how to handle money and people. And much of that is just common sense." Such myopic perceptions perpetuate images and practices that create student resistance to curricular change.

Third, the funding status of many programs in educational administration is not favorable. Compared to other professional preparation programs, those in school administration are usually underfunded (Twombly & Ebmeier, 1989). The fiscal ability of universities to provide a more comprehensive program of study remains in doubt.

Fourth, the broadening of graduate curricula raises serious questions about providing society with an adequate number of practitioners. Given the status and compensation of administrators, some are questioning if it is feasible to increase the academic requirements for entering practice (e.g., Browder, 1990–91). In this respect, market conditions also present a barrier to change.

Earlier in the book, it was noted that the preoccupation with management dates to the earliest days of school administration. The original purpose of administration was to have subordinates who would perform clerical and managerial tasks for school boards. This initial intention was sustained and fortified for many decades largely because of three primary factors: socialization, daily experiences, and graduate training (Cuban, 1988). In a sense, each served as a reinforcement for the others. Additionally, advances in management and social science during the late 1950s and early 1960s caught the attention of professors of school administration. This focus served to direct attention away from educational issues and toward technical and human skills in many preparation programs (Sergiovanni, 1991b).

IMPLICATIONS FOR PRACTICE

In planning your career, it is important for you to understand the academic requirements for entering practice. Also, you should understand that school administration is not a discipline in the traditional sense, but rather an eclectic field of study that concentrates on applying leadership and management in the organizational context of schools and school districts. Often students starting their studies in school administration ask, "Why is this course or that course required?" Since the curriculum encompasses study in several areas, this overview was designed to provide a basic explanation of some standard features of professional preparation. This information may prove useful as you contemplate your career goals, and it is especially cogent to deliberations regarding further academic study.

Your attitude toward professional preparation is something you need to think about. Do you want to get through courses as quickly as possible so you can obtain additional certificates and apply for higher paying positions? Or do you view administration as an opportunity to really make a difference in the education of thousands of students—or to find new challenges for yourself? These are not meaningless questions. You are more apt to approach your studies with enthusiasm if you have an appreciation for the importance of academic preparation. Students who see courses, regardless of whether they are highly technical or highly theoretical, as senseless hurdles are likely to gain little that will serve them in their career. After reading this chapter, you should have an understanding of the nature and purposes of professional study in school administration. You should comprehend the importance of questions surrounding reform in professional preparation.

Perhaps the most essential point that needs to be made relates to your expectations in studying school administration. You should not fall victim to the myopic notion that courses and internships will provide all the knowledge and skills needed for a lifetime. They will not. What they can provide are basic knowledge and skills and a deep appreciation for what it means to be a professional.

FOR FURTHER STUDY

1. Why do you believe there was so much emphasis placed on managerial roles of school administrators in the first half of the twentieth century?

2. What is meant by professional socialization? Does it occur with teachers? with principals?

3. Identify two areas of administrative responsibility that involve both management and leadership.

4. What are the differences between theory and reality?

5. List six attributes or characteristics that a major private manufacturing organization would have in common with school districts.

6. What do you think is the least important part of graduate study in school administration? Conversely, what do you consider most important? What leads you to your responses?

7. Should it be possible for persons who have no preparation and experience in teaching to receive a graduate degree in school administration? Why or why not?

8. Do you believe that an internship should be required for all graduate degrees in school administration? Why or why not?

9. In what ways would the study of the philosophy of education enhance the preparation of a school administrator?

10. Do you believe that many practitioners use the scientific method to study problems in their work? Why or why not?

OTHER SUGGESTED ACTIVITIES

1. Determine the degree requirements for being a principal or superintendent in your state.

2. Obtain the course of study for your current degree program. Determine if you understand the purpose of each of the courses listed.

3. Invite the chair of the department that houses school administration to visit your class to discuss his or her philosophy regarding preservice academic study.

4. Read the 1991 article, "The Dark Side of Professionalism in Educational Administration," by T. J. Sergiovanni (see references at end of this chapter for full citation). Discuss the major points he makes and how his arguments could affect professional education.

5. In recent years, a number of influential political leaders have questioned the value of persons completing courses in professional education to become teachers. Discuss whether you believe it is possible for someone who has not completed courses in school administration to be an effective principal.

REFERENCES

Anderson, M. E. (1989). Training and selecting school leaders. In S. Smith and P. Piele (Eds.), *School leadership: Handbook for excellence* (2nd ed.) (pp. 53–63). Eugene, OR: ERIC Clearinghouse on Educational Management.

Bell, E. D. (1989). The interaction of strategic planning, policy development, and settings in education: A case study. *Planning and Changing, 20* (4), 237–242.

Bennett, K. P., & LeCompte, M. D. (1990). *How schools work: A sociological analysis of education.* New York: Longman.

Black, J. A., & Champion, D. J. (1976). *Methods and issues in social research.* New York: Wiley.

Boyd, W. L. (1988). Policy analysis, educational policy, and management: Through a glass darkly? In N. Boyan (Ed.), *Handbook of research on educational administration* (pp. 501–522). New York: Longman.

Boyer, E. L. (1983). *High school: A report on secondary education in America.* New York: Harper & Row.

Browder, L. H. (1990–91). A critical essay on National Policy Board "Agenda." *National Forum of Educational Administration and Supervision Journal, 8* (1), 5–40.

Campbell, R. F., Corbally, J. E., & Nystrand, R. O. (1983). *Introduction to educational administration* (6th ed.). Boston: Allyn and Bacon.

Castetter, W. B. (1981). *The personnel function in educational administration* (3rd ed.). New York: Macmillan.

Chick, C., Smith, P., & Yeabower, G. (1987). Last in: First out maintenance budgets. *CEPF Journal, 25* (4), 4–6.

Clark, D. L. (1989). Time to say enough! *Agenda* (newsletter of the National Policy Board for Educational Administration), 1 (1), 1, 4–5.

Connor, P. E., & Lake, L. K. (1988). *Managing organizational change.* New York: Praeger.

Cooper, B. S., & Boyd, W. L. (1987). The evolution of training for school administrators. In J. Murphy and P. Hallinger (Eds.), *Approaches to administrative training in education* (pp. 3–27). Albany: State University of New York Press.

Crowson, R. L., & McPherson, R. B. (1987). Sources of constraints and opportunities for discretion in the principalship. In J. Lane & H. Walberg (Eds.), *Effective school leadership* (pp. 129–156). Berkeley, CA: McCutchan.

Cuban, L. (1988). *The managerial imperative and the practice of leadership in schools.* Albany: State University of New York Press.

Firestone, W. A., & Wilson, B. L. (1985). Using bureaucratic and cultural linkages to improve instruction: The principal's contribution. *Educational Administration Quarterly, 21* (2), 17–30.

Frase, L., & Hetzel, R. (1990). *School management by wandering around.* Lancaster, PA: Technomic.

Glass, T. E. (1991). The slighting of administration preparation. *The School Administrator, 48* (4), 29–30.

Glickman, C. D. (1990). *Supervision of instruction: A developmental approach* (2nd ed.). Boston: Allyn and Bacon.

Goldhammer, R., Anderson, R. H., & Krajewski, R. J. (1980). *Clinical supervision* (2nd ed.). New York: Holt, Rinehart & Winston.

Goodlad, J. I. (1990). *Teachers for our nation's schools.* San Francisco: Jossey-Bass.

Gorton, R. A. (1976). *School administration: Challenge and opportunity for leadership.* Dubuque, IA: Wm. C. Brown.

Griffiths, D. E., Stout, R. T., & Forsyth, P. B. (1988). The preparation of educational administrators. In D. Griffiths, R. Stout, & P. Forsyth (Eds.), *Leaders for America's schools* (pp. 284–304). Berkeley, CA: McCutchan.

Guskey, T. R. (1985). Staff development and teacher change. *Educational Leadership,* 42 (7), 57–60.

Guthrie, J. W., Garms, W. I., & Pierce, L. C. (1988). *School finance and education policy: Enhancing educational efficiency, equality, and choice* (2nd ed.). Englewood Cliffs, NJ: Prentice-Hall.

Hallinger, P., & Murphy, J. (1991). Developing leaders for tomorrow's schools. *Phi Delta Kappan,* 72 (7), 514–520.

Harris, B. M. (1980). *Improving staff performance through in-service education.* Boston: Allyn and Bacon.

Holliday, A. E. (1990). Revise the scope of your school-community relations program to enhance student achievement. *Record in Educational Administration and Supervision,* 11 (1), 54–59.

Johnson, W. L., & Snyder, K. J. (1989–90). A study on the instructional leadership training needs of school administrators. *National Forum of Educational Administration and Supervision Journal,* 6 (3), 80–95.

Justis, R. T., Judd, R. J., & Stephens, D. B. (1985). *Strategic management and policy.* Englewood Cliffs, NJ: Prentice-Hall.

Kerlinger, F. N. (1986). *Foundations of behavioral research* (3rd ed.). New York: Holt, Rinehart and Winston.

Kimbrough, R. B., & Burkett, C. W. (1990). *The principalship: Concepts and practices.* Englewood Cliffs, NJ: Prentice-Hall.

Kindred, L. W., Bagin, D., & Gallagher, D. R. (1990). *The school and community relations* (4th ed.). Englewood Cliffs, NJ: Prentice-Hall.

Kowalski, T. J. (1988). *The organization and planning of adult education.* Albany: State University of New York Press.

———. (1989). *Planning and managing school facilities.* New York: Praeger.

———. (1991). *Case studies on educational administration.* New York: Longman.

Lewis, A. (1989). *Wolves at the schoolhouse door: An investigation of the condition of public school buildings.* Washington, DC: Education Writers Association.

Lieberman, M. (1986). *Beyond public education.* New York: Praeger.

Liftig, R. (1990). Our dirty little secrets: Myths about teachers and administrators. *Educational Leadership,* 47 (8), 67–70.

Liston, D. P., & Zeichner, K. M. (1990). Teacher education and the social context of schooling: Issues for curriculum development. *American Educational Research Journal,* 27 (4), 610–636.

McCarthy, M. M., & Cambron, N. H. (1981). *Public school law.* Boston: Allyn and Bacon.

Mauriel, J. J. (1989). *Strategic leadership for schools.* San Francisco: Jossey-Bass.

Milstein, M. M., & Belasco, J. A. (1973). *Educational administration and the behavioral sciences: A systems approach.* Boston: Allyn and Bacon.

Milstein, M. M., Bobroff, B. M., and Restine, L. N. (1991). *Internship programs in educational administration.* New York: Teachers College Press.

Murphy, J. T. (1991). Superintendents as saviors: From the Terminator to Pogo. *Phi Delta Kappan* 72, (7), 507–513.

Nagel, S. S. (1988). *Policy studies: Integration and evaluation.* New York: Greenwood Press.

National Commission on Excellence in Educational Administration (1988). Leaders for America's schools. In D. Griffiths, R. Stout, & P. Forsyth (Eds.), *Leaders for America's schools: The report and papers of the National Commission on Excellence in Educational Administration.* (pp. 284–304). Berkeley, CA: McCutchan.

National Policy Board for Educational Administration (1989). *Improving the preparation of school administrators: An agenda for reform.* Charlottesville: University of Virginia.

Norton, M. S., & Levan, F. D. (1988). Doctoral studies of students in educational administration programs in UCEA-member institutions. In D. Griffiths, R. Stout, & P. Forsyth (Eds.), *Leaders for America's schools* (pp. 351–359). Berkeley, CA: McCutchan.

Oliva, P. F. (1989). *Supervision for today's schools* (3rd ed.). New York: Longman.

Owens, R. C. (1991). *Organizational behavior in education* (4th ed.). Englewood Cliffs, NJ: Prentice-Hall.

Pajak, E. F., & Glickman, C. D. (1989). Dimensions of school district improvement. *Educational Leadership,* 46 (8), 61–64.

Pitner, N. (1982). *Training of the school administrator: State of the art.* Eugene: Center for Educational Policy and Management at the University of Oregon.

———. (1988). School administrator preparation: The state of the art. In D. Griffiths, R. Stout, & P. Forsyth (Eds.), *Leaders for America's schools* (pp. 367–402). Berkeley, CA: McCutchan.

Popper, S. H. (1989). The instrumental value of the humanities in administrative preparation. In J. Burdin (Ed.), *School leadership* (pp. 366–389). Newbury Park, CA: Sage.

Portney, K. E. (1986). *Approaching public policy analysis.* Englewood Cliffs, NJ: Prentice-Hall.

Quade, E. S. (1989). *Analysis for public decisions* (3rd ed.). New York: North-Holland.

Rebore, R. W. (1991). *Personnel administration in education* (3rd ed.). Englewood Cliffs, NJ: Prentice-Hall.

Rossow, L. F. (1990). *The principalship: Dimensions in instructional leadership.* Englewood Cliffs, NJ: Prentice-Hall.

Rubin, L. (1984). Formulating education policy in the aftermath of the reports. *Educational Leadership,* 42 (2), 7–10.

Schubert, W. H. (1986). *Curriculum: Perspective, paradigm, and possibility.* New York: Macmillan.

Sergiovanni, T. J. (1991a). The dark side of professionalism in educational administration. *Phi Delta Kappan,* 72 (7), 521–526.

———. (1991b). *The principalship: A reflective practice perspective* (2nd ed.). Boston: Allyn and Bacon.

Smith, W. F., & Andrews, R. L. (1987). Clinical supervision of principals. *Educational Leadership,* 45 (1), 34–37.

Smith, W. F., & Andrews, R. L. (1989). *Instructional leadership: How principals make a difference.* Alexandria, VA: Association for Supervision and Curriculum Development.

Snyder, K. J., & Anderson, R. H. (1986). *Managing productive schools.* Orlando, FL: Academic Press College Division.

Stone, S. C. (1987). *Strategic planning for independent schools.* Boston: National Association of Independent Schools.

Stout, R. T. (1989). A review of criticisms of educational administration: The state of the art. In J. Burdin (Ed.), *School leadership* (pp. 390–402). Newbury Park, CA: Sage.

Twombly, S., & Ebmeier, H. (1989). Educational administration programs: The cash cow of the university? *Notes on Reform,* Number 4, The National Policy Board for Educational Administration. Charlottesville: University of Virginia.

Valente, J. (1980). *Law and the schools.* Columbus, OH: Merrill.

Verstegen, D. A., & Wagoner, J. L. (1989). Strategic planning for policy development— An evolving model. *Planning and Changing,* 20 (1), 33–49.

Wimpelberg, R. K. (1987). The dilemma of instructional leadership and a central role for central office. In W. Greenfield (Ed.), *Instructional leadership: Concepts, issues, and controversies* (pp. 100–117). Boston: Allyn and Bacon.

Yukl, G. A. (1989). *Leadership in organizations* (2nd ed.). Englewood Cliffs, NJ: Prentice-Hall.

CHAPTER 4

School Administration: Requirements and Opportunities

Chapter Content

Licensing/Certification Issues

Quality-of-Life Considerations

Contemporary Opportunities

Implications for Practice

At this point, you should have a basic understanding of school administration as a specialized area of study and practice. This chapter explores issues related to formally entering the profession. Is a license required? Do requirements vary from one state to another? What are the employment opportunities in school administration? What are the income possibilities?

In pursuing professional studies, you must make a number of critical decisions. Selecting a university, selecting a major, and even deciding which elective courses you will take serve as examples. In the previous chapter, the scope of academic preparation and current conditions that may affect professional preparation were discussed. In addition to this information, an understanding of licensing and employment practices, quality-of-life issues, and market conditions related to employment may assist you in making informed decisions about your career. As the material in Chapter 2 illustrated, there are many different roles included under the umbrella of school administration; this fact makes career planning a valuable tool.

Understanding the relationships between education, licensing, and practice also is made more critical by proposed changes flowing from school reform efforts. In writing about entry into practice in the United States, Gousha, LoPresti, and Jones (1988) observed:

Although there appears to be no specific common thread to the considerations of the states, districts, and campuses, it is obvious that there is much activity with respect to updating and revising programs and procedures for certification, employment, and preparation of school administrators. (p. 206)

The fact that universities, state governments, and school districts are developing independent agendas for change clearly makes career planning more difficult. What occurs in South Dakota may be quite different from the modifications promulgated in New Mexico. As you read this chapter, three observations should be kept in mind:

1. There are multiple areas of specialization within school administration.
2. Change in professional education and licensing is occurring at a rather rapid pace.
3. Not all changes are moving in the same direction.

LICENSING/CERTIFICATION ISSUES

Often the terms *certification* and *licensing* are used synonymously. This is the case in this book. Both words connote authorization to perform certain tasks and duties. An argument can be made that the terms are different in that licensing typically is used in conjunction with a mandatory process, whereas certification often refers to a voluntary procedure. Those who call for the national certification of educators, for example, refer to this distinction. They argue that state licensing permits one to practice, but national certification provides a certificate of competence (similar to board certifications in medicine). But at this time, a number of states officially use the word *certification* rather than *licensure* to refer to the documents issued to educators.

In the United States, most professions, including education, require a license to practice. But there was a time when such authorization was not required for teachers and administrators. Licensing of educators grew out of a belief that there was a need to set minimum standards for teachers as schools became larger and teaching more specialized (Armstrong, Henson, & Savage, 1989). The licensing of administrators and other education specialists (e.g., school counselors, psychologists) was an outgrowth of the licensing of teachers. Prior to World War II, a number of states did not even issue administrative certificates; and in states where licensing was mandatory, requirements for specific study in educational administration and supporting areas were not extensive (Campbell, Fleming, Newell, & Bennion, 1987).

The Relationship of Licensing and Professional Preparation

The granting of an administrative certificate does not automatically occur with the granting of a diploma for a graduate degree. Degree requirements are set by colleges and universities; certification standards are established by each of the fifty states (and other official territories of the United States), typically through a branch of the state department of education. Since the late 1980s, there have been efforts in several states to establish professional standards boards similar to those used in more established professions, such as law and dentistry. These state boards may be constituted to function in an autonomous regulatory capacity or as an advisory body (Shive, 1988). A major point of controversy with regard to establishing standards boards is the selection of board members. Several states (e.g., Connecticut and Indiana) have created licensing boards that ensure classroom teachers a majority of membership. This condition has sparked concerns among school administrators and professors of school administration that teacher unions may gain control of administrative licensing. If this were to occur, unions could either directly or circuitously establish requirements for the professional preparation of administrators. Similar concerns in other professions have resulted in multiple licensing boards. (For example, health providers often have separate boards for physicians, dentists, and nurses.)

Earlier in the book, it was noted that the two processes of earning a graduate degree and receiving a license to practice, although distinctively different, are related. Typically, universities establish degree requirements congruent with existing certification standards—public universities are especially prone to do so. Some may argue that the reverse is true—that certification standards flow from decisions made by major universities—but there is little evidence to support such a conclusion. Alterations in licensing promulgated by state officials essentially force universities to realign academic programs.

In 1987, the Texas legislature passed Senate Bill 994, a law limiting the number of credit hours students could complete in education courses to eighteen semester hours. This move was controversial for at least two reasons: (1) It set a maximum rather than a minimum, and (2) teacher educators and organizations were not a partner in the process of making this critical decision (Warner, 1990). But despite these shortcomings, universities in that state had little choice but to revise their professional preparation programs when the law was passed. This example shows just how powerful state government can be in determining directions for professional education.

During the reform debates spanning the past decade, several leaders in education have called for revisions that would reduce the cause and effect relationship between professional preparation and licensing. Not all critics, however, viewed the problem in the same way or proposed the same solutions. Boyer (1983) contended that "those who educate prospective teachers also control credentialing" (p. 180). He saw university professors as having too much power, and advocated a system where certification would depend on testing and an analysis of academic work—not on the recommendations of the university where the student completed academic work. By contrast, Goodlad (1990) viewed the problem as follows:

> Programs for the education of educators, in order to be vital and renewing, must be free from curricular specifications by licensing agencies and restrained only by enlightened, professionally driven requirements for accreditation. (p. 302)

Goodlad believed that licensing protects the public, certification connotes completion of academic preparation, and accreditation indicates that a program meets standards properly established by the profession. He argued that all three should be separate and that all are necessary to ensure competence.

The Legal Meaning of License

A certificate to practice as an educator, be it teacher or administrator, is not a property right. That is to say, it is not a contract between the individual practitioner and the state (Hessong & Weeks, 1991). This fact is critical because the state retains the right to change conditions of certification without legal concern for violating the property rights of certificate holders. Despite this condition, state leaders traditionally have been politically sensitive about establishing new requirements that would adversely affect those already in practice. Armstrong, Henson, and Savage (1989) wrote the following in this regard:

> . . . few substantial changes in certification requirements affect those with
> certificates in hand. For political reasons, state legislatures find it easier to pass
> changes in certification requirements by exempting those already holding
> certificates from many, if not all, of the new requirements. (p. 307)

This common practice of granting exemptions, referred to as "grandfathering," is one way of establishing new requirements while avoiding a political battle with those already licensed.

The topic of licensing is complicated by the fact that each of the fifty states and the District of Columbia sets its own standards for practice. Separate requirements also exist in territories of the United States (e.g., Puerto Rico). The net result of this individuality is a wide array of requirements, sometimes even dissimilar requirements, that confuse prospective school administrators. Today, it is very likely that many school administrators will work in two or more states during their careers. Increased mobility has resulted in a growing number of practitioners obtaining licensing in more than one state.

State Requirements

Baptist (1989) observed that administrative certification requirements are both an area of needed improvement and a vehicle for reform. Not only do these requirements vary among the fifty states, in some instances markedly, but things become even more muddled by their continual modification. Present practices by state licensing boards and legislatures serve to create a high level of instability (O'Reily, 1989). In large measure, impermanence is associated with diverse thoughts about what knowledge (and skills) is of most worth for school administrators—as noted in the previous chapter, a problem commonly recognized but not easily resolved.

Differences in state licensing requirements exist primarily in the types of certificates offered, academic degree required, and amount of professional experience required (e.g., classroom teaching experience). A valuable resource for reviewing exact specifications in each of the states is the *Manual on Certification and Preparation of Educational Personnel in the United States* prepared by the National Association of State Directors of Teacher Education and Certification (NASDTEC). This document is updated every few years and is available through certification advisors working with university-based programs. You should understand that state standards change frequently, and therefore, examples cited here are subject to modification.

Types of Licenses Issued.   Not only do specific requirements for administrative licensing vary, but the number and types of administrative licenses issued by the states also are heterogeneous. Some states, for instance, offer only one general administrative certificate that permits the practitioner to occupy any leadership position ranging from assistant principal to superintendent of schools. Other states issue separate certificates for principals and superintendents. In a growing number of states, separate certificates also are being issued for specializations such as business manager or director of special education. Until recently, Michigan was the only state not issuing administrative certificates. In the District of Columbia, administrators are certified by local educational agencies for current vacancies.

In Connecticut, for example, two administrative licenses are issued: superintendent of schools and intermediate administrator or supervisor. Each has two forms—a provisional license and a standard license. The superintendent's certificate is required for a superintendent, and the other covers all remaining administrative positions. Contrast this with Illinois, where one administrative certificate is issued—but with four different endorsements. The supervisory endorsement is required for curriculum directors, department chairs with administrative status, and other, similar positions; the general administrative endorsement is required for assistant principals, principals, and assistant superintendents; the chief school business endorsement is required for business managers; and the superintendent endorsement is required for superintendents.

In many states, separate certificates are issued for elementary and secondary school administrators (both principals and assistant principals). In a survey of state licensing officials, Gousha, LoPresti, and Jones (1988) found that nineteen of thirty- eight responding states issued separate certificates to elementary and secondary school principals. Very few states issue a separate certificate for the middle school principalship—fewer than 10 percent of middle school principals nationally hold such a license. Rather, about two-thirds of these principals hold a secondary principal's license (Edelfelt, 1988). In North Dakota, a rather unique licensing system exists for principals. There, three different levels of certificates are issued for both elementary and secondary school principals. The levels limit practice based on pupil enrollments (e.g., holding the lowest-level license limits holders to working in small schools).

Degrees.   The vast majority of the states require the completion of at least a master's degree to obtain an administrative license. Some states require higher levels of education for the superintendent's license. Baptist (1989) reported that forty-one states consider the completion of a specific graduate degree to be a minimum requirement for certification as a superintendent. Seven states require the completion of a specialist degree (or equivalent). Currently, no state requires the doctorate.

Although the major of the graduate degree may not be specified in the certification requirements, many states stipulate a minimum number of hours in administration and supervision that must be completed as part of, or in addition to, the graduate degree. For instance, the requirements for an elementary school principal's certificate in Arkansas requires a master's degree from a nationally accredited institution with no fewer than eighteen semester hours of graduate credit in administration, curriculum, supervision, and related fields in administrative work at the elementary school level.

Professional Experience.   Many of the states require teaching experience to obtain an administrative license. Often this requirement is accompanied by a stipulation that such experience must have been gained while the individual held a valid teaching license. The modal requirement is three years of teaching experience.

Many states also stipulate that one must possess administrative experience to obtain higher level licenses (i.e., higher than the initial license). This approach is often referred to as *layered certificates.* The two most common examples of this practice are (1) obtaining a superintendent's license after holding a lower level license (e.g., a principal's license), and (2) moving from a provisional certificate to a professional or life certificate. A provisional certificate is issued for a specified period (e.g., three years) and is the first license issued. A professional certificate typically is valid for a longer period (e.g., ten years). A life license does not require renewal in the state in which it is issued. Indiana provides one example of layered certificates. Moving from a standard administrative license to a professional license in that state requires five years of administrative experience. California, by comparison, requires only two years of administrative experience to move from a preliminary credential to a professional credential.

Duration of the License.   Variation also exists in the time parameters for licensing, regardless of whether they are provisional or more permanent. In Idaho, administrative certificates are valid for five years and are renewable. South Dakota issues a temporary endorsement to persons administering for the first time. These persons must work under the supervision of a three-member committee for one year. Successful completion of this experience permits the holder to then obtain other administrative certificates which are valid for five years. Mississippi issues administrative certificates that are valid for ten years; and in New Jersey, all administrative certificates are valid for life.

The practice of issuing life certificates is waning. In large measure, a reassessment of such licenses is prompted by recommendations that practitioners should engage in continuing professional education. Many states now require the completion of a specified number of university or continuing education credits for license renewal.

Special Requirements. In addition to standard criteria such as graduate degrees and professional experience, many states have special provisions for obtaining certification. Examples include specified scores on national or state tests, stipulating that one must hold a certain degree and also requiring that the degree be from an accredited institution, and completing an internship or comparable field-based experience. In New York, for instance, to obtain the provisional license one must obtain a certain score on the Core Battery Tests of the National Teacher Examination. Similarly, California requires a successful score on a state-devised basic skills test. According to Baptist (1989), thirteen of the fifty-one departments of education have some form of test requirement for obtaining the superintendent's license. (Such tests may be required for all administrative licenses in those states.) Certain states (e.g., Illinois) require tests on the U.S. Constitution, the state constitution, or both.

Slightly more than one-third of the states (37 percent) require some form of internship or practicum for potential superintendents (Baptist, 1989). Other states may require an internship year on a provisional or temporary license. Hawaii, for example, issues an initial school administrator's certificate for one year and requires individuals to complete the on-the-job phase of the Hawaii Department of Education's School Administrator Training Program.

National, regional, or professional accreditation also may be an issue in administrative certification. For this reason, one should note the accreditation status of a university before pursuing graduate work. Arkansas, for instance, requires applicants to have completed an NCATE-approved preparation program. A good number of the states require applicants to be graduates of regionally accredited institutions (e.g., North Central Association of Colleges and Schools, Southern Association of Colleges and Schools).

National Requirements

The tremendous diversity that exists in state licensing standards is partially responsible for recent calls for the establishment of a national certification program. Although currently no such program exists, several possibilities loom on the horizon. For one, a voluntary system of certification could be established by an independent agency, for example, the National Board for Professional Teaching Standards (Carnegie Forum on Education and the Economy, 1987). This initiative is being vigorously pursued for teachers, and it is likely that the effort will be extended to include other education professionals (e.g., counselors, administrators). Another possibility is that national organizations (e.g., AASA, NASSP) may decide to issue certificates of competency in given specializations.

The National Board for Professional Teaching Standards promotes a trilateral agenda for improving the certification of educators: (1) rigorous assessment, (2) an extended course of professional study, and (3) well-supervised practica. Although the immediate target of this board was teachers, their recommendations had a subsequent effect on recommendations for improving the preparation and licensing of school administrators (e.g., National Commission on Excellence in

Educational Administration, 1987). Regardless of the arguments presented by those who favor a system of national certification, which can range from more rigorous testing of applicants to reducing diversity among the states to increasing public confidence in educators, the advocacy of this program stems mainly from a judgment that the status quo (licensing by the states) contributes to a lack of confidence in education. There are several key political and economic questions, however, that cloud the future of national certification. Will states support a national program? Will employers show preference for those who hold national certificates? Will practitioners pursue them?

In the absence of national certification, the practice of *reciprocity* provides a mechanism that allows educators to move from one state to another. States typically have bilateral agreements ensuring that licenses issued in either of the two cooperating states are valid in both states. A number of states have negotiated reciprocity agreements with multiple states, but a small number of states have been unwilling to enter into such agreements. With these uneven conditions, it is advisable to secure information about certification and reciprocity for any state in which you may seek employment.

QUALITY-OF-LIFE CONSIDERATIONS

Although individuals are drawn to the profession of school administration by a host of extrinsic and intrinsic motivators, quality-of-life issues usually play a critical role. This category includes such factors as status, prestige, income, and job security. Unfortunately, it is difficult to generalize about positions and the degree to which they provide quality-of-life benefits. For example, the status, income, and security of an elementary school principal in suburban New York may be substantially different from that of an elementary school principal in rural Nebraska. Often the geographic location, wealth, and philosophy of a school district have more to do with compensation than does position itself. An elementary school principal in an affluent community may make a higher salary and receive greater fringe benefits than a superintendent in a small district with limited taxable property.

Income

Salaries for school administrators exhibit tremendous variance across the country and even within many states. Table 4–1 provides average salaries for administrative positions over a range from 1976 to 1989. You should note that these data are for school districts enrolling 300 or more pupils.

Average salaries can be misleading. For instance, it appears that salaries for deputy and associate superintendents are very close to those for superintendents. Deputy and associate positions exist primarily in larger school districts where it is likely that salaries would be above average. The actual differences between a superintendent's salary and an associate superintendent's salary in the same school district would tend to be greater than suggested in Table 4–1. Many

TABLE 4-1 Average Salaries for Administrators (in dollars)

Position	1976	1983	1985	1987	1989
Superintendent	30,338	50,260	56,954	64,580	71,190
Deputy/assoc. supt.	30,074	47,404	52,877	60,222	66,214
Asst. superintendent	26,460	42,194	48,003	53,656	59,655
Business manager	21,850	34,967	40,344	45,259	49,933
Principals					
High school	22,894	37,602	42,094	47,896	52,967
Jr. high/middle	21,136	34,996	39,650	44,861	49,427
Elementary	19,061	32,451	36,452	41,536	45,909
Assistant principals					
High school	18,939	31,252	35,491	39,758	44,002
Jr. high/ middle	17,868	29,746	33,793	37,958	42,292
Elementary	15,968	27,419	30,496	34,347	38,360

SOURCE: *Statistical Abstract of the United States: 1990.*
Note: Data are for school systems enrolling more than 300 pupils.

variables enter into salary decisions for school leaders. Consider some of the more cogent that appear in Table 4–2.

The examples in Table 4–2 help to explain why it is difficult to generalize about administrator salaries. These variables do not receive equal consideration from one school district to another. Since school boards are usually not restricted in devising compensation plans for administrators, personal biases, community standards, and past practices combine to create unique programs. In some school systems, for example, administrators are paid entirely on performance (merit), whereas in others, salary determinations are based on schedules similar to those used for teachers. There are even some districts that continue to link administrative salaries to the teachers'salary schedule, although collective bargaining has made this practice rare.

The very highest salaries paid to school administrators are generally in urban areas. Large-city school superintendents earn annual salaries far above the national average. During the 1990–91 school year, the average salary for superintendents in districts with 25,000 or more students reached six figures (American Association of School Administrators, 1991).

Salaries do not provide a complete picture of actual compensation. Much like managers in the private sector, school administrators increasingly are moving toward expanded compensation programs that infuse a range of fringe benefits (called collateral benefits). Historically, administrators and teachers received the same employment benefits. Although this practice is sustained in some school districts, the trend today clearly is toward separate employee-group benefit programs. In part, this trend is attributable to collective bargaining, a process that has purposefully sought to negotiate benefits for a single group of employees. Superintendents, in particular, are likely to receive a special employment contract outlining a unique fringe benefit package—one tailored to meet individual needs. It is not uncommon for the superintendent's employment contract to include

TABLE 4–2   Common Variables Affecting Administrative Salaries

Factor	Potential Implications
Geographic location of employer	Suburban or large city areas typically provide the highest salaries.
Size of school	Larger schools or school systems typically provide the highest salaries.
Level of administration	Salaries typically follow a bureaucratic pattern (i.e., salary is based on level of position in the organization).
Individual characteristics	Level of experience or education often plays some part in salary determination (however, less so than for teachers).
Supply and demand	Regional differences in supply and demand of qualified candidates often affect salaries.
Length of employment contract	Not all administrators are on twelve-month employment contracts.
Number of staff supervised	Administrative salary may be affected by the number of subordinates supervised.
Complexity of the curriculum	Salary adjustments may be made on the number of special programs or electives in a given school.
Sociological-economic status of students	Salary adjustments may be made on the nature of students supervised (e.g., a higher salary for being assigned to a school with a large number of students living in poverty).
Job performance	Merit salary adjustments may be made.

specific provisions covering annuities and deferred compensation (e.g., tax-sheltered programs), vacation, medical examinations, leave provisions, disability insurance, life insurance, professional growth support, professional dues, an automobile, and liability insurance (American Association of School Administrators, 1990). Additional fringe benefits that sometimes are given to administrators include retirement programs, provisions for permitting consulting work, and severance payments.

Although some school districts write unique contracts for each administrator, this is the exception rather than the rule. Often all administrators, with the exception of the superintendent, receive the same benefits package. In a growing number of large school systems, administrators are forming organizations and reaching formal agreements with school boards. In some of the largest urban systems (New York City, Boston, St. Louis, Detroit), administrative organizations have affiliated with national unions. The American Federation of School Administrators, an affiliate of the AFL-CIO, serves as an example of a national union whose membership consists of principals, assistant principals, directors, and supervisors. Since such organizations engage in collective bargaining, the exclusion of high-ranking officials (superintendent, assistant superintendents) is to be expected.

In general, administrators have higher incomes than the highest paid teachers; however, they typically have more responsibilities, work longer hours, and have less job security. The pressures of administrative work, especially in urban areas, have spawned major concerns about providing an adequate number of practitioners in the next ten to twenty years (Murphy, 1991). Superintendents who have been in the same position for more than seven years are becoming rare. To counter concerns related to mounting job pressures and decreasing job security, multiple-year contracts and higher salaries are becoming more common for all levels of administrators.

Status

Status is another topic about which generalizations are difficult. In some areas of the country, superintendents and principals maintain relatively high levels of social respect. In rural areas where there commonly are few professionals, the superintendent's level of education alone may provide social status. As America becomes a more highly educated society, educators are less likely to stand out just because they are college graduates.

Both the community and the school system set standards for administrators (Kimbrough & Burkett, 1990); in so doing, they help establish public perceptions regarding the importance of administrators in society. And since communities and school systems are unique entities, the status of administrators, professionally and socially, varies markedly. As you seek to determine the respect a community may have for educators, you should examine certain overt actions that provide clues as to the value the community places on education. Salaries paid to teachers, the quality of educational facilities, and the degree to which community agencies and the schools collaborate to meet societal needs serve as examples.

In general, the public has been uncertain about the professional status of educators. School leaders work in an environment that unmeditatedly hybridizes bureaucracy with professionalism. Administrators are educated professionals, yet their decisions are openly questioned and challenged by the public at large. This iteration, not generally experienced by health-care providers or most other professionals, unmistakably has an effect on the mental images the public develops of educators. It also has an effect on practitioner self-image. Are educational leaders to be accorded the dignity assigned to other professions, or should school administrators expect to be "fair game" simply because they work in the public domain?

A recent Gallup poll found that only one out of two parents would want his or her child to become a teacher. In 1969, this figure was three out of four (Elam, 1990). There are several possible explanations for this decline. For one, females (who constitute a large portion of education practitioners) have been attracted to a wider range of professions since 1970. Second, the continuous bombardment of criticisms against the schools and "educator bashing" may be taking their toll.

Gerritz, Koppich, and Guthrie (1984) point out that administrators generally are perceived as having higher status than teachers. Since self-image is affected by status, this is not an insignificant observation. It has long been recognized in education that seeking an administrative position is one of the few options educators have to increase income and yet remain in the profession. However, seeking advancement solely for this reason is a precarious practice, because the individual may be ignoring fundamental issues, such as those that affect job satisfaction.

There are many myths about school administrators that are related to the topics of status and prestige. Teachers, for example, often perceive principals and central office personnel as having a great deal of autonomy and power. In truth, administrators have limited autonomy, far less than teachers in many instances. When a teacher functions within the four walls of the classroom, he or she typically has latitude in using instructional strategies. By contrast, administrators interact more frequently with individuals and groups who exercise control over professional behavior. But most administrators have the opportunity to be power brokers—to make important decisions. In this respect, they can do some things (e.g., establish rules and regulations) that teachers cannot (Black & English, 1986). And for many, power—even limited power—is viewed as a source of status. Legitimate power (power that emanates from an organizational position) often is sufficient to produce a certain amount of status.

Public perceptions are also shaped by beliefs regarding the difficulty of entering a given profession. Put simply, the more difficult it is to enter a profession, the more likely the public will view its practitioners as having status. Spring (1985) summarized this conclusion as follows: "A claim to rigorous training and specialized knowledge is one of the most important ingredients in maintaining professional status" (p. 50). In this regard, it is noteworthy that many of the national reform reports of the 1980s were replete with concerns relative to the professional education and licensure of teachers and administrators.

Although school administrators as a group do not enjoy equal status with other learned professions in the United States, one should guard against sweeping generalizations. Status, like salaries and job opportunities, varies from one region of the country to another and from one school district to another. You should realize that status is often earned by educators on an individual basis, i.e., it is acquired through positive job performance. Many outstanding leaders in education continue to possess relatively high levels of professional status because they have demonstrated their worth through job-related accomplishments. In this regard, school administration differs from more highly compensated professions, where prestige is acquired automatically by receiving a license to practice. In discussing the status of American schoolteachers, Swart (1990) concluded that prestige was possible— but that it had to be earned. This judgment is equally valid for administrators.

Other Considerations

One issue that receives considerable thought from prospective administrators is *time requirements.* Many administrators spend sixty or seventy hours per week on job-related functions. High school principals, for example, frequently find it necessary to be at school three or more evenings every week. Research has identified time requirements as one of the least satisfying aspects of employment for principals (e.g., Johnson, 1988). A study of elementary schools in the late 1980s revealed that the average work week for the principal was about fifty hours (Doud, 1989). Time requirements, like salaries, tend to be idiosyncratic. One's ability to manage time, for instance, is a critical factor. Some administrators are able to delegate authority and focus on specific projects; others do not feel comfortable unless they are personally in charge of every function. In the final analysis, it is a combination of job and individual that determines how much time is devoted to work. For the poorly organized person, even the least demanding job can be overwhelming. By contrast, highly skilled leaders find ways to cope with what appear to be impossible work loads.

A frequently asked question of principals and superintendents is, "If you had it to do all over again, would you become a school administrator?" This query seeks to establish levels of *job satisfaction* among practitioners. Research outcomes on this topic are very mixed. Job satisfaction is difficult to measure because it is such a complex topic. Some practitioners derive satisfaction from completing certain tasks related to their position (e.g., maintaining financial records, developing schedules), whereas others find fulfillment in the social contacts associated with the job (e.g., meeting with parents, attending professional meetings).

A clear understanding of job satisfaction is attenuated by the tendency to use the terms *motivation* and *satisfaction* interchangeably. The former refers to the cause(s) of behavior and the latter to outcome(s). The two factors are, however, related (Miskel & Ogawa, 1988). Some individuals enter administration because they believe they can make a greater impact on the education of children. Others do so because they seek higher salaries and prestige. Work environments (school or school district) and administrators blend to create circumstances that ultimately determine job satisfaction.

Much has been written in the past two decades about the "burnout" of teachers and administrators. In part, growing pressures experienced by educational leaders can be attributed to changing conditions in society and in schools. Sarros (1988) noted that the three conditions most likely to contribute to administrator burnout were work overload, deteriorating status, and unsatisfactory relationships. The last of these is especially troublesome. Leadership relies on effective interpersonal communication (Hitt, 1988); and when an administrator cannot work in harmony with teachers or other administrators, job-related stress increases. In this regard, collective bargaining has been discomforting because principals and superintendents often are cast as "the enemy." Reform proposals that seek to create closer ties between administrators and teachers reflect these negative conditions that now exist in many schools.

Stress cannot be blamed entirely on the work environment. The individual's emotional well-being, physical health, and personality also are factors, as evidenced by the fact that not all practitioners react to stressors in the same manner. Many are able to make healthy adjustments to environmental changes and go on with their professional and personal lives. Some researchers have noted that individual personality differences play a critical role in stress management (e.g., Raith, 1988). This conclusion is most noteworthy because it supports the contention that not every teacher can become a successful and self-actualizing administrator. Too often those considering a career in school administration look only at the higher salaries and power-brokering opportunities. As you contemplate a career in school administration, you should engage in a candid self-assessment of your ability to cope with stress, criticism, and the other less-than-desirable by-products of leadership. In making a judgment about pursuing a career in administration, you must be honest with yourself. You ought to know your strengths and your weaknesses, your aspirations and your fears, and your needs and your abilities. Kimbrough and Burkett (1990) noted that "knowledge, acceptance, and truthfulness about yourself are prerequisites to effectiveness as a leader" (p. 32).

There is another rather potentially disturbing dimension of school administration that is worth mentioning. Blumberg and Blumberg (1985) refer to it as the notion of "administrator as public property." That is, the public expects administrators to be accessible at all times. As such, inadequate distinctions are made between the public and private lives of educational leaders. For many who enter the profession, life in a fishbowl is disquieting.

One of the commonly cited advantages of becoming an administrator is increased *career flexibility* (Blumberg & Blumberg, 1985; Gerritz et al., 1984). Compared to teachers, administrators tend to have more diversified career opportunities—they can change jobs more readily, and they usually have greater control of personal work. Superintendents in particular have latitude to determine how they will spend their work time. Teachers, by contrast, can exercise flexibility in teaching methods, but they have no choice but to be in the classroom teaching at specified times. In essence, escaping routine can be an issue for some who desire a career in school administration.

The potential for *instrinsic rewards* in the education profession is high. For those who genuinely like helping students, working with parents, and resolving conflict, jobs in school administration can be immensely satisfying. Many seasoned practitioners admit that their greatest job satisfaction comes from seeing former students go on to become successful citizens. Although quite influential, intrinsic motivators are the most difficult to describe and identify.

Finally, *job security* merits mention. Much has been written about the tenuous nature of leadership positions in education, but little notice is given to other side of the coin. Unlike managers in the private sector, school administrators almost always enjoy the privilege of tenure. Tenure is a product of state laws and regulations and is not uniform across the United States. Most states do not grant tenure to administrative positions per se (e.g., one could not acquire tenure as an assistant superintendent), but administrators are able to acquire tenure as teachers. In most instances, this gives the person an option of returning to teaching when they leave administration. Some states extend separate tenure to administrative posts, but rarely to the highest positions, such as superintendent (Valente, 1980). Especially in uncertain economic times, tenure is not an insignificant matter.

CONTEMPORARY OPPORTUNITIES

In the late 1980s, there were approximately 320,000 school administrators in the United States. Almost nine out of ten actually worked in schools or school systems (elementary, secondary, technical schools, or higher education). The remainder worked in child-care centers, state departments of education, religious organizations, job-training centers, or other agencies providing education (e.g., private businesses, military) (Hopke, 1990). Approximately half of the school-based administrators work specifically in elementary/secondary school settings. In the early 1990s, there were about 125,000 principals and assistant principals and about 23,000 superintendents and assistants in the United States (Hopke, 1990). It is estimated that about half of the persons holding positions as superintendents and principals in the United States in 1990 will retire between 1991 and the 1999. More noteworthy, it is anticipated that as these jobs become vacant, fewer qualified applicants will step forward to seek the positions (Murphy, 1991).

In studying job opportunities in school administration, one is faced with the problem of differentiating between quantity and quality. Often analysts cite licensing figures in conducting supply and demand studies; that is, the supply is equal to the number of persons licensed in a given state. But numbers alone do not present an accurate description of the supply side of the equation.

The Supply of Administrators

National supply-and-demand projections in the field of school administration vary markedly. When analysts have relied solely on licensing data, the result has usually been a conclusion that supplies are either adequate or too great. Such findings need to be considered in light of several circumstances. First, Bliss (1988) noted that the accuracy of data is often in question:

> The inability of many state certification directors to provide accurate data on the number of certificate holders is symptomatic of a widespread crisis of information management within state certification offices. (p. 198)

Second, many educators who complete leadership preparation programs and receive licensing never end up being employed in positions as building-level or central office administrators. In fact, many licensed individuals will never even apply for an administrative post. Therefore, simply relying on licensing numbers is a precarious method of determining supply. To understand why this is so, consider the following realities:

- Researchers have frequently noted that school administrators fall into one of two broad categories: career bound and place bound (Miklos, 1988). Career-bound leaders seek positions primarily for career advancement, with geographic location being a secondary consideration. By contrast, place-bound practitioners have little if any geographic flexibility. That is, they are neither geographically mobile nor interested in positions that become vacant outside of a given school, school district, or other restricted territory. Many who hold administrative licenses fall into the latter category. Two possible explanations can be offered for the high number of place-bound individuals in education. One is that many educators receive administrative licensing after spending three or more years as classroom teachers. Often, such persons become established in their respective communities, and relocation is either undesirable or impractical. The second possible explanation relates to family considerations. A large number of educators live under the "two-income syndrome." A job change requires that the spouse also seek new employment.

- In many school systems, graduate degrees and courses in school administration are acceptable for advancement on the teacher salary schedule. For example, an English teacher seeking to move to the master's degree plus thirty semester hours category on the salary schedule typically has several options. He or she could take additional work in English, additional courses in curriculum and instruction, or complete courses in specialized areas such as administration or counseling. Under these conditions, a teacher can gain monetarily from completing coursework in school administration even though there is no intention of becoming an administrator.

- Historically, admission to preparation programs in school administration has been based largely on traditional criteria related to previous academic study and scores on standardized tests. Individual traits such as personality, appearance, and attitude do not commonly receive equal consideration. Yet, these factors may be primary variables in initial employment and ultimate career success. In some respect, this same condition is true for practitioners in other professions who are not self-employed, but it is an especially weighty consideration for professionals who enter public employment.

- The structure of teacher salary schedules is such that many in the profession reach the income pinnacle long before it is time to retire. This condition circuitously serves as an inducement for teachers to pursue credentials in school administration even though professional and intrinsic motives to do so are missing. That is, these teachers are lured to study school administration by the potential for a higher salary. But in the absence of more potent motivators, many never apply for, or acquire, administrative posts.

- Compared to other professional schools, programs in school administration have been relatively low in cost, and student selection has been conducted with less than rigorous standards (Gerritz et al., 1984). Thus, school administration may attract a certain number of individuals who cannot enter other professions and who ultimately may not be competitive in the job market.

Recent efforts to measure the supply and demand condition for school administrators almost always result in conclusions of oversupply (e.g., Bliss, 1988; Gerritz et al., 1984). But we must remember that the supply-and-demand issue has two dimensions: sheer numbers and quality analysis. When one draws distinctions between all licensed candidates and real candidates, or between all licensed candidates and desirable candidates, the condition of oversupply changes markedly.

Many scholars in school administration (e.g., Clark, 1989) note that the field has entertained a series of programmatic accommodations over the past quarter-century in an effort to attract students. Many universities offer watered down courses to part-time students who take night classes after a full day of work (Murphy, 1991). Many scholars find these to be undesirable conditions for professional preparation. In large measure, a proliferation of programs is responsible for these conditions. Colleges and universities are enticed by the relatively low cost of administrator preparation and the fact that few bureaucratic barriers exist to implementation. By contrast, creating a medical school is expensive and often politically difficult. In parts of the country, growth in the number of administrator preparation programs heightened institutional competition for students and ultimately forced program accommodations among the competitors. In their research, Gerritz et al. (1984) noted how California was not producing an adequate number of able school leaders even though the number of licensees in that state far outnumbered available positions.

In the final analysis, decisions regarding the future of professional preparation in school administration will be a key determinant of the supply and demand of practitioners. Two opposing forces are very much alive in the United States. On one hand, there are advocates for reforms that would radically reduce the number of institutions that offer professional programs. But at the same time, a growing number of colleges and universities are attempting to either start administrator preparation programs or extend the ones that already exist (e.g., create a doctoral program).

Campbell, Cunningham, Nystrand, and Usdan (1990) noted that selection into the profession of educational administration occurs at two points: (1) when an individual is admitted to a university program, and (2) when a person is actually employed. It could be argued that licensing is rapidly becoming a third checkpoint, especially in those states where testing is already mandated. Each of these levels of scrutiny is likely to be influenced by contemporary conditions that raise expectations for practitioners and redirect traditional perceptions of job performance. Greater influence on leadership skills hopefully will result in improved screening devices to determine one's ability to work in instruction, resolve conflict, accommodate group decision making, and be politically astute. As this occurs, future projections of the supply and demand of school administrators may focus more directly on qualitative assessments.

Regional Influences

On a regional basis, demographics, economics, and organizational considerations usually play a big part in determining supply and demand. A recent study in New England, for example, noted that an expected shortage of administrators in that region was attributable to highpressure, long hours, low salaries, and high housing costs (Sullivan, 1989). Although the first two factors are rather common throughout the United States, the last two are more regionally unique.

One of the most powerful regional influences on job markets is demographic trends. States such as California, Florida, and Texas are growing rapidly, whereas other states, especially in the northern part of the country, are either stable or actually decreasing in population. Several factors have contributed to this condition. Energy, labor costs, and state laws have played a part in many relocations of industries from the Northeast and Midwest to the South and Southwest. Immigrants in recent years have come mostly from Central and South America, and many of these new residents have chosen to live in the warmer climates. Accordingly, states such as Florida are continuously building new schools and adding staff, whereas states such as North Dakota are losing school population.

Early retirement programs are another regional factor worth mentioning. Many states have enacted plans that permit practitioners to retire prior to age sixty. Indiana, for instance, has a retirement plan that allows educators to retire at age fifty-five if their combined age and years of service totals eighty-five. Early-retirement incentives coupled with a skewed demographic profile where most practitioners are nearing retirement age provide a promising outlook for job opportunities in the next ten to fifteen years.

Other Considerations

The reform reports of the 1980s clearly articulated a concern about the relatively low number of female and minority practitioners in education. The National Commission on Excellence in Educational Administration (1987), for example, took a strong stand that the recruitment and placement of ethnic minorities and women should be a high priority in the profession. This topic is reviewed in detail in Chapter 14; however, it is important to note here that gender and ethnicity are increasingly becoming important considerations with regard to job opportunities. Clearly, there is a gap between the professional literature and the practices carried out by university programs and employers. Even though ethnic minorities have increasingly made their way to the top positions in urban school systems, Afro Americans and Hispanics remain underrepresented in many regions. The same can be said for women. Although the majority of the teaching force is female, the majority of administrators—and the vast majority of top-level school executives—continue to be men (Sergiovanni, 1991).

The placement of minorities in top-level positions in education has many positive by-products and goes well beyond legal considerations. The benefits are especially visible in communities with large minority populations. (Some cities already have "minority majorities.") For example, a minority administrator may better understand the cultural diversity of a given community. Or he or she may be able to establish credibility with parents and students. The minority leader also may become a symbol of success—and hope—for the minority community (Campbell et al., 1990). Valverde and Brown (1988) summarized this potentiality:

> The importance of increasing the number and percentage of minority school administrators goes beyond the issue of underrepresentation and the need to enhance the influence and status of minority educators. Although individual achievement is important, the long-term benefit remains the potential for minority administrators to contribute to the improvement of educational opportunities for minority school pupils. (p. 154)

Increasingly, school board members in districts with large minority populations are heeding this advice.

Affirmative action programs are additional variables that have affected the market demand for female and minority school administrators. If nothing else, these programs have raised awareness regarding the underrepresentation of certain groups in public education. They are designed to remove barriers that commonly are associated with the outcomes of underrepresentation.

Finally, *alternative certification* needs to be mentioned. Certification was discussed in the first part of this chapter; however, a notation needs to be made here that state-level licensing decisions and the future supply of school leaders are related matters. In some states, legislators have responded to warnings about shortages of educators by advocating alternative licensing programs. This approach may provide temporary solutions, but it is viewed by many to be largely a bureaucratic and political notion that fails to examine the professional dimensions of teaching and leadership (e.g., Kowalski, 1988).

Overall Outlook

The outlook for jobs in school administration is favorable, and growth in demand is anticipated through the 1990s. Demand for elementary school principals will be greater than for secondary school principals. Demand will accelerate as older, experienced practitioners retire (Hopke, 1990). This forecast must be tempered, however, with several observations. They include the following:

- There is apt to be a growing reliance on assessment procedures in an effort to raise standards for professional study and admission to the profession. The degree to which such procedures will reduce the number of aspirants and practitioners remains uncertain.

- Geography, the economy, and demographic trends will continue to be major influences in the job market. Therefore, precise national projections remain extremely difficult.

- If current recommendations for improvements in preparation programs and licensing are actualized, fewer, but better prepared, practitioners will enter the workforce. The result will likely be higher stature and higher salaries. If, on the other hand, the number of institutions preparing administrators continues to grow and there is little escalation in licensing requirements, an opposite outcome may occur.

- School reform efforts could increase the number of leadership positions in education. Programs that reduce class size and principal-teachers ratios could create a significant number of new positions nationally. Additionally, calls for instructional leadership may encourage new positions, especially assistant principalships in elementary schools.

IMPLICATIONS FOR PRACTICE

The professional preparation of school administrators is in many ways unique. One novel facet relates to the variance in educational and licensing formats that exist throughout the United States. As you begin to study school administration, it may be helpful for you to know the requirements for the state or states in which you may seek employment. This information can be vitally important in selecting courses and even degree programs.

There are two critical assessments you should make as you plan your career. The first is of yourself. You need to candidly evaluate your strengths, interests, and limitations. Second, you need to develop a balanced image of school administrators. To do this, you must look at a multitude of practitioners. Seek out models of success—individuals who have accomplished a great deal and who exhibit personal satisfaction in their work. Do not rely solely on descriptions that portray conflict and failure.

You need to exercise care in examining data on employment opportunities in coming years. Quantitative data alone fail to provide a total picture of the demand for highly qualified leaders. For a variety of reasons, a number of states exhibit a statistical oversupply of administrators. Many of the individuals who hold licensure, though, will never apply for, or acquire, principalships and super-intendencies. Employment prospects appear most favorable for certain individuals. Clearly, minorities are in short supply—and the demand for them is high. Also, school districts that are rapidly moving to new concepts such as site-based management are seeking dynamic leaders who express a willingness to work closely with teachers and to balance leadership with management. Such circumstances help to explain why quantitative data do not describe sufficiently the supply and demand for educational leaders.

FOR FURTHER DISCUSSION

1. What are the potential benefits of a voluntary national certification program for school administrators?
2. Why do states rather than the federal government have the right to license school administrators?
3. What are some reasons that school leaders generally have less status in American society than do other professions?
4. In many communities, salaries of school administrators are published in the local newspaper. Do you think this is a good idea? Why or why not?
5. What is the tenure law in your state regarding school administrators?
6. Do you believe it would be a good thing if there was a critical national shortage of licensed administrators in the United States? Why or why not?
7. In what ways are decisions regarding academic preparation related to future supplies of school leaders?
8. Suppose that your state legislature passed a law giving all administrators a 35 percent increase in salary. Do you think public perceptions of administrators would improve? Why or why not?

9. What is meant by a property right with regard to tenure and licensing? Why is this concept important?

10. Do you believe that your state should establish a professional standards board to regulate the licensing of educators? Why or why not?

OTHER SUGGESTED ACTIVITIES

1. Structure a debate regarding the merits and problems associated with principals and assistant principals forming their own union and negotiating with the school board.

2. List three primary reasons why you want to be a school administrator.

3. Discuss the reasons why the demand for Afro American and Hispanic administrators is increasing in the United States.

4. Contact your university placement office and ask if data are available to show the supply and demand for school administrators in your state.

5. Contact administrative associations in your state and see if they maintain salary data for their membership.

6. Have a group discussion about ways that the stature of teachers and administrators could be raised in our society.

7. Debate the merits and potential shortcomings of alternative certification programs.

REFERENCES

American Association of School Administrators (1990). *Talking about the superintendent's employment contract.* Arlington, VA: Author.

American Association of School Administrators (1991). Urban superintendent salary averages 6 figures for 1st time in study. *AASA Leadership News* No. 82, April 15, pp. 1–2.

Armstrong, D. G., Henson, K. T., & Savage, T. V. (1989). *Education: An introduction* (3rd ed.). New York: Macmillan.

Baptist, B. J. (1989). *State certification requirements for school superintendents.* (ERIC Document Reproduction Service No. ED 318 107)

Black, J. A., & English, F. W. (1986). *What they don't tell you in schools of education about school administration.* Lancaster, PA: Technomic.

Bliss, J. R. (1988). Public school administrators in the United States: An analysis of supply and demand. In D. Griffiths, R. Stout, & P. Forsyth (Eds.), *Leaders for America's schools* (pp. 193–199). Berkeley, CA: McCutchan.

Boyer, E. L. (1983). *High school.* New York: Harper & Row.

Blumberg, A., & Blumberg, P. (1985). *The school superintendent: Living with conflict.* New York: Teachers College Press.

Campbell, R. F., Fleming, T., Newell, L. J., & Bennion, J. W. (1987). *A history of thought and practice in educational administration.* New York: Teachers College Press.

Campbell, R. E., Cunningham, L. L., Nystrand, R. O., & Usdan, M. D. (1990). *The organization and control of American schools* (6th ed.). Columbus, OH: Merrill.

Carnegie Forum on Education and the Economy (1987). *The National Board for Professional Teaching Standards: A prospectus.* Washington, DC: Author.

Clark, D. L. (1989). Time to say enough! *Agenda* (newsletter of the National Policy Board for Educational Administration), 1 (1), 1, 4–5.

Doud, J. L. (1989). *The K–8 principal in 1988: A ten year study.* (ERIC Document Reproduction Service No. ED 319 134)

Edelfelt, R. A. (1988). *Careers in education.* Lincolnwood, IL: VGM Career Horizons.

Elam, S. M. (1990) The 22nd annual Gallup poll of the public's attitudes toward the public schools. *Phi Delta Kappan, 72* (1), 41–55.

Gerritz, W., Koppich, J., & Guthrie, J. W. (1984). *Preparing California school leaders: An analysis of supply, demand, and training.* (ERIC Document Reproduction Service No. ED 270 872)

Goodlad, J. I. (1990). *Teachers for our nation's schools.* San Francisco: Jossey-Bass.

Gousha, R. P., LoPresti, P. L., & Jones, A. H. (1988). Report on the first annual survey of certification and employment standards for educational administrators. In D. Griffiths, R. Stout, & P. Forsyth (Eds.), *Leaders for America's schools* (pp. 200–206). Berkeley, CA: McCutchan.

Hessong, R. F., & Weeks, T. H. (1991). *Introduction to education* (2nd ed.). New York: Macmillan.

Hitt, W. D. (1988). *The leader-manager.* Columbus, OH: Battelle Press.

Hopke, W. E. (Ed.). (1990). *Encyclopedia of Careers and Vocational Guidance,* Volume 2: *Professional Careers.* Chicago: J. G. Ferguson.

Johnson, N. A. (1988). *Perceptions of effectiveness and principals' job satisfaction in elementary schools.* Unpublished Ph.D. diss., University of Alberta, Canada.

Kimbrough, R. B., & Burkett, C. W. (1990). The principalship: Concepts and practices. Englewood Cliffs, NJ: Prentice-Hall.

Kowalski, T. J. (1988). One case for the national certification of teachers. *The Teacher Educator, 23* (4), 2–9.

Miklos, E. (1988). Administrator selection, career patterns, succession, and socialization. In N. J. Boyan (Ed.), *Handbook of research on educational administration* (pp. 53–76). New York: Longman.

Miskel, C., & Ogawa, R. (1988). Work motivation, job satisfaction, and climate. In N. J. Boyan (Ed.), *Handbook of research on educational administration* (pp. 279–304). New York: Longman.

Murphy, J. T. (1991). Superintendents as saviors: From the Terminator to Pogo. *Phi Delta Kappan, 72* (7), 507–513.

National Commission on Excellence in Educational Administration (1987). *Leaders for America's schools.* Tempe, AZ: University Council for Educational Administration.

O'Reily, R. C. (1989). *The instability of certification for educational administration.* (ERIC Document Reproduction Service No. ED 307 575)

Raith, F. D. (1988). *Reported locus-of-control and level of occupational stress of elementary principals in Georgia.* Unpublished Ed.D. thesis, University of Georgia, Athens.

Sarros, J. C. (1988). Administrator burnout: Findings and future directions. *Journal of Educational Administration, 26* (2), 184–196.

Sergiovanni, T. J. (1991). The dark side of professionalism in educational administration. *Phi Delta Kappan, 72* (7), 521–526.

Shive, J. J. (1988). Professional practices boards for teachers. *Journal of Teacher Education, 39* (6), 2–7.

Spring, J. (1985). *American education: An introduction to social and political aspects* (3rd ed.). New York: Longman.

Sullivan, J. R. (1989). *Study shows administrative shortage.* (ERIC Document Reproduction Service No. EJ 398 959)

Swart, E. (1990). So, you want be a professional? *Phi Delta Kappan, 72* (4), 315–317.

U.S. Bureau of the Census (1990). *Statistical abstract of the United States: 1990* (110th ed.). Washington, DC: Author

U.S. Department of Labor (1990). *Occupational Outlook Handbook, 1990–91 Edition,* Bulletin 2350. Washington, DC: United States Department of Labor, Bureau of Labor Statistics.

Valente, W. D. (1980). *Law in the schools.* Columbus, OH: Merrill.

Valverde, L. A., & Brown, F. (1988). Influences on leadership development among racial and ethnic minorities. In N. J. Boyan (Ed.), *Handbook of research on educational administration* (pp. 143–158). New York: Longman.

Warner, A. R. (1990). Legislative limits on certification requirements: Lessons from the Texas experience. *Journal of Teacher Education,* 41 (4), 26–33.

PART II

Schools as a Workplace: Social, Political, and Historical Contexts

CHAPTER 5

Control and Authority in Public Education

Chapter Content

The system of public education in the United States is in many ways a unique amalgamation of values, beliefs, needs, and practices. Whereas most other countries operate a federal system of education, the United States maintains separate units of public education in each of the states, the District of Columbia, and territories (e.g., Puerto Rico). In all states except Hawaii, the authority to operate public schools is delegated to local school systems, making the governance of education even more diversified.

Since school leaders are expected to enforce myriad laws and regulations and to resolve a continuous flow of problems, their understanding of the evolution of the American system of education is foundational to effective practice. The intents of this chapter are to (1) examine the government's interest in public education, (2) highlight the roles of the federal, state, and local governmental units, and (3) provide an overview of why this information is critical to practice in school administration.

THE GOVERNMENT'S INTEREST IN EDUCATION

In colonial America, citizens often struggled to create a balance between freedom and order. Their experiences with oppression and war heightened their appreciation of freedom, but their strong religious and political values led them to fear that they might create a decadent and chaotic society (Spring, 1990). It was within this context that education became an important process. Education would free individuals to do virtuous acts, and it would create an enlightened citizenry—a necessary component of an emerging democracy.

The U.S. Constitution, drafted in 1788, made no mention of education. But this omission should not be construed as a lack of interest. Campbell, Cunningham, Nystrand, and Usdan, (1990) wrote:

> Despite the lack of specific mention of public education in the federal Constitution, the critical importance of the schools in preserving its meaning and heritage has been stressed throughout American history. (p. 42)

Although Americans from the earliest days of the country saw the value of a free public education, they did not necessarily agree on what knowledge should be stressed. Even today, we confront lingering questions such as Why do public schools exist? Over time, such queries resurface in the context of school improvement debates—and there have been many such debates since colonial days. Should schools enable men and women to be free? Should schools develop a workforce that ensures a healthy economy? Should schools ensure an educated citizenry capable of defending and protecting the Republic?

Governmental Interests in Colonial America

A distinguishing feature of colonial America was the constant clashes between old values settlers brought from Europe and new ideas emanating from those who sought to build a unique society. In this context, many leaders in colonial times discovered that traditional education outlooks were incongruent with values stemming from novel religious, philosophic, and scientific attitudes that surfaced in America. This conflict gave birth to a hybrid conception of education (Butts & Cremin, 1953).

Education for Christian salvation was a theme of the earliest schools (Brubacher, 1966). But religious ideals were not the only influences steering the development of public education. There also was a practical theme to colonial education, a theme that could be more closely tied to governmental interests. Thayer (1965) described this condition when he wrote:

> Even the lovers of scholarship were careful to emphasize its practical advantages. At no time have Americans established schools and colleges or organized curricula within these institutions purely out of respect for learning or scholarship. Rather has the justification been consistently pragmatic and curriculum—whether in the liberal arts or in frankly vocational education—been envisaged as an instrument of utilitarian value. (pp. 19–20)

Thus from its earliest days, American education was driven by a mix of aims and influences. Philosophy, religion, economics, and practical needs all played a part in the evolutionary process. Clearly, some of these factors constituted a government interest in promoting education.

This country was settled largely by the poor, the oppressed, and the religiously persecuted of Europe. Education emerged as an important commodity for these pioneers as they sought both freedom and a better life in a democratic society. But the high value placed on education went well beyond self-interests. There was a common faith in the notion that education advanced civilization; and accordingly, a belief emerged that the strength of a new nation would depend on the spread of learning and enlightenment (Counts, 1952). This constituted the primary interest of governmental officials in the establishment of public schools.

Evolving Purposes

Over time, the original purposes of a common education were altered as needs of the nation and its citizens changed and the profession of education became more enlightened. For instance, the Industrial Revolution created new needs and wants among the citizenry, leading to an emphasis on vocational education and a broadening of curriculum. Prominent philosophers such as John Dewey posed insightful questions about the nature of learners, the role of teachers, and the intentions of a public education. Wars, economic depressions, and more recently social ills, cultural heterogeneity, and worldwide economics helped to cast the directions of America's public schools. Partially because there is no federal system of education and partially because there are so many avenues by which groups and individuals can affect change in the schools, the overall purposes of education have proven to be less than immutable. Change, however, does not mean a lessening governmental interest. This should be especially obvious in the midst of recent intense efforts to improve our schools.

Meandering of curricula and instructional practices between the mid-1950s and today exemplifies how the aims and content of schooling can quickly be transposed. In the midst of the "cold war" in the late 1950s, the Soviet Union successfully launched Sputnik I. American society was stunned, and perceptions that this scientific accomplishment was a threat to national security quickly became apparent. Finger pointing ensued, and the public schools often were singled out for blame. Specifically, political leaders, journalists, and even educational leaders concluded that American schools had become second rate in preparing scientists and mathematicians—a judgment that was quickly tied to concerns for national security. The perceived threat was so great that the federal government enacted legislation making massive amounts of financial assistance available to public education in an effort to upgrade studies in selected areas. The result was a 1960 curriculum that emphasized science, foreign languages, and mathematics. Within a few short years, however, the passage of the Civil Rights Act refocused much of the public's attention away from foreign relations and toward domestic problems. By the mid-1960s, several of the nation's major cities were experiencing racial riots and other forms of social unrest. Again the schools shouldered a good bit of the blame for national problems—and again the federal government enacted legislation in hopes of making public education more responsive to current needs.

Events surrounding the launching of Sputnik I and the passage of the Civil Rights Act provide several messages:

1. The federal government is likely to intervene in public elementary and secondary education when such intervention is deemed to be in the national interest.
2. Schools are never separated from the problems of society as a whole. Whether it is national security, race relations, or poverty, schools are viewed as an integral part of the problem—and the solution.
3. Purposes of American education are not fixed. They are mutable and can be radically changed in a relatively short period of time.

More recent evidence supporting these conclusions is found in the legislation for the disadvantaged and the handicapped enacted during the 1970s. As advocate groups applied political pressure to gain rights for the handicapped, school administrators observed a familiar chain reaction—one that starts with societal needs and concerns, receives direction from federal legislation, and eventually alters elementary and secondary school programs.

In addition to being transitory, educational goals at any given time are less than universally embraced by the American public. Clearly, not all citizens agree on the aims of public schooling. This discord is visible in continuing debates in areas such as values clarification, prayer in the schools, and sex education. Americans generally acknowledge that the public schools should address the ever-changing needs of society and individual citizens, but there is significant disagreement with respect to how this should be accomplished, the parameters of curricular responsibility, and the focus of control of public education.

Among the various conceptions of the purposes of public education, there are four that are rather prominent. First, there is the view that the mission is one of promoting the intellectual attainment of learners. Here emphasis is placed on the individual student and the acquisition of knowledge. Second, there is the belief that the mission of public education is to create good citizens. Here the emphasis is on the collective interests of society, especially as those interests relate to the role of the citizen in a democratic country. Third, there is the view that the schools should prepare individuals for the workforce. Here the emphasis is largely economic and related to the linkages of capitalism and democracy in the United States. And fourth, there is the belief that the primary mission of schools is to foster the development of learners. Here the emphasis is on lifelong learning via the acquisition of learning skills, mental discipline, and the development of an appreciation for learning (Armstrong, Henson, & Savage, 1989). Although each of these aims is accepted by most taxpayers, there is certainly no common agreement as to their order of importance.

Environmental Influences

Actions of the American public, especially actions of those who promulgate and administer educational policy in an official capacity, are influenced by problems of the day. In this regard, movement to global economic competition over the past two decades has heightened interest among captains of industry and elected officials in the role of public schools in preparing students to enter the workforce. Priorities established for education are not, however, the product of any single influence. Environmental conditions and personal values and beliefs intermingle to produce contemporary initiatives. Table 5–1 provides examples of environmental influences currently creating needs and wants for consumers of public education.

The leverage of environmental conditions is certainly discernible in recent reform proposals. The National Governors' Conference in 1991, for instance, produced six goals for American education. These goals, to be reached by the year 2000, exemplify the range of purposes attached to public elementary and secondary schools:

1. All children in America will start school ready to learn.
2. The high school graduation rate will increase to at least 90 percent.
3. American students will leave grades 4, 8, and 12 having demonstrated competency in challenging subject matter including English, mathematics, science, history, and geography; and every school in America will ensure that all students learn to use their minds well, so they may be prepared for responsible citizenship, further learning, and productive employment in our economy.

TABLE 5–1 Examples of Factors Creating Needs and Wants in Public Education

Factor	Implications
Cultural diversity	A demand for multi-cultural education; bilingual education
Drug abuse	Substance abuse programs
Changing American family	A greater demand for schools to assume responsibility for social and moral development
Poverty	Compensatory programs for children reared in poverty—including provisions for basic needs (e.g., breakfast programs)
Technological advancements	Infusion of computers into the classroom; broadening of curricula
World economy	Greater pressures for academic competition; increased emphasis on comparing educational outputs with other countries; preparing students to enter the workforce (meet expectations of employers)
Nature of work	Emphasis on lifelong education to facilitate career changes; adult education
Concern for at-risk students	Alternative schools; alternative programs; new methods of instruction
Civil rights	Changes in employment practices; changes in policies governing programs and activities; greater access to programs

4. U.S. students will be first in the world in science and mathematics achievement.

5. Every adult American will be literate and will possess the knowledge and skills necessary to compete in a global economy and exercise the rights and responsibilities of citizenship.

6. Every school in America will be free of drugs and violence and will offer a disciplined environment conducive to learning.

These goals attempt to integrate the broad purposes of education that have been articulated over time. Collectively, they are aimed at the development of the learner, preparation of students to enter the labor force, social concerns, and the security and prosperity of the country.

In summary, the government of this country has had a continuing interest in a free system of public education. This fact is quite significant in light of the ways in which laws, regulations, and policies are developed for elementary and secondary schools. Examples of environmental influences presented here serve to verify that schools are not insulated from communities in which they exist. They are integral parts of social and political structures.

Purposes and Control

One weighty criticism of public education is that children do not have access to equal educational opportunities. That is, from school to school and school district to school district, there are significant differences in the quality of teachers, instructional materials, facilities, and so forth. Some conclude that this inequality is a product of a policy environment where there are no clear and concise national goals. Although this judgment may be partially valid, it by no means provides a full explanation of existing inequities. Even if all citizens and communities could agree on what should be accomplished in elementary and secondary schools, many doubt that this consensus would produce standardized experiences for students. As Cremin (1989) noted:

> For all of the centralizing tendencies in American schooling—from federal mandates to regional accrediting association guidelines to standardized tests and textbooks—the experiences students have in one school will differ from the experiences they have in another. (p. 44)

In part, variations in schools and schools districts are explained by the reality that everyday experiences in the classroom really determine what is emphasized and what is accomplished. In this regard, teachers, principals, superintendents, and school board members are key decision makers. They are protectors of the government's interests.

Control of American education is vested in legal foundations. This legal framework has three basic sources: federal and state constitutions, statutes, and case law. Constitutions delegate authority to legislative bodies to enact laws in the interest of the public; statutes provide the actual laws; and case law establishes interpretations of constitutions and legislative acts. Historically, laws governing education have been shaped by philosophical, political, and social traditions (Alexander & Alexander, 1985). Within this framework, the development of a public school system appears to have been guided by several basic principles: (1) the public believed that the citizenry should be responsible for schools; (2) the public believed that the federal government should not have direct control over public education and should not dictate the organization and operation of schools; (3) the public believed that each state should develop its own plan for providing public education; and (4) the public believed that the direct responsibility for providing and operating public schools should be a function of local government (Morphet, Johns, & Reller, 1967). These guiding principles help to shape a truly novel system of public education—one in which the balance of federal, state, and local control is ever changing.

THE ROLE OF FEDERAL GOVERNMENT

The role of the federal government in public education has been modified markedly since the nineteenth century. Almost every textbook discussion of this topic begins with the notation that the U.S. Constitution does not mention education; and accordingly under provisions of the Tenth Amendment (Powers not delegated to the federal government by the Constitution, nor prohibited by it to the states, are reserved to the states or to the people.), education is deemed a state's right. Based largely on this interpretation, each state has the charge of establishing a system of public schools.

Many scholars have speculated about the conspicuous absence of a reference to education in the U.S. Constitution. Common suppositions include the following:

1. Many of the framers of the Constitution were products of private schools, and as such, they viewed education as a family and church responsibility.
2. By 1789, some states had already made provisions for public education in their own constitutions, and state officials wanted to avoid federal intrusion into this activity.
3. The omission of education was by default. It was simply overlooked (Grieder, Pierce, & Jordan, 1969).
4. Much of the education offered in 1789 was private and limited to those who could afford it.
5. Education was not a high national priority in that era (Van Scotter, Kraft, & Haas, 1979).

Despite the omission, the federal government has had varying degrees of involvement with public education throughout the history of the county—but always in a manner that recognizes that the primary responsibility for this service rested with the states. During latter parts of the nineteenth century and continuing through the twentieth century, federal intervention in education expanded, and as it did, local apprehensions increased. As early as the start of the twentieth century, political cartoons appeared in education magazines expressing misgivings of local school officials relative to accepting federal assistance. There emerged a common belief that federal assistance always came with "strings attached." To this day, that attitude persists among many local educational leaders. Many see an imbalance between federal financial aid and requirements placed on local school districts if they accept the money.

Sources of Intervention

In the infant years of the United States, governmental powers were divided—they belonged to either the federal government or the states. Political and economic conditions of that era favored such an arrangement. But as the country developed, a shift from a dual federalism to a national federalism occurred (Campbell et al., 1990). No longer could issues be neatly labeled as either federal or state concerns. For one, the federal government became increasingly adamant about protecting constitutional rights of citizens and the welfare of the nation—especially when rights or welfare appeared to be eradicated or diminished by state statutes. A gray area between state and federal jurisdiction grew rapidly, and many aspects of public education fell into this zone of uncertainty.

The federal government can reach out and touch school districts through legislation, legal decisions, and policy (rules and regulations developed by agencies charged with enforcing federal statutes and court decisions). These avenues of power and authority are displayed in Figure 5–1, where they are associated with branches of the federal government—legislative, judicial, and executive (also called the administrative branch). Each branch performs unique functions; yet, the three intertwine to create operational and policy relationships. For instance, the courts interpret laws enacted by the legislative branch; the executive branch often influences legislation through political lobbying; and both the executive and legislative branches exercise control over judicial appointments. Each branch of the federal government is reviewed here.

Legislative. The promulgation of laws is the most visible form of federal activity and is a function of the U.S. Congress. The earliest interventions followed a pattern of providing financial assistance to create or augment programs associated with national interests. The establishment of land grant universities in the late nineteenth century exemplifies how a national concern, in this case agriculture, resulted in the enactment of federal law in an area that was officially designated as a state's right. Supporters of such acts did not intend to usurp the authority of state government; and they justified their initiatives on the view that indirect support to public education was possible without an erosion of state authority and control—a view held by many policy analysts (McCarthy & Cambron-McCabe, 1987).

In the past one hundred years, dozens of federal laws have been enacted in the area of education. Some were directly targeted at changing curricula; others merely had a tangential effect on public schools. An examination of action by the U.S. Congress in the area of education produces four overriding themes—

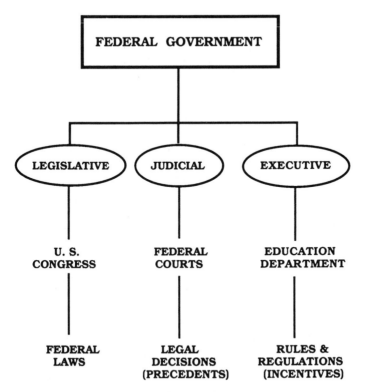

FIGURE 5-1 Avenues of Federal Intervention

constitutional rights of citizens, national security, domestic problems, and concerns for a healthy economy. Table 5–2 provides selected examples of legislation
and brief indication of implications for public schools.

The role of the U.S. Congress is largely to translate the intent of the federal
Constitution into actual practices. But intent is open to interpretation. Philosophical and political disagreements frequently result in divergent opinions about
the appropriateness of federal interventions. Since the reform reports first surfaced
in the early 1980s, a growing number of representatives and senators have taken
an active interest in elementary and secondary education. This attentiveness has
once again put the controversy of federal legislation affecting public education
in the spotlight.

Judicial.   The United States has a dual system of laws—federal and state. It is
possible for the two to come into conflict; and when they do, pertinent federal
law displaces inconsistent state law (Valente, 1987). For the most part, federal courts
have jurisdiction when a federal constitutional question or a federal statute is
involved, or when there is a diversity of state residence between litigants (Reutter,
1985). Since many aspects of public education involve constitutional rights, the
potential for the federal courts to hear cases related to education is rather high.

TABLE 5-2 Examples of Federal Legislation Affecting Education

Legislation	Year	Implications
Smith-Lever Act	1914	Provided support for teacher education in agriculture and homemaking
Smith-Hughes Act	1917	Federal support for vocational education
National Youth Administration	1935	Provided full-time employment to those between ages 16 and 24 who were in school full-time
National School Lunch Act	1946	Support to improve food services in schools
National Defense Education Act	1958	Financial assistance for the study of mathematics, science, foreign languages
Vocational Education Act	1963	Maintain, extend, and improve vocational education programs
Elementary and Secondary Educational Act	1965	Program support for the disadvantaged; inducements for innovative programs; and supplemental funding for libraries and state departments of education
Education for All Handicapped Children Act	1975	Federal assistance to provide special education programs

Essentially there are three divisions of the federal judicial system—district courts, courts of appeal, and the Supreme Court. Typically, cases heard by the first two receive far less public attention than those decided by the highest court in the land. Yet, decisions of all federal courts may have profound implications for public school administration.

Since the mid-1950s, the federal judicial system has increasingly adjudicated education-related cases. At first glance, a number of these legal disputes appear to have been unrelated to education because they did not address commonly recognized components of schooling (e.g., curriculum, tuition, textbooks). But they did address constitutional issues that unavoidably have implications for all public institutions (e.g., civil rights). As noted earlier, educational and social issues often are inextricably linked; and as a result, schools can become a battleground for settling legal disputes that are essentially related to individual and group rights (Hessong & Weeks, 1991). Matters decided in federal courts have included issues such as parental rights, student rights, rights and authority of school officials (school boards, administrators, teachers, and other employees), and rights of racial and ethnic minorities or other protected groups (e.g., racial discrimination, gender or age discrimination).

Legal disputes can make their way to the highest court in the country in two ways. First, cases may be heard by the U. S. Supreme Court if a federal or state statute is questioned as to its validity under the federal Constitution. Second, cases may be heard by this body if any title, right, privilege, or immunity is claimed under the federal Constitution (Alexander & Alexander, 1985). Both pathways are broad.

Several landmark cases serve to explicate the power of federal courts to influence public education. *Brown v. Board of Education,* decided by the United

States Supreme Court in 1954, struck down state laws that required public schools to be racially segregated. Even though public education is a state's right, this ruling restricted decisions of state government when those decisions were deemed discriminatory under the United States Constitution. The *Brown* decision was later extended to cover ethnic minorities (e.g., Hispanics, Native Americans). A second cogent example related to unionism. As teacher unions developed in education, circa 1960, disputes related to membership, fees, contract interpretation, and collective bargaining were settled in federal courts. Additionally, topics such as religious freedom, the funding of education, affirmative action, and tort liabilities have made their way into the federal judicial system.

Constitutionally, the federal judicial system does not have the right to formulate law—the courts are expected to interpret law. This issue has been central to many confirmation hearings held by congressional committees. Given that the Supreme Court often votes five to four, the values and beliefs of judges are deemed critical with respect to judicial interpretations. That is, even the best legal minds often disagree on interpretation of law; yet, their ultimate decisions have a profound effect on society.

Executive. Passage of laws providing federal support to education requires some form of regulation by federal agencies. For many years, education responsibilities were delegated to the Department of Interior; in 1939, the Federal Security Agency assumed responsibility; in 1953, education became part of the Department of Health, Education, and Welfare; and under the Carter administration in 1979, a separate Department of Education was established. In part, the evolution to a separate department (whose head is a member of the president's cabinet) reflected the rapid growth of federal involvement in public elementary and secondary education from 1950 to 1980. Throughout the planning phases for the new department, the question of the proper federal role in public education loomed as a point of controversy.

Immediately after being formed, the Department of Education had 17,000 employees, 11,000 of whom were part of the Department of Defense overseas schools. The Washington, D.C., staff comprised approximately 6,000 employees (Radin & Hawley, 1988). Responsibilities of the department were outlined by focused assignments given to six assistant secretaries:

- elementary and secondary education
- postsecondary education
- vocational and adult education
- educational research and improvement
- special education and rehabilitative services
- civil rights.

One primary function of the Department of Education is to enforce federal laws via the development of rules and regulations. The department also dispenses federal aid and grants. Often these functions intermingle. For instance, acceptance of federal aid places requirements on school districts to comply with standards initiated in legislation and defined by the Department of Education (e.g., awarding contracts to bidders who meet certain federal guidelines). The department has the additional charge of enforcing rules and regulations and ensuring compliance with federal laws.

In its brief existence, the Department of Education has spawned considerable controversy. For instance, disagreements abound regarding the role this agency should play in formulating policy and laws. The department is part of the executive branch of the government and the Secretary of Education is appointed by the president subject to approval by the Congress. Many believe that the mere existence of the department is symbolic of a belief that the federal government should exercise considerable control over the states and local school districts.

Shortly after being created, the department faced the strong possibility of extinction. The election of Ronald Reagan resulted in a significant philosophical change from the previous administration with regard to the role of the federal government in education (Marcus, 1990). This shift occurred at approximately the same time that critics began to call for a massive restructuring of public schools.

Present Role of the Federal Government

A number of authors describing the federal role in education during the early 1980s referred to the period as the "Reagan reversion" (e.g., Campbell et al., 1990). Ronald Reagan entered the presidency openly stating that the creation of the Department of Education was an error. Philosophically, he favored deregulation and a reduced role for the federal government in elementary and secondary education. His initial positions called for substantial reductions in federal expenditures for education and a decentralization of authority that would permit state and local units of government to have more autonomy. During the Reagan administration, the federal government for the first time in several decades retreated from the educational policy arena (Marcus, 1990).

Deemphasis of the federal role in education was occurring at the same time that the public's interest in schooling was being heightened by critical reform reports. A number of states chose not to rely on the federal government to take the lead; they assumed an aggressive posture of enacting laws and regulations designed to improve public education. Even though efforts to dissolve the Department of Education were abandoned before Reagan left office, the future of the federal government as a major influence in education remains uncertain. If state-initiated reforms prove successful, the less aggressive role of the Department of Education that evolved during the 1980s may continue. If on the other hand these efforts fall short, the failures will be used to advocate greater federal control. There are those who believe that a new and more aggressive form of federal intervention is the only hope for saving troubled school systems (e.g., Hill, 1990).

Unmistakably, public—and more precisely, elected—officials hold varying positions regarding the proper role of the federal government in public education. Radin and Hawley (1988) summarized this condition as follows:

The level of social agreement on the appropriate role of the federal government in education is, indeed, fragile and tends to vary from one education policy area to another. (p. 230)

Thus, the formulation of political beliefs regarding federal intervention tend to be issue-related. Many citizens perceive federal intervention to be good or bad depending on the issue in question. Political parties similarly vascilate. In the end, political ideology, philosophy, and tradition, buttressed by what the Constitution does not say, serve to restrict federal interventions (Burke, 1990).

In troubled times, advocates for greater federal control usually become more visible. Among the arguments they put forward to defend their case are the following:

- Other nations with federal systems of education have superior results as measured by higher student test scores (e.g., Japan).

- The present system of education has resulted in schools of varying quality. The federal government has a responsibility to ensure that all children have access to an equal education. Present conditions have been especially harmful to economically disadvantaged students.

- The record of educational achievements for state governments is inconsistent. Put simply, we may not be able to totally trust state governments to provide good schools (e.g., it was federal intervention that put a stop to segregation).

- Federal standards would lead to a national curriculum, and a national curriculum would improve student performance.

- Taxpayer revolts have restricted improvements in education.

By contrast, many continue to argue against greater federal control. Among the more visible arguments for this group are the following:

- A widening federal role is in direct contrast to the intentions of the Constitution.

- Federal intervention will result in greater levels of bureaucracy. This will make schools less effective and less responsive to real needs of the populace.

- The federal government will attempt to standardize educational programs; as a result, differences in community and student needs will be overlooked.

- Real improvements in education must come in the classroom. Centralizing control and authority is moving in the wrong direction. What is needed is greater authority for teachers and increased citizen participation in policy decisions.

In view of these diverse viewpoints, the future role of federal government in education is anything but certain.

THE ROLE OF STATE GOVERNMENT

From the very earliest years, promulgation of laws governing schools was the province of colonial legislatures—and this power has largely been delegated to local agencies. This governance structure has had its critics. Over these many decades, two essential concerns continue to linger with regard to permitting local districts to be largely independent of state control: (1) equalization of educational opportunities (providing every child within the state with equal educational opportunities), and (2) increased standards (changing rules, regulations, and curricula in pursuit of improved programming and outcomes). Each generates cogent questions about the ultimate legal responsibilities of state government for public education and the appropriate mix of power and authority between state government and local school systems. This form of questioning and changing economic, social, and demographic conditions in the country in the late nineteenth century contributed to decisions to expand state control. Movement in this direction was particularly visible in two initiatives—the advancement of the position of state superintendent and the creation of state boards of education (Butts & Cremin, 1953).

Evolution of the state's authority over local school systems was accompanied by considerable and protracted controversy. Over time, most citizens accepted, albeit some grudgingly, that state government was a legally legitimate partner in the provision of public education (Burke, 1990). In a great many legal decisions, the courts have uniformly held that education is essentially and intrinsically a state function. These judgments also stipulate that public education is a matter of state and not local concern (Garber & Edwards, 1970). But these affirmations have not totally eradicated convictions of school board members, educators, and other taxpayers who believe that state government ought not to get overly involved in controlling public elementary and secondary schools.

Avenues for state intervention in public education are similar to those at the federal level. State government, like the federal government, is divided into three distinct divisions—legislative, judicial, and executive. Judicial and legislative functions are quite similar at federal and state levels; however, the executive process of state government with regard to public elementary and secondary education is more complex.

The Legislative Function

Constitutions of individual states establish the authority of the legislature to enact statutes that give direction to public education. A state legislature has almost unlimited (plenary) power to determine basic policy questions within a given state (Kimbrough & Nunnery, 1976). No state may enact laws that violate provisions of either the U.S. Constitution or respective state constitution. For example, a state legislature could not pass a law that would abridge the privileges and immunities granted to a U.S. citizen (such as First Amendment free speech rights). It could not establish a statute that would deprive a citizen of life, liberty, or property without due process (Fourteenth Amendment rights). Nor could it pass a law that deprives a citizen of equal protection under the law (also a Fourteenth Amendment right).

In recent times, reform efforts have magnified the importance of the legislative role in formulating educational policy. Recommended improvements to public education, such as longer school years and longer school days, frequently are established by legislative acts. Yet, there are inherent shortcomings in strategies that seek reform exclusively with quick and simple mandates. Legislatures can, and often do, pass laws based on popular concerns with little or no consideration as to how a given law will affect the long-term initiatives of either the state department of education or local school districts. Coordinating legislative and executive initiatives at the state level remains one of the great policy challenges for public education.

The Judicial Function

The role of the state courts in providing direction and control of public education is becoming an increasingly popular topic among scholars. Two areas of litigation serve to exemplify the power of state courts—collective bargaining and state funding formulas. Legal decisions in these matters have had profound impact on local school districts. As noted in the discussion of federal courts, the purpose of judicial review is to interpret law, not to write it. Decisions rendered by state courts affect educational policy in two primary ways. First, decisions establish precedent that are likely to affect future judgments in similar cases. Second, decisions in landmark cases often lead to new legislation. In the late 1980s, for example, courts in the commonwealth of Kentucky ruled that all previous statutes pertaining to education were invalid. This ruling caused a flurry of legislative and administrative actions.

Historically, state judges have been somewhat reluctant to interfere with the authority of legislative and executive branches of state government in the area of education (Hessong & Weeks, 1991). The primary charge given to the legal branch of state government has been to determine the reasonableness of constitutional provisions and statutory law. There was little expectation that judges would question the wisdom or appropriateness of these provisions and statutes (Kimbrough & Nunnery, 1976). Despite this tradition, there are indications that a growing number of state court judges are willing to become immersed in educationally related policy matters.

The Executive Function

In many states, the executive branch of state government exerts considerable influence over education. Several key agencies and positions are standard in all states (e.g., chief school officer, state board of education); however, but the actual power and authority of the executive branch among states is less than uniform. In recent times, key players in state-level policy for public education have been the governor, the state board of education, the chief school officer, and the state department of education.

Governor.   Because of dissimilar statutes, the power of governors to affect educational policies varies among the states. But differences go well beyond the parameters of law. Partisan politics, tradition, aspirations, personality, and self-interests also are injected into key decisions. Powers of a governor over education policy may be exercised in several ways. Most obvious is the use of veto power over legislative action. Additionally, governors frequently formulate legislative proposals and engage in political persuasion to aid the passage of bills before the legislature. In a number of states, governors make key educational appointments—in some states this includes the appointments of members to the state board of education or the appointment of the chief school officer. They also have primary responsibility for formulating and administering state budgets (Campbell et al., 1990).

During the 1980s, many governors labeled themselves an "educational governor." In 1984, half of them made education the top priority in their state-of-the-state speeches (McDonnell & Fuhrman, 1985). Lamar Alexander, for example, achieved national recognition as an educational reform governor while serving as the chief executive of the state of Tennessee. In 1991, he was appointed secretary of education by President Bush. Unquestionably, the involvement of governors in the formulation of policy and control of public education is greater today than it was two or three decades ago.

State Board of Education.   By 1870, most states had some form of a state board of education (Knezevich, 1975). In some states, this body is authorized by constitutional provision, whereas in other states it is authorized by legislative action. In the earliest years of existence, state boards largely assumed the role of executing law enacted by the legislature. There is tremendous variance among states with regard to the size and functions of these bodies. In eleven states, members of the state board are elected. In other states, members are appointed by the governor or some other official as provided by law (Sergiovanni, Burlingame, Coombs, & Thurston, 1987). The primary purpose of the state board is to carry out state mandates. In several states, however, these bodies also function to formulate policy initiatives.

Duties and responsibilities of a state board of education may include the following:

- Influence the development of educational policy
- Coordinate the efforts of state government with regard to education
- Appoint commissions and other bodies as may be necessary to administer state laws, rules, and regulations
- Develop rules and regulations
- Oversee the operations of the state department of education and establish policy for its operations
- Engage in strategic planning
- Serve as a hearing board in adjudicating grievances and due process procedures related to state educational policies, rules, and regulations
- Recommend legislation, budgets, and other matters to the legislature or other state agencies.

In about half the states, the state board has authority to appoint the chief school officer (Sergiovanni et al., 1987).

Chief School Officer.   The first chief school officer took office in 1812. Over time, this position has had varying titles. They ranged from state superintendent of public instruction to commissioner of education. Both method of selection (appointment or election) and the scope of duties and responsibilities of this position vary from state to state. Variance also exists with regard to terms of office, salaries, and requirements to hold the position (it is possible in some states for the chief school officer to have no preparation or experience in the education profession). Duties include management and leadership for the state department of education. In some states, the state superintendent is an ex-officio member of the state board of education.

As the top official for education in the state, the chief school officer is expected to be a spokesperson for public education. Through appointments, fiscal decisions, and the administration of rules and regulations, he or she can exercise considerable authority.

State Department of Education.   In reviewing the evolution of state departments of education, three distinct levels are noteworthy. Until the twentieth century, these agencies were largely responsible for maintaining records. From 1900 to 1930, they assumed an inspectoral role—one in which officials determined if local school districts were complying with state laws. After 1930, many departments incorporated leadership activities—proactive functions designed to improve local schools (Knezevich, 1975). Today, these agencies perform a number of important functions as exhibited by the following examples:

- Ensuring compliance with state and federal laws for schooling
- Providing technical assistance to local school districts
- Serving as an agent for the distribution of federal assistance
- Maintaining adequate statistical data
- Filing necessary reports with other governmental agencies
- Providing staff development opportunities
- Developing and publishing curriculum guides
- Administering standards for school facility development
- Administering licensing standards for practitioners
- Establishing recommendations for the state board of education or the legislature
- Conducting needs assessments
- Completing program evaluations
- Establishing and administering accreditation standards for state-licensed schools
- Providing interpretations of laws, rules, and regulations
- Administering the state funding formula.

School improvement efforts are resulting in broader missions for most state departments. Today, there are growing expectations that these agencies become catalysts for change as well as regulatory agencies.

Present Role of State Government

Since the 1950s, state governments have been exerting more control and authority over public education. Two factors are largely responsible. First, litigation involving equal educational opportunities has resulted in greater state funding for public education in many states (e.g., between 1971 and 1981, twenty-eight states reformed their funding systems for public education). But in most instances, increased state funding has meant increased state control. Second, demands for improvement in elementary and secondary schools have been directed largely toward state government. During the 1980s, the political climate was very conducive for bold initiatives at the state level. For governors, legislators, and other state officials, the risks of acting decisively on educational reform were low— and the political costs for not doing so were high (McDonnell & Fuhrman, 1986).

The ability of state government to provide meaningful leadership in educational improvement is still in question. In reality, promulgation of state laws, rules, and regulations often is mired in politics, self-interests, and misperceptions. Additionally, evaluations of attempted innovations reveal that many factors unique to a given school or school district combine to facilitate or impede desired change (McGuire, 1985). Therefore, even the best-intentioned and best-designed state-wide initiatives face unavoidable hurdles related to differences among communities and students.

THE LOCAL SCHOOL DISTRICT

During the second half of the nineteenth century, there was a rapid expansion of the common school. Compulsory attendance laws resulted in more students' attending school. As common schools proliferated across the land, there were strong arguments for more centralized control—at the state level, at the county level, and at the school district level (Button & Provenzo, 1989). In all of the states except Hawaii, legislatures generally delegate authority to local government to establish units of school organization. In essence, local school districts are quasi-corporations that serve as instruments to oversee and manage public education—they are extensions of state government (Campbell et al., 1990).

Commonly, school districts include kindergarten through grade 12, but there certainly are exceptions. In some states several types of school districts exist. For example, Illinois has unit school districts (grades K to 12), elementary districts (K to 8), and high school districts (9 to 12). In California, some districts extend from kindergarten through grade 14 (the inclusion of community colleges in the school system). Distinctions may also be made among school districts within a given state according to legislation under which districts are established. In Indiana, for instance, school district classification (city district, metropolitan district), is based on the law used to create the district as a legal entity. In some states, the terms *independent* and *dependent* are used in conjunction with school districts. This connotes whether a district is free of legal affiliations with other governmental units. For instance, dependent school districts have their budgets established by other units of government (e.g., county government). Thus, school districts can vary in terms of the grade levels served, legislative statutes under which they are organized, and their association with other governmental units.

School districts also vary markedly in geographic size and enrollments. In several states (e.g., Florida, Kentucky, Louisiana), there is usually only one school district in each county. (There are a few exceptions in these states for large city districts.) In most states, there are several school districts in each county. Reorganization efforts eliminated many small school districts over the years. Yet, some states (e.g., Nebraska and Illinois), still have over 900 school districts each.

The School Board

Today, virtually all school districts are governed by school boards. (In some states, there remain unreorganized districts that are under the jurisdiction of township trustees.) In most instances, school board members are chosen in nonpartisan elections. The size of the school board and the method of member selection (appointment or election) are determined by state statutes under which the local school district is established. These statutes also identify qualifications, if any, for serving on a school board, the term of office for members, and other pertinent parameters regarding legal operations and scope of authority.

School boards in some states are officially called *boards of education* and in other states they are referred to as *boards of school trustees*. The authority and duties of this body vary depending on state statutes; however, common functions include the following:

- Employing a superintendent of schools
- Approving recommendations for the employment of all other personnel
- Establishing policy for the operation of the school district
- Becoming involved in adjudicating disputes (e.g., due process hearings, grievances)
- Collectively negotiating with employee unions
- Approving budgets and expenditures
- Evaluating the superintendent of schools
- Communicating with the public at large
- Approving capital projects (e.g., new facilities)
- Levying taxes and borrowing money
- Establishing attendance boundaries
- Determining curricula.

Officially, school board members are agents of state government. This is true regardless of whether they are appointed or elected to office. This fact is commonly misunderstood, because school districts are viewed as part of local government. For instance, in some communities school board members are appointed by mayors or judges. Citizens conclude that school board members appointed in this manner are answerable to those who make the appointments. Legally, this is not the case. Because school boards are extensions of state government, their powers may be extended or limited by state statute (Reutter, 1985).

Individual school board members do not possess power to administer schools. This fact comes as a surprise to many citizens. In some communities, superintendents and principals complain that it is common practice for school board members to behave as if they had administrative powers or as if they had the legal authority to make decisions individually. The school board must act a whole to exercise its powers. In some instances, persons simply do not receive a proper orientation when they become school board members; but there are others who reject the notion that school board members should restrict their activity to policy matters. Despite definitive statutes that address the powers of school boards, there is enormous discretion as to how active members wish to be, and on which issues (Sergiovanni et al., 1987).

Conditions surrounding the formation of the first school boards helped to shape functions of these governing bodies and their relationships with school administrations. First, the concept of meritocracy (the idea that one's social and occupational position is determined by merit, not politics or wealth) influenced decisions regarding schooling. Thus, those who had acquired special knowledge and skills were deemed qualified to be leaders in the schools. Second, there was a strong desire to keep public education out of politics. One way to do this was to grant powers to professional leaders (administrators). Third, the growth of school administration as a field of study fostered the notion of an appropriate separation of powers in local school districts. School boards were to set policy—administrators had the charge to enforce policy without interference from the school board (Spring, 1990).

For the most part, school boards have been successfully insulated from rough-and-tumble partisan politics (Sergiovanni et al., 1987). But in some larger cities, school board elections can get mired in partisan politics—although usually in an unofficial manner. That is, candidates are not listed on the ballot as Republicans or Democrats, but they seek the endorsement or fiscal support of local parties or their leaders. In a relatively small number of school districts, school board members are elected on a partisan ballot. Figure 5–2 provides a profile of board member selection based on a recent survey reported by the *American School Board Journal* (School board survey: Here's looking at you, 1990).

The typical school board member is a white male who is well educated and reasonably affluent. Slightly more than half currently have children of school age, and two-thirds hold some type of college degree. Only 10 percent have merely a high school diploma or less. Although the number of female board members reached a high of 39 percent in the late 1980s, there is no indication that it is steadily rising. In 1989, approximately one out of every three board members was a female (School board survey: Here's looking at you, 1990).

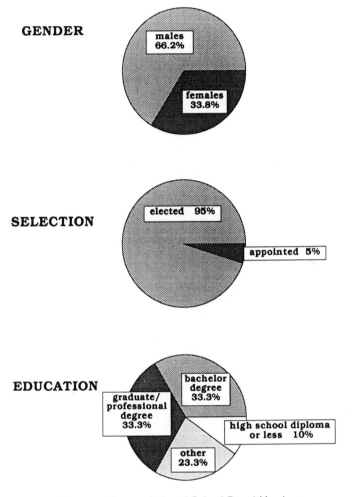

FIGURE 5–2   Characteristics of School Board Members
in 1990

SOURCE: *The American School Board Journal* (1990), 177 (1), 34.

In today's reform-minded environment, many of the traditional practices of public education are being challenged. Among them is the contention that school administrators, being professionals, should be left alone to make critical decisions about the operations of schools. In part, contemporary criticisms have re-ignited debates about professional control versus shared decisions in a democratic society. This is evidenced by the popularity of concepts such as school-based management and community-school councils. Yet, these challenges to operational procedures have had only limited impact on changing statutes that establish school board powers. One notable exception is the city school system in Chicago. The General Assembly of Illinois enacted a law in the late 1980s known as the Chicago School Reform Act. Among provisions of the statute is the requirement of establishing a local school council for every school in the district. These councils, consisting of six parents, two teachers, two community residents, and the principal, were given powers previously held by the school board and administration (e.g., planning, selecting/terminating the principal) (English, 1990). This radical effort to involve large numbers of citizens in the decision-making process has spawned legal battles that remain unresolved regarding individual rights and school board authority (e.g., a local school council taking action that may violate existing collective bargaining agreements).

Some states have laws requiring public governing boards to conduct official business in meetings open to the public. In Florida, for instance, such legislation is referred to as the "Sunshine Law." These statutes are based on the premise that all activities of the governing board should be open to public scrutiny. Not all open meeting laws are identical. In some states, school boards are allowed to hold executive sessions (meetings not open to the public) to discuss sensitive personnel matters, collective bargaining strategies, issues related to the acquisition of property, and other matters where public deliberations are deemed not to be in the best interest of a person or the state (including the school district as an agency of the state). Many states also require specified procedures for notifying the public of forthcoming meetings (e.g., ads in newspapers, postings).

The primary concerns of school boards vary from one community to another and from one state to another. In general, the greatest concern remains a perceived lack of financial support to operate the schools. A recent survey sponsored by the *American School Board Journal* (School board survey: Money woes, 1990) cited the following as the five highest concerns of school board members nationally:

- Lack of financial support
- State mandates
- Facilities
- Curriculum development
- Use of drugs.

The inclusion of state mandates serves as a reminder of the continuing friction that exists between state government and local school boards.

Administration

The nature of administrative positions within a school district was discussed earlier in the book. In drawing an analogy to federal and state governments, the function of the administration of a school district is to perform executive duties. This includes enforcement of policy, development of rules and regulations, formulation of policy recommendations, and professional leadership.

The power and authority of school administrators are not uniform across all districts. In part, differences are explained by the following factors:

- Philosophy of the school board
- Expectations of the school board

- Past practices in a community (or school district)
- Present needs and problems within the school district
- Ability, personality, and philosophy of the superintendent
- Relationship between the superintendent and the school board
- Adherence to certain standards (codes of ethics, accreditation standards, state statutes, rules, and regulations).

Communities and school districts are unique entities. This reality helps to explain why a practitioner can be highly successful in one job and be a failure in another. Although conditions under which administrative functions are performed vary substantially, the primary purposes of administration are universal. They are to provide professional leadership and to ensure that policies, laws, and other regulations are implemented. As Sergiovanni et al. (1987) noted, a superintendent is the board's agent, its expert on educational and management matters, and the leader of the professional staff.

The Present Status of School Districts

Some argue that there has been a serious erosion of local control, and as a result, school boards and administrators have very little latitude to make meaningful decisions. These individuals point out that curricular decisions are made primarily by state legislatures and departments of education and the real arbiters of disputes in education are state and federal courts. Even budgetary decisions, they contend, are now meaningless because available resources are largely consumed by employee salaries. Although there is a modicum of truth in these judgments, the reality is that local leadership often makes a substantial difference in educational outcomes. Decisions about staff development, a willingness to raise local taxes to generate additional revenues (where this option is possible), or an approval of a facility project serve as examples of locally driven decisions that often have positive effects on education. But beyond decisions that focus largely on financial resources, school boards and administrators can make a critical difference in educational programming. Noted policy analyst Michael Kirst believes that the role of local school boards would be enhanced if they became more involved in curriculum and instructional policies (Saks, 1990).

Many citizens, including a good number of influential policy developers, already have concluded that public schools no longer are capable of governing themselves. Demographic and political changes are major contributors to this skepticism. American society has become increasingly pluralistic and multicultural; the structure and functions of families have changed substantially; families have become more mobile; many economic, political, and social issues have been transfigured into global concerns; and the association of federal, state, and local policy development has reached new levels of complexity. These conditions fuel doubts as to whether a system of local control that worked well in the past can effectively serve future generations. Even within the ranks of the profession, there are those who argue that local control is passé (e.g., Lieberman, 1986). Those who see local control of public education as an outdated concept offer varying solutions that basically take two forms: centralization (giving the federal or state government more control) and competition (creating choice by allowing tax dollars to be used for private schools, even profit-seeking schools). By contrast, a good number of educational leaders are advocating a return to, rather than a retreat from, local control. These reformers believe that school boards still have the preeminent position for setting policy (Saks, 1990); and accordingly, they conclude that if meaningful improvement is to be realized, it must come from local school district initiatives. Because of this dichotomy of thought, the future of local control is somewhat uncertain.

THE INTERMEDIATE SCHOOL DISTRICT

Intermediate school districts exist in a number of states and are known by varying names (regional educational service agencies, regional service centers, boards of cooperative educational services). In essence, these organizations are downward extensions of state authority over public education, an intermediate administrative/service agency between local school districts and the state departments of education. The creation of the position of county superintendent was the earliest form of intermediate district. The primary function of this office was to provide services and management to weak and ineffective school districts (Knezevich, 1975). This was especially true in an era when many school districts were organized on a township basis and were controlled by the township trustee rather than a school board. In many counties, this condition resulted in numerous school districts, each with relatively small pupil enrollments.

Although varying forms of intermediate school districts have existed for some time, they remain an enigma to many. The concept underlying this organization is rather simple—the intermediate district provides services to school districts that are too small or too poor to offer complete programs (Campbell et al., 1990). Through cooperative purchasing, media libraries, equipment repair, shared staff development programs, and similar functions, the intermediate district can provide cost savings and program improvements.

Intermediate districts are often confused with two other forms of joint ventures. These are educational cooperatives and study councils. Cooperatives exist in some states to provide joint services (i.e., several school districts offering programs cooperatively). Typically these educational cooperatives have a single function, special education and vocational education being the most common examples. Study councils, by contrast, generally focus on collaborative research, staff development, and other functions designed to provide information and services rather than direct programming for students. Intermediate units differ from these two entities in that they are less restrictive in operations and exist as official extensions of state government. Some school districts simultaneously hold membership in a special education cooperative, a vocational education cooperative, a study council, and an intermediate school district. Not all states having intermediate districts require local school districts to participate in them.

In Indiana, for example, membership in regional service centers is voluntary; yet, the state government encourages and financially supports these centers as extensions of the state department of education. Some states permit private schools to participate in all or some services provided by intermediate units.

The funding of intermediate districts also varies among the states; however, revenues for most are obtained through a combination of state funding and local participation fees (usually established on a per-pupil basis). Intermediate units also may receive federal funding (in the form of support for special projects and grants), private gifts, and revenues generated through designated fees (e.g., charges for equipment repair).

Governance of intermediate units is usually prescribed by state statute. The typical arrangement is for the unit to have a director or superintendent (appointed in most states, but elected in some), a staff, and a governing board. The mode is for superintendents from participating districts to serve on the board (or representatives of the superintendents); some states elect board members in a fashion similar to local school board elections. These units may be fiscally independent or they may be linked to a school district that functions as its local educational agency (LEA).

One example of the growing value of intermediate units for many school districts is the prolifiration of computers in schools. Intermediate school districts often provide small school systems access to cooperative purchasing of computers, software libraries, staff development, and even equipment repair. These are opportunities that low-enrollment districts usually could not generate independently. But even financially capable small districts typically benefit from cooperative buying and other services provided by intermediate units.

The degree of control an intermediate district has over local school systems varies among the states. In Illinois, for instance, regional superintendents perform certain functions commonly provided by state government (e.g., registering licenses and certificates). In the past thirty to forty years, some states have consolidated regional units in an effort to achieve a more reasonable scale of economies (e.g., Wisconsin, Illinois). This has resulted in fewer but larger intermediate districts.

IMPLICATIONS FOR PRACTICE

Who controls public education in the United States? The answer is more complex than most imagine. In the past fifty years, the federal government has become more than a silent partner in elementary and secondary education. Likewise, state government has increased its control. What has evolved is a novel approach to establishing policy that sets the United States apart from virtually all other countries. Control flows from a mixture of federal-state-local government where roles and shares of power are fluid.

Concerns sparked by the distribution of authority among federal, state, and local governmental agencies have taken on new prominence in an era of school reform. Many who investigate ways of improving education quickly conclude that the issue of control is paramount to meaningful reform. Interestingly, three very different proposals for school improvement have surfaced. First, there are those who believe that local control is either a myth or an ineffective structure for promulgating necessary policy changes. These reformers suggest that a stronger state and federal role is the answer to improved policy. Second, some critics believe that schools will never improve unless they are (1) forced to compete in an open market and (2) freed from the bureaucratic quagmire in which they operate. For these reformers, deregulation of public education and giving parents the right to choose any school, public or private, appear to be the solution. Finally, there are those who urge increasing local control of schools. Greater decentralization is viewed as a means for creating increased citizen participation, a role for teachers in decision making, and a greater linkage between individual schools and neighborhoods. Site-based management and school-community councils exemplify initiatives embraced by this third group.

Clearly, the American public (and even professional educators) is less than uniform in its convictions regarding the future governance of public schools. As you prepare to enter practice in school administration, you should understand (1) how the control of American schools has evolved, (2) present mixes of federal, state, and local control, (3) origins of policy decisions, and (4) the potential for radical changes in the coming decades. In later courses, especially in the study of school law and policy analysis, you will examine these issues in greater depth.

Regardless of claims to the contrary, public education is immersed in political problems. Wiles, Wiles, and Bondi (1981) contended that this condition is defined by four primary questions:

What is legitimate?
Who controls decision making?
What is the nature of competition?
What is valued? (p. 4)

Practitioners continuously confront these queries, and they do so in an environment where other officials and taxpayers hold differing beliefs. This chapter has focused on the dimension of control—a critical variable that affects everyday decisions as well as major policy initiatives related to reform.

FOR FURTHER DISCUSSION

1. If the U.S. Constitution does not mention education, why has it been held to be a state's right?
2. In the past ten years, has the federal government become more or less involved in public education?
3. Does your state have a state board of education? If so, how are members selected and what are their terms of office?
4. Can the state legislature legally abolish local school boards? Why or why not?

5. If states have the authority to provide public education, can a state abolish mandatory attendance laws? Why or why not?

6. How is the chief school officer selected or appointed in your state?

7. What is the difference between an independent and a dependent school district?

8. What are the laws in your state regarding the selection of school board members for local school districts?

9. Intermediate school districts are least likely to be found in states that have all-county school districts. Why is this true?

10. Should a superintendent in a local school system be the chief representative of the school board? the chief representative of the professional staff? the chief representative of both?

OTHER SUGGESTED ACTIVITIES

1. Have a debate in your class relative to whether local control of education should be expanded or reduced.

2. Discuss the relationships between professional control and shared-decision making.

3. Discuss the issue of the role of federal courts in education. Can these courts make law?

4. Trace the development of the state department of education in your state.

5. Debate the topic of whether chief school officers (or state boards of education) should be elected in partisan elections.

REFERENCES

Alexander, K., & Alexander, M. D. (1985). *American public school law* (2nd ed.). St. Paul, MN: West Publishing.

Armstrong, D. G., Henson, K. T., & Savage, T. V. (1989). *Education: An introduction* (3rd ed.). New York: Macmillan.

Brubacher, J. S. (1966). *The history of the problems of education* (2nd ed.). New York: McGraw-Hill.

Burke, F. G. (1990). *Public education: Who's in charge?* New York: Praeger.

Button, H. W., & Provenzo, E. F. (1989). *History of education and culture in America* (2nd ed.). Englewood Cliffs, NJ: Prentice-Hall.

Butts, R. F., & Cremin, L. A. (1953). *A history of education in American culture.* New York: Henry Holt and Company.

Campbell, R. F., Cunningham, L. L., Nystrand, R. O., & Usdan, M. D. (1990). *The organization and control of American schools* (6th ed.). Columbus, OH: Merrill.

Counts, G. S. (1952). *Education and American civilization.* New York: Teachers College, Columbia University.

Cremin, L. A. (1989). *Popular education and its discontents.* New York: Harper & Row.

English, F. W. (1990). *Can rational organizational models really reform anything? A case study of reform in Chicago.* Unpublished paper presented at the University Council for Educational Administration, October 1990.

Garber, L. O., & Edwards, N. (1970). *The public school in our governmental structure.* Danville, IL: The Interstate Printers & Publishers.

Grieder, C., Pierce, T. M., & Jordan, K. F. (1969). *Public school administration* (3rd ed.). New York: Ronald Press.

Hessong, R. F., & Weeks, T. H. (1991). *Introduction to the foundations of education* (2nd ed.). New York: Macmillan.

Hill, P. T. (1990). The federal role in education: A strategy for the 1990s. *Phi Delta Kappan,* 71 (5), 398–402.

Kimbrough, R. B., & Nunnery, M. Y. (1976). *Educational administration: An introduction.* New York: Macmillan.

Knezevich, S. J. (1975). *Administration of public education* (3rd ed.). New York: Harper & Row.

Lieberman, M. (1986). *Beyond public education.* New York: Praeger.

McCarthy, M. M., & Cambron-McCabe, N. H. (1987). *Public school law: Teachers' and students' rights* (2nd ed.). Boston: Allyn and Bacon.

McDonnell, L. M., & Fuhrman, S. (1986). The political context of school reform. In V. D. Mueller and M. P. McKeown (Eds.), *The fiscal, legal and political aspects of state reform of elementary and secondary education* (pp. 43–64). Cambridge, MA: Ballinger.

McGuire, K. (1985). Implications for future reform: A state perspective. In V. D. Mueller and M. P. McKeown (Eds.), *The fiscal, legal and political aspects of state reform of elementary and secondary education* (pp. 309–324). Cambridge, MA: Ballinger.

Marcus, L. R. (1990). Far from the banks of the Potomac: Educational politics and policy in the Reagan years. In L. R. Marcus and B. D. Stickney (Eds.), *Politics and policy in the age of education* (pp. 32–55). Springfield, IL: Charles Thomas.

Morphet, E. L., Johns, R. L., & Reller, T. L. (1967). *Educational administration: Concepts, practices, and issues* (2nd ed.). Englewood Cliffs, NJ: Prentice-Hall.

Radin, B. A., & Hawley, W. D. (1988). *The politics of federal reorganization.* New York: Pergamon Press.

Reutter, E. E. (1985). *The law of public education* (3rd ed.). Mineola, NY: The Foundation Press.

Saks, J. B. (1990). Michael Kirst. *American School Board Journal,* 177 (11), 31–33.

School board survey: Here's looking at you. (1990). *American School Board Journal* 177 (1), 34.

School board survey: Money woes. (1990). *American School Board Journal* 177 (1), 34–35.

Sergiovanni, T. J., Burlingame, M., Coombs, F. S., & Thurston, P. W. (1987). *Educational governance and administration* (2nd ed.). Englewood Cliffs, NJ: Prentice-Hall.

Spring, J. (1990). *The American school, 1642–1990* (2nd ed.). New York: Longman.

Thayer, V. T. (1965). *Formative ideas in american education: From the colonial period to the present* (2nd ed.). New York: Dodd, Mead and Company.

Valente, W. D. (1987). *Law in the schools* (2nd ed.). Columbus, OH: Merrill.

Van Scotter, R. D., Kraft, R. J., & Haas, J. D. (1979). *Foundations of education: Social perspective.* Englewood Cliffs, NJ: Prentice-Hall.

Wiles, D. K., Wiles, J., & Bondi, J. (1981). *Practical politics for school administrators.* Boston: Allyn and Bacon.

CHAPTER 6

The Social, Political and Historical Context of Private Education

Chapter Content

A Historical Overview

The Status of Private Education in the United States

The Resurgence of Interest in Private Education

Types of Private Schools

Governance and Control of Private Schools

Legal Issues

Implications for Practice

Many think of the American educational system as consisting of the nation's public elementary and secondary schools and its colleges and universities. However, public schools in the United States currently are attended by only 85 percent of precollegiate students who attend school. The remaining 15 percent of kindergarten through twelfth-grade students attend an ever-increasing number of nonpublic schools.

The projected continued increase in the private school population, coupled with the fact that many nonpublic schools have smaller enrollments than their counterparts in the public sector, make it likely that one-fourth to one-third of all future administrators will work in private school settings during some point in their careers. The remaining two-thirds to three-fourths will have to work collaboratively with nonpublic schools and their administrators. Thus, it is in the best interests of prospective school administrators to have a working understanding of private schools.

Unfortunately, comparatively little has been written about the private school sector; and much of the existing private school literature is focused on Catholic schools, the largest segment of the private school population. This chapter will provide both historical and contemporary perspectives of private education.

A HISTORICAL OVERVIEW

Historically, private schools have been a refuge for those who dissented from the value system explicitly or implicitly promoted by public schools. More specifically, growth in the private school sector generally has been in response to a change in public school treatment of religious values (Lines, 1986).

Public school treatment of religious values has passed through three over-lapping periods. The first period, the evangelical Protestant period commenced with the beginning of public schools and lasted well into the nineteenth century. Subsequently, there was a brief period of nondenominational religious emphasis, which continues to be evident in some sectors today. The third period, that of secular education, has been the most dominant in recent years (Lines, 1986).

The formation of the Catholic school system during the nineteenth century was a response to the evangelical Protestant emphasis in public schools at that time. Evangelical Protestant values were incongruent with values Catholics wished to promote. Many Catholics were recent immigrants to this country and did not have the financial means to take advantage of existing private schools, most of which had high tuitions. Thus, their only option was to establish schools in which Catholic values were taught. Since most immigrants established permanent residences in the cities in which they arrived or in close proximity to them, the major eastern seaboard cities still retain the highest numbers of Catholic schools.

By the middle of the nineteenth century, Catholic schools were growing as rapidly as public schools. From this period until the mid-1960s, the vast majority of nonpublic schools were Catholic, and over 90 percent of private school students were enrolled in those Catholic schools (Lines, 1986).

The rapid growth of Catholic schooling was accompanied by considerable dissension. Many saw Catholic schools as a threat to public schools. Others perceived them to be inferior, overcrowded, undesirable, and even unpatriotic, since they were perceived to contribute to cultural pluralism rather than cultural unity. Some were simply motivated by prejudice against the immigrant groups who made up the major portion of Catholic school enrollments.

One state (Oregon) responded to the growth of Catholic schools and the substantial public sentiment against them by modifying its compulsory attendance law to require attendance at public schools. This law was challenged and eventually found unconstitutional in *Pierce* v. *Society of Sisters,* often referred to as the ''private school bill of rights'' (Lines, 1986).

Public schools responded to the rapid increase in Catholic schools by replacing traditional Protestant values with nondenominationalism. The underlying principle of this movement was that a set of core religious principles and values existed and could be identified and taught in public schools. Nondenominational prayer at the start of the school day, the posting of the Ten Commandments, and Bible reading are characteristic of this period.

Prior to and during the nondenominational period, there were those who felt that religion played no part in public schools. They believed that to protect the religious freedoms of all, the religious principles of none should be promoted. In the opinion of these secularists, even supposedly nondenominational religious principles were suspect, since they might violate the beliefs of those embracing Eastern religions, or of atheists.

The influence of secularists became increasingly evident in schools. For example, the *Cardinal Principals of Secondary Education* referred to "ethical character," but made no mention of religious training. The capstone events of the secularist movement occurred in the early 1960s. The *Engel* v. *Vitale* U.S. Supreme Court decision held that school prayer was unconstitutional. The following year the Court outlawed Bible reading in schools for all but literary, social, or historical purposes.

As schools became more secular, those embracing Protestant values responded by attempting to change the public school curriculum from its secular nature to its former evangelical Protestant roots. They perceived the removal of prayer and Bible reading from schools as the "collapse of consensus concerning the basic nature and function of our institutions and the values, traditions, and purposes undergirding them" (Carper, 1983, p. 135). However, the Supreme Court continued to rule in favor of secularization of schools in cases involving school prayer and other efforts to inject religious influences into the curriculum.

Failing in their efforts to evangelize the curriculum, evangelical Protestants formed their own schools (Cooper, 1984). These schools have variously been called evangelical, Christian, or fundamentalist schools and have been the fastest-growing sector of private education over the past two decades. A related response has been a dramatic increase in home schooling.

Cooper (1984) has argued that today's private schools essentially have become the new public schools. He argues that a social compact exists between families and schools. Families provide their support, trust, and children to schools in exchange for the schools' promotion of the mores and values of the home. Many of those fleeing the public schools for private schools do so because they feel public schools have broken the compact. They perceive the values and mores that public schools promote to be incongruent with those they want their children to learn. Conversely, they frequently they perceive today's private schools to embody these standards of appropriateness.

THE STATUS OF PRIVATE EDUCATION IN THE UNITED STATES

Although the percentage and total number of kindergarten through twelfth-grade students attending private schools decreased between 1965 and 1990, a closer look at demographic data points to some recent growth of the private school sector. This growth is projected to continue into the foreseeable future.

In 1989, 5.35 million students of the nation's kindergarten through twelfth-grade students attended private schools (U.S. Department of Education, 1991). This accounted for 11.7 percent of the nation's students in this age group. Although this was a slight decline from the 5.67 million private school students who made up 13.6 percent of total kindergarten through twelfth grade enrollment in 1960, data from the 1980s indicates some growth in the private school sector (U.S. Department of Education, 1980, 1991).

The slight increase in private school enrollments during the 1980s occurred despite a continued decline in the Catholic school population. By far the largest segment of the private school population, Catholic schools educated 88 percent of the students attending private schools in 1965. From 1965 to 1983, the number of Catholic schools decreased by 30 percent and the number of students attending Catholic schools by 46 percent (Cooper, 1984). The decline in Catholic school enrollments can be attributed to several interrelated reasons. Following the Second Vatican Council of the Catholic Church, there was a significant shift in the official thinking of the Catholic Church about a variety of topics. Questions were raised about the importance of Catholic schools to the mission of the Church. The result was that many bishops and pastors no longer advocated Catholic schooling as enthusiastically (especially since the schools were a drain on parish and diocesan funding).

The Second Vatican Council also gave members of religious orders greater liberty to choose service areas. Whereas nuns previously had served almost exclusively as Catholic school teachers and principals, they now branched out into other service areas at the same time that the number of females entering the convent decreased. In order to staff schools, lay teachers had to be hired at salaries much higher than had previously been required to cover living expenses for nuns. Many parishes were saddled with large convents that now housed only a handful of nuns but continued to be a costly maintenance expenditure.

As a result of these circumstances, many parishes and dioceses were forced to close their schools. Other Catholic schools found that church collections, which had been the primary source of school funding, no longer were adequate to meet rising expenditures. These schools implemented tuition plans. Parents of many Catholic school students were thus faced with situations where schools were either no longer in existence or no longer affordable. As a result, many of them had no option but to send their children to public schools.

Other reasons that have been cited as contributing to the decreasing Catholic school population include a declining birthrate and the migration of families from the central city (where Catholic schools generally are located) to the suburbs (where they are not) (Erickson, 1983). Recently, however, the situation has stabilized, with decline in Catholic school population leveling off (Cooper, 1984), although many Catholic schools continue to struggle with funding difficulties.

Meanwhile, between 1965 and 1980, the non-Catholic portion of the private school population more than doubled, going from 750,000 students in 1965 to almost 2 million in 1980 (Lines, 1986). The increase is largely attributable to the large number of new fundamentalist Christian schools (Lines, 1986). Whereas American Lutheran Church schools and conservative Jewish schools increased by over 250 percent during the period from 1965 to 1983, evangelical schools embracing the fundamentalist ideal increased by over 600 percent. These schools were educating almost 1 million students in 1983, a total larger than that of any other type of private school with the exception of Catholic schools (Cooper, 1984). Additionally, home schooling, although educating a relatively small portion of the total population of school-age children not attending public schools, is growing exponentially. The number of students being educated in home schools increased from an estimated 10,000 in 1975 to over 50,000 in 1985 (Lines, 1986), with more recent estimates placing the number between 120,000 and 1 million students (Knowles, 1988).

The growth of the non-Catholic private school population occurred simultaneously with a decline in the number of public school students. For example, public school enrollment decreased by 11 percent between 1969 and 1989 from 45.6 million students at the beginning of that period to 40.5 million at the end (U.S. Department of Education, 1980, 1991).

Larger private school enrollments, combined with several recent reports that have supported the effectiveness of private education, have given private school constituencies a growing political power base. Recently, school choice and other initiatives that would provide direct or indirect financial assistance to private schools have received great attention and increasing public and legislative support. Cooper (1984) has noted that the increased political power base of private schools has already resulted in "an impressive array of public policies in their favor" and may "in the future . . . gain direct federal aid" (p. 437).

The decreasing population of Catholic school students and the increase in fundamentalist and other religiously affiliated schools have increased the diversity of private schools both philosophically and geographically. Whereas the formerly Catholic private school population was largely ethnic, East Coast, and urban fundamentalist schools are located in all parts of the country (Cooper, 1984).

Generally, private schools are smaller than public schools. Private schools have an average enrollment of 234 students; public schools average 482 students. Averages vary dependent on level of school, with private elementary and secondary schools averaging 218 and 541 students, respectively. This compares to averages of 403 students in public elementary schools and 721 in public secondary schools. Catholic schools tend to be the largest private schools, averaging 363 students, and fundamentalist schools are the smallest, sometimes having fewer than 100 students (Ornstein, 1989).

Several studies have found size to be a significant factor in school outcomes, with smaller schools generally exhibiting more favorable outcomes (e.g., Fowler & Walberg, 1991), although others have argued that small schools restrict program offerings. However, expansive program offerings have also been criticized for contributing to school fragmentation and diffusion of purpose (Powell, Farrar, & Cohen, 1985). Research has indicated that the less extensive but more academic and focused curriculum offered by Catholic schools leads to greater academic achievement (Erickson, 1983).

Although many private schools have been criticized for accepting only white middle-class and upper-class students, this is an inaccurate perception, at least with regard to Catholic schools. Although there was a 37 percent decrease in

Catholic school enrollments between 1970 and 1987, minority enrollments increased 27 percent during this period. The percentage of minority students enrolled in Catholic schools increased from 11.5 percent in 1970 to 22.9 percent in 1987 (Ornstein, 1989). Meanwhile, member schools of the National Association of Independent Schools increased their minority enrollments from 9.1 percent of their student population in 1981 to 12.7 percent in 1990 (National Association of Independent Schools, 1990).

Not only are many minority students enrolling in private schools, but analysts have also noted that many of the brightest students living in urban areas are fleeing urban public schools for the perceived superiority and safety of urban private schools. This "bright flight" is illustrated by the more than 20 percent decline in many urban public schools during a time when urban private school enrollments remained stable (Ornstein, 1989, p. 198).

Within private schools, a number of additional demographic changes have occurred.

- Student-teacher ratios in private schools have declined from 31.5 in 1957 to 16.1 in 1987, a ratio superior to the public school ratio of 17.7.

- Approximately 96 percent of private school teachers held either bachelor's, master's, or doctorate degrees in 1986, a significant improvement since 1973 when only 89 percent of private school teachers held bachelor's or higher degrees. The 1986 figure still does not match the public school figure of almost 100 percent of the teachers with bachelor's or higher degrees.

- On average, private schools have a slightly longer school day than public schools. However, additional time may well be allocated to religious instruction or worship services. Nonetheless, analysts have hypothesized that, due to a variety of factors, private schools are likely to have more time on task.

- Private and Catholic school students receive more math, science, English, and social studies coursework than their public school counterparts (Ornstein, 1989).

- Although salaries of private school personnel have improved in recent years, they still remain 10 percent to 40 percent lower than those of their public school counterparts (Ballantyne, Chambers, & Lajoie, 1984).

THE RESURGENCE OF INTEREST IN PRIVATE EDUCATION

Traditionally, a substantial number of families turned to private schools because of the congruency between their religious beliefs and the schools religious affiliation (Lines, 1986). However, recent studies indicate that academic reasons have become a more important motivator for private school enrollment. For example, one source notes that the majority of parents cite academic reasons as the prime motivator for enrolling their children in Catholic schools, with only 20–30 percent listing religious reasons as the main reason (Convey, 1991, p. 28).

This may be due to the significant amount of attention that has been given in the past decade to several studies that support the effectiveness of private education. For example, studies have found that private schools have higher academic achievement, more instructional time, fewer student absences, more-effective discipline, more-committed teachers, and students who do more homework and watch less television than their public school counterparts (Coleman, Hoffer, & Kilgore 1982; Morton, Bassis, Brittingham, Ewing, Horwitz, Hunter, Long, Maguire, & Pezzullo, 1977; Morton, 1979; Lee, 1985, 1987; Lee & Stewart, 1989; Marks & Lee, 1989).

Numerous studies have also shown that minority students attending Catholic schools have higher educational aspirations, are less likely to drop out of school, and exhibit achievement levels closer to those of white students than do minority students attending public schools (Coleman et al., 1982; Coleman & Hoffer, 1987; Greeley, 1982; Lee, 1985, 1987; Lee & Stewart, 1989; Marks & Lee, 1989). Other data have indicated that 14.3 percent of public school tenth- through twelfth-grade students drop out of school, whereas only 3.4 percent of Catholic school students in these grade levels do so (Coleman, Hoffer, & Kilgore, 1982). Additionally, 84 percent of private school graduates attend a two- or four-year institution subsequent to high school compared to 64 percent of public school graduates (Ornstein, 1989).

The validity of many of these findings has been questioned by research methodologists (see e.g., Cain & Goldberger, 1983); nonetheless, many parents have been swayed to pursue perceived higher standards in private schools. For these parents, studies have simply substantiated what they have long believed— that standards in private schools are more rigorous than those in public schools.

The cultures of private schools have also been linked to effectiveness. Organizational scholars have found that strong, positively perceived organizational cultures contribute to effectiveness. Private schools have several natural advantages in ensuring the development of positive organizational culture. Private schools are formed to promote a central (frequently spiritually oriented) mission or set of values. This gives organizational members a sense of social cohesion (Erickson, 1983), of being involved in something that goes beyond self-interest. Parents become significant and involved stakeholders (sometimes at great financial sacrifice) by virtue of their conscious choice to send their children to private schools. Thus, private schools do not experience the degree of fragmentation that leads to diffused purpose and cultural ambiguity in many public schools.

The recent resurgence of interest in private education may, however, be more than academically and religiously motivated. Erickson (1983) has speculated that several additional factors have contributed to the flight of many public school patrons to private schools. He noted that school finance cases in many states that attempted to achieve an equitable distribution of funds for all students (e.g., the *Serrano* case in California) limited the discretionary powers of public school districts that were heavily populated by affluent families to subsidize the education of their students at high levels. Thus, parents who wanted a maximum level of educational services for their children were forced to send them to private schools that were not limited in their delivery of extensive and high-cost services.

Second, there has been a significant amount of case law during recent decades that has attempted to ensure equitable treatment of students by providing various protections of their rights (Erickson, 1983). Increased student rights litigation has restricted the discretionary powers of school personnel to maintain appropriate standards of school discipline. As a resulting, parents have sent their children to private schools, which they perceive to have more-rigorous and fair standards of discipline. The importance to parents of rigorous discipline is illustrated by its being cited for many years as the top issue confronting schools in the annual Gallup poll of public attitudes toward education (see e.g., Gallup, 1985).

Several trends have also increased the rights of teachers over recent decades. Perhaps most notable is the advent of collective bargaining for teachers. Teacher contracts have become increasingly expansive, going well beyond salary and fringe benefit issues to encompass a variety of working conditions. Additionally, extensive litigation has also protected the rights of teachers. The result has been that schools have had less ability to ensure that teachers embrace the values of the communities in which they are employed and of the families whose children they served. Consequently, many parents have removed their children from public schools that seemingly no longer embrace communal values or the ideal of the common school.

Additionally, increasing state regulation of schooling, greater school and district size due to consolidation efforts, and the empowerment and professionalization of public school personnel have served to disempower parents by giving them less input into public school values and purposes (Erickson, 1983).

Public schools have defended themselves against charges of private school superiority by claiming that the policies of private schools give them an unfair advantage. Public school advocates claim that private schools are extremely selective in their admission of students. This may hold true for elite, high-tuition private schools, but it appears less true for mainstream religiously affiliated schools. For example, data from the National Catholic Education Association indicate that over 90 percent of students applying to Catholic schools are accepted (Rachlin & Glastris, 1989). Another criticism has been that private schools readily expel students who do not comply with standards. Although accurate data are not available, Erickson (1983) has claimed that expulsion in private schools occurs "less frequently than is widely assumed" (p. 37).

TYPES OF PRIVATE SCHOOLS

Erickson (1983) classified private schools into four categories: high-tuition schools, religiously affiliated schools, fundamentalist schools, and other private schools. Additionally, home schooling could be classified as a fifth type of private education.

High-tuition private schools are generally thought of as elite schools for the affluent. Although they are found throughout the United States, they are predominantly located along the East Coast. There are two types of high-tuition schools:

day schools in which students attend school during the day and return to their homes in the evening, and boarding schools at which students both receive instruction and live during nonschool hours. High-tuition schools are patronized primarily for academic reasons by people who want and can afford the best. Additionally, some parents who send their children to high-tuition private schools are well aware of the importance of social connections and perceptions of quality that these schools foster (Erickson, 1983).

Mainline religious schools are affiliated primarily with Catholic, Lutheran, Baptist, Seventh-Day Adventist, and Jewish sponsors, although a variety of other religious affiliations are represented to a lesser degree. As would be expected, the primary reason most parents have for sending their children to religiously affiliated schools is that they want them to have a strong grounding in the tenets, values, and morals of a particular faith. However, for a sizable segment of the religiously affiliated school population, the primary reason for attendance is strong academic standards. For example, a portion of the 11.2 percent of Catholic school students who are not members of the Catholic faith may well be attending Catholic schools because of strong academic standards. A growing dissatisfaction with public education is likely to increase the percentage of private school patrons whose primary motivation for attending religiously affiliated schools is rooted in academics rather than religion.

Fundamentalist schools embrace values that at one time characterized American public schools. The formation and patronization of these schools is a response to litigation such as the outlawing of prayer and Bible reading in public schools, and school board policies in many districts that prohibit the teaching of creationism. Additionally, fundamentalists are offended by the legally protected, contemporary lifestyles of some public school teachers and wish to shelter their children from student subcultures that promote "drugs, sex, and rock and roll" (Erickson, 1983). Generally, fundamentalist schools are very small, and may be located in church basements or other spaces not specifically designed for instructional purposes.

A variety of other types of private schools exist. One type of school that encompasses both a religious mission and an ethnic mission is the Hebrew day school. These schools experienced a period of significant growth in the mid-1960s and early 1970s in response to a "fever of ethnicity" that was prevalent in the United States at the time (Erickson, 1983, p. 12). Recently, their growth has stabilized.

In 1989, the first Japanese high school was opened in the United States. The school serves a geographic area that has a high density of Japanese industry and is intended to provide the children of Japanese families residing in the area an education similar to what they would receive in Japan. The school differs from most American schools in a number of respects. The school day is longer and the school year has more days, resulting in over 25 percent more instructional time during the course of a year. Whereas most American schools have one teacher for approximately twenty-five students, the Japanese school has one teacher for every two students. Ironically, the school, whose tuition is $13,000 per year, is located in a community that the previous year had twice rejected a $25 vehicle tax that was intended to aid public schools (Tifft, 1989; The land of rising sons . . . , 1989).

Recently, in a controversial decision, the Detroit public schools established several all-male academies for African-American adolescents. These academies are staffed primarily by African-American male adults and were established in response to the low academic achievement and high dropout and incarceration rates of African-American males. The intent of the academies was to provide positive African-American role models for young black males. Issues of reverse racial discrimination and gender discrimination quickly surfaced, and a legal challenge against the academies was mounted. Although the legal process is likely to continue to higher courts, the initial ruling rendered by the U.S. District Court held that the academies were unconstitutional and must also admit females (Cuban, 1991).

Home Schooling[1]

Enrollment of students in private schools frequently is a parental response to the absence of public school values instruction, or instruction in values that the parents perceive to be incongruent with their own values. A large number of parents have taken the issue of values instruction to an extreme by choosing to educate their children themselves at home, rather than have them attend public or private schools. The actual number of children receiving their schooling at home has been estimated from 120,000 to over 1 million (Knowles, 1988).

Most home schoolers begin to teach their children at home because of objections to the nature of public schools (Marchant & MacDonald, 1992). These parents view public schools as grounded in secular humanist philosophy that does not include strong Christian values. They are concerned about what might be missing in the education of their children, and fear the negative effects of peers and incompetent teachers. Although often they are drawn to home schooling to avoid public and even private schooling, they continue to school at home because of the pleasure and satisfaction they get from the activities. Home-schooling parents often comment on how short-changed they now feel by their own education after the wonderful experiences associated with learning at home (Marchant & MacDonald, 1992).

For some, the choice to school at home has to do with a special situation or their geographic location. Parents who see their children failing or realize that the child is going to be labeled as requiring special education may choose to remove the child from the school. Some families choose home schooling because of their geographic isolation. Home-schooling families in Alaska and in rural areas of the United States school at home because it makes practical sense, owing to limited facilities and resources for the schools. Home schooling is also a logical choice for many military families and other very transient families.

Home schoolers are as different in their teaching style and ability as public school teachers. Many home-schooling parents attempt to recreate a school atmosphere and structure in their homes (Van Galen, 1988). These parents often rely heavily on commercially produced materials, purchasing packages that teach

---

[1] We would like to thank Gregory Marchant for authoring this section of the chapter. Dr. Marchant is currently involved in an extensive study of home schooling.

a subject across several grade levels. About half of home-schooling parents design their own curriculum (Lines, 1987). These parents tend to be more informal and experiential in their teaching. They buy or develop materials and organize activities inside and outside of the home designed to meet the needs of their children. There are some indications that home schoolers who start out emulating public schools become more flexible with experience (Marchant & MacDonald, 1992).

The amount of time spent on schooling also varies greatly among home schoolers. Although some home schoolers report spending as little as one and a half hours a day teaching, others consider their teaching to last as long as eleven hours (Marchant & MacDonald, 1992). Part of the discrepancy has to do with a definition of *teaching*. Ray (1988) estimated the average amount of formal schooling time to be about three or four hours a day, with additional time spent on individual learning endeavors. Although the mother serves as the home-schooling teacher the vast majority of the time, a supportive father usually is present in the family (Lines, 1987; Marchant & MacDonald, 1992).

Although home-schooling parents tend to be proud of their efforts and believe that their children benefit from the practice, many home schoolers are not eager to make their home schooling public. The question of who governs decisions concerning the education of a child—the parent or the state (Rakestraw & Rakestraw, 1990)—often puts home-schooling parents at odds with their local school district and their state government (Gordon, Miles, & Russo, 1991). Conflicts that arise can breed resentment in both the home-schooling parents and school officials. Interpretations of state laws governing compulsory education of children drive some home-schooling parents "underground" out of fear of legal problems.

Although home schooling is legal in every state, a number of states regulate home schools (Lines, 1987). Some states require parents to register their intent to school at home; others require the teaching parent to pass the state's teacher certification exam. Some states require home-schooling parents to submit a curriculum and bring their child to the school annually for standardized testing.

Questions and concerns persist about the quality of education attained through home schooling. Studies have suggested that home-schooled children achieve the same as or more than children educated in public schools. (See Ray, 1988, for a synthesis.) However, by taking their children out of schools, home-schooling parents may be depriving the children of certain resources and opportunities such as the opportunity for peer social interaction.

GOVERNANCE AND CONTROL
OF PRIVATE SCHOOLS

Private schools exhibit a variety of governance patterns. For example, Catholic and Lutheran systems have a governance hierarchy, whereas independent schools are generally loosely tied to the National Association of Independent Schools. Other types of private schools are unattached to any higher authority beyond local organizing and governance groups.

Generally, private schools have fewer levels in the governing hierarchy and thus are not subject to the fragmentation that conflicting demands from trying to serve too many masters has placed upon public schools. Control, authority, and decision making are generally located at the school level (Scott & Meyer, 1985).

Private school administrative staffs tend to be very small. Public schools have much larger central office administrative staffs, fostered by a web of funding sources, program requirements, and mandates—generally dictated from state or federal governments or other regulatory agencies. The impact on public schools has been less program coherence than in private schools (Scott & Meyer, 1985).

Little detailed research has been conducted on private school governance, with the exception of Catholic school governance. Most Catholic elementary schools are operated on a parish by parish basis. This has caused them to be affected by the uncertainties of single-parish finance, and in- and out-migration. Secondary schools span parish boundaries and are operated by dioceses and religious orders, and thus are less subject to minor fluctuations in the external environment. They have more diverse budgets and income sources and larger attendance areas (Erickson, 1983).

Catholic school governance has undergone a transition during the past twenty-five years. Prior to the Second Vatican Council of the Catholic Church, governance of Catholic schools was carried out primarily through traditional hierarchical authority structures of bishop, pastor or religious order, and principal in descending order of authority. Since the Council, governance has evolved into more collaborative arrangements that have included parents as members of advisory committees and school boards.

Under the new structure, parish school boards consisting of parents whose children attend the parish school have been developed in approximately 70 percent of the Catholic schools in America (Hocevar, 1991). These boards are of two types—a board with limited jurisdiction and a consultative board. Jurisdictional boards have power over policy in certain areas of educational concern, with bishops retaining control in matters of religion and Catholicity. These boards have final but not total jurisdiction. Consultative boards, on the other hand, are involved in the development of policy, but have no actual authority (Hocevar, 1991).

The parish pastor is entrusted with pastoral care for the diocese, but his relationship with the principal has not been formally delineated. Generally, the principal fulfills responsibilities such as employment, supervision, and evaluation of teachers and other school employees; the formulation of policies for consideration by the school board; oversight of the instructional program; and the preparation of a school budget. The pastor retains ultimate financial control, supervises and evaluates the principal, and oversees the religious instruction program of the school (O'Brien, 1987).

Catholic schools also have a diocesan education office, generally with a very small administrative staff (Scott & Meyer, 1985). Diocesan offices, however, have no formal authority, although superintendents may have authority if they have been appointed episcopal vicar by the bishop. In either case, a fundamental principle of Catholic canon law holds that decisions regarding a parish are most appropriately resolved at the parish rather than the diocesan level (O'Brien, 1987).

Informally, however, the relationship of the diocesan office with the bishop and parish pastors, and its ability to grant or withhold resources or services in some instances, gives it a degree of power over individual schools whether or not the superintendent has been appointed episcopal vicar.

Similar to the perceptions of power loss felt by many public school administrators in response to calls for greater teacher involvement in school decision making, many bishops and religious orders have viewed the change in Catholic school governance relationships as a "diminution of their lawful authority" (Hocevar, 1991, p. 10).

LEGAL ISSUES

Regulation of Private Schools

Recently, there has been a great increase in the number of legal cases involving regulation of private schools. Litigation of this type was rare before the 1950s, but the number of cases increased rapidly during the 1970s and 1980s. In fact, whereas the early 1900s was characterized by three to four cases per decade of this type, the first three years of the 1980s involved fifty-one such cases. Some projections have predicted that the 1990s will result in four to five times as many cases involving regulation of private schools (Lines, 1986).

The increase in regulatory actions against private schools can largely be attributed to the growth of fundamentalist Christian schools. Although the right of parents to satisfy compulsory attendance requirements by sending their children to private schools was established in 1925 by *Pierce* v. *Society of Sisters,* the court also ruled in that case that the state has an interest in regulating the quality of private education to ensure an educated citizenry. However, for the government to intervene with parents' decisions regarding their children's education, the government must show that intervention is necessary to protect the child or the state (McCarthy & Cambron-McCabe, 1987).

The refusal of many Christian school administrators to make any efforts to comply with the standards of schooling established for public schools has stimulated much of the current litigation. Although Catholic, Lutheran, and other religiously affiliated schools in recent years have attempted to meet public school standards in order to enhance their credibility as strong academic institutions, many fundamentalist Christian school heads have viewed public school standards as an infringement on their right to educate their students as they best see fit. They see the school as an extension of the church, and thus not subject to state regulation.

Governmental Aid to Private Schools

States provide a variety of types of aid to private schools. Private schools receive about 26 percent of their total income directly or indirectly from government funding (Scott & Meyer, 1985). In 1985, thirty-eight states provided public aid to education including transportation services (twenty-three states), the loan of textbooks (eighteen states), state-required testing programs (fourteen states), special education services (thirteen states), and guidance counseling (ten states) (McCarthy & Cambron-McCabe, 1987).

Public aid to private schools has been the subject of extensive litigation. Although an exhaustive treatment of relevant cases is beyond the scope of this book, several significant principles that prospective school administrators should keep in mind will be highlighted here.

The primary argument against public aid to private education is that it violates separation of church and state as established by the Constitution, since most private schools are church-related. The courts have approved several types of aid that primarily benefits students rather than institutions (e.g., transportation services). Court approval, however, simply means that services are constitutionally permissible; it does not mean that services must be provided (McCarthy & Cambron-McCabe, 1987).

One court ruling that continues to create logistical headaches for public and private schools is *Aguilar* v. *Felton.* In this case, the U.S. Supreme Court ruled that Title I services (now Chapter I), which public schools are required to provide for all qualifying students regardless of school type, could not be provided by public school teachers in parochial school buildings since this constituted excessive entanglement between church and state. The Court did not strike down the provision that these services be provided for parochial school students, but rather required them to be provided in public schools or at neutral sites. It has been widely assumed that this ruling also applies to other federal programs that provide services for parochial school students (e.g., special education services) (McCarthy & Cambron-McCabe, 1987).

Recently, the concept of choice has received much attention as a reform initiative to improve education. (See the discussion in Chapter 12.) Although there are different forms of choice, one type involves providing parents with a voucher that can be used at any school, public or private, to pay for the education of their child. The end result of the voucher system is that religiously affiliated schools receive government funding for students who choose to attend their schools, although the aid is indirect in the sense that it is first funneled through the student. At issue is whether the primary beneficiary of government funding is parents and students or religiously affiliated institutions.

The U.S. Supreme Court has ruled on several cases that hold implications for the constitutionality of choice. In *Mueller* v. *Allen,* the Court upheld the constitutionality of a Minnesota tuition tax credit plan that allowed parents to claim a tax deduction for educational expenses incurred for their children. The court ruled that since the benefit was provided for all students, regardless of whether they attended private or public schools, the plan "evidences a purpose that is both secular and understandable" (McCarthy & Cambron-McCabe, 1987, p. 53). In *Witters* v. *Washington Department of Services for the Blind,* the Supreme Court ruled that aid that went directly to a handicapped student who then transmitted the funds to a religiously affiliated institution for educational services was constitutional since the aid was provided to the student, who exercised personal choice about which institution should receive the funds. Thus, although courts have not directly ruled on the constitutionality of choice plans, it appears that in order to uphold constitutionality, plans should provide *all* students a choice and should provide assistance facilitating such choice directly to students or their parents rather than to the educational institution.

IMPLICATIONS FOR PRACTICE

Scholars have noted that the lines between public and private schools increasingly are becoming blurred (Ornstein, 1989): many private schools now promote what once were mainstream public school values; there is greater public support for private schools than for public schools; and government increasingly has become involved in the regulation of private schools. Many have argued that the private school now more closely resembles the ideal of the common school than does the public school—a school that promotes the values and beliefs of the dominant culture, where "moral instruction and civic learning occur with the greatest intensity" (James, 1985, p. 2).

Whether or not empirical research proves the efficacy of private schools, it remains clear that:

- Internal and external conditions differ for public and private schools.
- Private school patrons are more satisfied with their schools than are public school patrons.

For public schools, many of the conditions that affect them are beyond their control. Nonetheless, rather than practicing defensive posturing, public school administrators would do well to study the reasons for increased private school satisfaction levels and emulate practices as appropriate and possible. Erickson (1983) has noted, "One of the most compelling reasons for studying private schools may be that by isolating the factors responsible for their particular strengths . . . strategies [may be generated] for the improvement of all schools, public and private" (p. 40). One analyst has suggested that what public schools lack is "something analogous to religious commitment, an 'excitement, spiritual fulfillment and enrichment'" in the way people approach their work (James, 1985, p. 2).

The decline in the number of school-age children, the increased elderly population, and the growing disenchantment with public education may result in a crisis of social support for all schools (Cooper, 1984). Yet, educational authorities at different levels of governance (e.g., teaching versus administration) and in different sectors of education (e.g., public and private) often work at cross purposes, thus fragmenting educational authority in the competition for resources and the establishment of appropriate policy (Scott & Meyer, 1985). When public and private schools war over issues such as tax relief for private school patrons, attention is diverted from increasing sums of money spent on defense and programs for the elderly (Cooper, 1984). In the interests of all children, public and private school personnel and constituents need to cooperate in order to present a unified front in competing with other societal groups for scarce resources.

FOR FURTHER DISCUSSION

1. One of the oft-cited reasons families choose to patronize private schools is that they promote values. Discuss the issue of values instruction in public schools. Should values be taught in public schools? If so, what values should be taught? Is it possible for teaching to be value-free?
2. With the exception of Catholic schools, other segments of the private education sector are growing. What are the advantages and disadvantages of private school growth for education? for children?
3. How do you feel public schools should respond to the growth of private education?
4. What can public schools learn from private schools? What can private schools learn from public schools?
5. What are the implications of *Aguilar* v. *Felton* for public school administrators?
6. Discuss the benefits and pitfalls of home schooling. What should be the responsibility of public schools to home-schooled children?
7. Discuss the concept of choice. Should vouchers be implemented to give parents a choice of schools to which to send their children?
8. Research and discuss the concepts of American-Japanese schools and African-American male academies. What are the advantages and disadvantages of each type of school?

OTHER SUGGESTED ACTIVITIES

1. Research citing the effectiveness of private schools has been argued to be methodologically flawed. Review several research studies supporting private school effectiveness and critiques of the research. Discuss your findings.
2. Develop a set of interview questions for interviewing public and private school administrators, based on discussion in this chapter. Interview several administrators employed in public schools and several from private schools and analyze and compare their responses.
3. Develop a list of advantages and disadvantages of public schools. Do the same for private schools. What implications for modifying practice in each sector do the lists suggest?
4. The chapter has provided an overview of the current private school context with the concluding section suggesting several implications for practitioners. Develop a list of additional implications.
5. Spend a few hours visiting and observing in both private and public schools. Take field notes during your visit. Analyze your notes and compare both settings. Develop working hypotheses of similarities and differences in the two types of schools and discuss what can be learned from them.
6. Review research on existing school choice programs. In what ways have they been successful? In what ways have they been unsuccessful?

REFERENCES

Ballantyne, M., Chambers, J. G., & Lajoie, S. (1984). *A comparative study of public and private schools in the San Francisco Bay Area: A descriptive report.* (ERIC Document Reproduction Service No. ED 269 905)

Cain, G. G., & Goldberger, A. S. (1983). Public and private schools revisited. *Sociology of Education,* 56 (October), 208–218.

Carper, J. C. (1983). The Christian day school movement. *Education Forum* (Winter), 35–149.

Coleman, J. S., & Hoffer, T. (1987). *Public and private high schools: The impact of communities.* New York: Basic Books.

Coleman, J. S., Hoffer, T., & Kilgore, S. (1982). *High school achievement: Public, Catholic, and private schools compared.* New York: Basic Books.

Convey, J. J. (1991). Catholic schools in a changing society: Past accomplishments and future challenges. In *The Catholic School and Society.* Washington, DC: National Catholic Educational Association.

Cooper, B. (1984). The changing demography of private schools. *Education and Urban Society,* 16 (4), 429–442.

Cuban, L. (1991, November 21). Desperate remedies for desperate times. *Education Week,* 36, 30.

Erickson, D. A. (1983). *Private schools in contemporary perspective.* (ERIC Document Reproduction Service No. ED 231 015)

Fowler, W. J., & Walberg, H. J. (1991). School size, characteristics, and outcomes. *Educational Evaluation and Policy Analysis,* 13 (2), 189–202.

Gallup, A. (1985). The 17th annual Gallup poll of the public's attitudes toward the public schools. *Phi Delta Kappan,* 67 (1), 35–47.

Gordon, W. M., Miles, A., & Russo, C. J. (1991). *Home schooling.* (ERIC Document Reproduction Service No. ED 332 291)

Greeley, A. M. (1982). *Catholic high schools and minority students.* New Brunswick, NJ: Transaction Books.

Hocevar, R. A. (1991). Catholic school governance. In *Catholic school governance and finance.* Washington, DC: National Catholic Educational Association.

James, T. (1985). *Public & private schools.* (ERIC Document Reproduction Service No. ED 017 682)

Knowles, J. G. (1988). The context of home schooling in the United States. *Education and Urban Society,* 21, 5–15.

Lee, V. E. (1985). *1983–84 National Assessment of Educational Progress reading proficiency: Catholic school results and national averages.* Washington, DC: National Catholic Educational Association.

———. (1987). *1983–84 National Assessment of Educational Progress writing proficiency: Catholic school results and national averages.* Washington, DC: National Catholic Educational Association.

Lee, V. E., & Stewart, C. (1989). *National Assessment of Educational Progress proficiency in mathematics and science: 1985–86.* (ERIC Document Reproduction Service No. ED 307 132)

Lines, P. M. (1986). The new private schools and their historic purpose. *Phi Delta Kappan,* 67 (5), 373–379.

———. (1987). An overview of home instruction. *Phi Delta Kappan,* 68, 503–517.

McCarthy, M. M., & Cambron-McCabe, N. (1987). *Public school law: Teachers' and students' rights* (2nd ed.). Boston, MA: Allyn and Bacon.

Marchant, G. J., & MacDonald, S. C. (1992, April). *How home schoolers school.* Paper presented at the annual meeting of the American Educational Research Association.

Marks, H. M., & Lee, V. E. (1989). *National Assessment of Educational Progress proficiency in reading 1985–86: Catholic and public schools compared.* Washington, DC: National Catholic Educational Association.

Morton, D. S. (1979). Examining the differences between public and parochial education: The Rhode Island experience. In T. Vitullo-Martin (ed.), *Catholic inner-city schools: The future.* Washington, DC: United States Catholic Conference.

Morton, D. S., Bassis, M., Brittingham, B. E., Ewing, P., Horwitz, S., Hunter, W. J., Long, J. V., Maguire, J., & Pezzullo, T. R. (1977). *A comprehensive analysis of differences in public and parochial school student performance on standardized tests of achievement.* Paper presented at the annual meeting of the American Educational Research Association, New York.

National Association of Independent Schools (1990). *NAIS statistics, 1989–90. Enrollment, staff, people of color.* (ERIC Document Reproduction Service No. ED 330 075)

O'Brien, J. S. (1987). *A primer on educational governance in the Catholic church.* (ERIC Document Reproduction Service No. ED 289 250)

Ornstein, A. C. (1989). Private and public school comparisons. *Education and Urban Society,* 21 (2), 192–205.

Powell, A. G., Farrar, E. & Cohen, D. K. (1985). *The shopping mall high school: Winners and losers in the educational marketplace.* Boston: Houghton Mifflin.

Rachlin, J., & Glastris, P. (1989, May 22). Of more than parochial interest. *U.S. News & World Report.* Pp. 61–62.

Rakestraw, J. F., & Rakestraw, D. A. (1990). Home schooling: A question of quality, an issue of rights. *Educational Forum,* 55, 67–77.

Ray, B. D. (1988). Home schools: A synthesis of research on characteristics and learner outcomes. *Education and Urban Society,* 21, 16–31.

Scott, W. R., & Meyer, J. W. (1985). Autonomy, authority, & administration: Differences in school organizations. In *Public & private schools.* Stanford University: Institute for Research on Educational Finance and Governance. (ERIC Document Reproduction Service No. ED 017 682)

The land of rising sons and daughters (1989). *U.S. News & World Report,* May 22, pp. 12–13.

Tifft, S. (1989). Rising sun over Sweetwater. *Time,* May 22, p. 92.

U.S. Department of Education (1980). *Digest of education statistics.* Washington, D.C.: Author, Office of Educational Research and Improvement.

————. (1991). *Digest of education statistics.* Washington, D.C.: Author, Office of Educational Research and Improvement.

Van Galen, J. A. (1988). Ideology, curriculum, and pedagogy in home education. *Education and Urban Society,* 21, 52–68.

CHAPTER 7

The Organizational Dimensions of Schools

Chapter Content

Defining Organizations and Organizational Behavior

Critical Features of Organizations

Schools as Organizations

A Contemporary Context for Schools

Implications for Practice

Joan Andrews has been principal of Lincoln Middle School for three years. During her tenure, she became frustrated by the fact that she could not get a teacher to serve as cheerleader sponsor. Each time she found a teacher to assume the task, that person would decline after giving the matter further consideration. What truly confused Joan was the fact that newly hired teachers often expressed enthusiasm about working with cheerleaders; but once they started working at the school, their enthusiasm for this assignment quickly waned. Joan decided to investigate the matter. She quickly discovered that a small but influential group of teachers was discouraging other faculty from accepting this assignment. Members of this group believed that cheerleading should be treated as a sport; and as such, they argued that sponsors for this activity should receive stipends equal to those paid to coaches. By dissuading faculty members from accepting the assignment, the group believed they could force school officials to adopt their position on this matter. Joan's problem provides an excellent example of how conditions in an organization can affect worker behaviors.

Understanding and influencing behavior are critical elements of leadership. When an employee decides to do something, or not do something, his or her decision usually is predicated on collective influences. Individual beliefs, wants, and needs often intertwine with social pressures and political considerations to determine a person's course of action. Thus, when a faculty member tells the principal that he or she does not want to be cheerleader sponsor, the principal needs to realize that any number of factors may have contributed to the decision. This awareness allows the principal to develop contingency solutions. Three critical tasks—understanding employee behavior, problem identification, and the development of solutions—are facilitated by a leader's knowledge of schools and school districts as organizations.

DEFINING ORGANIZATIONS AND ORGANIZATIONAL BEHAVIOR

We commonly recognize that General Motors and Delta Air Lines are organizations. These institutions are vast; they have hierarchies of authority and divisions of labor. Their ultimate goal—profit—is no mystery to the public. Structure, product, and the quest for profit are attributes we readily acknowledge and associate with organizations. But what about churches or schools? Do they qualify as organizations?

There are literally hundreds of ways to define an organization. There are, however, two recurring elements in virtually all formal definitions: (1) the social nature of these entities and (2) the fact that these entities exist to achieve specific purposes. The two are evident in the following brief definitions:

> Organizations are social inventions accomplishing goals through group effort (Johns, 1988, pp. 9–10).

> An organization can be defined as a social unit that has been deliberately designed to achieve some specific goals (Reitz, 1987, p. 13).

In its most basic form, organizations can be viewed as integrated systems of independent structures known as groups. And in all organizations, these groups are composed of individual employees (Berrien, 1976).

Hall (1991) described the pervasiveness of organizations in contemporary society:

> Organizations surround us. We are born in them and usually die in them. Our life space in between is filled with them. They are just about impossible to escape. They are as inevitable as death and taxes. (p. 1)

Yet, many of us spend our entire lives really not understanding how these entities help shape our values and beliefs, and ultimately our behavior. Our contact with organizations, and our reliance on them, stretches well beyond our world of work. A multitude of organizations ranging from governmental agencies to churches to country clubs to manufacturers of goods affect our lives virtually every day.

To help explain organizations, a number of authors have relied on metaphors. Owens (1991), for instance, summarized comparisons of organizations to the human organism. He noted that the groups and individuals within them function much like cells and molecules in our bodies. A malfunction in part of the system may have repercussions for all other parts. There is an interdependency among the components. Over time, none is able to stand alone. A system, whether it is the human body or a school, is a set of interrelated parts, each functioning as an element of the whole.

Morgan (1986) offered two additional metaphors for organizations. He likened bureaucratic organizations to machines—entities where some parts were purposely designed to interface with other parts, and to do so with a minimum loss of energy. He also postulated that organizations could be viewed as systems of political activity. In this context, organizations can be studied from the perspective of human behavior. More precisely, analysis occurs by systematically focusing on the relationships among interests, conflict, and power.

Recurring themes of these metaphors are that (1) organizations are unique entities composed of individuals and groups, (2) there is an interdependency among the various components of the organization, and (3) human interactions are inevitable. Behavior of those within the organization is a critical concern for leaders who have the responsibility of directing and managing people to facilitate the achievement of determined organizational goals. A principal, for instance, can better lead the school toward desired change if he or she can anticipate employee responses to change initiatives.

Organizational behavior is the term used to identify the attitudes and behaviors of individuals and groups who compose the organization (Johns, 1988). For organizational behavior to occur, three elements must be present: individuals, an organization, and interaction between individuals and the organization. This is illustrated in Figure 7–1.

FIGURE 7–1 Components of Organizational Behavior

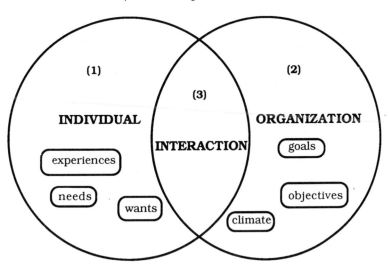

Production line workers, for example, bring personal attitudes, beliefs, needs, wants, and experiences to the workplace. The employer also has needs and wants, and these are expressed in formal and informal goals. At times, interaction between workers and employer is harmonious (i.e., the needs and wants of both are basically congruent). But at other times, conflict emerges when workers want to go in one direction and the employer in another. Recognizing this potentiality, manufacturing organizations may go to great lengths to control employee behavior. This is attempted through training, indoctrination, or other forms of persuasion intended to condition employees to perform in certain ways. If this is successful, employee behaviors become routine and are performed without reflection (Hall, 1991). When this condition exists, conflict between worker and employer interests is less likely.

Relationships between an employee and the organization are made even more complex by the fact that individuals are members of both formal and informal groups. Groups embrace common values, needs, wants, and so forth—just like individuals and the organization. Figure 7–2 illustrates the interactions that occur among individuals, groups, and the organization. Labor unions or a division of

FIGURE 7–2   Interactions among Individuals, Groups, and Organizations

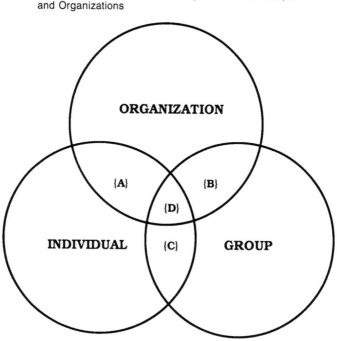

A = interactions between organization and individual
B = interactions between organization and group
C = interactions between individual and group
D = interactions among individual, group, and organization

an organization exemplifies a formal group, and five employees who eat lunch together every day may constitute an informal group. In the context of organizational behavior, the five workers become an informal group when their association results in commonly held needs, expectations, values, beliefs, or wants.

A large part of leadership entails understanding how organizations function and how interactions occur among individuals and groups. These insights provide information critical to directing or redirecting worker behavior. This is true regardless of the intent and purposes of the organization. A school principal, like a division manager in a large corporation, is expected to steer subordinate performance toward the attainment of organizational goals. This responsibility becomes less of a burden if the leader understands organizations generally, and the immediate work environment specifically.

Two of the most common problems facing organizations are uncertainty and inadequate strategies to cope with uncertainty (Thompson, 1967). *Organizational uncertainty* is created by ambiguity in philosophy, mission, structure, purposes, and so forth. In other words, the organization's intentions and operational procedures are unclear, even for those who hold top leadership positions. This condition intensifies the risks of leadership, particularly in decision making (March & Simon, 1958). Overall, public schools still possess a large measure of uncertainty. This comes as no surprise given that the general public continues to hold varying perceptions of what schools should accomplish and how administrators and teachers should perform their responsibilities.

CRITICAL FEATURES OF ORGANIZATIONS

All organizations have some type of structure that facilitates the division of tasks or operations related to achieving goals and objectives (Knezevich, 1984). Although all organizations share such common attributes, you should not conclude that all are identical. They vary in size, environmental conditions, incentive systems, leadership and authority, and goals (Knoke & Prensky, 1984). Like human beings, organizations share common features, but they can be distinguished from one another by visible and invisible characteristics that make each unique. Thus, a given school district not only differs from General Motors, it also possesses characteristics that separate it from all other school districts.

You may have observed that policies and operations in small rural districts often are substantially different from those in large urban districts. Likewise, small and large high schools often differ in many respects. This variance illuminates the importance of organizational context in relation to administrative behavior. Since organizations are not identical, leadership behaviors that work in one setting may not be equally effective in another.

Basic understandings of organizational behavior are fundamental to the study of school administration. For this reason, five foundational topics are reviewed in this chapter. These are organizational theory, culture, climate, adaptability, and centralization of authority. In more-advanced courses, you should have opportunities to extend your understandings of the organizational dimensions of schooling.

Organizational Theory

Organizational theory involves the systematic ordering of knowledge accumulated in the context of organizational behavior. The process includes the study of interactions among institutional structures, individuals, groups, and the general environment (Kowalski, 1988). Too often, leaders become wed to a single view of how organizations function; and when this occurs, a full understanding of behavior is virtually impossible (Bolman & Deal, 1989). Organizational science seeks to describe and explain individual and group behavior in organizations. Its ultimate aim is the production of theory. Hoy and Miskel (1984) noted that educational administration theory is defined as:

> a set of interrelated concepts, assumptions, and generalizations that systematically describes and explains regularities in behaviors in educational organizations. (p. 20)

Organizational theory is the product of research. Initially, the influence of classical theory (bureaucracy) created images of a rational organization where scientific management was viewed as the key factor related to institutional success. But as analysts discovered that organizational life was really more complex and less predictable than first thought, their efforts to describe and forecast organizational behavior drifted toward human relations. This shift was predicated on the belief that the fundamental problem in all organizations was the development and maintenance of dynamic and harmonious relationships (Hoy & Miskel, 1984). More recently, those attempting to describe organizational life have infused the study of behavioral sciences, noting that neither classical nor human relations efforts were sufficiently comprehensive to explain all behavior. In their seminal book, *Toward a General Theory of Action,* Parsons and Shils (1951) exhibited how various social scientists could work together to formulate frameworks to explain behavior. Subjects such as anthropology, psychology, political science, and sociology have much to offer in this regard. The importance of behavioral studies also is illuminated by systemic views of organizational life. As mentioned previously, an organization is much like a human organism: All parts are interrelated.

Organizational Culture

As previously noted, every employee brings values, beliefs, needs, wants, and motivations to the workplace. Over a period of time, organizations, driven by formal and informal goals, socialize employees (Owens, 1991). That is, personal variables interact with organizational forces to affect behavior. The symbolic dimension of an organization is referred to as *culture.* Deal and Kennedy (1982) pointed out that every organization has a culture. It may be fragmented and difficult to determine, but it does exist. Culture affects practically every decision made within the organization. It is largely the product of basic concepts and beliefs that constitute cherished values of the organization. In other words, culture is an invisible framework of standards representing beliefs and values that are perceived as having worked well in the past. Culture also includes rites and rituals that provide visible and potent examples of what the organization deems important. And it includes role models who provide examples of expected work performance (Deal & Kennedy, 1982).

Norms are a product of culture, and they help employees to interpret everyday occurrences and to sort out the confusion, uncertainty, and ambiguity of work life (Goens & Clover, 1991). Beneath norms are assumptions representing what people in the organization hold to be true or false, sensible or absurd, and possible or impossible (Owens, 1991).

Cultures are not static—but neither are they prone to change easily. To bring about culture change, leaders must possess technical knowledge (strategic planning, human resources development knowledge, and the ability to join the two) (Burack, 1991). You may have observed a new principal who brings to the school values that are incongruous with existing norms. This may not be a problem if teachers, school board, and superintendent deem that change is needed. If, however, there is a strong desire to preserve the status quo, disharmony between the principal and the existing culture is likely to create serious problems. The culture of the school is not apt to change simply to accommodate the administrator. Hart (1991) observed that leader succession (the process of replacing key officials) does not ensure organizational change. She wrote:

> Organizations, however, protect against the intrusion of new members, values, and beliefs by routinization and through formal and informal social mechanisms, one of which is socialization. (p. 469)

Culture change is especially difficult in organizations where strong beliefs and values have existed over a period of time.

Culture can be a very positive influence. It may provide the glue that binds components of the organization so that they work toward commonly accepted objectives. Conversely, culture can be dysfunctional. That is to say, it can produce negative influences with regard to organizational goal achievement (Goens & Clover, 1991). One dimension of culture in school districts that you may readily understand relates to practices for employing administrators. Do you know of a school district that has a reputation for not hiring "outsiders"? This is a school district with a strong bias that current employees should receive preferential consideration for promotion to leadership positions. Such a manifestation of culture may be predicated on the belief that loyalty and service should be rewarded or that organizational stability is more likely when internal promotions are the norm.

Each school and each school district develops its own culture. Culture survives because there are persons who protect it. Deal and Kennedy (1982) referred to these individuals as "high priests." They are employees whose personal values and beliefs are most congruent with the present culture. Thus, employees who believe that internal promotions are best will directly and indirectly fight to preserve this norm—and the intensity of their efforts is fueled by personal conviction.

Organizational Climate

Organizations have leaders, policies, methods for making decisions, and other facets that collectively help to establish a climate within the workplace. Organizational climate may be expressed as understandings and expectations held in common by a majority of leaders and employees. This common acceptance results in uniformities in leadership and subordinate behaviors (Frederiksen, Jensen, and Beeton, 1972). Owens (1991) referred to organizational climate as "the study of perceptions that individuals have of various aspects of the environment in the organization" (p. 175). Take, for instance, the way teachers and principals dress for work. In some organizations, dress codes for teachers and administrators may be enforced (e.g., men must wear ties). Although the organization's position on such matters may be embedded in formal policy and rules, perceptions also may be a product of informal rules. Employees are quick to sense what types of behaviors are rewarded, tolerated, discouraged, or even punished.

The climate of an organization often is discussed in terms of a continuum ranging from totally open to totally closed. This designation refers to the degree to which the organization interacts with its external environments (environments external to the organization such as the community, county, or state government). For public schools, this is a critical factor. The closed nature of many profit-seeking companies can be seen when they resist governmental interventions in their operations (e.g., lobbying against legislation that would affect manufacturing procedures). External interventions often create inefficiency for the companies; thus, an effort is made to avoid them. Schools, by contrast, are generally expected to be open institutions. Taxpayers, based on the notion of public ownership, demand to have some say in setting goals, monitoring resources, and overseeing other administrative functions.

Clearly, public schools differ in their willingness to encourage employee or organizational interaction. Some principals actively solicit teacher and parental input in critical decisions, whereas others believe that major determinations are the sole prerogatives of management. In some school districts, every effort is made to collaborate with other community agencies; but in others, such linkages are avoided because they are viewed as potential sources of conflict. This variance in organizational climate among schools and school systems is often overlooked when we explore ways of improving leadership, and ultimately education outcomes.

Organizational Adaptability

Especially in recent times, many school administrators have come to the conclusion that maintaining the status quo is not really an option. With the deployment of technology and demands for reform, an organization either moves forward or it falls behind. In these conditions, change becomes an important element in organizational life. It can be induced by a myriad of factors, including those external to the organization (e.g., governmental interventions, market demands). Change also may be induced by factors that are internal to an organization. For example, a company alters the way it markets automobiles in an effort to attract a different type of buyer.

Schools too are shaped by external as well as internal forces (Verstegen & Wagoner, 1989). Operations are directed by school board policy and administrative rules, but they also are influenced by external factors such as laws, governmental regulations, pressure groups, and community needs. Adaptation is the process of organizational modifications carried out in an attempt to remain relevant. It constitutes a process of using organizational assets to respond to environmental needs and wants.

One of the current criticisms of public education is that schools are not adaptable institutions. In the past decade, calls for transforming the structure of public education reflect perceptions that inflexibility has caused schools to become outdated. The topic of change is discussed in detail in Chapter 13.

Centralization of Authority

Authority is considered to be legitimate power (i.e., power acquired solely through one's position in the organization). Simon (1957) described authority as the power to make decisions that guide the behavior of subordinates. Authority generally is described along a continuum ranging from highly centralized to highly decentralized. A school system that has high levels of centralized authority would be one in which major decisions are made by the superintendent and only one or two other high-ranking officials. Decentralization, by contrast, diffuses authority, dispersing it among units of the organization (e.g., giving individual principals greater autonomy in making decisions about curriculum and instruction).

Those who defend centralization view the structure as a source of protection against disasters, confusion, and conflict. This is accomplished by reducing uncertainty in decisions (i.e., if only a few individuals are making key decisions, the decisions are likely to be more consistent). Centralization, however, can be demoralizing for lower-level executives. These individuals often have the knowledge necessary to make proper decisions, yet must defer to higher-ranking officials who may be out of touch with specific situations (Mintzberg, 1979). On the other hand, decentralization attempts to accomplish three very different goals: flexibility, accountability, and productivity (Brown, 1990). Consider the present conditions facing public schools. There are growing demands for organizational change; taxpayers continue to ask for evidence of accountability; and critics of education are insisting on improved outputs. Given these circumstances, site-based management, a form of decentralization, has gained popularity in recent years.

SCHOOLS AS ORGANIZATIONS

Even though they are not profit-seeking entities, and even though they provide services rather than products, schools (and school systems) are every bit as much organizations as are major private enterprises. The common thread is a social dimension (i.e., schools are complex social organizations possessing many of the same attributes found in all organizations) (Bennett & LeCompte, 1990). For example, an elementary school and American Air Lines are both composed of people and groups. Although motives, goals, and structure in these two organizations are quite different, leaders share common interests with regard to human behavior and goal achievement. In this regard, organizational studies have a universal value for all institutions.

The Social Dimension

The concept of a social system is based on the idea that a group of individuals whose relationship is more than random create interactions that affect behavior (Hoy & Miskel, 1984). As previously noted, two types of groups are found in organizations: formal and informal. Formal groups are those that have a legal status. The English department in a high school exemplifies an entity formally recognized by the school. As noted earlier, informal groups often are less obvious. The formation of social units within an organization is sometimes referred to as the *informal organization* (Blau & Scott, 1962). Figure 7–3 provides a depiction of the range of formal and informal groups that could exist in a high school.

FIGURE 7–3   Examples of Groups Common in Secondary Schools

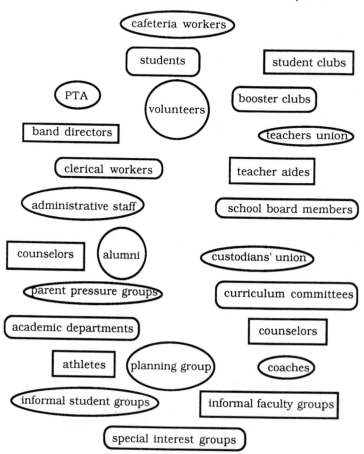

Hoy and Miskel (1984) identified two sources for processes that socially organize human beings: "(1) the *structure of the social relations* in the group; and (2) the *culture* of the group" (p. 51). Structure relates to patterns of interaction (e.g., how and where members meet), and culture comprises the shared values, beliefs, and possibly needs of the members.

The organizational format of most schools isolates teachers for much of the workday. Especially in elementary schools, there is very limited time for peer interactions. In viewing the social dimension of schools, two important points should be noted: (1) Teachers consider themselves to be professionals, and (2) historically teachers have had little power to affect governance in schools (Stinnett & Henson, 1982). The frustration that grew out of these two conditions sparked interest in bold actions such as unionization. Although many teachers feared that union membership would deter their quest for recognition as a profession, they nevertheless joined the movement because they wanted a greater voice in the control of schools (Bennett & LeCompte, 1990). Interestingly, school-improvement initiatives often include notations that teachers need to spend more time with other teachers—to share information, ideas, and problems.

After groups are formed and membership established, three characteristics usually are observable. First, the group's culture becomes a force that affects the behavior of its members. When members conform to the established norms, they in essence create a degree of interdependence among themselves. Second, the members derive satisfaction of individual needs via participation in the group. For example, membership may result in a sense of security or prestige. Third, members share common aims. Although they may not agree on everything, they embrace goals specifically endorsed by the group (Owens, 1991). Research on small groups emphasizes the critical role the group occupies between the individual and the organization. Bolman and Deal (1989) wrote:

> Small groups influence how well individuals perform, how well their needs are met, and how they view their work and the organization. (p. 204)

The group becomes the reference point for defining many work related issues. For this reason, administrators need to understand the social dimensions of organizational behavior and they ought to be able to identify ways in which prevailing conditions in schools help shape employee behavior.

The Professional Dimension

There are unique characteristics that set public schools apart from other types of organizations. They are publicly owned; they evolve in the context of communities (each of which is a novel amalgam of values and beliefs); they provide services and set goals that are substantially different from those commonly found in profit-seeking companies; and there exist multiple lines of power and control (Bennett & LeCompte, 1990). Additionally, there are characteristics that set schools and school districts apart from each other (e.g., size, geographic location, philosophy). Thus, the detailed study of organizational theory in school administration necessarily includes (1) common elements of organizational behavior, (2) characteristics of schools and school districts that differentiate them from other types of organizations, and (3) characteristics that differentiate schools and school districts from each other.

Schools frequently are cited as bureaucratic-type organizations. In our society, the term *bureaucracy* has for many become synonymous with inefficiency and waste; thus, this description has negative connotations (Kowalski, 1988). But are schools really bureaucratic? And, if they are, how did they get that way?

Much of American industry, especially during the Industrial Revolution, was influenced by the writings of Max Weber, a German sociologist. Weber was a major contributor to the creation of the bureaucratic organization; his work sought to establish the ultimate model of organizational efficiency. Among his fundamental beliefs were that managerial authority was essential to maintaining control and that control was necessary if organizational goals were to be met. These principles resulted in features that characterized the bureaucratic organization such as hierarchy of authority, a division of labor, a reliance on formal rules, and the priority of efficiency over interpersonal relationships (Weber, 1947). As American industry molded itself around these principles, leaders of public service organizations were continuously reminded of the perceived successes of industrial managers. Public school systems, in particular, were prodded to adopt business practices. Such an outcome was not unexpected, given that many captains of industry held influential positions on the school boards of major cities during and immediately following the Industrial Revolution (Callahan, 1962). Over time, schools and school systems embraced many attributes of bureaucracies, and as a result, they acquired reputations as rather inflexible institutions.

One difficulty in determining whether schools are bureaucracies stems from the use of varying definitions by researchers. For example, some studies were predicated on the judgment that the presence of centralization in authority and decision making was sufficient for such classification. However, labeling schools in this fashion ignores consequences of centralization and normative elements of the organization (Abbott & Caracheo, 1988). For instance, it is possible for a school district to have highly centralized authority and still interact at high levels with the environment. And it is possible to have decentralization of authority but a culture that embraces many other aspects of the bureaucracy.

Close examination of schools and school systems often reveals patterns of behavior that defy rational explanations (Owens, 1991). Largely for this reason, a number of theorists have questioned whether schools truly are bureaucratic-type institutions. Pellegrin (1976), for one, argued that schools are really loosely coupled organizations composed of subsystems that have their own identity and often act independently. Likewise, management control and the enforcement of rules controlling employee behavior often are less intense than in a factory. Such distinctive elements have led some writers to reject the idea that schools are bureaucracies. Corwin and Borman (1988), however, argued that it is preposterous to conclude that school districts are not organized as bureaucracies. They viewed complex organizations such as schools as being composites of bureaucratic, professional, and political variables.

Schools are also viewed as sociopolitical systems—systems composed largely of human elements competing for power and resources. The discovery that informal groups could direct human behavior in organizations proved to be a monumental development for theorists. Whereas classical theory sought to identify how organizations ought to function, sociopolitical theory emphasized descriptions of the actual behaviors of organizations. In the real world, administrators do not possess complete power and employees do not always behave rationally. In many schools, teachers—and groups to which they belong—exert tremendous influence over peer behavior—and even the principal's behavior. Such findings cast serious doubts about rational control in organizational life and led to a new ideology called human relations. This movement maintained that employees would be most productive when they embraced organizational goals and took pride in their work (Hanson, 1985). Keith and Girling (1991) wrote:

> The human relations/behaviorist approach views productivity, efficiency, and effectiveness as social rather than simply technical concerns. It focuses on the manager's style of interaction with employees. (p. 16)

Often, bureaucratic and human resources perspectives of schools have been compared as ideal cases for purposes of exposing differences between them. In reality, schools are neither totally bureaucratic nor totally sociopolitical systems. More precisely, they are accurately described as possessing attributes of these ideologies (Owens, 1991).

Schools are human-intensive organizations in which a majority of the employees are classified as professionals. In this regard, they are similar to hospitals or mental health clinics. Some authors (e.g., Mintzberg, 1979) refer to these organizations as professional bureaucracies. This classification has evoked a number of questions about the relationship between administrators and teachers. In some professional organizations, the relationship between administrator and employee is one of parallel authority. In schools, however, teachers typically have far less power to control major policy decisions that affect their practice and work environment than do staff physicians in a hospital (Brown, 1990). Genuine professional organizations tend to have unique lines of authority where the practitioners are empowered to perform certain functions independently.

Two characteristics are used to identify professional organizations: (1) the presence of goals that relate to the production, application, or communication of knowledge, and (2) 50 percent or more of the staff being classified as professionals (Etzioni, 1964). Within these parameters, one could argue that public schools are professionally dominated institutions. But are teachers truly professionals? In seeking an answer, there have been many attempts to equate teaching with more established professions. Etzioni (1964) classified teachers (along with social workers and nurses) as semi-professionals. In semi-professions, practitioners have less freedom from supervision or societal control than the traditional professions. Bennett and LeCompte (1990) described this condition:

> Practitioners of the semi-professions are not typically self-employed; rather, they are "bureaucratized" existing within the confines of service bureaucracies and paid by means of salaries instead of client fees. (p. 124)

Despite schools' being considered professionally dominated organizations, there is substantial evidence that society does not treat teachers as true professionals.

Two critical questions are most cogent to the future of schools as professionally dominated organizations. First, will society raise the status of teachers and truly accept them as professionals? This question will not be resolved by textbook analyses or academic debates; it is an issue that will be determined in the realm of public perception. Second, will administrators and teachers view themselves as members of the same profession?

The Political Dimension

In more recent times, the study of schools has placed great emphasis on organizational politics. Sergiovanni, Burlingame, Coombs, and Thurston (1987) noted that analyzing the political dimension of schools is not related to partisan politics; rather, it focuses on the realization that schools continuously face political questions. Knezevich (1984) described educational politics in this way:

> Politics deals with decision-making power, its distribution and limitations, among persons who are part of the organization, community, state, region, and nation. (p. 491)

Consider the following examples of problems that have political implications for school administrators:

- A school district desperately needs to build an addition to its high school. State law requires voter approval for capital projects. After three failed referenda, the superintendent is asked to develop yet another campaign to win public support.
- A group of parents organize to lobby the school board to approve offering French and Spanish in the district's elementary schools. Adequate funding for the initiative, however, is not available. The superintendent is directed to seek a compromise with the parents.
- The state legislature intends to make school districts responsible for providing free textbooks—but does not intend to provide additional funding for this responsibility.

The political dimension frequently deals with interactions between the school and political systems in which the school exists. But there is also an ample amount of internal politics in which administrators, teachers, and other employees compete for power and recognition (Knezevich, 1984). Teacher unionization, for instance, is both a professional and a political issue for administrators.

Organizational politics are tied together by several basic assumptions. First, organizations do not possess all of the resources necessary to do everything that is desired. Second, organizations are composed of individuals and coalitions (groups) possessing varying values, beliefs, needs, preferences, perceptions, and wants. Third, organizational goals and decisions emerge from an ongoing process of negotiations in which the various individuals and coalitions exercise power (Bolman & Deal, 1989).

A review of research on the politics of education led Burlingame (1988) to write:

> The work since 1960 has displayed the heterogeneity of local school districts and the complexity of politics and policy at the local level. The school districts of this nation vary widely; the economic, social, political, religious, and educational traditions of these districts are remarkably different. (p. 449)

Despite many differences, schools share multitudes of common political concerns. For example, all are subjected to community, state, and national pressures; all are forced to recognize political interventions in establishing policy. Because of such commonalities, there has been an increasing amount of attention given to the behavior of public-sector administrators (i.e., institutional administrators functioning in the public domain). Continuing quests to mix rationality with politics—to force schools and other public organizations to use models developed for the private sector even though public organizations face higher levels of extraorganizational interventions—exemplify a contemporary issue for public-sector administrators. Superintendents, for example, often are encouraged to adopt efficiency programs such as *management by objectives* (M.B.O.) only to find that the political dimensions of their organizations and environment prevent desired outcomes (Kowalski, 1984). Studies examining behaviors of public administrators frequently conclude that management decisions are framed largely by political considerations (e.g., Clark & Schrode, 1979).

A CONTEMPORARY CONTEXT FOR SCHOOLS

Increasingly, American society is accepting the contention that public education cannot be reformed unless there is a fundamental restructuring of curriculum, instruction, and organizational patterns that have existed for decades. This conclusion provides added importance to understanding schools as formal organizations. For instance, the belief that schools cannot escape tenets of bureaucracy is apt to produce reform ideas compatible with bureaucratic structure. Top-down mandates, the imposition of rules and regulations, and stronger management control are strategies that can be anticipated from individuals who see schools essentially as business organizations. In this regard, two critical elements—perceptions of organizational context and planning the future—are inextricably allied. Conley (1991) observed that this association was present in early 1980s reform ideas. Intensification mandates such as lengthening the school year and the school day were largely bureaucratic strategies for bringing about change. More recently, however, school-improvement initiatives have focused more directly on the primary providers of education—teachers. To many analysts, this has not been an insignificant conversion. It signifies a changing perception of the organizational foundations of public schools. Giving teachers more autonomy and a greater voice in district-wide decisions and allowing them to share in the governance of their workplace will require pithy institutional transformations. For most school districts this will necessitate remolding culture and climate. A school district organized around a vision of schools as professionally dominated organizations will be less reliant on regulations, provide greater teacher autonomy, and advance the practice of group decision making. Leaders in these educational environments will need to strike a careful balance between the centralization and decentralization of authority. Issues of educational reform are explored in greater depth in Chapter 12.

The Importance of Organizational Adaptability

Foremost among issues facing school administrators is organizational adaptability. Public schools repeatedly are criticized for being static institutions that fail to keep pace with a rapidly changing society. These rebukes have encouraged studies of cultures and leadership styles in an effort to identify variables that enhance organizational change. Such knowledge is critical for leaders who are expected to transform public education. Restructuring necessitates a radical approach to rethinking how we improve schools:

> Restructuring is distinguished as much by its philosophical underpinnings as it is by its structural or operational components. Its most salient characteristics are influenced by a belief system and a vision that require radically different responses to the problems of education than are possible with current forms of schooling. (Mojkowski, 1991, p. 9)

In essence, restructuring is not possible unless schools acquire high levels of organizational adaptability.

Michael, Luthans, Odiorne, Burke, and Hayden (1981) hypothesized that the first step to meaningful change was a recognition by leaders that the environment consists of opportunities and problems that eventually manifest themselves as a set of demands for organizational performance. For schools, this means that communities, and even the larger environments of state and nation, continuously formulate pressures that must be addressed. Often, these demands evolve as proposals for substantive change. Schools that are highly isolated from their environments (i.e., schools that have little interaction with the community) are faced with a high probability of criticism and public frustration. Leaders help to make organizations adaptable by maintaining an awareness of environmental needs and wants.

Public organizations are not alone in facing the need to create adaptable organizations. Hahn (1991), writing to managers in private industry, noted that change will be ubiquitous in the 1990s. As a result, three basic conflicts can be expected: (1) innovation versus tradition, (2) self-fulfillment versus participation, and (3) decentralization versus integration. These conditions are already visible in public education. Calls for reform often clash directly with inflexible organizational cultures; staff development programs frequently address only organizational concerns; and suggestions for decentralization spark concerns about authority and control.

Change requires intensive and well-planned strategies to alter ways in which practitioners look at their world of work. Most importantly, change requires risk takers in leadership positions—administrators who involve others, create support networks, effectively communicate, tolerate mistakes, provide reinforcement, set high expectations, and lead by example (Myers & Robbins, 1991). Research on effective schools repeatedly identifies effective leadership as a necessary component in instructional change and improvement (Hall & Hord, 1987). Traditionally, school administrators have not been perceived as risk takers. In part, this is attributable to the fact that public education has rarely faced life-threatening challenges. Quite to the contrary, public schools remain quasi-monopolies, and many still consider one of the primary missions of public education to be the preservation of societal values and beliefs.

World conditions are having a dramatic effect on American society and its educational institutions. Technology, economics, and changing family structures exemplify catalysts that are altering the environment. In these less-than-static conditions, three goals appear to be essential for organizational success. First, administrators must achieve credibility as leaders. This means that their responsibility must extend beyond management. Second, the organization must be motivated to change. This is a particularly cogent point for public schools, given their continuing status as quasi-monopolies. Third, schools must create a functional relationship with their environments that permits them to respond to external stimuli that suggest the need for change (Gabris & Mitchell, 1991). These goals emphasize the desirability of moving away from closed climates and toward the creation of an organizational format that is highly adaptable.

The Management of Professionals

As noted previously, schools are considered professionally dominated organizations. Despite this characterization, teachers historically have had limited freedoms in practicing their profession. Their relationship with administration has largely been one of subordinate. In essence, teachers have been expected to acquire and use technical knowledge in a rather confined manner. Their charge has been to present an established and rigid curriculum—and to do so while teaching twenty-five to thirty-five students with varying needs. In the traditional classroom setting, many teachers have had to live with conflicting institutional and professional ideals. They are repeatedly reminded that they are professionals, but they are given little freedom to determine what they teach.

In reality, the teacher's world of work is filled with ambiguity and conflicting goals (Griffin, 1985). As is the case with all professions, teaching entails challenges that simply defy technical solutions (Schon, 1987). If this were not the case, the use of basic managerial approaches by administrators would be sufficient. Effective teachers, however, assume multiple roles and make countless decisions about students. In determining a child's real needs, teachers examine social, psychological, emotional, and physical conditions as well as the more commonly recognized educational variables. Performing such complex tasks, teachers need human and material resources that permit them to make proper judgments.

Administration in a professionally dominated organization is considered to be a substantial challenge. This is especially true when administrators are selected from the ranks of the professionals to be supervised (Bywaters, 1991)—a condition certainly prevalent in education. In Chapter 1 of this book, distinctions were made between management and leadership. It was noted that contemporary administrators are expected to perform both roles. We know from history, however, that this ideal has not been fully achieved. Many principals and superintendents concentrate almost exclusively on management functions and continue to view teachers as subordinates. Lieberman (1986) explained that unionism is advanced by feelings of helplessness when employees realize that their own resources provide insufficient protection against unfair actions. For many teachers, group membership, in unions or other associations, constitutes a justifiable quest for professional autonomy (Newman, 1990)—a rather ironic situation since unionism is considered to be a factor that detracts from professional status.

Unquestionably, the decision of teachers to affiliate with powerful local, state, and national organizations has affected operations in most school districts. Although collective bargaining agreements have provided teachers with opportunities to voice their opinions, the process has done little to raise the professional stature of teachers (Lieberman, 1986) or to improve relations between teachers and administrators. Administrators, however, have had to modify their behavior. To quote Drake and Roe (1986):

> As teachers have gained strength and obtained a larger share of decision making, school administrators have found that they must accommodate themselves accordingly and alter their pattern of decision making. This is creating a re-examination of administrative and managerial rights and a re-evaluation of faculty participation in the decision-making process. (p. 57)

But do such adjustments reflect mere political accommodation? Or do they reflect a more fundamental change in belief about teachers and the relationship between teachers and administrators?

More recent efforts to achieve teacher autonomy have been advanced under the label of *teacher empowerment*. Since the early 1960s, collective bargaining between teacher unions and school boards served as the medium through which teachers attempted to gain power (i.e., to have a voice in ratifying policies, rules, and regulations). Advocates of empowerment take a markedly different approach—one that attempts to create power by virtue of knowledge. If teaching is accepted as a profession, and if entry into that profession is based on high standards of knowledge and skills, teachers would gain power as experts in performing their duties. In essence, empowerment creates a sense of self-worth and an elevation of the importance of professional knowledge and competence (Bennis, 1989). Compared to union-based power struggles of the past twenty-five years, teacher empowerment offers an opportunity for erecting new relationships between teachers and administrators.

The Quest for the Professional Organization

A number of authors have drawn contrasts between the bureaucracy and the professional organization. Campbell et al. (1990) noted that aspects of the bureaucracy simply are not compatible with professionalism. The establishment of countless rules and regulations that govern teacher behavior serves as an example. Professional organizations, by contrast, tend to rely far less on formal rules (Bywaters, 1991). In part, this is true because professionals are prone to use voluntary associations for the purpose of self-control (e.g., bar associations for lawyers). Conley (1991) described the professional model as one in which:

> . . . the teacher is a decision maker who creatively adapts knowledge to unique and varied problem situations, expands skills beyond "textbook knowledge," and continuously refines professional judgment, initiative, and decision making. (p. 48)

In such work environments, the administrator would largely manage things, lead the organization, and support and augment the efforts of teachers.

The transformation of schools to professional organizations is still very much in question. One of the primary concerns continues to be teacher unionism (or administrator unionism where it exists). Lieberman (1986) contended that union contracts often blocked reform initiatives, especially when proposed changes adversely affect interests of union members (e.g., requiring a longer school year). For such critics, unionism and professionalism are simply not compatible. They fear that a diffusion of authority, as in site-based management, will produce added power to unions and do little to empower individual teachers. In response to such concerns, the unions say that they function no differently than the American Medical Association or other professional associations. And like other professional associations, they argue that they look out for their members and their members' clients (Newman, 1990).

The movement from bureaucratic-like structures to professional cultures also can be deterred by the presence of a policy mechanism that allows various national, state, and local agencies to govern schools. Even if administrators and teachers come together as one profession expressing mutual respect, their practice will be restricted by laws and policies coming from legislatures and local school boards. Without question, governmental agencies repeatedly pass laws ranging from new curriculum mandates to textbook selection to the number of minutes in a school day. The vulnerability of the school system to outside agencies makes purposeful change difficult, because many of the new mandates are unrelated to any long-term vision or plan of what schools are to become.

Restructuring may be sidetracked by administrators who are incapable of producing or managing change. In summarizing a number of studies on successful schools and effective leadership, Sergiovanni (1991) observed that the individual who occupies the principalship makes a critical difference. Faced with the same barriers and constraints, effective principals exhibit an ability to adjust, whereas the less effective do not. Thus, administrators who neither support change nor possess the knowledge and skills necessary to create adaptable organizations may constitute a major barrier to creating professional environments.

Increasingly, scholars in business administration are focusing on the unique elements found in organizations that employ large numbers of salaried professionals (e.g., engineering firms, accounting firms). The primary question driving this inquiry is how to provide employees autonomy while ensuring adequate control of the organization (Raelin, 1989). This attention has produced recommendations for the use of novel reward systems, task rather than role orientations, alternative communication methods that allow professionals to bypass the hierarchy of authority, and greater emphasis on self-regulation (Segal-Horn, 1987). Many of these alterations will be particularly difficult to infuse into public organizations. Beyond the presence of traditional structure, change agents also must confront extraorganizational interventions that tend to be especially intense in public education (e.g., taxpayer dissatisfaction, pressure groups).

Finally, change that would give teachers greater autonomy could be slowed by antifeminism (Newman, 1990). The profession is composed of a majority of female teachers, and to the extent that many still view women as second class and subordinate, the concept of a professional organization has political ramifications. This condition is even more relevant when you consider that a majority of school administrators are male.

IMPLICATIONS FOR PRACTICE

There are several key messages that you should have received from this chapter. First, schools clearly are organizations. They share certain attributes that are found in all organizations; yet, they also are unique entities. That is, schools (and school districts) possess characteristics that set them apart from most other organizations. For instance, schools are professionally dominated institutions, more than half of whose employees are classified as professionals.

Second, schools and school districts are somewhat unique. When they are placed under a microscope, differences in culture, climate, leadership, and so forth, become apparent. For this reason, one must be careful about sweeping generalizations. As a practitioner, each institutional environment in which you work should be viewed from two perspectives: (1) What makes this organization like all other organizations? and (2) What makes this organization unique?

Why should prospective school administrators study organizations and organizational behavior? Organizations surround us and become a critical part of our personal and professional lives. They become a primary tool for achieving a better society (Hall, 1991). But more precisely, your behavior as a leader will occur in an organizational context. Your success will be enhanced by an understanding of how individual employees interface with the organization, of how individuals become members of formal and informal groups, of how groups interact and exercise power, and of how you can lead individuals and groups toward the achievement of institutional goals.

Perhaps at no previous time has the organizational dimension of schooling been more critical. As we strive to restructure and improve education, we face the realization that existing cultures and climates can either facilitate or hinder our goals. Increasingly, critics are pointing fingers at administrators and accusing them of being unwilling or incapable of reshaping our educational system to accommodate the needs of the twenty-first century.

FOR FURTHER STUDY

1. Identify several reasons that American business exerted influence over the organizational culture of public schools during and immediately following the Industrial Revolution.

2. Identify formal and informal groups that exist in an organization in which you have been employed.

3. Do you believe that teachers deserve to be treated in a similar manner to practitioners in other professions? Why or why not?

4. Do you believe that administrators should occupy most or all of their time with management tasks? Why or why not?

5. Have unions succeeded in creating teacher empowerment?

6. Is organizational climate something that can be changed by a new superintendent?

7. Do all organizations seek change?

8. Why are some organizations better able to cope with change?

9. Do you believe that teachers should be subordinate to principals?

10. A principal once noted, "Teachers do whatever they want once they close their classroom door. What more freedom do they want?" Do you agree with this assessment? If it is true, what are the organizational implications?

11. Identify myths and rituals that are common to schools.

12. Do you believe that the transformation of schools to professional organizations will be hindered by feelings of antifeminism in society?

13. When organizations, such as schools, are subject to high levels of external intervention, does this make organizational behavior more or less predictable?

14. Are there any benefits to a centralized system of authority in a school system?

OTHER SUGGESTED ACTIVITIES

1. Compare two school districts with which you are familiar. Identify organizational commonalities and differences.

2. Prepare a list of characteristics you would examine if you wanted to identify the culture and climate of an unfamiliar school district.

3. School systems clearly have hierarchies of authority. Discuss why this one feature alone is insufficient to determine whether the system is a bureaucracy.

4. Interview an executive in private industry and a school administrator to ascertain their perceptions of whether their jobs entail solely management or a combination of management and leadership.

5. Discuss the differences between organizational culture and organizational climate. How are they different? How are they related?

REFERENCES

Abbott, M. G., & Caracheo, F. (1988). Power, authority, and bureaucracy. In N. Boyan (Ed.), *Handbook of research on educational administration* (pp. 239–257). New York: Longman.

Bennett, K. P., & LeCompte, M. D. (1990). *How schools work: A sociological analysis of education.* New York: Longman.

Bennis, W. (1989). *Why leaders can't lead.* San Francisco: Jossey-Bass.

Berrien, F. K. (1976). A general systems approach to organizations. In M. Dunnette (Ed.), *Handbook of industrial and organizational psychology* (pp. 41–62). Chicago: Rand McNally.

Blau, P. M., & Scott, W. R. (1962). *Formal organizations: A comparative approach.* San Francisco: Chandler.

Bolman, L., & Deal, T. (1989). *Modern approaches to understanding and managing organizations.* San Francisco: Jossey-Bass.

Brown, D. J. (1990). *Decentralization and school-based management.* London: The Falmer Press.

Burack, E. H. (1991). Changing the company culture: The role of human resources development. *Long Range Planning, 24* (1), 88–95.

Burlingame, M. (1988). The politics of education and educational policy: The local level. In N. Boyan (Ed.), *Handbook of research on educational administration* (pp. 439–451). New York: Longman.

Bywaters, D. R. (1991). Managing professionals. *Executive Excellence, 8* (2), 7–8.

Callahan, R. E. (1962). *Education and the cult of efficiency.* Chicago: University of Chicago Press.

Campbell, R. E., Cunningham, L. L., Nystrand, R. O., & Usdan, M. D. (1990). *The organization and control of American schools* (6th ed.). Columbus, OH: Merrill.

Clark, T. D., & Schrode, W. A. (1979). Public sector decision structures: An empirically-based description. *Public Administration Review, 39,* 343–354.

Conley, D. T. (1991). What is restructuring? Educators adapt to a changing world. *Equity and Choice* 7 (2–3), 46–51.

Corwin, R. G., & Borman, K. M. (1988). School as workplace: Structural constraints on administration. In N. Boyan (Ed.), *Handbook of research on educational administration* (pp. 209–237). New York: Longman.

Deal, T. E., & Kennedy, A. A. (1982). *Corporate cultures.* Reading, MA: Addison-Wesley.

Drake, T. L., & Roe, W. H. (1986). *The principalship* (3rd ed.). New York: Macmillan.

Etzioni, A. (1964). *Modern organizations.* Englewood Cliffs, NJ: Prentice-Hall.

Frederiksen, N., Jensen, O., & Beeton, A. A. (1972). *Predictions of organizational behavior.* New York: Pergamon Press.

Gabris, G. T., & Mitchell, K. (1991). The everyday organization: A diagnostic model for assessing adaptation cycles. *Public Administration Quarterly, 14* (4), 498–518.

Goens, G. A., & Clover, S. I. (1991). *Mastering school reform.* Boston: Allyn and Bacon.

Griffin, G. (1985). The school as a workplace and the master teacher concept. *Elementary School Journal,* 86 (1), 1–16.

Hahn, D. (1991). Strategic management: Tasks and challenges in the 1990s. *Long Range Planning,* 24 (1), 26–39.

Hall, G. E., & Hord, S. M. (1987). *Change in schools: Facilitating the process.* Albany: State University of New York Press.

Hall, R. H. (1991). *Organizations: Structures, processes, and outcomes* (5th ed.). Englewood Cliffs, NJ: Prentice-Hall.

Hanson, E. M. (1985). *Educational administration and organizational behavior* (2nd ed.). Boston: Allyn and Bacon.

Hart, A. N. (1991). Leader succession and socialization: A synthesis. *Review of Educational Research,* 61 (4), 451–474.

Hoy, W. K., & Miskel, C. G. (1984). *Educational administration: Theory, research, and practice* (3rd ed.). New York: Random House.

Johns, G. (1988). *Organizational behavior: Understanding life at work* (2nd ed.). Glenview, IL: Scott, Foresman and Company.

Keith, S., & Girling, R. H. (1991). *Education, management, and preparation.* Boston: Allyn and Bacon.

Knezevich, S. J. (1984). *Administration of public education* (4th ed.). New York: Harper & Row.

Knoke, D., & Prensky, D. (1984). What relevance do organizational theories have for voluntary associations? *Social Science Quarterly,* 65 (1), 3–20.

Kowalski, T. J. (1984). The debilities of MBO in educational organizations. *NASSP Bulletin,* 68 (472), 119–123.

———. (1988). *The organization and planning of adult education.* Albany: State University of New York Press.

Lieberman, M. (1986). *Beyond public education.* New York: Praeger.

March, J. G., & Simon, H. A. (1958). *Organizations.* New York: John Wiley.

Michael, S. R., Luthans, F., Odiorne, G. S., Burke, W. W., & Hayden, S. (1981). *Techniques of organizational change.* New York: McGraw-Hill.

Mintzberg, H. (1979). *The structuring of organizations: A synthesis of the research.* Englewood Cliffs, NJ: Prentice-Hall.

Mojkowski, C. (1991). *Developing leaders for restructuring schools: New habits of mind and heart.* Washington, DC: The National Leadership Network, U.S. Department of Education.

Morgan, G. (1986). *Images of organization.* Newbury Park, CA: Sage.

Myers, K., & Robbins, H. (1991). Ten rules for change. *Executive Excellence,* 8 (5), 9–10.

Newman, J. W. (1990). *America's teachers.* New York: Longman.

Owens, R. G. (1991). *Organizational behavior in education* (4th ed.). Englewood Cliffs, NJ: Prentice-Hall.

Parsons, T., & Shils, H. A. (1951). *Toward a general theory of action.* New York: Harper & Row.

Pellegrin, R. J. (1976). Schools as work settings. In R. Dubin (Ed.), *Handbook of work, organization and society* (pp. 343–374). Skokie, IL: Rand McNally.

Raelin, J. A. (1989). An anatomy of autonomy: Managing professionals. *Academy of Management Executive,* 3 (3), 216–228.

Reitz, H. J. (1987). *Behavior in organizations* (3rd ed.). Homewood, IL: Irwin.

Schon, D. A. (1987). *Educating the reflective practitioner.* San Francisco: Jossey-Bass.

Segal-Horn, S. (1987). Managing professionals in organizations. *International Journal of Manpower,* 8 (2), 11–19.

Sergiovanni, T. J. (1991). *The principalship: A reflective practice perspective* (2nd ed.). Boston: Allyn and Bacon.

Sergiovanni, T. J., Burlingame, M., Coombs, F. S., & Thurston, P. W. (1987). *Educational governance and administration* (2nd ed.). Englewood Cliffs, NJ: Prentice-Hall.

Simon, H. A. (1957). *Administrative behavior* (2nd ed.). New York: Macmillan.

Stinnett, T. M., & Henson, K. T. (1982). *America's public schools in transition.* New York: Teachers College Press.

Thompson, J. D. (1967). *Organization in action.* New York: McGraw-Hill.

Verstegen, D. A., & Wagoner, J. L. (1989). Strategic planning for policy development: An evolving model. *Planning and Changing,* 20 (1), 33–49.

Weber, M. (1947). *The theory of social and economic organizations* (translated by A. Parsons and T. Parsons). New York: The Free Press.

CHAPTER 8

The Roles of School in Society

Chapter Content

Schools as a Mirror of Society

Emergence of the Management Role

Relationship of Management and Other Administrative Roles

The Varying Purposes of Schooling

Implications for Practice

The relationship between schools and society is characterized by three roles that reflect philosophical viewpoints of reproduction, readjustment, and reconstruction (Johnson, Collins, Dupuis, & Johansen, 1988). The reproductive role of schools involves transmission and preservation of the existing culture, values, traditions, and norms. Readjustment involves responding to changes in society and adjusting curriculum and instruction as appropriate. Reconstruction requires a more proactive stance, since it views the school as an agent of societal change. These three philosophical viewpoints are carried out through school purposes and goals that have been classified as political, social, economic, vocational, intellectual, and personal (Goodlad, 1984; Spring, 1991).

Similar to the interrelationship between schools and society is the interrelationship between administrators and their schools. Administrators both shape their school's philosophy and purpose and are shaped by it as well as by society.

This chapter will discuss the role of schools in society. Although schools undoubtedly shape and are shaped by society, the significant issue is the extent to which each of these should occur. That is, should schools focus primarily on reproduction of culture or on transformation of culture? The chapter will explore this issue by providing a historical perspective of how schools have served as a mirror of society. Following the historical perspective, the multiple and often incongruent purposes of schooling will be examined. The chapter will continue by examining how societal influences have shaped conceptions of the school administrator's role as well as what the implications of varying purposes of schooling are for administrative practice.

The second part of the chapter will address how schools can serve as an agent of societal change. The perspective of those advocating a societal change agent role for schools will be examined. Finally, implications for administrative practice will be explored.

SCHOOLS AS A MIRROR OF SOCIETY

A Historical Perspective

In their discussion of public school leadership in America, Tyack and Hansot (1982) provided an insightful portrait of how schools have reflected societal norms and values. They noted that, to this day, as one travels across America, evidence of the legacy left by various periods of American schooling can be observed in the architecture of school buildings. For example, they noted that facilities showing the influence of early American education reflect the dominant values of church and the Protestant ethic in their simplicity with the focal point of the building frequently being a steeple-like bell tower. The smallness and simplicity of the buildings reflect the relatively uncomplex nature of government of that period. The nation had been created to protest excessive government regulation, and early schools reflected this in the lack of bureaucracy and government regulation. Remaining schools of this vintage are generally located in nonurban areas, reflecting the rural nature of American society of the period during which these facilities were constructed.

The purpose of these early American schools was to prepare individuals for leading a godly life, and to teach reading for purposes of studying the Bible and laws. During this early period, schools were elitist institutions with access to education provided only to the wealthy. In post-Revolution America, the elitist conception of education broadened. Education began to be perceived as a vehicle that could be used to serve not only religious needs, but also human needs. Those in positions of power and authority realized that education could be used to promote political and cultural values. In essence they saw universal education as a means of creating a perfect society.

A tension that continues to this day in American education developed almost immediately. On the one hand, there was a desire to use education as a means of promoting independence, that is, helping individuals acquire the intellectual tools to think for themselves and select their own moral and political values. This was especially salient given the new nation's recent fight for independence from a ruling aristocracy whose religious values had been forced upon everyone. On the other hand, there was a desire to use education to create virtuous, patriotic, and well-behaved citizens who would embrace the culturally dominant values.

The change in school purpose from serving elitist functions to being an instrument for the promotion of public policy had implications for access to education. Education was no longer simply a luxury for the wealthy, but now became a necessity for the masses.

During this period, two additional societal trends highlighted the need for universal schooling. As large groups of immigrants descended on the country, each group bringing with it its own cultural values, it was felt necessary to ensure that the cultural values that had come to characterize the new nation remain dominant. Universal schooling for the children of immigrant families helped accomplish this. Education once again served conflicting purposes. For immigrant families it provided hope for achieving equality of economic opportunity and thus social mobility. For those in power it was a means of social control and stability. However, in order to ensure uniformity in the cultural values that were promoted, it became necessary to increasingly centralize and control schooling.

The second factor that necessitated universal schooling was suffrage. The right to vote was being extended to an ever-increasing segment of American society. Suffrage required a literate society. Education was a means of ensuring literacy (Pounds & Bryner, 1973).

Thus, while the new nation was involved in a process of creating itself, one essential piece of the creation was the construction of a public school system. Pounds and Bryner noted that the emerging educational system took on four characteristics that reflected the democratic spirit of the country: it was free, public, nonsectarian, and universal.

The school system became nonsectarian not out of a sense of atheism on the part of the people, but to the contrary, in order to protect the religious freedom of all. The people were largely God-fearing but were characterized by heterogeneity in terms of their religious beliefs. Thus, the question became, What religion should be taught? In order to protect the beliefs of all, no beliefs were taught. The separation of church and state continues to this day and has been the subject of great controversy, legal battles, and frequent headaches for school administrators. Unfortunately, many individuals do not understand that the religious beliefs they want to promote in schools deny the right of others to their beliefs.

Although schools were nonsectarian in the sense that they were not formally associated with any religious sect, they were nonetheless grounded in religious ideology. Tyack and Hansot (1982) described the creation of a system of public schooling as a social movement that was concerned with instilling a Protestant-republican ideology in the hearts and minds of individual citizens. They note that among school leaders there was a ''common religious and political conception of the role of public education in shaping a Christian nation'' (p. 5). This sense of common purpose and, in a sense, spiritual mission, galvanized and mobilized the creation of a nonsectarian, universal, and free system of public schooling that remains with us to this day.

The Era of Scientific Management and Big Business.   A second era of American education corresponds roughly with the late nineteenth century and early twentieth century. This period can be characterized by the emergence of the specialist. Similar to the business sector, which was developing a body of expertise, so also did school people begin to perceive themselves as experts. Much of the business expertise was grounded in the tenets of scientific management. Scientific management assumed there was one best way of accomplishing tasks and focused on identifying this way. The most scientific way became synonymous with the most efficient way of accomplishing tasks, and resulted in the initiation of activities such as time and motion studies.

The era was also marked by the rise to wealth and power of big business tycoons such as the Carnegies and Rockefellers. These power barons achieved great prominence in society. The combination of emerging big business and scientific management had a great effect on American public schools. Schools developed their own power barons, who came to be known as the education trust (Tyack & Hansot, 1982) and were able to define school norms and values through controlling access to administrative positions, particularly school super-intendencies. The values that this educational trust promoted were the tenets of scientific management and gave rise to school administrators who could be characterized as professional managers.

Nonetheless, although the vision for schools was more secular than pre-viously, it was still utopian. The educational trust felt that schools could shape the evolution of an emerging complex urban-industrial society. In a sense, they may have felt a degree of omnipotence—through managing schools, they could manage society. The sense of purpose in American schooling was no longer to create an educational system, but rather to redesign it.

The emergence of a wealthy urban elite also signaled the intensification of class divisions in American society. The rise of class divisions coupled with scientific management's focus on efficiency resulted in school redesign that now focused on differentiation rather than common denominators. That is, whereas formerly everyone had received the same education, students now began receiving a differentiated education based on their perceived merit. Some students were channeled into a vocational track, and others received advanced instruction. The differentiation of students according to merit changed the meaning of equality of educational opportunity in American schools. Formerly the educational system had attempted to provide an equal education for everyone and then allowed the social race for power and economic goods to begin. Opportunity decisions now were made by schools rather than by competition in society.

The practice of tracking continues to this day in many American schools, although its adverse effects on students have been well documented. For example, Oakes (1986) notes:

> There is little evidence to support any of the assumptions about tracking. The effects of tracking on student outcomes have been widely investigated, and the bulk of this work does not support commonly held beliefs that tracking increases student learning . . . . students who are not in top tracks suffer clear and consistent disadvantages from tracking . . . . the net effect of tracking is to exaggerate the initial differences among students rather than to provide the means to better accommodate them. (p. 14)

A student's merit and subsequent curricular placement was determined through recently developed scientific means of measuring intelligence. The continued and perhaps increasingly prevalent use of the progeny of these early measures is evident in today's schools in the variety of intelligence, achievement, competency, and other forms of standardized testing to which students are subjected.

Although the overriding societal purpose for schooling had been modified, schools continued to be regarded as "museums of virtue" (Tyack & Hansot, 1982). The previous era of schooling had been characterized by a spiritual focus that had provided the moral capital for the current era. This had resulted in a sharply defined sense of purpose which was now combined with a scientific management perspective and resulted in schools that were characterized by a "blend of science and missionary zeal . . . the rhetoric of moral charisma . . . complemented . . . the language of science and evolutionary social efficiency" (Tyack & Hansot, 1982, p. 7).

The Era of Diversification and Fragmentation.   From the mid-twentieth century on, the hard-edged factory appearance of schools that had characterized the previous business and scientific management era changed to a sprawling, one-story school, divided into segments and united only by a parking lot. The mid-twentieth-century school frequently resembled a shopping mall, both in appearance and in its attempt to provide something for everyone. Powell, Farrar, and Cohen (1985), in describing modern secondary schools, write:

> High schools take few stands on what is educationally or morally important. Yet one thing they cannot be neutral about is diversity itself. Pluralism is celebrated as the supreme institutional virtue, and tolerating diversity is the moral glue that holds schools together. But tolerance further precludes schools celebrating more focused notions of education or of character. "Community" has come to mean differences peacefully coexisting rather than people working together toward some serious end. (p. 3)

The eclectic nature of the school results in satisfying individual tastes and needs, but blurs the sense of purpose that characterized earlier American schools (Tyack & Hansot, 1982).

The fragmented nature of contemporary schools is evident not only in course offerings, but also in leadership and policymaking. As individuals in society have become more focused on self-interest, single-issue reformers have been born and seemingly multiplied exponentially. These individuals have had a strong effect on school policymaking through the formation of special-interest groups formed by recruiting similarly minded individuals. Groups have applied pressure through various forms including politically through election to school board posts and legally through litigation. Although the efforts of special-interest groups have resulted in laudable social gains for women, handicapped individuals, Afro Americans, Hispanics, and other minority groups, they have also resulted in a fragmentation and politicization of educational decision making and policy-making, and resultant loss of clear-cut purpose.

Also contributing to fragmentation have been an increasing number of state and federal programs, frequently initiated in response to pressure from special-interest groups or in response to historical or social events. For example, 1958 witnessed the Russian launching of Sputnik, the first successful manned spaceflight. Subsequently, American schools were bombarded with demands for increased emphasis on science and mathematics. The call for additional school accountability has also been a recurring emphasis that was once again resurrected with the school reform movement of the 1980s. Generally, additional mandated programs have been accompanied by increased regulation and bureaucracy.

In many cases, responsibilities of schools have been expanded beyond educational functions to encompass functions such as health care, nutrition, counseling, day care, and other functions that formerly were the responsibility of the family or the church. On the social front, increased rates for teenage pregnancy, venereal disease, and the spread of AIDS have resulted in mandated sex education programs. In some states events such as injuries or deaths resulting from children and adolescents' playing with guns has resulted in schools' being required to add gun safety education to their curriculum.

Internally, the increasing labor unrest that marked American society in the early twentieth century also affected schools, with the most visible effects occurring in the last several decades. Lines have been drawn between teachers and administrators and, rather than being united by a common sense of educational purpose, a "we-they" relationship has emerged and crystallized.

The internal and external forces that have impinged upon school leadership has resulted in a delegitimization of leadership. Whereas formerly school administrators led by "aristocracy of character" (Tyack & Hansot, 1982) or by their perceived expertness, the fragmentation and discord of recent years has resulted in a seeming inability to lead. Bennis and Nanus (1985) in their observations of societal leadership in general have termed this a *credibility gap*.

Wirt and Kirst (1989) have noted that six societal core constituencies have emerged during recent years, each affecting schools and school leaders through key issues that they embrace. Students, one core constituency, are most interested in issues of governance, expression, dress, behavior, and other student rights. Teachers are interested in issues of collective bargaining; parents in issues dealing with parental involvement in school governance; taxpayers in the reform of school financing, particularly as it affects them at the local level; minorities in issues of desegregation and equal employment; and federal and state authorities in a variety of areas that are addressed in laws or mandates. This categorization may be overly simplistic on two levels. On one level, members of one constituency (e.g., teachers) may also belong to another constituency (e.g., the teacher may be a parent). On a second level, members of one group may be interested in issues listed for a different constituency (e.g., a teacher may also be interested in governance, an issue listed as being of prime importance to parents). The point is that school leaders are bombarded by a variety of groups that have varying interests and different viewpoints.

The delegitimization of leadership coupled with the increasing complexity of society has resulted in accountability's becoming a myth. Clark and Astuto (1988) have argued that the statement "The buck stops here" is no longer true. Due to the complexity of modern organizations, any effect has multiple causes, which means the buck never stops—it just keeps circulating from one cause to another. The result has been that many have wondered if *anyone* was in charge. School and organizational scholars such as Clark and Karl Weick would likely argue that not only is no one in charge, but that no one *can* be in charge in the traditional sense. This argument obviously has significant implications for those preparing to be school administrators.

EMERGENCE OF THE MANAGEMENT ROLE

Just as American schools have been affected by the nature of American society, society has also had a significant impact on school administrators. The most pervasive effect on school administrators, one that continues to this day, is the effect of scientific management. Frederick Taylor is generally credited with being the father of scientific management. The principle underlying scientific management is that there is one best way of doing any job, and that this way can be determined using scientific methods. Specifically, Taylor advocated that job analysis consisting of time and motion studies be performed to determine the most efficient way of performing any job. Efficiency was defined as the way that had the best cost-benefit ratio. Once the optimum way of performing a job had been determined, the best person had to be selected and trained to perform the job in this manner. Managers needed to make certain that work conditions permitted the task to be accomplished in this manner and that the work was indeed completed in the predetermined manner (Sergiovanni, Burlingame, Coombs, & Thurston, 1987).

At the same time that Taylor and others were developing the principles of scientific management, big business was gaining ascendancy in American society and business tycoons were being revered. Without paying heed to differences between the tasks of business organizations and schools, school administrators quickly and heartily embraced the tenets of scientific management. School administrators began to look upon themselves as school executives rather than as scholars or educational philosophers. The result was an emphasis on the management aspects of administrative positions and a neglect of the educational aspects. Many argue that this emphasis continues to this day.

Callahan (1962) attributed the adoption of scientific management principles to the simultaneous occurrence of four historical factors:

1. America was in the midst of an era of reform, which was stimulated by muckraking journalists and was critical of all public institutions including schools.
2. Principles of scientific management were being developed, and its label appeared to have credibility and appeal.
3. Business and society were advocating for the adoption of business methods for other institutions.
4. The profession of school administration was in its formative stage and had not developed a strong knowledge base that would counteract external influences.

Callahan noted that school administrators' adoption of scientific management principles was not surprising, but that the strength and prevalence of these principles in schools was surprising. He attributed this primarily to the vulnerability of school administrators. He argued that vulnerability is built into our pattern of local support and control. In most school districts in America, school administrators are appointed (and terminated) by locally elected school boards. When schools are being criticized, school board members are in political jeopardy unless they can give the appearance that they are taking action to improve the situation. Perhaps the most visible action they can take is the termination of the superintendent or other school administrators. Thus, when schools are criticized, school administrators are vulnerable and must respond with whatever measures are in vogue at the time. In the early twentieth century, these measures involved the adoption of scientific management principles for schools.

Button (1991) disputed Callahan's vulnerability theory. He argued that businessmen were a higher status group in American society and thus became a reference group for school administrators who emulated the business way of doing things. Greenfield (1991) has argued that this has resulted in the exclusion of values, conceptions of the human and the humane, and passion and conviction from the study of school administration. Fundamental and difficult questions dealing with purpose, morality, the imposition of one person's will upon another, and the congruence of means and ends are neither asked nor answered. The focus instead is on "pallid consensus and illusory effectiveness (Greenfield, 1991, p. 6). By default, the ideology of school administration became that of business and scientific manager (Button, 1991).

There were numerous ways in which scientific management was evident in schools of the early twentieth century. For example, Callahan (1962) noted that attempts were made to measure which courses were of most economic value, with the result that courses such as Greek were dropped because they were perceived not to have any economic value. Impossible teaching loads were imposed on teachers because scientific school managers were interested in cost-benefit ratios and did not understand the need for study and preparation. The era saw the development of quantitative ways of evaluating both student achievement and teaching ability. School surveys that involved extensive quantification of a school's or district's characteristics became extremely popular. Quantitative characteristics were then equated to a judgment of the school's or district's efficiency.

Schooling at the university level also showed evidence of scientific management. School administrator preparation programs were constructed around various technical aspects of school administration, resulting in an "empire of courses built on a foundation of sand" (Callahan, 1962, p. 247). Disregarded were fundamental issues of leadership dealing with the shaping of people and organizations, the search for better values, and the justification of the application of power and decisionmaking (Greenfield, 1991). Elaborate offices were constructed for college administrators, whereas professors were sometimes crammed six to a small office and had access to only minimal libraries (Callahan, 1962).

Callahan noted that the real tragedy of scientific management's adoption of a business philosophy was not so much that this occurred, but rather that educators did a poor job of applying the philosophy. Whereas the underlying business principle was "the finest product at the lowest cost," the educational application focused on the lowest cost with little concern for the finest product. This indiscriminate application of business philosophy to public schooling resulted in the subordination of educational questions of values and purposes to considerations of business. An already prevalent anti-intellectual climate was strengthened. Scholars such as John Dewey were dismissed as harmless fellows, with the Fords and Carnegies held up for emulation. The result was that educators were produced who were not educators.

Unfortunately, the legacy of scientific management continues to be evident in today's schools and administrators. Many would argue that today's public school teaching loads of seven to eight classes daily for approximately 30 students at the elementary level, and five classes involving three or four preparations daily for 150 different students at the secondary level, do not provide adequate time for scholarly study and reflection. The continued and increasing reliance on standardized achievement and competency testing for students, teachers, and administrators is a vestige of scientific ways of evaluating an individual's worth. State and national school accreditation instruments that link accreditation status with a school's quantitative characteristics are a contemporary progeny of the school survey. At the university level, many administrator preparation programs continue to focus on budgets, buses, and buildings, and ignore the larger questions of purpose and value.

RELATIONSHIP OF MANAGEMENT AND OTHER ADMINISTRATIVE ROLES

Although management of technical aspects of school operations is an essential component of administrative positions, it is simply a prerequisite for effective schooling. Sergiovanni (1984, 1991), for example, has persistently argued that attention to only the technical aspects of schooling may not lead to even competent schooling. He argued that in order to guarantee even minimal competence, school administrators must effectively utilize human and educational leadership in addition to technical leadership. In order to attain excellence in schooling, administrators must also emphasize symbolic and cultural leadership. That is, they must help the school develop its sense of purpose or mission and then call attention to it in symbolic and cultural ways.

Findings from research conducted in business, industrial, and school settings have consistently found that effective organizations have strong leaders with well-defined visions of what they are trying to accomplish. Indeed, effective schools research has consistently highlighted the importance of strong principal leadership to school effectiveness. Dwyer, Barnett, and Lee (1987) have found that a distinguishing characteristic of effective principals is that they have developed personal overarching perspectives of the purposes of schooling.

The purposes school administrators hold for the units in their charge are likely to have a direct effect on the purposes members of the unit hold and thus on purposes that are achieved by the unit. Thus, it is imperative that prospective school leaders contemplate what schools should attempt to accomplish and what their administrative role is in helping schools attain these purposes. Unfortunately, scholars have argued that today's educational leaders are characterized more by fragmentation than by clear-cut purpose (Tyack & Hansot, 1982).

THE VARYING PURPOSES OF SCHOOLING

Many prospective administrators may feel that discussing the purposes of schooling is an inconsequential issue. After all, they may argue, schools exist to educate students—what else is there to discuss? This outlook, however, would have to be classified as naive. Espoused as well as actual purposes of schooling are much more diversified than simply educating students.

Imagine, for example, the following scenario. You recently have become principal of an elementary school in a small, rural community nestled in the hills of a midwestern state. The community traditionally has been very stable, with most young people following their fathers' footsteps, working in the nearby stone quarries. The past decade has seen a slight diversification of career paths with some young people moving from high school to manual labor positions in the auto manufacturing plant that recently was built in the town.

The community has always considered the purpose of the local public school system to be that of providing the young people of the community with a basic level of education that equips them with sufficient literacy to function productively in the stone quarries, as homemakers, and as community citizens. The arrival of the auto plant, however, brought with it a number of middle- and upper-level management personnel. Although small in number, their control of a significant percentage of the community's employment and economic welfare provided them with an instant power base in the community. The purpose these high-level executives had for the community's schools was to equip their own offspring with the intellectual skills to pursue whatever opportunities they chose in the larger realm of society. Additionally, they were concerned that the school upgrade its educational programs in order to provide auto plant workers who left high school with the higher level of technological skill required of many positions in the plant.

In addition to management personnel, a number of manual laborers who had been employed by the auto manufacturer at other plants in the country transferred to the community when the new plant began operations. Many of these workers came from large urban areas and brought different values with them. Shortly after their arrival, the crime-free community experienced a sudden and drastic increase in crime. An ad hoc women's club, formed primarily of spouses of auto plant management personnel, began to lobby the superintendent of schools for a program of moral education that would teach young people that crime was wrong. Meanwhile, the superintendent, who was hired a year after the new plant opened, was concerned with his career goal of moving to superintendencies of progressively larger school districts. He knew that the political reality of accomplishing this was to focus school purpose on increasing standardized test scores. As principal, you feel strongly that instruction should be focused on higher-level thinking and problem-solving skills rather than on the lower-level skills that standardized tests are able to assess. The dilemma you face is which set of school purposes to pursue.

As is evident from the scenario, there are a diversity of school purposes. The community traditionally held civic goals for the local schools. They expected graduates to be prepared to be productive members of the local community. The new purposes brought in by the auto plant management included intellectual goals for their own children and economic goals for the children of the community. The women's group advocated social and moral purposes, and the superintendent was focused on personal political goals. As principal, you are in favor of intellectual purposes for the school.

Scholars have provided various classifications for school purposes. Spring (1991), for example, has categorized school purposes as political, social, or economic. Potential political goals of schooling include educating citizens, providing education to help citizens select political leaders, helping achieve political consensus by instilling a common political creed in individuals, maintaining dominant power relationships, and socializing children for the political system (Spring, 1991, pp. 6–10). Spring noted that schools can be used both as a means of exerting political control and as a means of teaching citizens how to use their political rights. Thus, schools can be an instrument of oppression or of freedom.

Schools also frequently pursue purposes that emanate from political processes present in the school, district, community, state, or nation. Additionally, the political aspirations of parties directly or indirectly involved in the schooling process may influence school purpose. For example, in this scenario the career ambitions of the superintendent provide a narrow focus to the academic purpose of the school by emphasizing achievement on standardized tests. This is likely to result in practices such as teaching to the test, the purchase of curricular materials focused on rote responses similar to those embodied in standardized tests, and staff development that emphasizes skill-based instruction. Given the limited amount of instructional and staff development time available, the opportunity cost of these practices is the diversion of attention from instruction dealing with creativity, liberal arts, and higher-level skills.

Social purposes of schooling include social control, improving social conditions, and alleviating social tensions caused by reducing economic inequalities (Spring, 1991). The women's club's efforts in the scenario to focus on moral education is an example of a social goal. Moral education brings another set of varying purposes into play; that is, which of many—sometimes conflicting—values should be taught? Fundamentalists have criticized schools for their hesitancy to take stands on many moral issues and to promote specific values. The attempted neutrality of schools on religious and moral issues, however, is a recognition of the diversity of opinion that exists on these issues, and a protective safeguard of the religious freedom that was instrumental in the founding of this country and is granted in the Constitution. The promotion of any religion or religious values would remove the rights of those of other persuasions to adhere to their religious beliefs.

The astute reader will note that the previously listed purposes of social control and reducing economic inequalities appear incongruent. Social control involves passing on existing cultural values and norms. The objective is social stability—that is, to perpetuate current societal conditions. Critical theorists and others who advocate a radical theory of schooling argue that society is clearly characterized by inequitable relationships with regard to race, class, and gender. Thus, when the purpose of schooling is social control, it perpetuates rather than reduces social inequities.

Critical theorists argue that schools perpetuate or reproduce the existing inequitable economic relationships in textbooks, curriculum, and practices such as tracking. In essence they protect established economic and class relations such that students from working-class families become working-class adults, middle-class students become middle-class adults, and so on. As a result, schools promote the continued dominance of groups that are in power. Critical theorists argue that rather than focusing on reproducing social conditions (and thus, inequities), the purpose of schools should be to empower students to transform existing social conditions. McLaren (1989) advocated that schools take "the problems and needs of students themselves as the starting point" (p. 226) in accomplishing this. In general, however, critical theorists have been criticized for lacking specificity in how empowerment and transformation might be accomplished.

Underlying the economic purposes of education are the dual objectives of increasing national wealth and advancing technological development (Spring, 1991). In the scenario described earlier in this chapter, management of the auto plant advocated economic purposes for the local schools. They wished the local schools to provide a continual pool of well-trained workers for their plant in order that the plant could produce automobiles in an efficient and effective manner that would result in continued and increasing profits. Although their concern was not so much with national wealth as with company wealth, the financial well-being of their company ultimately would contribute to national wealth.

Many of the national reform reports of the past decade have been rooted in economic purposes for schools. For example, *A Nation at Risk,* a report prepared by the National Commission on Excellence in Education that served as a springboard for the most extensive period of school reform in our nation's history (Murphy, 1991), bases a large part of its criticism of America's schools in economic terms. The central argument of the report is that our nation is at risk of becoming a second-class economic citizen of the world if our schools do not begin doing a better job of educating students. McLaren (1989) observed that the reform reports "define academic success almost exclusively in terms of capital accumulation and the logic of the marketplace" (p. 5). He noted that this has resulted in the elimination of concern for social issues and for nurturing citizens who are committed to our country but accept responsibility for keeping it strong by questioning policies and practices that they feel are inappropriate.

Not all scholars use the political, social, and economic classifications for school purposes. Goodlad (1984), for example, in his study, *A Place Called School,* categorized school purposes as vocational, social, intellectual, and personal. Vocational purposes are those that prepare students for work. Intellectual purposes differ from vocational purposes in that they focus on academic skills and knowledge. For example, in the scenario, auto plant management personnel advocated vocational purposes for "the masses" but seemed more concerned with intellectual school purposes for their own children. Additionally, the scenario exemplifies the diversity of purposes that can exist within a category. For example, the intellectual purposes the superintendent held for the schools (that is, high achievement test scores) differed from the intellectual goals the principal favored (higher level thinking skills).

Goodlad described social purposes as those that prepare students for the social life of a complex society. The purposes that the community traditionally held for its schools in the scenario—that is, providing young people with a basic level of education that equipped them with sufficient literacy to function productively in the stone quarries, as homemakers, and as community citizens—would be classified as social goals. The focus was less on intellectual or vocational success than on overall productive citizenship. According to Goodlad, personal school purposes are those that focus on the development of individual responsibility. In Goodlad's categorization, the moral educative purposes that the women's club in the scenario held for schools would be classified as personal rather than social (as they were classified in Spring's [1991] categorization).

Some scholars have classified school purposes according to philosophical schools of thought (Pounds & Bryner, 1973). Most of these purposes have already been discussed in Spring's and Goodlad's classifications and are presented in summary form in Table 8–1.

School Goals versus School Purpose

The previous discussion has used the terms goals and purposes interchangeably. However, distinctions do exist between the terms. Organizational goals can be thought of as specific objectives that an organization is attempting to accomplish. In contrast, organizational purpose is a more general statement that indicates what

TABLE 8–1 Purposes of Schooling According to Various Philosophies (adapted from Pounds & Bryner, 1973)

Philosophy	Purposes of Schooling
Humanism	World is unchanging; purpose of school is to pass on unchanging truths of universe and to cultivate the intellect
Essentialism	World is evolving and changing; purpose of schools is to pass on cultural elements that are essential and can be recognized as thoroughly established by previous history
Social Realism	Purpose of school is to make sure that currently prevailing ideas and values are passed on to students and to help them adjust to present society; current society is source of curriculum
Experimentalism	Change is certain; purpose of schools is to develop critically minded individuals who are able to solve problems
Reconstructionism	Change is certain; purpose of schools is to determine what future society should be like and to prepare students who are able to transform society into this future state

the organization stands for and provides a rationale for the organization's existence. For example, integrating computers into the curriculum is a goal; providing students with the academic skills to function productively in society is a purpose.

Traditionally, organizational theorists have held that (1) goals are prospective, (2) they guide action, (3) progress toward goals can be measured and monitored, (4) appropriate feedback based on the results of measuring and monitoring can be constructed, and (5) individuals and organizations are willing and able to make adjustments that help achieve greater congruency between goals and organizational behavior. Recently, however, organizational theorists have questioned the accuracy of these assumptions. These scholars argue that goals are retrospective and are constructed after the fact based on action determined largely by happenstance (e.g., March & Olsen, 1979; Perrow, 1982; Weick, 1979). For example, improvements in the computer program are more likely to occur as the result of a budding interest in computers on the part of a newly hired teacher than because of a formally stated school goal. In conversation about the computer program, a principal may attribute the improvement to "a goal that we had for this year."

Theorists also argue that progress toward goal achievement cannot be measured due to the ambiguity of what constitutes effectiveness. For example, school effectiveness often is measured on the basis of standardized test scores. However, standardized tests provide only a very limited indicator of what a school may be trying to accomplish and may be influenced by many factors beyond the school's control. Even if accurate measurement can occur, accurate feedback may not be able to be designed due to the multiple causes responsible for any event. Finally, even if all of these conditions were able to be met, individuals or organizations may not be willing or able to implement feedback due to lack of skill, competing agendas (e.g., insufficient time due to family commitments or other personal interests), or the loosely structured nature of schools (e.g., although schools may have elaborate, articulated curriculums, what is taught in one classroom at a particular grade level may have little relationship with what is being taught in another classroom at the same grade level).

Sergiovanni (1991) has suggested that multiple goals can mean no goals. The effect of too many goals is the fragmentation and diffusion of purpose (Tyack & Hansot, 1982). Unfortunately, the history of American schooling is characterized by a policy of inclusiveness and expansiveness. That is, schools have continually added new goals as interests and societal pressures changed. For example, as noted earlier, the Russian launching of Sputnik resulted in the goal of improving science and mathematics achievement. The publication of *A Nation at Risk* resulted in the goal of increasing standardized test scores. High rates of teenage pregnancy and the spreading of AIDS have resulted in goals of sexual awareness and caution for young people.

Seldom have new goals displaced previous goals; rather, schools have been in a continual add-on situation (Sergiovanni, 1991). In a sense, providing something for everyone allows administrators to avoid conflict by keeping everyone happy. However, it also skirts the necessity of addressing difficult questions of what should be the overarching purpose of the school.

Recent research questions the efficacy of goals, but highlights the importance of purpose. Clark and Astuto (1988), for example, have referred to the goal-purpose issue as the choice leaders have between intention (that is, achieving productivity through goal setting) and distinction (that is, defining the core values and beliefs for which the organization stands). They noted that current literature highlights the efficacy of distinction. Indeed, it is distinction that motivates and galvanizes people (Sergiovanni, 1991). One example of this is provided by Peters and Waterman (1982) in their book about outstanding business organizations. They wrote, "Every excellent company we studied is clear on what it stands for, and takes the process of value shaping seriously. In fact, we wonder whether it is possible to be an excellent company without clarity of values" (p. 280).

Organizations with a strong and clear purpose are likely to develop practices that are congruent with the values, beliefs, and assumptions embedded in their sense of purpose. The sum of these practices has been described as "the way we do things around here" (Deal & Kennedy, 1982) and has been termed "organizational culture." Strong, positive organizational cultures have been linked to effectiveness in several ways.

1. They provide an unwritten set of informal norms that inform what actions are appropriate in most situations (Deal & Kennedy, 1982). Specifically, the beliefs, values, and assumptions that constitute an organization's culture guide employee action and behavior. Actions that are incongruent with these cultural norms become inappropriate; those congruent with them are pursued.
2. In the sense that culture provides informal norms that guide action and behavior, it increases the intelligence level of the organization. New rules do not have to be developed to handle each contingency. Hall (1981) referred to this as "contexting" and noted that it was similar to "programming the memory of the system" in order to help it avoid information overload in an increasingly complex environment (pp. 85–86).
3. Culture provides a positive identity for employees by linking them with excellence (Deal & Kennedy, 1982; Smircich, 1983). Just as athletic teams (especially those with winning records) engender fan support, so also do organizations with strong cultures gain support from their employees. Employees feel pride in being associated with an organization they, or others, perceive in a positive light. Similar to the way in which fans cheers more rabidly for a winner, employees put forth greater effort for positively perceived organizations.
4. Culture provides meaning for individuals' engendering a sense of commitment that goes beyond self-interest (Smircich, 1983). When individuals accept the values, beliefs, and assumptions of the organization's culture as their own, they become "true believers" (Hoffer, 1951) in what the organization is attempting to accomplish. Their degree of commitment to fulfilling organizational tasks resembles that of a spiritual or political activist's more nearly than that of a typical organizational employee. Individual needs become subordinate to organizational needs.

Although goals may not guide organizational action to the extent that a strong organizational culture grounded in a common sense of purpose does, they do serve as symbols that portray schools as rational and legitimate to outsiders (Sergiovanni, 1991). In the words of Tom Sawyer in an organizational parody of *The Adventures of Huckleberry Finn,* "Goals is there only so's you can tell them to people when they ask you what your goals are. You don't have to follow them or nothing like that. It don't look right if you don't have no goals" (Reitzug, 1989, p. 147).

IMPLICATIONS FOR PRACTICE

This chapter has provided a historical perspective of the relationship between society, schooling, and school administrators.

The roots of the traditionally strong managerial emphasis that has been prevalent in courses that prepare educational administrators as well as in the practice of school administrators can be at least partially traced to the era of scientific management. The issue for present-day school administrators is how they define and practice their role. Key issues are (1) To what extent should administration be management-oriented, and to what extent should it be leadership-oriented? (2) Given the increased regulation of today's schools, how can an overemphasis on management be avoided? (3) How can management tasks be used to further the purposes of the school? (4) With the increasing advocacy of teacher involvement in school governance, should administrators concentrate their efforts on management and relegate leadership responsibilities to teachers?

One key consideration for school administrators with regard to purpose is the extent to which schools should pursue a single, focused purpose versus a diffused, multiplicity of purposes. The advantage of a key purpose is that it galvanizes followers and provides a sense of direction that helps inform action. The advantage of a multiplicity of purposes is that it offers "something for everyone" and leaves few people dissatisfied (Powell, Farrar, & Cohen, 1985, p. 3).

A second issue of purpose is the extent to which leaders should involve followers in defining school purpose. Chapter 9 will discuss this second issue in greater detail.

FOR FURTHER DISCUSSION

1. To what extent should administration be management-oriented and to what extent should it be leadership-oriented?
2. Given the increased regulation of today's schools, how can an overemphasis on management be avoided?
3. How can management tasks be used to further the purposes of the school?
4. Traditionally, reasons that have been given for homogeneously grouping students according to ability (tracking) have focused on its being an efficient way of meeting students' needs. Oakes (1986), however, found that tracking limited the educational

opportunity of students who were placed in lower tracks. What alternatives to tracking exist that achieve tracking's traditionally stated purposes?

5. Business, particularly through the practice of scientific management, greatly influenced schools and school administrators in the early part of this century. What evidence remains in today's schools of the influence of business and of scientific management? What are the positive and negative aspects of these influences?

6. Should schools pursue a single purpose or a multiplicity of purposes? Is it possible to have a focused direction and still provide something for everyone? Is it desirable to provide something for everyone?

7. American public education has been torn between (a) helping individuals acquire the intellectual tools to think for themselves and select their own moral and political values and (b) creating virtuous, patriotic citizens who embrace culturally dominant values. Which purpose do you think education should pursue?

8. Respond to the following statements:
   a. It is the right of school administrators to decide what should be the purpose of their school/district.
   b. School administrators have a responsibility to place students in classes with other students of similar ability in order for all students to be able to maximize their potential.
   c. The primary role of a school administrator is to be a school executive.
   d. The primary role of a school administrator is to be a scholar.
   e. The primary role of a school administrator is to be a philosopher.
   f. The primary purpose of schools is to pass on dominant cultural norms and values.
   g. With the increasing advocacy of teacher involvement in school governance, school administrators should concentrate their efforts on management and relegate leadership responsibilities to teachers.

OTHER SUGGESTED ACTIVITIES

1. Interview several principals or other school administrators about their roles and responsibilities. Decide whether their roles are more management- or leadership-oriented. Ask them about their perceptions regarding the ideal and the reality of the management and leadership aspects of their role.

2. Examine school philosophy statements and other documents to determine the stated purpose(s) of your school. Determine whether formal documents are characterized more by singular purposes or by a multiplicity of purposes.

3. Study your school to determine the actual purpose(s) it pursues. Determine whether school practices are characterized more by singular purposes or by a multiplicity of purposes. Decide whether the school's purpose is characterized more by helping individuals acquire the intellectual tools to think for themselves and select their own moral and political values, or by creating virtuous, patriotic citizens.

4. Compare statements of purpose in formal school documents with purposes implied by policy and practice in your school and determine the degree of congruency. If incongruencies exist, attempt to identify reasons for the incongruencies.

5. Study a school-business partnership in your community. Identify the advantages and disadvantages for schools and for businesses. What values does the partnership promote both directly and indirectly?

REFERENCES

Bennis, W., & Nanus, B. (1985). *Leaders: The strategies for taking charge.* New York: Harper & Row.

Button, H. W. (1991). Vulnerability: A concept reconsidered. *Educational Administration Quarterly, 27* (3), 378–391.

Callahan, R. E. (1962). *Education and the cult of efficiency: A study of the social forces that have shaped the administration of public schools.* Chicago: The University of Chicago Press.

Clark, D. L., & Astuto, T. (1988). Paradoxical choice options in organizations. In D. E. Griffiths, R. T. Stout, & P. B. Forsyth (Eds.), *Leaders for America's schools* (pp. 112–130). Berkeley, CA: McCutchan.

Deal, T. E., & Kennedy, A. A. (1982). *Corporate culture: The rites and rituals of corporate life.* Reading, MA: Addison-Wesley.

Dwyer, D. C., Barnett, B. G., & Lee, G. V. (1987). The school principal: Scapegoat or the last great hope? In L. T. Sheive & M. B. Schoenheit (Eds.), *Leadership: Examining the elusive* (pp. 3–15).

Goodlad, J. I. (1984). *A place called school.* New York: McGraw-Hill.

Greenfield, T. B. (1991). Foreword. In C. Hodgkinson, *Educational leadership: The moral art* (pp. 3–9).

Hall, E. T. (1981). *Beyond culture.* New York: Doubleday.

Hoffer, E. (1951). *The true believer: Thoughts on the nature of mass movements.* New York: Harper.

Johnson, J. A., Collins, H. W., Dupuis, V. L. , & Johansen, J. H. (1988). *Introduction to the foundations of American education* (7th ed.). Boston: Allyn and Bacon.

McLaren, P. (1989). *Life in schools: An introduction to critical pedagogy in the foundations of education.* New York: Longman.

March, J. G., & Olsen, J. (1979). *Ambiguity and choice in organizations.* Bergen, Norway: Universitetsforlaget.

Murphy, J. (1991). The effects of the educational reform movement on departments of educational leadership. *Educational Evaluation and Policy Analysis, 13* (1), 49–65.

Oakes, J. (1986). Keeping track, The policy and practices of curriculum inequality. *Phi Delta Kappan, 68* (1), 12–17.

Perrow, C. (1982). Disintegrating social sciences. *Phi Delta Kappan, 63* (10), 684–688.

Peters, T. J., & Waterman, R. H. (1982). *In search of excellence: Lessons from America's best-run companies.* New York: Warner Books.

Pounds, R. L., & Bryner, J. R. (1973). *The school in American society.* New York: Macmillan.

Powell, A. G., Farrar, E., & Cohen, D. K. (1985). *The shopping mall high school: Winners and losers in the educational marketplace.* Boston: Houghton Mifflin.

Reitzug, U. C. (1989). Huck Finn revisited: A 19th century look at 20th century organizational theory. *Organization Studies, 10* (2), 145–148.

Sergiovanni, T. J. (1984). Leadership and excellence in schooling. *Educational Leadership, 41* (5), 4–13.

———. (1991). *The principalship: A reflective practice perspective* (2nd ed.). Boston: Allyn and Bacon.

Sergiovanni, T. J., Burlingame, M., Coombs, F. S., & Thurston, P. W. (1987). *Educational governance and administration.* Englewood Cliffs, NJ: Prentice-Hall.

Smircich, L. (1983). Concepts of culture and organizational analysis. *Administrative Science Quarterly, 28,* 339–358.

Spring, J. (1991). *American education: An introduction to social and political aspects* (5th ed.). White Plains, NY: Longman.

Tyack, D., & Hansot, E. (1982). *Managers of virtue: Public school leadership in America, 1820–1980.* New York: Basic Books.

Weick, K. E. (1979). *The social psychology of organizing.* Reading, MA: Addison-Wesley.

Wirt, F. M., & Kirst, M. W. (1989). *Schools in conflict* (2nd ed.). Berkeley, CA: McCutchan.

PART III

Leadership in Education

CHAPTER **9**

Challenges of Leadership

Chapter Content

Leadership has previously been described in this book as a social influence process in which a person steers members of a group or organization toward a specific goal. Although conceptually this may seem like a straightforward and relatively simple task, in reality it is much more complex. Indicative of leadership's complexity is that it has been called one of the most observed and least understood phenomena (Burns, 1978). Bass (1981) cited over 5,000 studies related to leadership in his review of leadership research.

This chapter will provide an overview of some of the challenges that confront leaders. Specifically, the chapter will discuss the complexity of leadership as evidenced in decision making, change, motivation, communication, and time management. The chapter is written from the premise that leadership is a problematic undertaking with few easy answers. The presentation of chapter topics attempts to blend a sampling of the most significant theory and research, problematic aspects, and practical advice.

THE COMPLEXITY OF LEADERSHIP

The complexity of leadership is illustrated by the following example.

> Mr. Jones is the principal of a large elementary school in an affluent suburban area of a large city. Several weeks into the school year, Mr. Jones received a complaint from the father of a third-grade student in Mrs. Smith's class, expressing concern that his child never had any homework. When Mr. Jones discussed the complaint with Mrs. Smith, she explained that she did not feel that homework was appropriate for third-graders after spending a full day in school. She felt that after-school hours should be spent in play and related activities that were developmentally appropriate. Believing that teachers should be given as much freedom as possible to determine instructional philosophy and methodology, Mr. Jones dropped the matter, simply sending a note to the complaining parent to indicate that he had spoken to Mrs. Smith.
>
> A number of weeks passed before Mr. Jones received any more complaints about Mrs. Smith. This time, several parents visited him simultaneously to complain not just about the lack of homework but also about the "low academic standards" in Mrs. Smith's classroom. They complained that students were engaged in far too many physical activities and in discussion, and were essentially given a free hand in choosing what they read and wrote about. The parents were very concerned that students were missing the skills that were included in workbooks, worksheets, and basal readers and would not perform well on the upcoming standardized tests. This could have a ripple effect in years to come and ultimately affect their access to the best universities. Mr. Jones responded that Mrs. Smith was concerned with the total needs of the child—academic, social, and emotional.
>
> The parents were not satisfied with this response. They noted that the school was biting off more than it could (or should) chew. The school should be concerned with academics, and as parents they would provide the rest. The parents threatened to take the matter to the superintendent and the school board if a satisfactory resolution was not accomplished immediately.
>
> After the meeting Mr. Jones contemplated possible courses of action. He agreed with Mrs. Smith—they must be concerned for the total child. On the other hand, the parents had a point about the importance of standardized test scores in the "real" world. Students certainly were rated by how well they scored on standardized tests. Financially, the school's merit money, which made many of the enrichment programs possible, was dependent on the students' overall performance on the tests. Complicating the situation even further was Mr. Jones's current status in the superintendent's dog house regarding an unrelated matter. The easiest solution might be simply to tell Mrs. Smith to toughen up and focus on skill-oriented instruction. But . . . was that the right thing to do?[1]

The decision Mr. Jones faces is illustrative of the problematic nature of leadership. Although Mr. Jones may fully intend to influence Mrs. Smith or the parents in a specific direction, in whose direction does he influence them? Does he support his teacher (right or wrong), or does he side with the parents? Does he follow what he personally believes in, or does he do what is consistent with

---

[1] Adapted from Kowalski (1991).

the school's or district's philosophy? Does he do what's politically expedient, or does he do what is right and just?

Schon (1987, 1989) noted three characteristics that make the work of professionals in fields such as education especially challenging. First, he noted that these "minor" professions frequently are characterized by an absence of widely accepted, unambiguous purpose. The preceding example clearly illustrates the ambiguity of purpose faced by educational leaders. Should the goal of schooling be high test scores? Or should the goal be the development of the total person? Educational historians have observed that unlike early nineteenth-century educational leaders who shared a common religious and political conception of the role of public education and the purposes of schooling, today's public school leader "resembles an heir receiving a handsome legacy from a distant relative whose purposes now seem unclear or even quaint" (Tyack & Hansot, 1982, p. 4).

Second, Schon noted, social sciences such as education lack a basis in systematic, scientific knowledge; and even if such knowledge were available, the nature of social reality has created problems of complexity and uncertainty ill suited to traditional cause-and-effect solutions. Others have described the era in which we live as one characterized by "rapid and spastic change" (Bennis & Nanus, 1985, p. 10) in which traditional ways of addressing problems are ineffective. The discrepant views regarding appropriate instructional content and methodology held by Mrs. Smith, Mr. Jones, and the parents in the previously cited example provide one example of the uncertainty of professional knowledge in education.

Finally, Schon argued that there are two types of problems and that leaders have a choice about which type they will choose to spend the bulk of their time addressing. The first type of problem is simple and manageable, has a clear solution, and thus lends itself to research-based or technical solutions. Scheduling, budgeting, accounting, facilities management, and miscellaneous paperwork and managerial tasks are typical problems of this type that educational leaders would face. The second type of problem is complex, messy, and time-consuming, and is incapable of being solved with a clear-cut solution. Problems dealing with motivation, conflict, organizational direction, ethical behavior, and other "people" issues are typical of this type of problem.

The dilemma faced by leaders is that characteristically the easily solved problems are relatively unimportant, whereas the complex problems with only ambiguous solutions generally are critically important. Thus, leaders have a choice. They can choose to spend their time addressing "high hard ground" problems or they can immerse themselves in the messiness of "the swamp" (Schon, 1987, 1989). Principals and superintendents frequently choose to immerse themselves in the former type of problem because they are solvable and thus provide a sense of safety, comfort, and the satisfaction of seeing what has been accomplished. In effect, principals and superintendents who select this choice relegate themselves to being little more than managers who only minimally fulfill the leadership responsibilities of their position. However, opting for more complex problems is likely to lead to frustration due to frequently unsatisfactory solutions, and ambiguity resulting from indiscernible effects of actions.

THE NATURE OF DECISION MAKING

One aspect of the complexity of leadership is the nature of decision making. Traditionally, decision-making research has been predicated on the dual assumptions that decision making is an orderly rational process of choosing from alternative means of accomplishing objectives and that the steps in the decision-making process follow each other in a logical, sequential flow (Owens, 1987). For example, Simon (1977) has divided decision making into four phases: (1) intelligence activity, which involves identifying problems; (2) design activity, which consists of identifying possible courses of action; (3) choice activity, which involves deciding on a course of action; and (4) review activity, which is the evaluation of the results of choices made. In a similar vein, Drucker (1974) listed the following steps in the decision-making process:

1. Define the problem.
2. Analyze the problem.
3. Develop alternative solutions.
4. Decide on the best solution.
5. Convert the decisions into effective actions.

An Alternative View of Decision Making

Recently, however, scholars have noted a widespread disparity between rational models of decision making and the way practitioners actually make decisions. For example, some scholars have likened the decision-making process to a garbage can that attracts problems, solutions, and participants, and results in choice opportunities (Cohen, March, & Olsen, 1972). Unlike the assumption that decisions are the result of a consciously determined selection of alternatives to achieve objectives, the garbage can process holds that solutions may precede problems and individual participation is determined more by happenstance than by reason for participation.

The following example is illustrative of the garbage can model of decision making.

> Washington Elementary School is in need of a kindergarten teacher. Suzy, a college senior completing her work for a kindergarten certification, is returning to her dorm from her student-teaching assignment at a nearby school. On a whim she decides to stop by Washington School and introduce herself to the principal. The principal, who is in a meeting with the school's single, young, male art teacher, interrupts his meeting to call Suzy into his office since the secretary has already gone home for the evening. He is impressed with Suzy and decides that she is an outstanding prospect. Aloud, he muses to the art teacher, who has remained in the office, that he might hire Suzy, and what did he think of her. The art teacher thinks Suzy is cute and agrees that she should be hired.

The example illustrates a solution (Suzy) finding a problem (a kindergarten opening), with one of the participants in the decision (the art teacher) being involved not for rational reasons but simply because he happened to be in the principal's office at the time.

The Political Model of Decision Making

A third view of decision making is the political model. This model argues that decisions are the result of bargaining among competing interest groups. Rather than organizational goal achievement, achieving the goals of special-interest groups is the basis for making decisions (Estler, 1988). In the political model of decision making, Suzy would have been hired not because of a happenstance matching of a solution with a problem, but rather because her father was an influential school board member who agreed to support the principal's bid for a district-level post if he hired Suzy for a teaching position.

Limitations of Individual Decision Making

Other scholars have discussed the limitations of individuals as rational decision makers. For example, Simon (1957) concluded that people, at best, are "boundedly rational." He argued that in order to make objectively rational decisions, an individual must (1) view all decision *alternatives* in panoramic fashion prior to making a decision, (2) consider all *consequences* that would follow each choice, and (3) assign *values* to each alternative and select one alternative from the set. Simon noted that actual behavior falls short in at least three ways:

1. Rationality requires a choice from among all alternatives when in actuality only a few of the alternatives come to mind.
2. Rationality requires a complete knowledge of all the consequences that will follow each choice when in actuality knowledge of consequences is only fragmentary.
3. Values attached to consequences can only be imperfectly anticipated.

Additionally, scholars have noted that frequently decisions made are the result of "satisficing," that is, choosing the first acceptable solution rather than searching for the best possible solution. March and Simon (1958) describe satisficing as "the difference between searching a haystack to find the sharpest needle in it and searching the haystack to find a needle sharp enough to sew with" (pp. 140–141).

Suzy's hiring in the previously cited example is an example of satisificing. The principal hires her because she is an acceptable solution to his problem. Searching for the best solution would have required an extensive screening and selection process of all available candidates.

Participative Decision Making

Recently, increased attention has been given to involving teachers more extensively in school decision making. Although some principals have long used a participative decision-making style, the concept did not receive widespread attention until the publication of *A Nation Prepared: Teachers for the 21st Century* (Carnegie Forum on Education and the Economy, 1986), which advocated extending teachers a role in school governance. Some principals perceived the advocacy of increased teacher participation in school governance as an attempt to rob them of their power.

Arguments for expanding the scope of teacher decision making are grounded in several reasons:

1. It will make teaching a more stimulating and professional occupation.
2. It will increase teacher autonomy and thus result in better attitudes and resulting improved performance.
3. As human beings we should have a right to control our own destiny.
4. Increasing teacher participation in school decision making will expand the scope of expertise that is brought to bear on decisions and, thus is likely to result in improved decision making.

Research on participatory decision making has been inconclusive in verifying the validity of the arguments extended on its behalf. Firestone and Herriott (1981) have cited the need for further research to clarify participatory decision making's effects.

INSTITUTING CHANGE VERSUS MAINTAINING STABILITY

As effective school leaders engage in the process of making decisions, they attempt to set a consistent direction for their schools or districts. Clark and Astuto (1988) have noted that in setting school direction, leaders are faced with sets of conflicting choice options that are paradoxical in that either choice is supportable by research and theory. One choice option that poses a particular challenge for school leaders is the choice between activity and stability (Clark & Astuto, 1988). Activity can be described as initiating or stimulating change, or promoting attempts to innovatively alter curriculum or instructional delivery. In contrast, stability is a focus on maintaining the core of existing programs and delivery. The two choices can be illustrated by the slogan "Do it, fix it, try it" (Peters & Waterman, 1982, p. 13) as contrasted with "Why fix it if it isn't broken?" Contemporary critics would, of course, argue that the American system of public education is "broken."

School leaders opting for activity are faced with several considerations:

1. What should be the extent and nature of the leader's role in the change effort? That is, should leaders initiate and mandate change, or should they stimulate and support good tries in subordinates? How active should the leader's involvement and support be in tries initiated by subordinates?
2. What role should followers play in initiation and implementation of change? Since they are most closely involved in the technical core of education (i.e., teaching), should they initiate grass-roots efforts to

improve programs and delivery? Or should they simply be supportive of change efforts originating from formal organizational leadership?

3. How does one balance what is best for the organization in terms of sought-after organizational outcomes, with ethical and moral responsibility to honor the professional beliefs of individuals working in the organization?

Research on Planned Organizational Change

One of the key findings of research on planned organizational change in schools is that the principal's support is integral to successful change efforts. Tasks that principals can perform to facilitate successful change include obtaining resources, buffering the project from outside interference, encouraging and supporting staff, and modifying standard operating procedures to fit the project where necessary (Firestone & Corbett, 1988). Peters and Waterman (1982) found that leaders of excellent business organizations promoted "a bias for action"; that is, they encouraged and stimulated employees at all levels of the organization to attempt innovative practices and supported successful tries as well as aborted attempts.

In instances where leaders initiate and mandate change, it is important for them to analyze the match among the intervention, the context, and the characteristics of the intervention itself. Fullan (1982) found that the presence of four characteristics enhances the potential for successful implementation: necessity, clarity, complexity, and practicality.

Although it may seem obvious that to be successful a change intervention should be needed, realistically many change efforts are not initiated in response to necessity. For example, the extensive Rand Corporation-sponsored change studies (Berman & McLaughlin, 1975) found that many change efforts were opportunistically initiated in response to available grant funding. The Rand studies found that these projects were far less likely to be successful than those initiated in response to organizational need.

A second characteristic noted by Fullan (1982) that enhances a change effort's potential for success is clarity of purposes and procedures. Those implementing the change should be clear about the purposes of the change and the procedures for implementing it. On the other hand, too rigidly packaged innovations may detract from success. The adaptation of the innovation to local conditions and the development of materials to address local needs have been found to be characteristic of successful innovative program implementation efforts (Berman & McLaughlin, 1975).

A third characteristic for successful change efforts is complexity. Clark, Lotto, and Astuto (1984), in a synthesis of change research, noted that an innovation is more likely to be *adopted* if it is simple, that is, easy to understand and use. An innovation, however, is more likely to be *implemented* if it is complex, that is, if it is perceived as being ambitious. They hypothesized that a change has to be worth the effort to attract the energies of those adopting and implementing it, and thus the relative advantage of complexity outweighs the obvious advantage of simplicity.

Practicality is the fourth characteristic cited by Fullan (1982) as essential for successful change. Practicality can be thought of as the extent to which an innovation is capable of being put into practice (Firestone & Corbett, 1988). For example, if a school attempts to go from a half-day kindergarten program to an all-day program but has grant funding to pay the salaries of the additional teachers for only the first year of the change, the innovation is unlikely to stand the test of time. On the other hand, if the change in the kindergarten program is to modify curricular philosophy and subsequent practice from a skills-based approach to a developmental focus, and grant funding is available to make the initial purchase of nonconsumable materials required by the developmental program, then the innovation has greater practicality since future additional funding will not be required.

Leaders initiating and mandating change must also be cognizant of the appropriate time to involve subordinates, in order to increase the probability of the intervention's success. Although some previous research on change (for example, Berman & McLaughlin, 1975) indicated that teachers needed to be actively involved in decisions to adopt change interventions, more recent research argues that it is more essential for them to be involved at the stage where the change most directly affects them (Clark, Lotto, & Astuto, 1984). In most cases this would correspond with the implementation phase of the change effort.

The necessity of involving teachers in change efforts at the point in time where the change has personal ramifications for them highlights the essential concern that most individuals have early in any change process—that is, how will the change affect me? What will it mean to my life? Will I have to work harder or smarter? What benefits does the change hold for me?

Ethical Considerations of Change

As administrators strive to improve the attainment of organizational outcomes through stimulating, initiating, or mandating change, they must be cognizant of ethical issues involved in planned organizational change. For example, what responsibility do school administrators have to honor (and, indeed, solicit) the professional beliefs of individuals working in the organization? Is appointment by a school board sufficient warrant for school administrators to assume that their beliefs and plans of action are superior to those of subordinates?

Sergiovanni (1991) called change a form of "social engineering" and asked, "Are we talking about leadership, or are we really talking about manipulation?" (p. 267). The implication is that whether change is mandated or whether subordinates are in some fashion "sold" on the value of a change may not be essentially different since both are socially engineered manipulations of individuals' beliefs.

An Alternative Model of Change

Sirotnik (1989) suggested that schools and the people working in them traditionally have been viewed as centers *for* change rather than centers *of* change. The distinction is that in the former case people and schools are the targets at which change is directed from some external source (e.g., government regulation, school board, superintendent, or principal mandate). In the latter case, individuals and schools become the sources in which change is generated and developed. Sirotnik suggests that this might occur by schools' becoming centers of inquiry where teachers critically study their practice and that of their school in collaboration with appropriate others (for example, colleagues, principals, university researchers). The objective would be to challenge dominant ideas and ideologies as well as taken-for-granted assumptions of schooling for purposes of exploring new arrangements (Foster, 1986).

No matter what change philosophy and strategies leaders adopt, they would be well served by remembering the following story Eric Hoffer (1952) told in his discussion of change.

> Back in 1936 I spent a good part of the year picking peas. I started out early in January in the Imperial Valley and drifted northward, picking peas as they ripened, until I picked the last peas of the season, in June, around Tracy. Then I shifted all the way to Lake County, where for the first time I was going to pick string beans. And I still remember how hesitant I was that first morning as I was about to address myself to the string bean vines. Would I be able to pick string beans? Even the change from peas to string beans had in it elements of fear. (p. 1)

The point is that all changes, even minor changes like switching from picking peas to picking beans or from teaching math from one textbook rather than another, invoke a degree of fear in individuals. School leaders must be sensitive to this factor if they are to lead schools that are both productive and humane.

MOTIVATING FOLLOWERS

Argyris (1964) noted that organizations are formed when tasks needing to be accomplished are too complex for one individual to achieve. As society became less agrarian, the educational needs of the populace changed and the concept of universal education emerged. Individuals sought positions in schools for reasons similar to those for which individuals joined other organizations. Primary, of course, was the need to earn a living. However, since multiple options existed for earning a living, individuals also looked to organizations to fulfill other personal needs.

The need for individuals to fulfill diverse personal needs frequently clashes with the organization's need to accomplish a specific task. In striving for efficiency, organizations develop rules, regulations, standard operating procedures, and other mechanisms that prescribe how individuals in the organization must comport themselves and accomplish their tasks. For example, schools and school districts have policy manuals and teacher handbooks that specify how teachers should conduct themselves in various situations, and curriculum guides that indicate what should be taught. Compliance with organizational policies and practices is enforced by an individual who is the "boss" (in schools, the principal). Regularly, the organization's need for standardization of employee behavior, and the individual's desire to be autonomous, come into conflict.

Argyris (1957) likened the relationship between employees and organizations to a developmental continuum from infancy to adulthood. He noted that the more formally structured the organization, the more its tendency to force employees to be like infants, that is, to be dependent and submissive to the organization. Adults, on the other hand, seek autonomy, independence, and control over their immediate worlds. Discussions in recent years about school site-based management and teacher empowerment have been based in part on efforts to establish greater congruence between the adult developmental needs of teachers and the way schools are governed.

Principals, superintendents, and other school leaders face the challenge of motivating teachers and other subordinates when organizational needs may be incongruent with their individual needs. The challenge lies in structuring daily school life in a manner that allows schools and districts to accomplish the organizational need to educate students while still satisfying the personal needs of individuals.

Hierarchy-of-Needs Theory

Maslow (1970) theorized that the behavior of individuals is motivated by a number of needs, which are arranged in hierarchical order from basic physiological needs such as food, clothing, and shelter at the lowest level to self-actualization at the highest level. Intermediate-level needs are security and safety (physical and financial), social affiliation (love, belonging, acceptance), and esteem (recognition by others). (See Figure 9–1.) Once a need has been satisfied, it no longer serves as a motivator, with the next-higher-level need becoming the prepotent motivator. For example, teachers who are considering school administration as a career are likely to have fulfilled basic physiological needs and to feel relatively safe, physically and financially. In most cases they have also achieved a degree of personal and professional acceptance by others, fulfilling the need for social affiliation. In some cases these individuals are motivated to pursue school administration because of a striving for esteem or recognition from peers which they feel the visibility of a position in school administration will provide them. In other cases, individuals may have achieved adequate esteem as teachers but see administration as an opportunity that provides greater autonomy and more opportunity for self-direction, and that increases the likelihood for them to reach their fullest capabilities.

Maslow's hierarchy-of-needs theory has achieved great popularity and is widely accepted, although little research exists to support it (Miskel & Ogawa, 1988). Some attribute the dearth of supporting research to definitional and methodological problems, but it is also possible to imagine practical difficulties. For example, although many teachers who are considering a school administration career are undoubtedly motivated by the needs outlined in the figure, others may have achieved social affiliation and simply see school administration as an opportunity to receive a bigger paycheck, reflecting a lower level of need on Maslow's hierarchy.

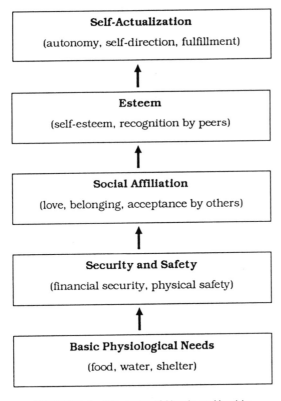

FIGURE 9-1 Hierarchy of Needs as Used in Maslow's Theory of Motivation

Two-Factor Motivation Theory

Herzberg, Mausner, and Snyderman (1959) provided a different conceptualization of job motivation. Their theory states that two separate factors are involved in motivation and employee satisfaction. These have been termed *motivators* and *hygienes*. Motivators include achievement, advancement, the work itself, growth, responsibility, and recognition. Hygiene factors include the work environment (for example, organizational climate, physical conditions), the type of supervision, salary, job security, status, and attitudes and policies of superiors. Simply stated, improving hygiene factors causes employees to be less dissatisfied but does not motivate them to better job performance; improving motivators motivates employees to perform better and feel more job satisfaction. (See Figure 9–2.) Thus, hygiene factors have little to do with employee performance, since improving them will not motivate employees to perform better. However, if hygienes are too strongly negatively present, they block motivators from having an effect. In essence, they serve as a prerequisite for motivators. That is, adequate satisfaction with hygiene factors is necessary before other factors can be put into play to

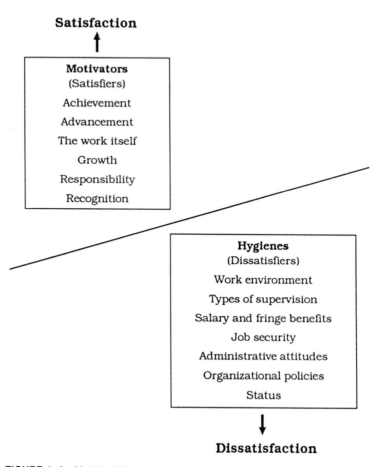

FIGURE 9–2   Model of Herzberg et al., 1959 Two-Factor Motivation Theory

motivate employees to improved performance. Similar to the hierarchy-of-needs theory, the two-factor theory is popular yet highly criticized.

Perhaps more important for school administrators than analyzing motivators and hygienes, or studying the operating needs levels of individual employees and attempting to develop congruent motivational strategies, is simply to be cognizant that physiological needs, security, salary, supervisory style, organizational climate, affiliation, responsibility, opportunities for growth, esteem, and self-actualization all are factors that motivate employee behavior. Individuals likely are motivated by several needs in varying strength valences in any given occurrence. For example, an individual who is considering accepting a job offer is likely to include factors dealing with finances, affiliation with colleagues, esteem, and opportunities for self-actualization in his or her deliberations.

A Contemporary Perspective

Peters and Waterman (1982) have developed a more simplistic but practical notion of motivation based on their study of excellent business corporations. They note that "all of us are self-centered suckers for a bit of praise and generally like to think of ourselves as winners" (p. 55), and that "none of us is really as good as he or she would like to think, but rubbing our noses daily in that reality doesn't do us a bit of good" (p. 55). Peters and Waterman found that excellent companies are characterized by their ability to deal with this paradox. These companies recognized that people are very responsive to external rewards, but that they are also strongly motivated from within to serve organizations that provide meaning for them. Excellent companies set achievement quotas that are attainable by the vast majority of employees rather than only by the elite few, have frequent celebrations of success, and provide many symbolic rewards (for example, certificates, ribbons, buttons).

Efficacy versus Accountability

Although frequently rewarding employees is consistent with the concept of positive reinforcement that prospective teachers learn in their preservice preparation, the norm in schools for administrators in dealing with teachers and for teachers in dealing with students frequently is incongruent with this concept. That is, meaningful praise of performance is the exception rather than the rule. Even those administrators who make conscious and continual efforts to recognize and reward employee performance find themselves in a paradoxical situation that forces them to choose between bolstering subordinates' feelings of efficacy (that is, professional effectiveness) and serving formal and informal demands for accountability (Clark & Astuto, 1988). The paradoxical nature of the choice between efficacy and accountability can be illustrated by the following example.

Almost every principal has been faced with considerations of how to motivate the marginal teacher. On the one hand, principals can take the route of efficacy— providing positive supervision, opportunities for professional development, and praising even minute examples of productive teaching performance. However, most school districts have policies that require principals to administer a formal evaluation to each teacher annually. If the principal practices consistent efficacious behavior, then the evaluation must be positively based, no matter how marginal the teaching performance. The positively based evaluation, however, does not serve accountability since it does not hold the teacher responsible for marginal teaching performance. If the principal opts to accurately portray the teacher's marginal teaching, then the evaluation does not serve efficacy since it will be negatively based.

Principals who may in the future be faced with initiating formal dismissal procedures against marginal teachers are confronted with an additional consideration. Past positive evaluations in a teacher's personnel file or examples of principal praise intended initially to develop feelings of efficacy may be cited by the teacher as evidence of teaching effectiveness. The principal will be hard-pressed to explain the sudden dramatic change in teaching performance suggested by the discrepancy between the past positive evaluations and the recent negative ratings. Dismissal proceedings are likely to be even more of a problem than usual.

If the principal chooses from the outset to hold the teacher accountable for marginal teaching performance, the chances of the teacher's improving teaching performance are decreased. One study cited found that 70 percent of the individuals surveyed rated themselves above average in leadership ability. Only 2 percent rated themselves below average. On other tasks, 60 percent rated themselves in the top 10 percent, 25 percent rated themselves in the top 1 percent, and none rated themselves below average (Myers, 1980, pp. 23–24). As individuals we engage in sensemaking behavior that helps us to rationalize those aspects of our lives that are not totally understandable. Teachers who are judged by principals to be poor performers are unlikely to accept this external judgment. They are more likely to question the principal's knowledge of teaching, ability to be a principal, motives, or character, and develop a negative attitude toward teaching resulting in even lesser performance.

COMMUNICATING WITH OTHERS

As was mentioned previously, individuals will sacrifice a great deal to organizations that provide meaning to their lives. Given the noble, service nature of education, developing meaningful organizations would seem a relatively easy task for school administrators to achieve. After all, one would assume that parents and most educators, whether teacher or administrator, have the best intentions of students in mind. Indeed, this may well be the case. What, then, prevents school faculties from developing strong core sets of beliefs that provide meaning and direction to daily life?

One of the difficulties may lie in the school's communication process. Although, on the surface, communication seems to be a relatively straightforward responsibility, Lysaught (1984) has noted that "problems of language, and meaning, and their transmission are among their [administrators'] most important, persistent, and ubiquitous organizational difficulties. More frequently than not, failures in communication lie at the heart of problems in organization, goal-setting, productivity, and evaluation" (p. 102).

Elements of Communication

There are a number of considerations related to communication that administrators must keep in mind. Lasswell (1948) succinctly stated these as "Who says What, to Whom, in Which channel, with What effect?" (p. 37). An additional consideration administrators may want to add is, "When should it be said?" Lasswell's formulation, however, captures only one side of the communication equation. The other side might be stated as "Who *heard* What, from Whom, When, through Which channel, with What effect?" This dual formulation of communication illustrates a number of aspects of the communication process. Communication includes a sender, a receiver, a sent message, a time when it was sent, a medium, and an outcome.

The school administrator has responsibility for sending messages to several different audiences. The most frequent audiences include teachers, parents, students, and the local community. In some cases, the principal may be responsible for communication but may decide that another party should do the actual communicating. For example, the principal may opt to let a teacher communicate information about a student's progress since the teacher has a more comprehensive understanding of the student's work. Likewise, the principal may let PTO officers communicate information about an upcoming PTO meeting.

Although principals should not feel the need to assume guilt for all that goes wrong in a school, ultimately they are the overseers of the entire operation and thus should be sensitive to all aspects of school operations. Thus, whereas teachers and PTO may accept primary responsibility for communicating the above information, the principal assumes secondary responsibility. Many principals require all written communication from the school or staff members to be funneled through their office for approval prior to being sent into the home or community. This helps the principal make sure that necessary information is being communicated and to ensure that a professional format is being used. The downside of following this procedure is that it may communicate a nonverbal message to teachers and others that the principal does not trust the quality of their communication.

Decisions over whether messages should be communicated in writing or orally; in person or by telephone; by informal note, memo, or formal letter are dependent on the substance of the message. For example, simply scrawling a note of reply or approval directly onto a letter of inquiry saves time and is acceptable in many cases. Replies that require greater length, might be publicly shared, or are written to outsiders or superiors who are not close acquaintances require a more formal response. Delivering a message in person (or even using the telephone) adds a personal touch to communication but should be followed up with written communication where documentation might be required or where misunderstanding could occur.

Simply communicating information is insufficient. Consideration should also be given to the appropriate time at which information should be communicated. For example, informing teachers on Monday that the school carnival is on Friday and that their class is expected to have a booth provides inadequate lead time. On the other hand, telling teachers in September that a booth is required in March should be succeeded by follow-up reminders as March approaches.

There will be instances when the answer to the question of when information should be communicated is "never." Principals are privy to various bits of information that need not go beyond them. A useful rule of thumb to follow is that if communicating information will not improve relationships or the process or product of schooling, then little is served by passing it on.

Problems and Strategies

Scholars of communication processes have identified a number of reasons why messages that are received do not always resemble messages that are sent. This section will briefly discuss several of these problems as well as present some practical communication strategies for school administrators.

Communication Oversight. A frequent communication problem is that administrators are closely involved with a number of different projects and may overlook communicating with some outsiders who are stakeholders but do not have direct involvement in the project at that time. For example, a principal may be working with a committee that is developing innovative math programming but neglect to keep math teachers not on the committee informed about the committee's progress. In such instances, the final recommendations of the committee may come as such a shock to noncommittee members that there is strong reactionary backlash against otherwise positive recommendations.

The problem of communication oversight is especially prevalent in school-to-home communication. For example, after working on a school project for several months and informing parents of the outcome only to meet with objections of "Why didn't you tell us you were working on this?" principals may wonder how it is possible that parents did not know about the project. After all, staff members had spent hundreds of hours on the project. Frequently it is easy to forget that the intimate familiarity we have with projects in which we are immersed is matched only by the total ignorance outsiders have of our work.

One strategy for minimizing communication oversight is to establish a written schedule of regular (and frequent) written communication with various audiences. This strategy provides several benefits. Establishing a schedule helps ensure that communication will take place on a regular basis. Having communication be in written form provides a record of what was communicated, and frequently permits mental review of noteworthy items that have occurred since the last communication.

Composing a written teachers' bulletin daily or every other day, although time-consuming, may actually save time in the long run by preventing misunderstandings and needless questions. It forces principals to ask themselves, "What is it that the teachers should know today? What should they know for the remainder of this week? next week? Of what previously mentioned items do I need to remind them today?" Daily communication allows details that contribute to the smooth operation of the school and might otherwise be overlooked to be noted.

Similarly, a written parent bulletin should be sent home every week with a more extensive newsletter monthly or quarterly. Questions to be addressed include "What is it that parents need to know? What is it that parents might want to know? What are we doing that shows that this school is moving forward? What good things have happened to teachers or students?" Consideration should be given to placing newsletters in businesses and stores in the school's attendance area.

Message Interpretation. Perhaps the most problematic aspect of communication is the effect it has on others. One would be naive to assume that the messages we send are always the same messages that are received. Frequently, there is a discrepancy between what an individual thinks is being communicated and the message that another individual is receiving. Conceptual models of communication refer to the factors that cause a discrepancy between the sent message and the received message as "noise" (Lysaught, 1984). Noise can be thought of as the influence of contextual factors on the message as it is received and decoded. For example, certain words such as *redistricting, busing,* or *AIDS* may engender emotional reactions in some individuals and cloud the substance of the message.

Symbolic interactionists have long held that the meaning of any event is not inherent in the event itself, but arises out of the interaction of the individual with the event. For example, a principal may frequently visit classrooms because of a strong interest in what students are learning and a desire to show teachers that he or she is interested in their work. Teachers, on the other hand, may interpret the principal's frequent presence in their classrooms as a lack of trust in them to do their jobs as they best see fit. The teacher who has received poor evaluations from the principal for marginal teaching performance may interpret the principal's classroom visits differently than the teacher who has become a friend of the principal through their working together on various professional committees. Some principals may decide to stay out of classrooms because of a concern that they will be perceived as distrustful or meddling. Conversely, teachers in these schools may perceive their principals as not being interested enough in them or the students to see how they spend their day. Obviously, the messages that are being received vary and may be different from the messages that are being sent.

Information Overload. Another barrier to effective communication is information overload. When the amount of information becomes more than can be dealt with effectively, the overload of communication engenders a response that results in less-than-optimal information processing. The complexity, specialization, and increasing regulation of today's schools result in principals and teachers being bombarded with information from a variety of sources. The amount of information coupled with time constraints on educators are likely to result in teachers and principals being periodic victims of information overload. Typical responses to information overload include omitting, erroring, queuing, filtering, generalizing, employing multiple channels, and escaping (Miller, 1960). Descriptions and examples of each response are provided in Table 9–1.

Given the variety of ways in which communication can and is likely to be distorted, principals would be wise to regularly solicit feedback from message recipients regarding their understanding of the message that was communicated.

MANAGING TIME

One of the biggest challenges faced by principals and other school administrators is managing time in a manner that allows them to accomplish those tasks which they feel are most important. Studies of managerial work (Mintzberg, 1973) and the principalship (e.g., Sproul, 1976, cited in Sergiovanni, Burlingame, Coombs, & Thurston, 1987; Wolcott, 1973) indicate that administrative work is characterized by many brief encounters generally of several minutes or less in length. Additionally, administrative work is fragmented; that is, the administrator deals with many different issues during the course of the day, but sees few of these to immediate completion. Work occurs at an unrelenting pace with one interaction followed in immediate succession by another.

TABLE 9-1 Responses to Information Overload and Representative Examples

Response	Description and Example
Omitting	Failure to process some information Teacher overlooks some sections of a teacher bulletin
Erroring	Processing information incorrectly Teacher reads "Tuesday at 10 AM" instead of "Thursday at 10 AM" as the time for a school-wide assembly
Queuing	Delaying the processing of information until a lull occurs Teacher delays reading the teacher bulletin because of other mail and demands
Filtering	Separating out less-relevant information Teacher skims teacher bulletin and only reads those sections that are personally most relevant
Generalizing	Reducing the level of specificity In response to a request for information, a teacher uses the same general response for a number of questions even though to be completely accurate the specifics of each response should vary somewhat
Employing multiple channels	Introducing alternative channels for information flow A teacher uses an instructional aid to read the mail with instructions for routing as appropriate
Escaping	Avoiding the information A teacher decides not to read teacher bulletins since they always result in additional tasks

Given the frenetic nature of administrative work, it is little wonder that studies have found a substantial discrepancy between how principals feel they should spend their time and how they actually spend it. For example, a study conducted by McCleary and Thomson (1979) found that secondary school principals ranked program development as the task area on which they would ideally spend the most time, but actually spent more time on school management, personnel, student activities, and student behavior. (See Table 9–2.) Increasing regulation of schools, changing demographics resulting in more at-risk students, and other factors that are increasing organizational complexity conspire to rob principals of an even greater percentage of their discretionary time in the future.

Time Management Tips

There are several strategies principals can adopt to shrink the discrepancy between the ideal and the reality of time expenditure. One strategy is simply to become proficient in time management techniques. The following list provides tips that have been cited by time management studies (e.g., Center for Educational Policy and Management, 1983) or proven in the authors' experience to result in more efficient use of time:

1. Delegate.
2. Say "no."

TABLE 9–2 Rankings of Ideal and Actual Time Allocations of High School Principals*

Task Areas	Ideal Time Planned	Actual Time Spent	Difference
Program development	1**	5	4
Personnel	2	2	0
School management	3	1	2
Student activities	4	3	1
Planning	5	7	2
Professional development	6	9	3
Student behavior	7	4	3
Community	8	8	0
District office	9	6	3

*Data from McCleary & Thomson (1979).
**On scale of 1 to 5 with 1 being most important, 5 being least important

3. Double up; that is, do two things at one time (for example, complete paperwork while on hold on the telephone).
4. Achieve closure; that is, stop meetings, conversations, and other activity at the point where productivity breaks down.
5. Do not procrastinate.
6. Use creative time wisely; that is, use the time of the day when you work best to complete your most complex tasks.
7. Establish a tickler file to remind you of upcoming deadlines.
8. Have someone screen your phone calls.
9. Keep a "to-do" list.
10. Handle paper once (for example, dispense with routine mail and memos the first time you handle them).
11. Write brief letters and jot replies directly on incoming letters and memos where appropriate.
12. Do not sit down after greeting "unwanted" visitors (for example, a salesperson in whose products you have no interest).
13. Always carry a small notepad to jot reminders and follow-up items.
14. Use "down" time (for example, catch up on professional reading or go through mail while waiting in the doctor's office).
15. Skip meetings where appropriate (when you have little substantive or symbolic information to communicate).
16. Have someone screen your mail and separate it into piles (for example, personal correspondence, bulk mail, reply required)
17. Speed-read and skim where possible.
18. Get an excellent secretary.
19. Reduce sleep.
20. Decide how you want to spend your time and then do it.
21. Do not assume unnecessary "monkeys."

The final item bears further explanation. As principal, it is not your responsibility to take care of all teacher, student, and parent needs that are brought to your attention. Many of these "monkeys" can be returned to the back of the person who tried to place the monkey on your back by directing that person to the appropriate information source or resources and letting him or her retain responsibility for follow-up. Be certain, however, that such people know it is their responsibility to follow up and are not assuming that you will do so. You can indicate your genuine interest in their well-being by asking them at a later time if they were successful in tracking down the information or resources.

Efficient time management is unlikely to totally provide principals with the curriculum and instructional development time they desire. Chapter 10 will discuss the concept of "overarching frameworks" (Dwyer, Barnett, & Lee, 1987, p. 33) and how they might serve as purposeful organizers to guide and connect administrator responses to the frequent, routine, frenetic, and seemingly fragmented interactions of which their days consist.

Finally, similar to the way solutions have a way finding problems in the garbage can decision-making model discussed earlier, so do additional tasks and problems have a way of finding principals who spend excessive time in their offices completing managerial responsibilities.

IMPLICATIONS FOR PRACTICE

This chapter dealt with some of the challenges of leadership. The central thesis of the chapter was that leadership is a complex and problematic undertaking. Those considering a career in school administration should be forewarned that it is not a profession for the light-hearted. Prospective school leaders should expect to encounter ambiguity in making optimal decisions and uncertainty in terms of who must, who might, and who should be involved in decision making. In their quest to keep organizational members working at peak performance and to move their schools forward through planned organizational change, future school administrators may face instances where issues of productivity confront issues of ethics. The nature of communication makes it likely that there will be instances where intents are misunderstood. Finally, in attempting to deal effectively with the various challenges of leadership, the school administrator can expect to confront role ambiguity brought on by the discrepancy between what is expected in terms of instructional leadership and what is required in terms of school management.

In a sense, a career in school administration is similar to the paradoxes of practice that school leaders frequently confront. Although the challenges and complexity of the people portion of the position make it difficult and periodically frustrating, they simultaneously provide the stimulation and the opportunity for service that make school administration an interesting and rewarding career.

FOR FURTHER DISCUSSION

1. What are the characteristics of effective school leaders with whom you have worked? Contrast these with the characteristics of ineffective school leaders with whom you have worked. Based on these characteristics develop a personal definition of leadership.

2. Do you agree with Schon (1987, 1989), and Tyack and Hansot (1982) that today's schools do not have a clear sense of purpose? Provide examples to support your argument.

3. As you make decisions and take action in your professional practice, what information guides your decision making and actions? Do you agree with Schon (1987, 1989) that social sciences such as education lack systematic, professional knowledge? Support your answer.

4. Which model of decision making (rational, garbage can, political) do you feel is most frequently true of educational decision making? Identify examples that support each model.

5. How extensively do you feel teachers should be involved in school decision making? How can schools overcome the logistical difficulties inherent in shared decision making (for example, lack of teacher time)?

6. Which more closely resembles your philosophy of change: "Do it, fix it, try it" or "Why fix it if it isn't broken?"?

7. Do you agree with change research findings that indicate that the appropriate time to involve teachers in planned organizational change is at the implementation stage rather than at the decision stage? What are the advantages and disadvantages of teacher involvement at each stage?

8. How do you feel about Sergiovanni's (1991) statement that change is a form of "social engineering"? Is there a difference between leading people in the change process and manipulating them to change? If so, provide key distinctions and supporting examples.

9. What is motivating you to consider a career in school administration? How do your motivational needs compare with Maslow's (1970), Herzberg et al.'s (1959), and Peters and Waterman's (1982) theories of motivation?

10. What are some ways that schools can more effectively communicate with parents and local communities?

OTHER SUGGESTED ACTIVITIES

1. Interview a principal in terms of (a) how he or she feels his or her time ideally should be spent and (b) how he or she feels his or her time actually is spent. Shadow the principal and compare how his or her time actually is spent with (a) how he or she perceives it is spent and (b) how he or she would ideally spend it.

2. Shadow a principal and record the types of situations he or she must address. Classify these situation according to degree of complexity and importance. Does Schon's (1987, 1989) hypothesis regarding simplicity/insignificance and complexity/importance hold true? What factors are involved in problems you classified as complex?

3. Analyze the main purpose of your school as reflected in the school's philosophy or mission statement (for example, high test scores, development of the total person). Recall some recent or significant school decisions and study instructional practices in your school. What do these suggest is the school's main purpose?

4. Study a recent decision that was made in your school. What was the process that was used to arrive at a decision? Who was involved in the process? What factors were taken into consideration in making the decision? Did the process most closely resemble the rational, garbage can, or political model of decision making?

5. Analyze policy and practice in your school and district to determine whether they are characterized more by change or by stability. When change occurs, how does

the change process compare with the various characteristics of change discussed in this chapter?

6. What are the formal and informal communication channels in your school? Do they seem adequate to communicate needed and desired information? How do various audiences (for example, teachers, parents, students, community) perceive communication from the school?

7. Analyze a situation in your school where communication went awry. What factors led to the miscommunication? How could the likelihood of future occurrences of this type of miscommunication be minimized?

8. Practice some of the time management tips provided in this chapter. Do they seem to provide you with additional time?

REFERENCES

Argyris, C. (1957). *Personality and organization: The conflict between system and individual.* New York: Harper.

———. (1964). *Integrating the individual and the organization.* New York: Wiley.

Bass, B. M. (1981). *Stodgill's handbook of leadership.* New York: Macmillan.

Bennis, W., & Nanus, B. (1985). *Leaders: The strategies for taking charge.* New York: Harper & Row.

Berman, P., & McLaughlin, M. W. (1975). *Federal programs supporting educational change.* Vol. 4: *The findings in review.* Santa Monica, CA: Rand.

Burns, J. M. (1978). *Leadership.* New York: Harper & Row.

Carnegie Forum on Education and the Economy (1986). *A nation prepared: Teachers for the 21st Century.* Washington, DC: The Forum.

Center for Educational Policy and Management (1983). *Managing brevity, variety, and fragmentation.* Eugene, OR: Author, University of Oregon. (ERIC Document Reproduction Service No. ED 271 846)

Clark, D. L., & Astuto, T. A. (1988). Paradoxical choice options in organizations. In D. E. Griffiths, R. T. Stout, & P. B. Forsyth (Eds.), *Leaders for America's schools* (pp. 112–130). Berkeley, CA: McCutchan.

Clark, D. L., Lotto, L. S., & Astuto, T. A. (1984). Effective schools and school improvement: A comparative analysis of two lines of inquiry. *Educational Administration Quarterly,* 20 (3), 41–68.

Cohen, M. D., March, J. G., & Olsen, J. P. (1972). A garbage can model of organizational choice. *Administrative Science Quarterly,* 17 (1), 1–25.

Drucker, P. F. (1974). *Management: tasks, responsibilities, and practices.* New York: Harper & Row.

Dwyer, D. C., Barnett, B. G., & Lee, G. V. (1987). The school principal: Scapegoat or the last great hope? In L. T. Sheive & M. B. Schoenheit (Eds.), *Leadership: Examining the elusive* (pp. 30–46). Reston, VA: Association for Supervision and Curriculum Development.

Estler, S. (1988). Decision-Making. In N. J. Boyan (Ed.), *Handbook of research in educational administration* (pp. 305–319). White Plains, NY: Longman.

Firestone, W. A., & Corbett, H. D. (1988). Planned organizational change. In N. J. Boyan (Ed.), *Handbook of research in educational administration* (pp. 321–340). White Plains, NY: Longman.

Firestone, W. A., & Herriott, R. E. (1981). Images of organization and the promotion of educational change. In R. Corwin (Ed.), *Research in sociology of education and socialization* (Vol. 2, pp. 221–260). Greenwich, CT: JAI.

Foster, W. (1986). *Paradigms and promises: New approaches to educational administration.* Buffalo: Prometheus Books.

Fullan, M. (1982). *The meaning of educational change.* New York: Teachers College Press, Columbia University.

Herzberg, F., Mausner, B., & Snyderman, B. (1959). *The motivation to work.* New York: John Wiley.

Hoffer, E. (1952). *The ordeal of change.* New York: Harper & Row.

Kowalski, T. J. (1991). *Case studies on educational administration* (pp. 122–130). New York: Longman.

Lasswell, H. D. (1948). The structure and function of communication in society. In L. Bryson (Ed.), *The communication of ideas* (pp. 39–51). New York: Harper & Brothers.

Lysaught, J .P. (1984). Toward a comprehensive theory of communication: A review of selected contributions. *Educational Administration Quarterly,* 20 (3), 101–127.

McCleary, L. E., & Thomson, S. D. (1979). *The senior high school principalship.* Vol III: *The summary report.* Reston, VA: National Association of Secondary School Principals.

March, J. G., & Simon, H. (1958). *Organizations.* New York: John Wiley.

Maslow, A. H. (1970). *Motivation and personality.* New York: Harper & Row.

Miller, J. G. (1960). Information input, overload, and psychopathology. *American Journal of Psychiatry,* 116 (8), 697–711.

Mintzberg, H. A. (1973). *The nature of managerial work.* New York: McGraw Hill.

Miskel, C., & Ogawa, R. (1988). In N. J. Boyan (Ed.), *Handbook of research in educational administration* (pp. 279–304). White Plains, NY: Longman.

Myers, D. G. (1980). *The inflated self: Human illusions and the biblical call to hope.* New York: The Seabury Press.

Owens, R. G. (1987). *Organizational behavior in education* (2nd ed.). Englewood Cliffs, NJ: Prentice-Hall.

Peters, T. J., & Waterman, R. H. (1982). *In search of excellence: Lessons from America's best-run companies.* New York: Warner Books.

Schon, D. A. (1987). *Educating the reflective practitioner: Toward a new design for teaching and learning in the profession.* San Francisco: Jossey-Bass.

Schon, D. A. (1989). Professional knowledge and reflective practice. In T. J. Sergiovanni & J. H. Moore (Eds.), *Schooling for tomorrow: Directing reforms to issues that count* (pp. 188–206). Boston: Allyn and Bacon.

Sergiovanni, T. J. (1991). *The principalship: A reflective practice perspective.* Boston: Allyn and Bacon.

Sergiovanni, T. J., Burlingame, M., Coombs, F. S., & Thurston, P. W. (1987). *Educational governance and administration.* Englewood Cliffs, NJ: Prentice-Hall.

Simon, H. A. (1957). *Administrative behavior.* New York: Macmillan.

———. (1977). *The new science of management decisions.* Englewood Cliffs, NJ: Prentice-Hall.

Sirotnik, K. A. (1989). The school as the center of change. In T. J. Sergiovanni & J. H. Moore (Eds.), *Schooling for tomorrow: Directing reforms to issues that count* (pp. 89–113).

Sproul, L. S. (1976, November). *Managerial attention in new educational systems.* Paper prepared for seminar on organizations as loosely coupled systems. University of Illinois-Urbana.

Tyack, D., & Hansot, E. (1982). *Managers of virtue: Public school leadership in America, 1820–1980.* New York: Basic Books.

Wolcott, H. J. (1973). *The man in the principal's office.* New York: Holt, Rinehart and Winston.

CHAPTER **10**

Leadership Styles

Chapter Content

Common Leadership Style Conceptualizations
Influence of Contextual Factors on Style Orientation
Additional Leadership Style Considerations
The Art of Reflective Practice
Implications for Practice

Chapter 9 discussed several of the challenges that confront school leaders. Leaders respond to these challenges based on personal action dispositions, which are commonly referred to as leadership styles. Leaders vary in the types of styles they embrace as well as in how strongly they believe in and adhere to these styles.

This chapter will explore various leadership styles and discuss implications of these styles for leader behavior. An examination of contextual factors that influence leadership style will follow. The chapter will discuss the concept of reflective practice and propose a heuristic for helping leaders and prospective leaders examine how contextual factors and personal professional beliefs influence their practice. Finally, the chapter will explore the implications of four concepts embedded in the previous discussion for school leadership.

COMMON LEADERSHIP
STYLE CONCEPTUALIZATIONS

Leadership style has been defined as an "action disposition, or set or pattern of behaviors, displayed by a leader in a leadership situation" (Immegart, 1988). The most popular conception of leadership style has centered around whether the leader is task-oriented or people-oriented (Stodgill & Coons, 1957). Other popular conceptions have revolved around the leader's predisposition toward democratic or autocratic governance, and toward directive versus nondirective behavior.

Task-Oriented versus People-Oriented

Imagine that you are the new principal of a medium-sized elementary school in an average American community. You have been on the job for several months and are adjusting well to your new responsibilities. During these initial weeks you have actively been trying to learn as much as possible about the school and the surrounding community. You have made some initial assessments about the ability and performance of the teaching staff and are wrestling with your first significant problem. Mrs. Smith, a veteran third-grade teacher, has not been teaching at the level of competence that you would expect. You have visited her classroom several times, and on each occasion she has shown poor lesson preparation and has been short-tempered with the students. In your discussions with her, she seems to show little interest in her teaching but constantly turns the discussion to her pending divorce and what an emotional struggle this is making her life. You have communicated your empathy to her but have also reminded her of her responsibility to her students. She, in turn, has asked for your continued patience, understanding, and support as she works through this difficult period in her life.

Nonetheless, her teaching remains poor. Complicating the situation further is that Mrs. Smith has long been considered one of the outstanding teachers in the school and has strong support from parents of past students, many of whom have become Mrs. Smith's personal friends. During your brief tenure at the school, however, you have had several parents of her current students complain about her teaching.

A few minutes ago you received a telephone call from a parent who issued the ultimatum that if the situation in Mrs. Smith's classroom did not improve immediately, she wanted her child placed in the other third-grade teacher's classroom, barring which she would issue a formal complaint to the superintendent and school board.

The situation illustrates the classic tension that exists for leaders between balancing the need to accomplish tasks and meeting the human needs of individuals in the organization. As a principal, you are torn between being supportive and understanding of the needs of a faculty member caught in a personal crisis and being concerned for the accomplishment of the instructional tasks of the school.

Although the particular case illustrated may be an extreme, it is representative of situations regularly faced by educational leaders. Furthermore, on a smaller scale, many of the numerous, seemingly routine daily decisions that constitute administrative work involve choices between human needs and task accomplishment.

A significant amount of research has been conducted on the people and task orientations of leaders. One of the best-known studies was conducted at Ohio State University and was the basis for many subsequent studies (Halpin, 1966). Not surprisingly, the study found that leaders whose behavior was high in both task orientation and people orientation were generally viewed as effective.[1] People and task orientation should be understood to exist on a continuum from low to high rather than as absolutes that are or are not present. That is, leader behavior in most situations is likely to embody both task orientation and people orientation, with the degree of each varying from situation to situation.

Research on the effectiveness of task-oriented versus people-oriented leadership has not conclusively supported either orientation. Leaders high in consideration tend to have more satisfied subordinates (Fleishman & Harris, 1962). On the other hand, the effects of consideration on group productivity vary greatly (House & Baetz, 1979). Conversely, leaders who are very task-oriented achieve greater group productivity (Schriesheim, House, & Kerr, 1976) but experience greater employee turnover and higher employee grievance rates (Fleishman & Harris, 1962).

The ethical issue that choosing task orientation versus people orientation raises for leaders is a variation of the age-old question, "Does the end justify the means?" Specifically, is it justifiable for a leader to achieve greater organizational productivity at the expense of the satisfaction of those who do the work of the organization? Or, conversely, is it justifiable for a leader to jeopardize organizational productivity in order to keep organization members satisfied? Obviously, ethical leaders strive toward both organizational productivity and employee satisfaction. Problematically, decisions must regularly be made that sacrifice one at the expense of the other.

Authoritarian versus Democratic

A second common conceptualization of leadership style is the extent to which leaders practice authoritarian versus democratic methods of governance. The tendency is to associate people-oriented leaders with a democratic leadership style and task-oriented leaders with an authoritarian style. Although this correlation may exist in many cases, people-oriented leaders may be authoritarian, just as task-oriented leaders may be democratic.

There are distinct differences between the task-people and the authoritarian-democratic dimensions of leadership. Authoritarianism and democracy refer to the extent to which followers are permitted to participate in the making of decisions. People orientation refers to the degree of consideration a leader has for individual needs, and task orientation to the extent a leader provides structure for tasks needing to be accomplished.

Authoritarian leaders are those who allow little or no employee participation in organizational decision making and may even severely restrict employee decision making about the most effective ways of accomplishing the tasks within their jobs. Democratic leaders, on the other hand, encourage individual and group input into organizational decision making. They encourage employees to make suggestions about how task requirements of their position might better be accomplished.

---

[1] Halpin (1966) used the concepts consideration and initiating structure in his studies. These concepts correspond closely to, and are frequently referred to as people orientation and task orientation, respectively.

Studies initially conducted on the effectiveness of authoritarian versus democratic leadership styles found that subordinates most preferred democratic leaders. Authoritarian leadership elicited either aggressive or apathetic behavior but resulted in greater productivity (Lewin, Lippitt, & White, 1939). However, subsequent studies have found that the initial increase in productivity experienced under authoritarian leadership diminishes sharply over time and ultimately results in lower productivity levels than in democratically led groups (Bowers, 1977). Overall, reviews of research on productivity levels of democratically versus autocratically led groups have been inconclusive (Bass, 1981; Jago, 1982). However, research reviews have consistently indicated that satisfaction and morale are likely to be higher in democratically led groups.

Opting for a purely democratic leadership style creates a potential quandary for school leaders. Democratic leadership implies a commitment to the group's goals for the organization rather than to a leader's individual goals for the organization. What course of action does a leader take when consistent discrepancies occur between the leader's goals and the group's goals? Kutner (1950) argued that in such instances in order for the group to remain democratic, the leader must be replaced. Obviously, purely democratic leadership requires a strong philosophical commitment from leaders!

Directive versus Nondirective

Leaders may also employ different styles during different phases of a situation. For example, Muczyk and Reimann (1989) distinguished between the act of making a decision and the process of *executing* the decision. In their conceptualization, the authoritarian-democratic dimension refers to the extent to which the leader involves employees in making decisions, whereas the leader's style in executing a decision falls on a continuum from directive to nondirective. Thus, their conceptualization has four distinct leadership styles:

- Authoritarian and nondirective leaders provide employees little input into decision making, but great discretion in how to execute decisions.
- Authoritarian and directive leaders allow neither input into decision making nor employee discretion in how to execute decisions.
- Democratic and nondirective leaders permit and solicit employee input into decision making and allow great discretion in how to execute decisions.
- Democratic and directive leaders permit and solicit employee input into decision making, but allow little discretion in terms of executing a decision.

Muczyk and Reimann argued that situational factors determine when each of the four styles is most appropriate. Table 10–1 provides an overview of preferred style situation.

TABLE 10-1   Democratic/Authoritarian-Directive/Nondirective Leadership Styles and Situational Factor Matches

Style	Situational Factors
Authoritarian-Directive	Quick action required Small organization Unstructured tasks Leading new, inexperienced, or underqualified subordinates Adversarial situations where coercion required
Authoritarian-Nondirective	Quick action required/simple, structured tasks Leading well-qualified, motivated employees Extrinsic factors exist to ensure task execution (e.g., clear task structure, incentive systems)
Democratic-Directive	Complex undertakings Quick action not required Leading inexperienced,underqualified or unreliable, lackadaisical employees Leader predisposed to shared decision making/marginally reliable employees
Democratic-Nondirective	Employee participation has informational or motivational benefits Highly qualified employees Presence of effective substitutes for personal direction Sufficient time for reaching consensus Leader predisposed to shared decision making/trusts subordinates' abilities

INFLUENCE OF CONTEXTUAL FACTORS ON STYLE ORIENTATION

Effective leaders appear to be those who are able to blend task and people orientations and decide in which instances an emphasis on one or the other should predominate. Immegart (1988) noted that most effective leaders demonstrate style variability.

Much of the research that has been conducted using the two-dimensional leadership theory has focused on determining in which situations people versus task orientations are more appropriate. Fiedler (1967), for example, developed a model in which an effective leadership style orientation in a situation is contingent on three variables inherent in the situation. These variables are the position power of the leader, the relative structure of the task, and leader-member relations. Depending on the combination of strong/weak position power, structured/unstructured task, and good/poor member relations, the leader chooses either a task or a people orientation as the most appropriate style to adopt for that situation. (See Table 10–2.)

Hersey and Blanchard's (1977) situational leadership theory bases the choice of people versus task orientation on the maturity level of the followers with regard to the specific task to be accomplished. Task maturity is based on followers' technical skill in being able to accomplish the task (including interpersonal skills if these are required) and their willingness to fulfill task goals. (See Figure 10–1.)

TABLE 10-2   Fiedler's Contingency Leadership Model

Leader Position Power	Task Structure	Leader-Member Relations	Style Orientation
Strong	Structured	Good	Task
Weak	Structured	Good	Task
Strong	Unstructured	Good	Task
Weak	Unstructured	Good	Relations
Strong	Structured	Poor	Relations
Weak	Structured	Poor	Relations
Strong	Unstructured	Poor	Relations
Weak	Unstructured	Poor	Task

SOURCE: (Fiedler, 1967)

As is the case with the people versus task dimensions of leadership style, some scholars have argued that situational factors should determine when democratic or autocratic leadership is more appropriate. Vroom and Yetton's (1973) normative contingency theory, for example, is based on seven situational factors: the quality requirement of a decision, the degree of available information relevant to the decision, the degree of structure the situation has, the criticalness of employee acceptance of a decision for effective implementation, the likelihood of subordinate acceptance of the decision without their involvement in making it, the degree of congruence between employee goals and organizational goals reflected in the decision, and the likelihood that the decision will result in conflict among subordinates. One of five leadership styles, ranging from autocratic to purely democratic, is chosen for use in the situation based on the leader's response to questions reflecting the seven factors.

Overall, research indicates that if tasks are clear and highly structured, there does not seem to be much benefit in soliciting employee input into how they should be accomplished, since a clear conception of this already exists. However, when tasks are ambiguous, complex, or ill defined, or when subordinates are ego-involved with the task, employee input is of greater benefit (House, 1971; House & Dressler, 1974). Subordinate participation also is of greater value when employees exhibit a willingness to participate, see benefits accruing from their participation, and receive satisfaction from participation (Duke, Showers, & Imber, 1980; House & Baetz, 1979).

Although the situational variables identified by Fiedler (1967), Hersey and Blanchard (1977), Vroom and Yetton (1973), and others are helpful in sensitizing leaders to situational variables of which they should be cognizant as they engage in daily practice, leaders who attempt to use them heuristically are likely to confront several problems.

1. What criteria does the leader use to decide how to rate a particular variable in a situation? For example, does a principal have strong or weak position power? Principals certainly have the power to make organizational work conditions less comfortable for employees but, conversely, employees also have the power to retaliate in legitimate ways to make principals'

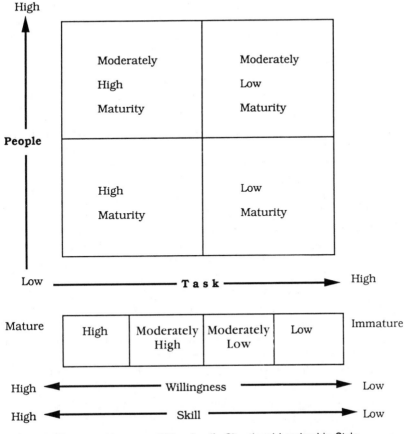

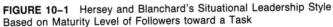

FIGURE 10-1 Hersey and Blanchard's Situational Leadership Style Based on Maturity Level of Followers toward a Task

work conditions less comfortable. If principals thus decide that they have "moderate" position power, where does the situation fit in a model that provides the discrete choices of "strong" or "weak"?

Similar examples can be provided for other situational variables. Where does one categorize a situation where one has good member relations with some of the individuals involved in a situation, mediocre relations with others, and poor relations with still others? How does one interact with a group of subordinates when some individuals in the group have high maturity toward a task, some have moderate maturity, and still others have low maturity? How does one categorize tasks that have some very structured parts and other unstructured parts?

2. What other contextual factors are essential in determining the appropriateness of either a task or a people orientation? Dwyer, Barnett, and Lee (1987), for example, found that community factors, personal beliefs and experiences, and characteristics of the institutional context shaped

principals' behaviors. Even if the most essential situational factors could be identified, how does the leader determine in which situations these factors constitute the critical mass necessary to dictate one leadership style over another?

3. Given the frequently frenetic, fragmented, and unexpected nature of administrative work, how does an administrator remember which situational variables call for which orientation? For example, if it had been determined that a situation embodied good leader-member relations, high task structure, and weak position power, would the leader instantly remember whether the situation called for a people or a task orientation?

4. How does a leader respond when different situational leadership models call for conflicting style orientations? For example, the situation outlined in item 3 calls for a task-oriented style in Fiedler's (1967) model. Conceivably, if leader-member relations are good, there will be a willingness to achieve task goals, and with high task structure, skills necessary to accomplish the task are likely to be present. This would result in a high degree of follower maturity toward the task and call for both low people and low task orientation in Hersey and Blanchard's (1977) model. What degree of task orientation then does the leader use—high as suggested by Fiedler, or low as suggested by Hersey and Blanchard?

5. Can an individual's basic leadership style orientation be altered? Even if all of the obstacles cited can be surmounted, it is debatable whether an individual's basic orientation to be task-oriented or people-oriented can be changed. Undoubtedly, effective leaders will respond to different situations with different degrees of emphasis on task or people, but the variance is likely to one of degree rather than one of total orientation. In other words, strongly people-oriented leaders in situations where they are exhibiting their strongest degree of task orientation may well still be less task-oriented than task-oriented leaders in situations where they are exhibiting their least degree of task orientation.

ADDITIONAL LEADERSHIP STYLE CONSIDERATIONS

Additional considerations for leaders as they reflect on leadership style are the task and philosophical objectives of their interactions with others. Discussion about the task objective of school administration has frequently centered around the extent to which the school administrator's style is focused on management (for example, scheduling, budgeting, building maintenance) or upon instruction (for example, supervision of instruction, curriculum and program development). One seminal conceptualization of the philosophical objective of leadership interactions is the notion of transactional versus transformational leadership (Burns, 1978).

Management Oriented versus Instructionally Oriented

The school administrator's work has often been characterized as consisting of the dual tasks of managing the school building or district and providing instructional leadership. Chapter 2 provided a list of common school management tasks including operating school lunch programs, budgeting, purchasing, operating the school plant, scheduling, discipline, and administering policies. Instructional leadership frequently is associated with tasks such as curriculum development, program development, staff development, instructional supervision, program evaluation, and teacher evaluation. Although all administrators must engage in both management and instructional leadership tasks in order to fulfill their position requirements, most will emphasize an action disposition, or leadership style, that gives precedence to one type of task over the other.

The literature on school administration has frequently emphasized the importance of instructional leadership for school administrators. Smith and Andrews (1989), after a review of instructional leadership research, found that principals displaying strong instructional leadership:

- placed priority on curriculum and instruction;
- were dedicated to the goals of the school and district;
- had the ability to rally and mobilize resources to accomplish school goals;
- created a climate of high expectations and respect;
- were directly involved in school instructional policy;
- continually monitored student progress and teacher effectiveness in attaining it;
- demonstrated a commitment to academic goals developed through goal and vision setting;
- involved faculty and other groups in school decision processes; and
- protected instructional time by creating order and discipline, and minimizing disruptions of the learning process.

Additionally, the authors found a correlation between teachers perceptions of strong principal instructional leadership and high student academic achievement. In high achieving-strong instructional leadership schools, interactions between principals and teachers centered around the four areas of the principal as resource provider, as instructional resource, as communicator, and as visible presence.

Studies of principals, however, have shown that they (1) spend more time on management tasks than they think they do (Montgomery County Public Schools, 1975, cited in Campbell, Corbally, & Nystrand, 1983) and (2) would prefer to spend considerably more time on instructionally related matters (McCleary & Thomson, 1979). A number of reasons can be cited for the discrepancy between how principals are exhorted to spend their time and how they spend it.

- Administrative work has time constraints and is fragmented in nature.
- Realistically, principals are much more likely to be evaluated negatively or lose their jobs for being poor managers than for being poor instructional leaders.
- Evidence of results is less tangible for instructional tasks than for management tasks.

- There is less security and greater potential for conflict in dealing with people-oriented matters such as instruction than with thing-oriented matters such as management tasks.

- There is a lack of understanding about what constitutes the role of an instructional leader.

- There is a lack of skills to execute the tasks of the instructional leader's role.

An additional factor that has recently emerged is the perceived conflict between strong principal instructional leadership and teacher empowerment and autonomy. The recent emphasis on providing teachers a greater voice in school decisions has resulted in a call from some teachers for principals to leave instructional leadership to teachers. Those advocating this viewpoint argue that since teachers are most closely involved with instruction, they are likely to be the most knowledgeable about appropriate instructional decisions, policies, and practices, and are also most severely affected by them. Although this argument presents some valid points, it also assumes an adversarial "either-or" perspective. That is, it makes the assumption that instructional leadership must come from either the principal or the teachers. The challenge for principals is to determine how instructional leadership can come from both teachers and administrators.

Several recent studies imply that the predominance of time seemingly spent on management tasks may be partially the result of a too-narrow conceptualization of instructional leadership. The traditional conceptualization focuses only on behaviors directly tied to instruction and ignores the antecedents and consequences of the "undifferentiated jumble" of routine, fragmented interactions that constitute the majority of a principal's day (Dwyer, Barnett, & Lee, 1987).

A recent study found that there were no consistent differences in the types of instructional leadership activities in which effective versus less effective principals engaged. What did distinguish effective from less effective principals were the meanings they ascribed to their actions (Scott, Ahadi, & Krug, 1990). For example, whereas a less effective principal viewed monitoring the lunchroom as a strictly managerial function, the more effective principal viewed it as an opportunity to promote instructional improvement by informally recognizing students for achievement, communicating school goals to students, or checking with students on their achievement.

In essence, effective principals develop "overarching perspectives" of what they hope to accomplish in their schools and are able to connect the routine interactions and experiences of their day to the more global objectives they envision (Dwyer, Barnett, & Lee, 1987). They send symbolic messages to followers about what is instructionally important in the school via their actions in carrying out management and other routine noninstructional tasks (Reitzug & Reeves, 1992). For example, a principal's allocation of surplus budget funds to math manipulative materials sends a symbolic message that indicates instructional priorities that are very different from those that would have been highlighted had the money been allocated to phonics worksheet masters (or to new office furniture).

Unfortunately, many principals enter administration without having developed clear conceptions of what they value and how this might be reflected in their daily actions. Once they are embroiled in the daily, frantic routine of their positions, they become so caught up in responding to the many demands upon them that they do not take (or create) the opportunity to systematically reflect upon their practice. Later in this chapter, the importance of a systematically reflective approach to practice will be discussed.

Transactional versus Transformational

In his seminal work on leadership, Burns (1978) distinguished between two types of leadership interaction—transactional and transformational. Transactional leadership involves an exchange between leader and follower for purposes of achieving individual objectives. For example, a principal may agree to let a teacher attend a national reading conference in exchange for the teacher's work on a textbook-adoption committee. In this case, the individual objective of the principal to fill committee slots is achieved, as is the teacher's individual objective of being able to attend the conference. Bennis and Nanus (1985) have noted that much of the work in organizations is accomplished through transactional leadership where tasks are completed for rewards such as money, security, or other jobs. They argued that the level of commitment engendered by transactional leadership is compliance at best, and "spiteful obedience" at worst (p. 218).

In contrast to transactional leadership, transformational leadership is the pursuit of higher-level goals that are common to both leader and followers. There are two components to transformational leadership:

1. It elevates the motives of individuals toward a common goal.
2. It focuses on higher-order, intrinsic, and moral motives.

The notion of common goal commitment underlies the recently popular conceptions of organizational vision and culture. Vision has been described as "a blueprint of a desired state . . . an image of a preferred condition that we work to achieve in the future" (Sheive & Schoenheit, 1987, p. 94). An organization's culture consists of the beliefs, values, and assumptions for which the organization stands. A more homely description is "the way we do things around here" (Deal, 1987, p. 5). The assumption is that the way things are done reflects and is congruent with the values and beliefs for which the organization stands. Recent research on effective organizations and effective leaders has consistently cited strong visions and cultures as key characteristics (e.g., Blumberg & Greenfield, 1980; Peters & Waterman, 1982; Sheive & Schoenheit, 1987).

The natural progression from the identification of vision and culture as key effectiveness components has been to identify ways in which leaders can develop strong visions and cultures in their organizations. This has resulted in a backlash of criticism that the concepts have become just one more way for leaders to manipulate followers to achieve organizational goals. In fact, some have argued that culture-building behaviors are morally less appropriate than more autocratic forms of achieving organizational goals, since they constitute a more subtle and more pervasive form of control that attempts to control mental as well as physical processes (Bates, 1987; Foster, 1986). Those arguing in favor of culture-building behaviors would question whether it is better for organizations to believe in something and reflect those beliefs, or to believe in nothing and reflect happenstance reaction to daily life.

Central to the moral appropriateness of culture-building behaviors are questions of process and substance. Specifically, what process is used to determine what the organization's core beliefs and values are to be? Second, what is the substance of the core beliefs and values?

The question of process contains several potentially problematic elements. Should the vision be determined by the leader and articulated and "sold" to followers? Or should the vision be created with input from all organizational members? If the former is the case, what happens when there are severe discrepancies between the leader's vision and followers' visions? If the latter is the case, how does one reach consensus without a resulting product that is so watered down that it does not mean anything, or so inclusive that it provides no focus?

Simply satisfying process issues and holding a common goal is insufficient to ensuring moral appropriateness or transformation. The point has been made that *democratic processes* do not justify *undemocratic ends* such as inequitable or dominance relationships (Quantz, Cambron-McCabe, & Dantley, 1990). For example, maintaining the economic superiority of our nation over Japan is unlikely to promote moral commitment. Nor is the currently popular goal of achieving higher standardized test scores likely to qualify.

For leadership to be transformational, the substance of organizational beliefs and values must show a concern for higher-order, intrinsic, and moral motives. Transformation implies change. To engender commitment, the change must be an improvement over current affairs that appeals to the heart as well as the head. Sergiovanni (1991) noted that to be morally elevating, leadership must be concerned with psychological needs for esteem, autonomy, and self-actualization, and moral needs such as goodness, righteousness, duty, and obligation.

The concept of transformational leadership is nested in a larger debate regarding whether the purpose of schooling should be the transmission and reproduction of the existing culture, or the empowerment of individuals to transform existing unjust and inequitable components of society. Critical theorists hold that current society is characterized by inequitable relationships between races, social classes, and genders, and that societal institutions serve to reinforce these inequitable relationships. For example, they argue that textbooks used in schools present the "correct" world view of the dominant upper- and middle-class culture and either ignore minority viewpoints or relegate them to inferior status. Those embracing this viewpoint advocate that rather than passing on cultural knowledge, schools should begin with the personal cultural knowledge individuals bring with them and then empower them to "appropriate knowledge" outside their immediate experience for purposes of "transforming the taken-for-granted assumptions about the way we live" (McLaren, 1989, p. 186).

What does all this mean for school administrators and what implications does it have for the practice of those who wish to move from a transactionally dominated leadership style to one that is more transformational? Logically, before students can be helped to challenge the taken-for-granted assumptions with which they live, teachers and administrators must examine, challenge, and transform the assumptions that guide their practice as educators. Sirotnik (1989) has suggested that this might be accomplished by making schools "centers of inquiry and change" (p. 107). One suggested way of accomplishing this is by making schools action research centers where (1) individual teachers study their personal professional practice not for purposes of generalizing to a more universal audience, but simply for the sake of improving their practice, and (2) faculties engage in dialogue about school-wide policies and practices related to teaching and learning, asking such questions as "What are we doing now? How did it come to be that way? . . . Whose interests are (and are not) being served by the way things are? . . . What information and knowledge do we have (or need to get) that bears upon the issues?" (Sirotnik, 1989, pp. 99–100). The next section on reflective practice provides additional detail on how principals might facilitate this in schools.

THE ART OF REFLECTIVE PRACTICE

It should be evident to the reader at this stage that leadership includes many challenges and great complexity. By now you are probably wondering about the practical and ethical issues of decision making, change, communication, and motivation. As a prospective administrator, you may be examining your assumptions about administrative roles, styles, forms of governance, directiveness, and interaction with followers. You may be wondering how you will know which style is most appropriate for a given situation. Additionally, you may be curious about how you develop an "overarching framework," and how you transform your school into a "center of inquiry and change."

Unfortunately, no easy answers are available for your ponderings. However, the complexity and ambiguity of professional practice has caused an increasing number of scholars and practitioners to abandon purely rational, scientific searches for nonexistent solutions, and turn to studying the residues of art and craft in education and administration (Blumberg, 1989; Eisner, 1983). Simultaneously, the concept of reflective practice has received much attention (e.g., Schon, 1983, 1989, 1990; Sergiovanni, 1991).

As professionals engage in the daily routine actions of their practice they frequently cannot describe how they know what to do next or why they take the actions they do. They are guided by an embedded, tacit knowledge of their practice. Occasionally, however, they must improvise or modify their routine actions in response to external stimuli. For example, teachers make on-the-spot adjustments in their lesson plans or their line of questioning, based on immediately prior student responses. When this occurs, the professional is engaging in reflection-in-action (Schon, 1989).

Over time, professionals encounter certain types or elements of situations on a recurring basis. They build an implicit repertoire of techniques and strategies for responding to these elements. Simultaneously, they develop a mental image of expected outcomes for their actions. When things go as planned and expected results materialize, no further thought is given to the event. However, occasionally surprises occur. Expected results do not materialize and outcomes are incongruent with what has previously occurred in seemingly similar situations. These unexpected results trigger both reflection-in-action and reflection-on-action, causing the individual to reflect on what is causing the unanticipated consequences both as they are occurring and later, after the heat of the moment has dissipated. The individual contemplates questions of how the situation compares with past similar experiences, ways in which it was the same and different, and what may have affected altered outcomes in this situation from previous, seemingly similar situations.

Frequently, the focus in reflective practice must shift from problem solving to problem definition. The perceived apparent problem in a situation may not be the real or the only problem. The apparent problem in the example provided at the beginning of this chapter deals with the perceived low academic standards in Mrs. Smith's room. Potentially, the real problem may be any of a number of other things ranging from a misunderstanding of Mrs. Smith's standards and methodology to the provocative way in which she dresses. Obviously, the way problems are defined has a direct effect on the alternative solutions that are generated and on the degree of success those solutions are likely to experience. If Mrs. Smith's manner of dress is the problem, an improvement in her teaching skills will make little impact on solving the problem!

Schon (1989) took the concept of problem definition a step further, arguing that leaders need to be as concerned with problem finding as with problem solving. The question, he wrote, may not be "how to pour concrete for the highway, but what highway makes sense?" (p. 190). A school-based example might suggest that the frequently addressed problem, "How do we raise standardized test scores?" might alternately be defined as, "Why do we want to raise standardized test scores?" or "What measures of school effectiveness make sense?"

A Heuristic for Reflective Practice

Teachers and administrators are likely to acknowledge that they have always thought informally about their practice both as they were engaged in it and perhaps as they drove home from work in the evening, but that they simply never knew that the label for what they were doing was "reflective practice." They may wonder, "Now that I know what it is called, so what?" Indeed, one of the difficulties with the concept of reflective practice has been that, although it helps explain how professionals think about their practice, some have found it to have little practical utility. This section will present a heuristic for how administrators (and teachers) can use reflection to more systematically examine their practice.

The reflective practice heuristic[2] centers on (1) an examination of an event and (2) thoughts that occurred prior to, during, and after the event. What distinguishes it from the informal reflection in which many practitioners engage is the addition of more a formal postevent reflective period. (The reader is urged to refer to Figure 10–2 throughout the discussion of the heuristic.)

Imagine that a particular event and an individual's thoughts related to the event could be separated into boxes. The first box would contain the individual's plan for how he or she intended to respond to an event and his or her thoughts during this planning period. In many cases this planning period may have consisted of only a few seconds or minutes prior to an unexpected event. In other cases, it may be more extensive, such as when a teacher plans a lesson for the following day.

The second box would contain a "script" of the actual event and the thoughts that occurred during it. In a sense, this box can be conceived of as containing not only audio and visual images of what occurred but also mental images.

The third box would contain the thoughts about the event that occurred during a more formal, planned reflective period—a "debriefing"—taking place subsequent to the event. Included in the third box are (a) the spontaneous reflections that occurred about the event after it had occurred (for example, subconscious thoughts about an interaction with a student while walking down the hall, sitting in the faculty lounge, or driving home at night) and (b) thoughts and insights that occur as the individual explores the contents of the first two boxes during the debriefing.

---

[2] The refelctive practice heuristic is adapted from Cornett (1990), and Reitzug and Cornett (1991).

FIGURE 10–2   A Heuristic Model for Reflective Practice

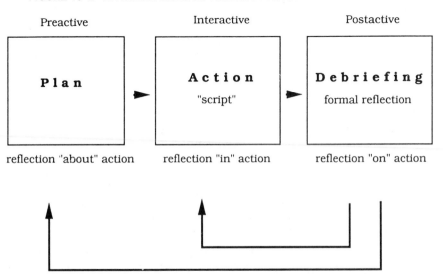

In order to systematize reflection and make it more professionally informing, the more formal, postevent reflective session is essential. Procedurally, the session would begin by recapturing as much of the detail of planning and the actual event as possible (boxes 1 and 2). Video- or audiotaping, where appropriate, would serve to capture an audio and visual record of the event and serve as a stimulus to recall the mental record.

Subsequently, postevent reflections occurring shortly after the event would be recalled. After these first two steps had been accomplished, the reflective practitioner would (a) record his or her thoughts about the event now that it had percolated for awhile, and (b) record any additional thoughts, observations, or insights that occurred during the completion of boxes 1 and 2 (box 3).

Additionally, a variety of other, more specific factors can be examined during the debriefing. For example, the individual could examine the role contextual factors and personal beliefs had played in the event. Dwyer, Barnett, and Lee (1987) cited the importance of factors such as community locale, socioeconomic status, ethnic composition, transiency, parent support, institutional context factors, and personal beliefs and experiences as strongly influencing principal behavior. Using this set of factors, questions that the reflective practitioner might ask include:

- During the event, of which community and institutional factors was I aware? Which did I take into consideration? Which influenced my actions? Did I identify any additional contextual factors while reflecting-on-action (box 3)? Which factors am I aware of now that I was not previously? Which other factors conceivably could have been relevant?

- What beliefs did my actions reflect? Are the reflected beliefs congruent with my espoused beliefs? If not, are my espoused beliefs or the beliefs reflected by my actions responsible for the incongruency? How could I have acted more congruently with my espoused beliefs? How should I modify my espoused beliefs to become congruent with my actions?

An additional piece of the debriefing session should involve problem restatement and the generation of alternative solutions. Questions the reflective practitioner would ask during this exercise would be:

- How did I define the problem in this situation? Does this seem to be the apparent problem? Is it the only problem, or are there other related problems? How else might the problem be defined? Are there political, ethical, or moral problems involved?

- What was my response to the situation? How else might I have responded? How could I respond to the alternative ways in which the problem can be defined?

Although formal postaction reflective sessions may seem cumbersome and undoubtedly are time-consuming, they need not be done daily. Even occasional use is likely to yield insights into practice and help practitioners become sensitive to relevant contextual factors. A focus on the congruency between personal beliefs and actions may facilitate the development of vision and "overarching frameworks" that previously have been noted to be of prime importance in effective leadership.

Additionally, postaction reflective sessions need not always be an add-on to busy days. They can serve as a framework for principals and teachers to use for supervision of instruction or for formal teacher or administrator evaluation. The inclusion of personal beliefs as a key factor in informing behavior recognizes and honors the professionalism of the individual much more than is possible with rationalistic, technically based observation and evaluation forms. On a school-wide basis, the heuristic can serve as a framework to examine congruency of school-wide policies and practices with school goals, values, beliefs, and assumptions.

IMPLICATIONS FOR PRACTICE

This section of the book has explored the style orientations from which leaders respond to the challenges and complexity of leadership. Several concepts have emerged from the discussion that can be connected in a manner that is useful for prospective school leaders. (See Figure 10-3.)

It seems evident that effective leaders must have a clearly defined set of beliefs about the purposes of schooling and what they hope to accomplish as school leaders.

FIGURE 10-3 A Model of School Leadership Connecting Overarching Frameworks, Symbolic Leadership, Organizational Culture, and Organizational Vision

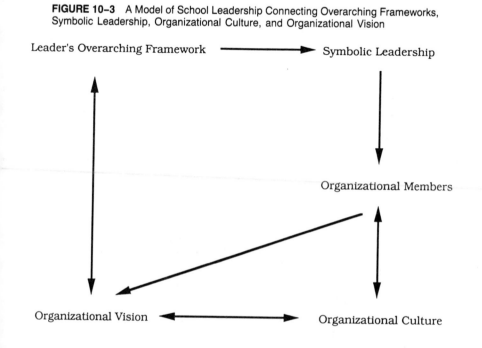

This *overarching framework* informs their routine and nonroutine daily actions and serves as a connecting glue for seemingly disjointed events and interactions. As a result, school leaders communicate their values and beliefs about schooling to followers not only through verbal articulation but also through the symbolic messages they send through their responses to everyday events. Sergiovanni (1991), in discussing this form of *symbolic leadership,* noted, "Very often it is the little things that count. One does not have to mount a white horse and charge forward in a grand dramatic event in order to be a symbolic leader. Simple routines and humble actions . . . can communicate very important messages and high ideas" (p. 107). The heuristic discussed in the previous section serves as a resource in helping leaders examine the congruency between their beliefs and their daily actions, and as a result develop and refine overarching frameworks of school purpose.

The symbolic messages that leaders send about what is important in the school shape the *organizational culture* of the school by indicating to followers what is important. If the messages sent by the leader are acceptable to followers, future actions of followers will be guided by these values and beliefs. In turn, the values and beliefs will gain even greater strength in the school's culture. Thus, organizational culture both shapes behavior and is shaped by behavior.

Studies of outstanding organizations have consistently found that they are characterized by a clear *organizational vision* that is known and held by all organizational members. A key piece to the success of this leadership model is congruency between the leader's personal vision, followers' visions, the organizational vision of the school, and the school's culture. That is, the policies, practices, and "way things are done" (i.e., the school's culture) should be consistent with the values and beliefs that are jointly held by leader and followers. If this is not the case, leaders will be marching in their own parade, and followers will be confused about which route they should take—the one they think is correct, the one the leader says is correct, the one others say is correct, or the one on which everyone seems to be marching.

Indeed, congruency among all four pieces of this model—overarching framework, symbolic leadership, culture, and vision—is essential. This requires continual examination on the part of individuals and the organization as a whole of beliefs, values, and assumptions, and how they match with organizational policy and daily practice.

Each component of this model raises issues for school leaders. For example, leaders must address questions such as What are the implications of my overarching framework for my daily practice? How does my overarching framework inform my responses to routine and nonroutine actions? Are the symbolic messages being sent to followers manipulating them to adopt my way as the best way? What role does "their way" play? Is the vision I am promoting my vision, or the organization's vision? Does the culture of the school reflect the vision, or do we think we believe one thing but reflect another in the way we do things?

It may seem to the reader that the past two chapters about leadership have raised more questions than they have provided answers. To have done otherwise would have done an injustice to a concept and practice as complex as leadership. It was not the authors' intent to resolve issues of leadership for the reader, since over 5,000 past studies have not accomplished this (Bass, 1981). Rather, the intent can be accurately expressed in the words of one anonymous sage, "I am still confused . . . but my confusion is now on a higher level."

FOR FURTHER DISCUSSION

1. Some studies have indicated that a people-oriented leadership style results in greater employee satisfaction, but that task orientation results in greater productivity. Do you think it is justifiable for a leader to achieve greater organizational productivity at the expense of the satisfaction of the employees of the organization?

2. What strategies can leaders pursue when their goals for the school or school district are consistently different from the goals of their followers?

3. Do you think it is possible for individuals to modify their leadership style based on situational factors, or do you feel that leadership style is ingrained, similar to one's personality?

4. What do you feel are the key contextual factors that inform which leadership style is most appropriate for a situation?

5. What do you feel is a principal's prime responsibility—school management or instructional leadership? Is a superintendent's prime responsibility school district management or instructional leadership? Support your answers.

6. Do you feel the purposes of schooling should be reproduction or transformation of culture?

7. Should the vision of a school be determined by the school administrator and "sold" to subordinates, or should all members of the organization be involved in setting the vision? What are the advantages and disadvantages of each approach?

8. Does your school have a vision? How do you know? Cite some examples of how school policies and practices reflect the vision.

9. From your past informal observation of your principal or superintendent, what would you deduce are his or her values, beliefs, and assumptions about school purpose? How does this compare with your and your colleagues' values, beliefs, and assumptions about school purpose?

OTHER SUGGESTED ACTIVITIES

1. Analyze your personal leadership style. Do you perceive yourself to be more people- or task-oriented? more democratic or authoritarian? directive or nondirective? Check with several of your colleagues to determine whether their perceptions of you match your own.

2. Analyze the leadership style of your superiors. Chart several of their actions and classify them in terms of people, task, democratic, authoritarian, directive, and nondirective dimensions.

3. Examine a decision you recently made to determine which contextual factors influenced your people-task orientation, degree of authoritarianism, and directiveness.

4. Study several interactions between school administrators and their subordinates. Do transactional or transformational interactions dominate?

5. In one paragraph, attempt to state your overarching framework for schooling.

6. Use the reflective practice heuristic to study your teaching or administrative decision making for several events. Study how the overarching framework you developed in item 5 is reflected in your actions.

7. List several problems that you or your school have faced recently and actions that have been taken in response to each problem. Develop alternative statements of the problem and generate solutions for these alternative problem statements.

REFERENCES

Bass, B. M. (1981). *Stodgill's handbook of leadership.* New York: Macmillan.

Bates, R. J. (1987). Corporate culture, schooling, and educational administration. *Educational Administration Quarterly,* 23 (4), 79–115.

Bennis, W. B., & Nanus, B. (1985). *Leaders: The strategies for taking charge.* New York: Harper & Row.

Blumberg, A. (1989). *School administration as a craft: Foundations of practice.* Boston: Allyn and Bacon.

Blumberg, A., & Greenfield, W. (1980). *The effective principal: Perspectives on school leadership.* Boston: Allyn and Bacon.

Bowers, D. G. (1977). *Systems of organization: Management of human resources.* Ann Arbor: University of Michigan Press.

Burns, J. M. (1978). *Leadership.* New York: Harper & Row.

Campbell, R. E., Corbally, J. E., & Nystrand, R. O. (1983). *Introduction to educational administration* (6th ed.). Boston: Allyn and Bacon.

Cornett, J. W. (1990). Utilizing action research in graduate curriculum courses. *Theory into Practice,* 29 (3), 185–195.

Deal, T. E. (1987). The culture of schools. In L. T. Sheive & M. B. Schoenheit (Eds.), *Leadership: Examining the elusive* (pp. 3–15). Reston, VA: Association for Supervision and Curriculum Development.

Duke, D. L., Showers, B. K., & Imber, M. (1980). Teachers and shared decision-making: The costs and benefits of involvement. *Educational Administration Quarterly,* 16 (1), 93–106.

Dwyer, D. C., Barnett, B. G., & Lee, G. V. (1987). The school principal: Scapegoat or the last great hope? In L. T. Sheive & M. B. Schoenheit (Eds.), *Leadership: Examining the elusive* (pp. 30–46). Reston, VA: Association for Supervision and Curriculum Development.

Eisner, E. (1983). The art and craft of teaching. *Educational Leadership,* 40 (4), 4–13.

Fiedler, F. E. (1967). *A theory of leadership effectiveness.* New York: McGraw Hill.

Fleishman, E. A., & Harris, E. F. (1962). Patterns of leadership behavior related to employee grievances and turnover. *Personnel Psychology,* 15, 43–56.

Foster, W. (1986). *Paradigms and promises: New approaches to educational administration.* Buffalo, NY: Prometheus Books.

Halpin, A. W. (1966). *Theory and research in administration.* New York: Macmillan.

Hersey, P., & Blanchard, K. H. (1977). *Management of organizational behavior: Utilizing human resources* (3rd ed.). Englewood Cliffs, NJ: Prentice-Hall.

House, R. J. (1971). A path-goal theory of leader effectiveness. *Administrative Science Quarterly,* 16, 321–338.

House, R. J., & Baetz, M. L. (1979). Leadership: Some empirical generalizations and new research directions. In B. Straw (Ed.), *Research in organizational behavior,* Vol. 1 (pp. 341–423). Greenwich, CT: JAI Press.

House, R. J., & Dressler, G. (1974). The path-goal theory of leadership: Some post hoc and a priori tests. In J. G. Hunt & L. L. Larson (eds.), *Contingency approaches to leadership* (pp. 29–62). Carbondale: Southern Illinois University Press.

Immegart, G. L. (1988). Leadership and leader behavior. In N. J. Boyan (Ed.), *Handbook of research on educational administration* (pp. 259–277). New York: Longman.

Jago, A. G. (1982). Leadership: Perspectives in theory and research. *Management Science, 28* (3), 315–336.

Kutner, B. (1950). Elements and problems of democratic leadership. In A. W. Gouldner (Ed.), *Studies in leadership: Leadership and democratic action,* pp. 459–467.

Lewin, K., Lippitt, R., & White, R. K. (1939). Patterns of aggressive behavior in experimentally created "social climates." *Journal of Social Psychology,* 10, 271–299.

McCleary, L. E., & Thomson, S. D. (1979). *The senior high school principalship.* Vol. III: *The summary report.* Reston, VA: National Association of Secondary School Principals.

McLaren, P. (1989). *Life in schools: An introduction to critical pedagogy in the foundations of education.* New York: Longman.

Montgomery County Public Schools (1975). *Report of findings of a study of the principalship in action in the Montgomery County Public Schools.* Rockville, MD: Author.

Muczyk, J. P., & Reimann, B. C. (1989). The case for directive leadership. In R. L. Taylor & W. E. Rosenbach (eds.), *Leadership: Challenges for today's manager* (pp. 89–108). New York: Nichols Publishing.

Peters, T. J., & Waterman, R. H. (1982). *In search of excellence: Lessons from America's best-run companies.* New York: Warner Books.

Quantz, R. A., Cambron-McCabe, N., & Dantley, M. (1990). Preparing school administrators for democratic authority: A critical approach to graduate education. *The Urban Review* 24 (3), 243–262.

Reitzug, U. C., & Cornett, J. W. (1991). Teacher and administrator thought: Implications for administrator training. *Planning and Changing,* 21 (3), 181–192.

Reitzug, U. C., & Reeves, J. E. (1992). "Miss Lincoln doesn't teach here": A descriptive narrative and conceptual analysis of a principal's symbolic leadership behavior. *Educational Administration Quarterly* 28 (2), 185–219.

Schon, D. A. (1983). *The reflective practitioner.* New York: Basic Books.

———. (1989). Professional knowledge and reflective practice. In T. J. Sergiovanni & J. H. Moore (eds.), *Schooling for tomorrow: Directing reforms to issues that count* (pp. 188–206). Boston: Allyn and Bacon.

———. (1990). *Educating the reflective practitioner.* San Francisco: Jossey-Bass.

Schriesheim, C. S., House, R. J., & Kerr, S. (1976). Leader initiating structure: A reconciliation of discrepant research results and some empirical tests. *Organizational Behavior and Human Performance,* 15, 197–321.

Scott, C., Ahadi, S., & Krug, S. E. (1990). *An experience sampling approach to the study of principal instructional leadership II: A comparison of activities and beliefs as bases for understanding effective school leadership.* Urbana: The National Center for School Leadership, University of Illinois.

Sergiovanni, T. J. (1991). *The principalship: A reflective practice perspective.* Needham Heights, MA: Allyn and Bacon.

Sheive, L. T., & Schoenheit, M. B. (1987). Vision and the work life of educational leaders. In L. T. Sheive & M. B. Schoenheit (eds.), *Leadership: Examining the elusive* (pp. 93–104). Reston, VA: Association for Supervision and Curriculum Development.

Sirotnik, K. A. (1989). The school as the center of change. In T. J. Sergiovanni & J. H. Moore (eds.), *Schooling for tomorrow: Directing reforms to issues that count* (pp. 89–113). Boston: Allyn and Bacon.

Smith, W. F., & Andrews, R. A. (1989). *Instructional leadership: How principals make a difference.* Alexandria, VA: Association for Supervision and Curriculum Development.

Stodgill, R. M., & Coons, A. E. (1957). *Leader behavior: Its description and measurement.* Columbus: Bureau of Business Research, The Ohio State University.

Vroom, V. H., & Yetton, P. W. (1973). *Leadership and decision-making.* Pittsburgh: University of Pittsburgh Press.

PART **IV**

Contemporary Issues

CHAPTER 11

American Society in Transition

Chapter Content

Present-day school administrators are a graying profession. Demographers forecast a large number of position openings in school administration in the next decade due to school administrators who are currently in their fifties or early sixties. These graying professionals have been called on to respond to the vast changes that have occurred in American society since the days when they went to school and commenced their educational careers.

Consider, for example, today's fifty-year-old school administrator. This individual attended elementary and secondary school in the period between World War II and the late 1950s. This was a period of great prosperity in America. Socially, we had not yet confronted the Kennedy and King assassinations; we had only begun to be embroiled in racial strife and confrontation; and the nation had not yet been torn asunder by the Vietnam war. The typical American family of this era consisted of a working father, a stay-at-home mother, and two children. The father was likely to have a high school education and work in a local factory, making adequate wages to comfortably support his family. The American dream of a ranch-style home in the suburbs was widely affordable. The entire family frequently gathered around the television set in the evening to view their favorite program. It was likely that the family lived in the northern half of the United

States, and, if they took a long vacation trip, it might well be to a location in the southern half of the United States.

A common problem that faced school administrators of this era was dealing with the occasional ruffians who engaged in a fist fight. Other than that, keeping the school lavatories smoke-free was the most significant problem. Students generally came to school healthy, well-dressed, well-fed, and respectful.

Anyone who has recently visited today's urban school or worked with children and adolescents from the typical American family of the 1990s, is aware of the differences that characterize today's schools and students. Not only must graying administrators address a myriad of problems that are complex under any circumstances, they must do so from the perspective of someone who grew up in a society and culture that could at best be described as alien to that of today's youth.

This chapter will discuss the nature of changes that have occurred in American society. An extensive demographic portrait of society and the life-world of today's youth will be presented. The responses schools have made to societal changes will be discussed as well as implications and suggestions for future responses.

A CHANGING SOCIETY

Fertility Rates

In 1790, 5 percent of the U.S. population lived in urban areas; by 1890, the proportion of urban dwellers increased to 35 percent; and by 1990, the figure reached 70 percent (Kimbrough & Nunnery, 1988).

In addition to becoming increasingly urban, our country has also become increasingly populated by minority group members. Although nonwhites make up only 16 percent of the U.S. population, they accounted for almost 50 percent of nation's population growth between 1980 and 1990. It is projected that between 1990 and 2010, the nonwhite component of the U.S. youth population will increase from 30 percent to 38 percent. In fact, twelve states will contain almost half of U.S. youth and eight of these will have youth minority majorities (Hodgkinson, 1991a).

The increasing minority representation in our society has been mirrored in public schools. According to one source, minority group members made up 38.7 percent of public school enrollment in 1989 (Education vital signs, 1991). Some urban school districts have even larger percentages of minority group students attending their schools. For example, school districts in Atlanta, Washington DC, Newark, and San Antonio have over 90 percent minority enrollment (Tanner, 1989). Recently, the fastest-growing minority group in public schools has been Asian students, whose school population increased 40 percent between 1976 and 1986 compared with a 13.2 percent growth rate among Hispanics, the second fastest growing group.

The reason for the continued growth of minority populations can be understood when one looks at fertility rates. Hispanics have the highest fertility rate with an average of 86.1 births per 1,000 women, followed by blacks[1] with a rate of 72.2 births per 1,000 women. Whites have the lowest birth rate at 64.6 births per 1,000 women. Hispanics are also the youngest subgroup with a median age of 25.0 compared with 26.3 for blacks and 32.2 for whites (McKay, 1986). The high fertility rates, young median age (resulting in a large number of women of child-bearing age), and high immigration rates, ensure continued growth in the Hispanic population.

Birth rates may have less to do with minority group membership than with socioeconomic status. Low-income groups have the highest fertility rate, with the "short cycle" family being a prime cause. The short cycle family is one in which females give birth to their first child at a very young age with their daughters also producing offspring at a young age so that there may be only fifteen years between generations. These families are almost always poverty families.

Immigration has also had a significant impact on the make-up of the American population. More immigrants now come to the United States than ever before, and these immigrants are coming from different geographic locations than immigrants during previous generations. Whereas in 1910 89 percent of U.S. immigrants were European, currently Europeans make up only 10 percent of new immigrants. Immigration policy during the 1970s and 1980s has focused on reuniting families that already had some members residing in the United States. This has resulted in Asians and Hispanics being the largest immigration groups (America's changing face, 1990). Many adult immigrants from this group are low skilled and their children frequently have language difficulties (The hunt for new Americans, 1990). Others are kept from employment for which they are qualified by credential requirements and must accept lower-level work.

Language difficulties may partially explain why Hispanics are the most undereducated major group of Americans. Many Hispanic students are placed in lower tracks early in their school careers before they have mastered the English language. Frequently they get stuck in these tracks even after they are able to do higher-level work.

Currently, 39.5 percent of the Hispanic students are enrolled below the modal grade for their age compared to 37.3 percent of blacks and 24.9 percent of whites (Orum, 1986). In 1984, the median number of school years completed by Hispanics twenty-five and over was 11.3 compared to 12.2 for blacks and 12.6 for whites. Only 8.2 percent of Hispanics had completed four or more years of college compared to 10.4 percent of blacks and 19.8 percent of whites. Additionally, 29.8 percent of Hispanics had completed less than eight years of school compared to 15.7 percent of blacks and 6.7 percent of whites (McKay, 1986).

Hispanic children are also less likely to be put into gifted or honors classes than white or black students. In 1978, only 5 percent of students in gifted or honors classes were Hispanic, although at that time they made up 6.8 percent of the school population. Compare these figure with those for white students who, according to one source, make up 75.3 percent of the total school population, but comprised 81.0 percent of the students in these classes (Orum, 1986).

---

[1] Term used here is as reported in demographic references.

Geographic Population Shifts

Over the past decade there has been a steady migration of population from northern and eastern parts of the United States to the southern and western parts. This movement has been due, in part, to economic misfortunes of northern and eastern industries devoted heavily to manufacturing and, specifically, affiliated with the auto industry. Many automobile plants and auto-related manufacturers laid off thousands of workers due to several periods of economic recession, the affordability and availability of Japanese automobiles perceived to be of higher quality, and increasing automation and use of robotics in factories. This downsizing continues; General Motors recently announced a long-term plan of laying off thousands of assembly line workers and middle management personnel.

The loss of jobs caused many laid-off workers to pursue sunnier climates and economic fortunes. This has resulted in the continued growth of warm- weather states and decline of population in northern and eastern states. Hodgkinson (1991a) has noted that 90 percent of the 23 million increase in the U.S. population between 1980 and 1990 occurred in the South and West. Texas, Florida, and California accounted for almost half of the nation's growth. All three of these states have large ethnic populations. Whereas southern and western states continue to gain population, population in other states has stabilized recently due to decreased out-migration.

The shift in population from one part of the country to another has caused problems for school administrators. Administrators in areas of population decline have been faced with closing schools and downsizing programs. For example, the school district in Anderson, Indiana, a community tied heavily to auto-related industries, has seen student population decline from approximately 20,000 students to its current level of just over 10,000 students. This has resulted in emotional battles to close a number of schools, steeped in tradition but located in sections of the community hardest hit by out-migration. Although staff has been reduced through attrition, teachers' contracts and the effort to maintain positive labor relations with the teachers' association have resulted in schools that are overstaffed. With the largest item in school district budgets being personnel costs (usually 70 to 85 percent), overstaffing has resulted in financial difficulties for the district. Compounding financial problems is the fact that the downsizing and flight of auto-related industries has significantly lowered the property tax base of the district. With local school funds making up approximately 50 percent of total school funding and property taxes being the dominant source of local funds, administrators have had to battle financial problems and placate the public while continuing to try to improve the education of students.

School administrators in high-growth states and districts are confronted by a different set of problems. For example, the Orlando, Florida area has seen tremendous growth since the opening of Disney World two decades ago. The once-sleepy community has been transformed into a bustling, major metropolitan area in a relatively short period of time.

The tremendous growth has created major problems for all public services, including schools. Many school districts in the area have doubled in size every few years. Funding does not exist to construct schools at the rate needed to keep up with the exponential growth. Existing funding frequently is tied up in extensive state regulation and bureaucracy. As a result, many schools are so overcrowded that a number of severe measures are necessary. Many schools have subdivided single classrooms into multiple classrooms, essentially squeezing twice the number of students as desirable into spaces. Others have converted stage areas into classrooms, or even held classes in hallways. Not only does this limit instructional delivery, but it may also result in other deleterious effects that psychologists have observed in people when they inhabit overcrowded areas.

Other responses to overcrowded school conditions have included double sessions and year-round schooling. Double sessions resemble a two-shift factory model, with one group of students attending from early in the morning until early afternoon (e.g., 7 AM to 12:30 PM) and the second shift attending from early afternoon until early evening (e.g., 12:45 PM to 6:15 PM). Year-round schooling does not mean that an individual student attends school all year long, but rather that the school is more fully utilized during the summer months by reconfiguring the school calendar so that groups of students are in attendance all twelve months of the year. Essentially, year-round schooling permits schools to increase their capacity by one-third by utilizing the three summer months. Each set of responses has brought with it a series of related problems, not the least of which has been parent opposition to forms of schooling that violate the traditional mode of schooling with which they grew up.

An Information Society

American society has changed in ways other than demographic make-up during the past several decades. Perhaps the most significant labor force change during that period has been the shift from a manufacturing base to an information, service orientation. Between 1979 and 1985, 1.7 million manufacturing jobs were lost. One projection placed manufacturing jobs at 9 percent of the labor force in the year 2000, down from 24 percent in 1984 (Cetron & Rocha, 1988). Conversely, nearly 75 percent of U.S. workers currently are employed in service jobs, up from 55 percent in 1948. It has been estimated that service jobs will account for 88 percent of the workforce by the year 2000.

Many jobs in the service industry are part-time and low-paying and have replaced high-paying manufacturing jobs. However, there are two segments to the service economy: personal services (e.g., hair stylists) and information services (e.g., bankers, insurance agents, lawyers, journalists) (Wright, 1990). It is in the latter segment that growth has occurred, and these positions generally have a somewhat higher rate of pay than personal service positions.

As might be concluded, most information service positions have a "voracious appetite for information technology" (Wright, 1990, p. 84). For example, the information content of a piece of pizza (i.e., advertising, legal expenses, and so on) accounts for a larger percentage of its cost than does the edible content (Wright, 1990). One high-ranking official at AT&T has noted that they are in the IM&M business—information movement and management (Wright, 1990).

The implication for schools is that information processing and computer proficiency have become the new basics. Information processing includes skills such as research, thinking, problem solving, and decision making (Caissey, 1990).

THE NEW AMERICAN YOUTH

Changing demographic patterns have implications for school management and the shift to an information society affects curriculum; changes in the lives of American children and adolescents also have pervasive implications for schools. The set of elements that shape a child's experiences include the level of family income, parental employment, family structure, racial and ethnic background, health care, availability of alcohol or drugs, and family support systems such as child care or mental health services. These have changed significantly in recent years (Kirst & McLaughlin, 1990).

Compared to previous generations, today's young people are more likely to come from a family living below the poverty level, underperform at school, commit suicide, need psychiatric help, suffer a severe eating disorder, bear a child out of wedlock, take drugs, and be a victim of violent crime (Hewlett, 1991). In fact, an index that measures the social health of children has declined from 68 in 1970 to 37 in 1987 (Hewlett, 1991).

Consider what *Time* magazine calls our "legacy" to youth in America. Every day in America 6 teenagers commit suicide, 9 children or adolescents die because of guns, 27 children die because of poverty, 206 young people are arrested for a drug offense, 1,375 teenagers drop out of school, 1,849 children are abused, 2,740 teenagers get pregnant, 2,987 young people's parents divorce, 3,288 run away from home, and 135,000 bring guns to school (Everyday in America, 1991; Gibbs, 1990). Additionally, in our society a violent crime is committed every twenty-five seconds, a murder every twenty-eight minutes, a rape every six minutes, and a robbery every minute (Kimbrough & Nunnery, 1988).

About one-third of America's youth are destined for school failure due to poverty, neglect, sickness, handicap, or lack of adult protection and nurturance (Hodgkinson, 1991). Essentially, these children have the deck stacked against them before they even begin school. Their problems have not gone unnoticed by the nation's teachers. A recent survey commissioned by the Metropolitan Life Insurance Company indicated that prior to their first year of teaching, 75 percent of teachers believed many students are too overwhelmed by family and other outside problems to succeed in class. After their first year of teaching, this figure had increased to 89 percent (The American teacher 1990, 1990).

Hodgkinson (1991a) used the analogy of a leaky roof to discuss the educational status of American schools. He likened the tremendous changes that have occurred in the conditions of childhood and the responses of schools to a building with a leaky roof. Schools have fixed the plaster, the electricity, and the windows through reforms such as higher academic standards and longer school years but have neglected to fix the roof. However, until we fix the roof, our work will be for naught since the next rain will ruin the new plaster and the effects of other repairs. Similarly, until we pay attention to the conditions of childhood, "tinkering with the rest of the house will continue to produce no important results" (p. 10). Hodgkinson noted that the conditions of childhood are not an educational problem; rather, they are a societal problem. Educators cannot fix the roof by themselves—a total and collaborative effort by all societal agencies is necessary.

The Changing Family

Contributing greatly to the changing conditions of childhood is the nature of today's family. The archetypical nuclear family of the 1950s—a working father and stay-at-home mother—has given way to various other arrangements. In fact, the traditional family structure currently comprises fewer than one-third of families (Kirst & McLaughlin, 1990).

Perhaps the most significant change in family structure is the increase in single-parent families. In 1990 there were 9.7 million single parents in the United States, a 41 percent increase since 1980 and a 257 percent jump since 1970. In fact, single-parent families are quickly becoming the modal family structure for America's youth. Hodgkinson (1991a) noted that almost 50 percent of youth will spend some years before the age of 18 being raised by a single parent.

Eighty-seven percent of single parent-families are headed by women, and this percentage is likely to increase. Since 1970, the number of children living with a single, never-married mother increased 678 percent (Hodgkinson, 1991a). Although single-parent households currently are four times more common among black families than among white families (10 percent of Asian, 12 percent of white, 24 percent of Hispanic, and 52 percent of black children are living in such family structures), this discrepancy is likely to shrink; between 1980 and 1988, the birthrate among unmarried white women between thirty and thirty-nine increased over 68 percent (Smolowe, 1990).

Most single mothers find it necessary to work to support their families. However, most are not able to attain high-paying positions. In 1985, the average income of single mothers was $11,400, within $1,000 of the poverty line (Kirst & McLaughlin, 1990). In fact, females over the age of twenty-five with children to support (not teenagers, as might be thought) account for the largest proportion of low-wage workers (Hodgkinson, 1991a).

Not only are single-parent mothers finding it necessary to work outside the home, but mothers in two-parent families are also increasingly entering the labor force. In 1987, half of the mothers with kids under six and 70 percent with children between the ages of six and seventeen worked or were seeking employment outside the home (Hodgkinson, 1991a). In 46 percent of today's families both or the only parent is working (Kirst & McLaughlin, 1990).

This has resulted in what Hewlett (1991) cited as the primary at-risk factor for nondisadvantaged children—the time deficit. The time deficit refers to the decreasing amount of time that parents spend with their children. Hewlett noted that since 1960, children have lost ten to twelve hours of contact time with their parents per week. This has been due to a variety of factors including more mothers in the workforce, an escalating divorce rate, divorced fathers' abandonment of their children, single parenthood, and an increase in the number of hours required on the job. Consider the following facts:

- The number of mothers in the workforce has more than doubled in the last three decades, going from 30 percent in 1960 to 66 percent in 1988.

- Working mothers spend less than half the amount of time in primary care activities with their children as do nonemployed mothers, with single, working mothers spending only one-fourth as much time.

- Three out of four parents never visit their child's school (compared to Japan where mothers visit their children's schools every two weeks).

- The divorce rate has doubled between 1950 and 1989.

- The number of children growing up without fathers has doubled since 1970, increasing from 12 percent to 24 percent.

- The number of single-parent families has more than doubled since 1970.

- The forty-hour work week now averages fifty-two hours, with the typical worker today spending six hours more per week on the job than the typical worker in 1973 (Hewlett, 1991).

Overall, the total contact time parents have with their children (including time spent in primary care activities and time spent with children while engaged in other activities like shopping) has decreased 40 percent during the last twenty-five years (Hewlett, 1991).

The increasing number of families whose adult members are employed full-time in the labor force has resulted in a large number of latchkey children, that is, children who have no adult supervision after school. Sources have estimated the number of latchkey students under the age of thirteen to be anywhere from 2 million (Hodgkinson, 1991a) to 20 million (Hall, 1991). Studies have found that latchkey children are twice as likely to take drugs and drink alcohol as children who have adult supervision after school. In fact, one study found a correlation between the number of hours young people take care of themselves after school and substance abuse. These findings hold true regardless of race, sex, socio-economic status, or family structure (Hewlett, 1991).

Many schools have responded by providing extended-day programs that provide adult supervision for students before and after school. However, the percentage of families who have access to such programs is small, and even the best extended day care cannot substitute for the emotional bonds that the care of a parent provides. Gibbs (1990) has noted that "for the vast majority child care is like a game of Russian roulette: rotating nannies, unlicensed home care, unregulated nurseries that leave parents wondering constantly: Is my child really safe?" (p. 44).

One factor that has threatened the safety of America's youth is the youths themselves. The suicide rate for fifteen- to nineteen-year-olds tripled between 1960 and 1986, and doubled for younger adolescents. In 1986, one out of every ten teenage boys and one of five teenage girls attempted suicide (Hewlett, 1991). In most cases, suicidal youth come from middle-class and affluent families—families frequently characterized by a time deficit.

Yet, a recent poll indicated the acceptance of changes in family structure. Sixty-five percent of those polled felt it acceptable for mothers of preschool children to work full-time outside the home; 61 percent to have families with young children in which only one parent lives in the home; 46 percent for parents with young children to divorce; and 27 percent for women to have children out of wedlock—yet 78 percent favored a return to traditional values and old-fashioned morality (Groller, 1990). Seemingly, a large segment of society yearns for a return to the past, but is overcome by a sense of helplessness in the face of economic and social pressures.

The environment within homes has also not always been positive for children. One source has described home as "an impoverished place, little more than a dormitory, a spot for a shower and a change of clothes (Elmer-Dewitt, 1990, p. 74). Due to the increasingly stressful nature of many present-day jobs, the time spent by parents with their children is frequently more stress-filled (Hewlett, 1991). This is reflected in the increase in child abuse, which went from 600,000 cases in 1979 to 2.4 million cases in 1989 (Gibbs, 1990). Not only do children suffer from child abuse, but eventually society also suffers. Currently, four out of five death row inmates in the United States were abused as kids (Gibbs, 1990). Exemplifying the underfunded and overextended nature of child welfare services in the United States is the fact that in California, one-fifth of child abuse emergency response calls go unanswered for a week or more (Kirst & McLaughlin, 1990).

Poverty and Homelessness

In addition to the influence of a changing family, a second factor that significantly influences the childhood experience of an increasing number of America's youth is growing up in poverty. The United States has the highest child poverty rate among industrialized nations, three times that of most other economically advanced nations (Reed & Sauter, 1990).

Children are poorer than any other single age group in America (Reed & Sauter, 1990). Currently, one out of every five American children overall and one of every four children under the age of six lives in poverty (The fraying fabric, 1989; Hodgkinson, 1991). Projections indicate that as many as half of the children born today will live in poverty for part of their lives. Most black children will spend four or more years in poverty during the first ten years of their lives (the fraying fabric, 1989). Overall, 40 percent of America's poor people are children (Hodgkinson, 1989).

Race, ethnicity, gender, and family structure are strongly associated with poverty. For example, whereas only 14 percent of white children are poor, approximately 27 percent of Asian children, 37 percent of Hispanic children, and 44 percent of black children live in poverty (Reed & Sauter, 1990). Half of single women with children live in poverty compared to 11.4 percent of two-parent families (Kirst & McLaughlin, 1990). The average annual income for a single mother living in poverty with one child is less than $3,000 (Reed & Sauter, 1990). Additionally, the persistently poor (i.e., those unlikely to ever find a decent job or marriage partner) are heavily concentrated in two groups: black households and female-headed households. Although blacks constitute 12 percent of poor people, they make up 62 percent of the persistently poor (The fraying fabric, 1989).

Poverty is not just relegated to urban areas. In 1990, almost one-fourth of rural children were living in poverty (Cohen, 1992). Overall, the poverty rate for rural areas is 50 percent higher than in urban areas (O' Hara, 1988). Additionally, rural children living in poverty are less likely to have access to, or qualify for, government assistance (Cohen, 1992).

Sociologists have identified six poverty populations:

- the physically or psychologically impaired who are unemployable;
- those undergoing personal upheaval (e.g., divorce, job loss)—for individuals in this group, poverty is generally a temporary condition;
- the working poor, that is, those who are employed but unable to break through the poverty line;
- the long-term unemployed who want work but cannot find it;
- the unemployed who are so discouraged they no longer look for work;
- the chronically unemployed, usually young minority males, and welfare mothers and their children concentrated in inner-city neighborhoods (The fraying fabric, 1989).

A recently escalating side effect of poverty has been homelessness. Conservative estimates placed the U.S. homeless population at 2.5 million in 1988. One study estimated that there will be 18 million homeless by the year 2003 if present trends continue—more than seven times the current number of homeless individuals (Erickson, 1990). Currently, 51 percent of the homeless population is black, 35 percent is white, and 14 percent is made up of other races (U.S. Conference of Mayors, 1989).

Typically, the single mother with housing will pay over 50 percent of her income for housing costs (Hodgkinson, 1991a). By comparison, approval ratios for home mortgages used by lending institutions are generally between 25 percent and 28 percent—indicating the percentage of income that should be spent on housing. Thus, it is easy to see that for many single mothers and others living in poverty, something as minor as a missed bus or a broken-down car can set off a series of circumstances that causes them to become homeless.

The lack of affordable housing is illustrated by the fact that there are 8 million qualified low-income households vying for 4 million low-income housing units. Between 1984 and 1986, the number of households with real income under $5,000 increased by 55 percent while the number of low-rental housing units decreased by over 1 million (Hodgkinson, 1989). Yet, since the Reagan administration, virtually no additional low-income housing units have been built. During this period, federal assistance for low-income housing decreased 76 percent.

Children make up a sizable portion of the homeless population. Over the course of one year as many as 1 million youth under the age of eighteen lack a permanent home or live on the streets for some period of time (Reed & Sauter, 1990). Forty percent of homeless shelter users are families with children (Hodgkinson, 1991a) with most homeless families headed by single women with two or three children under the age of five (Hodgkinson, 1989). However, a significant number of homeless youth live outside the family structure. In one study of seventeen major cities, unaccompanied youth under age eighteen accounted for over 10 percent of the homeless population in a number of cities, with cities reporting this segment of the homeless population to be increasing (U.S. Conference of Mayors, 1989).

The impact of homelessness on children includes health problems, psychological problems, and school-related problems. Homeless children are much more likely to have anemia, malnutrition, and asthma than are nonhomeless children and are less likely to receive adequate health care. They experience more instances of depression, hyperactivity, listlessness, anxiety, and aggression, and have lower self-esteem than do children of the same socioeconomic groups who reside in homes with their families (U.S. Conference of Mayors, 1989).

Approximately 36 percent of homeless children do not attend school (Erickson, 1990). Those who do attend have various school-related problems, including lower school attendance than nonhomeless children. Meanwhile, the societal expectation for schools is that they teach children of poor and homeless families even though these children have irregular school attendance, have few opportunities to establish peer friendships, and may be dealing with catastrophic circumstances such as lack of long-term housing or major changes in their housing.

Many problems faced by homeless children are also characteristic of poor children in general. Incidental risks of poverty include death in infancy, serious illness, generally poor physical health, teenage pregnancy, dropping out of school, lower self-reports of happiness, and lower academic achievement. (Socioeconomic status is the single greatest predictor of performance on standardized testing as well as of adult self-sufficiency; Kirst & McLaughlin, 1990).

The health problems of many poor children commence prior to birth. One-third of pregnant mothers do not receive adequate prenatal care, many because of insufficient financial resources (Hewlett, 1991). About 20 percent of handicapped children would not be impaired if their mothers had gotten even one exam during the first trimester of pregnancy which could have detected potential problems (Hodgkinson, 1989, 1991a). Receiving no prenatal care increases a mother's risk of giving birth to a low-birthweight, or premature baby, at risk for developmental disability, by three to six times (Reed & Sauter, 1990). Ironically, the cost of providing an expectant mother with effective prenatal care for nine months is approximately $400; the cost of neonatal intensive care for just one premature infant can be as much as $100,000. As Reed and Sauter (1990) have noted, "The willful neglect of America's poor children is not only immoral; it is just plain stupid" (p. K3).

Health problems for poor children continue after their birth with problems caused by inadequate prenatal care exacerbated by insufficient care subsequent to birth. One source estimated that 18 million children have never seen a dentist, and half a million suffer from malnutrition (Hall, 1991). Another source noted that one of every five preschool age children has not been vaccinated against polio. The effects of this are that children from poor families spend approximately twice as many days in hospitals as do other children (Kirst & McLaughlin, 1990). It can only be hypothesized how many more poor children who required hospitalization did not visit the hospital due to inadequate financial resources or lack of health insurance. (One-fourth of the children in the United States are not covered by health insurance; Kirst & McLaughlin, 1990.)

The near poor—that is, those with incomes between 100 percent and 150 percent of the poverty level—are perhaps worse off than the poor; they are ineligible for many services at public expense and thus simply do without medical, dental, mental health, and other services (Erickson, 1990). Kirst and McLaughlin (1990) have noted that essentially we have two medical nations within the United States—one with the latest technology, the other that matches those in Third World countries.

Many policymakers have been advocating extensive implementation of preschool services for children from low income families; however, this strategy may be a case of too little, too late. To prepare at-risk children to be ready for school by age five requires more than preschool. It also requires health care for them during the first five years of their lives as well as for their mothers before their birth.

Although childhood poverty is increasing, government funding for services related to poverty populations is decreasing. Since 1970, the median Aid to Families with Dependent Children (AFDC) grant has fallen 23 percent in constant dollars (Reed & Sauter, 1990). In fact, in 1985-1986, families of fewer than half of the poor children nationwide received AFDC. Additionally, 39 percent of eligible children did not receive free or reduced lunches; 38 percent did not receive food stamps; and public housing was available to accommodate only 21 percent of poor families (Kirst & McLaughlin, 1990). Meanwhile, between 1980 and 1989, the poorest 20 percent of Americans saw their real income drop 3.2 percent and their federal taxes increase 16.2 percent (The fraying fabric, 1989).

Apparently, increased taxes were funding programs for the elderly and for defense. Federal spending for the elderly increased 52 percent between 1978 and 1987, and spending for defense rose 37 percent during roughly the same period. Meanwhile, federal expenditures for children decreased by 4 percent (Hewlett, 1991; Reed & Sauter, 1990).

Although stereotypes frequently portray poor people as lazy good-for-nothings, interested more in collecting public money than employment, facts indicate otherwise. Eighty-seven percent of children living in poverty are from families where at least one member is employed at least part-time (Reed & Sauter, 1990). Nearly half the heads of household of poor families and 24 percent of homeless adults are employed in full-time or part-time jobs (U.S. Conference of Mayors, 1989). Unfortunately, employment in a minimum-wage position earns a full-time worker who is the head of a household of three $2,500 less annually than the poverty line. In 1964 the same minimum-wage position would have put the family at 104 percent of poverty level (Erickson, 1990).

Prominent demographer Harold Hodgkinson (1991a) notes that trying to teach sick or hungry kids is an exercise in futility. For children, growing up in poverty means living in shabby surroundings where violence, drug use, and physical abuse are common. Additionally, poverty is closely linked with low academic achievement, dropping out of school, teenage pregnancy, poor physical health, and general childhood unhappiness. The Children's Defense Fund estimates that the cost of eliminating child poverty in the United States is $17.22 billion ($51.65 billion for eliminating poverty for all persons in the United States). Although this may seem like a major expenditure, the figures become much more reasonable when one considers that the U.S. Congress recently committed $325 billion to bail out the savings and loan industry (Reed & Sauter, 1990).

In view of the seeming lack of will to solve the problem of child poverty, school administrators must find other solutions to reduce its pervasive, negative effects. Subsequent sections of this chapter will discuss some commonly proposed solutions.

Influence of Television and Pop Culture

A third pervasive effect on the nature of childhood during recent decades has been television and related forms of pop culture (e.g., video games, pop music, music videos). One observer of popular culture noted that television, movies, tapes, and electronic games are replacing parents as the key acculturizing agent for many children (Frost, 1986). Indeed, *Time* magazine, in a story on the status of childhood in the 1990s, has questioned how values will be passed on from one generation to the next when the key cultural influences on children are television, pop music, and Nintendo (Elmer-Dewitt, 1990).

Studies have found that watching television occupies more time in children's lives than any other leisure activity, with more than half of all the leisure time of children being spent in this way (Comstock & Paik, 1987). By the time a child reaches high school, he or she will have spent more time watching television than in the classroom. The A. C. Nielsen Company estimates that children between the ages of two and eleven watch an average of 28 hours of television per week, with teenagers averaging 23.5 hours of television consumption per week (Comstock & Paik, 1987). This adds up to 15,000-16,000 hours of television watching during the school age years of six to eighteen compared to 13,000 hours spent in school during these years (Frost, 1986).

By the time youth reach age eighteen, they have been exposed to 350,000 commercials and 18,000 murders on television (Frost, 1986). Two decades ago, a study of television violence showed that regular programs averaged eight acts of physical violence per hour, and cartoons averaged twenty-two acts per hour (Steinfield, 1973). By 1985 the most violent regular programs averaged forty violent acts per hour, with many cartoons averaging more than this. A longtime childhood staple, *Bugs Bunny,* averaged fifty-six violent acts per hour, and even "socially redeeming" programs such as the *Smurfs* and *Muppet Babies* averaged eighteen and six violent acts per hour, respectively (Frost, 1986).

What has been the effect of the sum and substance of adolescent television viewing? One expert noted that television is robbing children of childhood by bringing every taboo out of the closet for children to see, including divorce, promiscuity, adultery, sadism, murder, homosexuality, and incest (Postman, 1981). Television watching has been blamed for increased levels of violence in children, decreased levels of academic achievement, and a higher percentage of childhood obesity. (Twenty-seven percent of youngsters aged six through eleven are obese, up from 18 percent twenty-five years ago; Hewlett, 1991). Although research findings are not totally conclusive, evidence exists to support each of these accusations.

Studies have found that the amount of time spent watching television and scholastic achievement are inversely related in children and teenagers. In a California study, this held true regardless of grade level and socioeconomic status. However, the *degree* of the effect does vary by socioeconomic status of the student's family. The higher the socioeconomic status of the family, the more television negatively affected achievement. For poorer socioeconomic class students as well as among limited-English-proficiency students, there was an increase in achievement at low levels of television watching. As the amount of television exposure was increased, achievement decreased. Television watching also had a greater negative effect on achievement at higher grade levels. Additionally, the amount of time spent on homework and reading outside the classroom decreased as the amount of television watching increased (Comstock & Paik, 1987).

These findings suggest that whereas television watching negatively affects academic achievement, limited amounts of television exposure can have a positive effect on some groups. Seemingly, television watching negatively affects achievement when it displaces an intellectual or experientially rich activity, positively affects it when it provides such an activity (Comstock & Paik, 1987).

Television has been argued to be such a strong socializing force that it competes with parents, teachers, and other agents in providing models that influence a child's beliefs and values. Indeed, children learn both prosocial and antisocial behaviors from television viewing (Tregoning, 1986). In one study, a large majority of children and teenagers reported that they got most of their information about public events from television—more so than from parents, teachers, and peers (Comstock & Paik, 1987).

Numerous studies have cited negative beliefs and behaviors influenced by television. For example, in one study preschoolers tripled their violent acts of kicking, choking, hitting, and pushing after being exposed to two weeks of violent television (Steinfield, 1973). A study of one hundred juvenile offenders found that twenty-two of them had copied their criminal techniques from television (Frost, 1986). Another study found that a relationship existed between the amount of violent television watched by boys when they were in elementary school and their aggressive behavior at age nineteen (Tregoning, 1986). Other studies have found that children were more accepting of aggressive behavior in their peers after watching violent television programs (Tregoning, 1986), and that college undergraduates were more accepting of the "rape myth" (i.e., that women enjoy involuntary sex) after extensive exposure to violent and pornographic films in which women are the victims (Comstock & Paik, 1987).

Syntheses of research on the influence of television on values, beliefs and actions have found that:

- Children learn aggressive behavior from television.
- Children who watch violent television are more aggressive than children who watch less violent television.
- Effects of seeing violence on television are cumulative; that is, children who watch a lot of violent television are more likely to think that aggression is a good way to solve problems (Tregoning, 1986).
- Television desensitizes people to deviant behavior (Comstock & Paik, 1987).
- Behaviors learned from television are not necessarily displayed at the time they are acquired but may remain dormant until circumstances similar to what was observed on television arise, at which time the behavior will be displayed (Tregoning, 1986).

Research syntheses have also examined in what circumstances television seems to be most influential. These syntheses have found that television is most potent in influencing beliefs, values, and behavior when:

- Events or circumstances are portrayed repeatedly (Comstock & Paik, 1987).
- What is observed on television is not part of previously formed schemes of behavior—for this reason, children and adolescents are especially vulnerable, since their beliefs are still in formation (Comstock & Paik, 1987; Tregoning, 1986).
- Portrayals of violence are rewarded, go unpunished, are justified, resemble real-life situations, occur without victim pain, are sexual and inflicted on a female who eventually relinquishes and enjoys it, or are viewed by someone who is angry or frustrated prior to seeing it (Comstock & Paik, 1987).

Findings on the influence of television are consistent with several psychological theories. For example, Bandura's social learning theory holds that capability of performing an act is enhanced by observing its performance by others, especially if the act is wholly unfamiliar to the observer. Berkowitz's disinhibition and cue theory holds that television and film portrayals raise or lower inhibition regarding internal states such as anger and affect the response regarding the state; that is, television viewing may teach that specific modes of response (such as the use of physical force) are appropriate when one is angry. Finally, Tannenbaum and Zillman's arousal theory holds that excitation created by an experience (e.g., an event viewed on television) may transfer to subsequent behavior (i.e., a real-life situation) (Comstock & Paik, 1987).

Substance Abuse

Another part of the childhood and adolescent experience of a significant number of youths is exposure to drugs and alcohol. The percentage of students who use drugs and alcohol has declined slightly in recent years, perhaps due to extensive campaigns to discourage their usage.

During the past two years the number of high school seniors using alcohol decreased by 5 percent. Marijuana usage declined 24 percent since its peak in 1979, and cocaine usage decreased 8 percent since its peak in 1985. Nonetheless, a significant percentage of high school seniors continue to use these substances. In 1990, almost 81 percent of surveyed high school seniors reported using alcohol during the previous twelve months, while 27 percent reported using marijuana and 5.3 percent reported using cocaine (Education vital signs, 1991). Almost 2 million teenagers are regular user of illicit drugs (Krantz, 1990).

Perhaps more significant than the total percentage of students who consume alcohol are the frequency and amount of consumption. Thirty-five percent of all adolescents are regular consumers of alcohol, and 40 percent of high school seniors fit this category (Kirst & McLaughlin, 1990; Education vital signs, 1991). Thirty-two percent of high school seniors surveyed reported engaging in at least one bout of heavy drinking (five or more drinks in a row) during the past month (Education vital signs, 1991). U.S. Department of Health and Human Service data reported that 5.4 million seventh- through twelfth-graders have binged at least once (fifteen drinks per week), that more than 3 million students binge each month, and that almost half a million teenagers are regular binge drinkers.

Even though there has been an extensive national "Just Say 'No' " anti-drug campaign during the past few years, 36 percent of fourth-graders surveyed indicated that students their age felt some or a lot of pressure to try beer, wine, or liquor. Twenty-five percent of fourth-graders and 51 percent of sixth-graders reported some or a lot of pressure to try marijuana or cocaine (Krantz, 1990).

An additional aspect of the substance abuse problem involves children born to parents who are substance abusers. Each year 350,000 children are born to cocaine-addicted mothers (Hodgkinson, 1991a). Gibbs (1990) reported that the number of drug-exposed babies entering the foster care system in Los Angeles rose 453 percent between 1984 and 1987. Children who grow up in families with drug- using parents are likely to have a variety of physical and mental problems. For example, drugs are involved in two of three child abuse or neglect cases. Children in these situations are faced with life with abusers or life at the mercy of a system filled with strangers (Gibbs, 1990).

Schools in some urban areas are beginning to see the effects of a flood of "crack" babies. These children are likely to have a variety of physical and mental handicaps requiring extensive and expensive special services. Preparing a child born to a cocaine-addicted mother for kindergarten costs approximately $40,000 per child (Hodgkinson, 1991a).

Dropouts

Similar to the decline in the rate of substance abuse, the dropout rate has declined slightly during recent years. The dropout rate for white students has declined from 15 percent in 1968 to 12 percent in 1989. For black students the rate has declined from 27 percent in 1968 to 14 percent in 1989; the rate for Hispanics in 1989 was 33 percent, a rate that has been fairly steady over the years (Education vital signs, 1991).

Nonetheless, a significant number of students continue to drop out of school. Poor academic performance, truancy, and in-school delinquency are strong predictors of early school leaving (Pallas, 1984) and frequently can be detected during elementary school years.

For those who choose to drop out, there is an array of social and personal costs (McDill, Natriello, & Pallas, 1986). Financial costs of dropping out have been estimated at $71 billion due to lost tax revenues, welfare and unemployment costs, and expenditures associated with crime and crime prevention (Levin, 1972).

Dropouts typically have poor job prospects, high unemployment rates, and lower earnings than those who complete high school. About one in four dropouts is unemployed compared to one in ten high school graduates. In 1986, on average, high school graduates earned 54 percent more annually than did those who completed only one to three years of high school (U.S. General Accounting Office, 1986). One source conservatively estimated lifetime earnings for high school graduates to be $107,500 more than for dropouts (McDill et al., 1986). Additionally, dropouts are also more likely to be in semiskilled manual jobs, and in lower-quality jobs (i.e., jobs with poorer intrinsic and extrinsic working conditions) (U.S. General Accounting Office, 1986).

One of the significant social costs related to dropping out is an increased likelihood of incarceration. Eighty percent of America's 1 million prisoners are dropouts. Almost without exception, states with the highest dropout rates also have the highest incarceration rates, while those with lowest dropout rates have the lowest incarceration rates. For example, Florida leads the nation in dropout rate and incarceration rate, whereas Minnesota is fiftieth in dropout rate and forty-ninth in incarceration rate (Hodgkinson, 1989).

Each prisoner costs taxpayers more than $20,000 per year. This can be compared with $3,300 of taxpayer money spent on a college student per year. Hodgkinson (1991) is fond of highlighting this relationship by noting that it costs six times as much per year to send someone to the state pen as it costs to send him or her to Penn State. The cost of prisons is growing more rapidly than any other social service including education and health, yet return is dismally low. Sixty-three percent of those released from prison return within three years (Hodgkinson, 1989).

The correlation between dropping out of school and criminal activity becomes understandable when one considers that high school dropouts who are able to obtain employment are likely to earn the minimum wage. This translates to about $9,000 a year, too little to attain the American Dream—unless they turn to a life of crime. Obviously, the best solution for reducing the crime rate is increasing the education rate. Unfortunately, in the short-sighted world of political policymaking this is a long-term solution whose benefits will not become evident for years, and thus is not as politically expedient as the "get tough" policies communicated by building more jail cells (Hodgkinson, 1991a).

Reasons for dropping out of school can be categorized as school experiences, family circumstances, and economic factors (McDill et al., 1986). Specific reasons cited within these categories include poor grades, difficulty adjusting to the institutionalized school environment, employment, difficulty getting along with teachers, having to support a family, and expulsion. Additionally for females, pregnancy and marriage plans were prevalent reasons for dropping out (U.S. General Accounting Office, 1986), with 80 percent of teen mothers under seventeen never completing school (Neill, 1979).

Several studies have found that increased academic standards spawned by the reform movement have influenced some students to drop out of school. In one study, 27.7 percent of schools surveyed attributed increased academic standards as being directly related to increased dropout rates. The study found that although longer school days were correlated with increased dropout rates, longer school years were not. This may be because longer school days prohibit students from keeping their after-school jobs (Tanner, 1989). This hypothesis is supported by other studies that have found that working more than twenty hours per week is associated with higher rates of dropping out. Studies have also found that, although higher academic standards may result in higher achievement for better students, it comes at the cost of a narrower curriculum and increased probability of dropping out for at-risk students (Fetler, 1989).

RESPONSES OF SCHOOLS

A landmark study by Coleman (1966) concluded that family background matters far more in determining student achievement than any attributes of the formal educational system. The study estimated that the home is almost twice as powerful as the school in determining student achievement. Given the extensive changes in families, including the effects of poverty and the influence of television and other forms of popular culture, it becomes obvious that the challenges faced by schools in meeting the needs of today's children and adolescents are different than they were several decades ago.

Schools are responsible for educating an ever-growing number of students who are at risk of educational failure, psychological failure, or social failure. The impact these students have had on schools has resulted in lower standardized test scores, an increased dropout rate, more extensive abuse of substances, a dramatic increase in gang activity, and greater violence toward students and teachers. Although some of these conditions have improved slightly in the past few years, the challenge of educating students to be productive members of society is greater now than it has ever been.

This section will explore several of the more significant responses to demographic changes that schools have implemented during the past several decades.

Responses Associated with the Reform Movement

The extensive changes in the nature of childhood and adolescence have resulted in more students coming to school with extensive and pervasive physical, mental, and emotional problems stemming from family or societally based dysfunctions. Educating students has become more difficult with the result that schools increasingly have been blamed for students who perform academically at less than desired levels. This would appear to make logical sense, but, in essence, changes in academic performance have been caused more by changes in society than by decreasing performance of schools. The decade of the 1980s could be termed the "reform decade" in reference to the many reports and recommendations intended to improve the performance of schools and students.

Hodgkinson (1991b) has argued that when the public thinks of poor schools, it is not thinking about the middle-class school in suburbia, but rather about the low-income inner-city school. Inner-city schools contain the highest proportion of at-risk kids, yet reform reports have conspicuously not addressed their problems (Hodgkinson, 1991; Orum, 1986). Instead, reforms have focused on competency testing, increased academic standards (including more rigorous academic content of courses, more homework, and stricter grade promotion policies), longer school days and years, and restructuring to promote site-based management and teacher involvement in school decision making. None of these reforms directly address the needs of poor students and, in fact, may exacerbate some poverty-related problems such as dropping out of school. (See the previous section on dropouts.)

Results of reform initiatives have been marginal at best. More rigorous academic content has been somewhat effective for students overall in increasing SAT test scores, but has had little effect on scores of the lowest-performing youngsters (Alexander & Pallas, 1984). In general, higher demands have been effective for low-ability students only when they have been accompanied by additional assistance (McDill et al., 1986). As previously discussed, the impact of increasing the time demands of schooling may increase the dropout rate by forcing students to choose between time requirements of their jobs and school.

Additionally, increased time demands may limit participation in athletics and other extracurricular activities, which have been shown to have positive effects on some students (McDill et al., 1986).

Hodgkinson (1989) has argued that attention to the demographics of childhood and adolescence suggests a reform agenda focused on improvement of the bottom third of students, a reduction of youth poverty, mandated and funded Head Start for all eligible children, and integrated services for kids at risk on several factors.

Compensatory Education (Chapter I)

One long-existing response that has attempted to address the instructional needs of students from low-income families is the compensatory education program, commonly referred to as Chapter I. Chapter I originated with the Elementary and Secondary Education Act of 1965 and as Title I was the largest program funded by the act. Its purpose as stated in the act was:

> To provide financial assistance . . . to local educational agencies serving areas with concentrations of children from low income families; and to expand and improve their educational programs by various means . . . which contribute particularly to meeting the special educational needs of educationally deprived children. (Public Law 89-10, Section 201)

During the past five years, funding for Chapter I has increased 90 percent from $3.5 billion to $6.7 billion largely because Congress has perceived it as a program that works. Indeed, most districts that receive Chapter I funds have reported net achievement gains for their Chapter I students since regular reporting of such results began.

However, gains have been reported as measured on standardized achievement tests—tests that typically are able to measure only basic-level skills to the exclusion of higher-level thought processes. It has been the traditional view that in order to work effectively with students coming from culturally deprived environments, they must first be provided with basic skills that lay the foundation for more advanced work. Basic skills were provided through instruction in discrete skills taught in linear sequence. Unfortunately, many Chapter I students never advanced beyond this basic skills instruction.

Recent advances in cognitive psychology suggest that this may not be the most appropriate means of instruction for disadvantaged students. Cognitive psychology suggests that instruction should begin with what students know and "expose them to explicit applications of what has traditionally been thought of as higher-order thinking" (Means & Knapp, 1991, p. 283).

A new set of curricular assumptions for compensatory education has emerged from this research. Specifically, curriculum should focus on complex, meaningful problems that make connections with students' out-of-school experiences and culture. Basic skills instruction should be embedded in the context of these more global tasks (Means & Knapp, 1991).

Appropriate instructional techniques to facilitate curricular assumptions include modeling thought processes for students, honoring multiple approaches for accomplishing tasks, scaffolding, and dialogue between teacher and students (Means & Knapp, 1991). For example, the process approach to writing uses modeling by imitating the process that writers use in composing, revising, editing, and polishing manuscripts. In scaffolding, students are assisted in completing complex tasks by the teacher's completing part of the task. For example, the teacher may complete the computation involved in a difficult math problem while the student focuses on the operations and process of the problem.

The Hawkins-Stafford amendments of the most recent Chapter I reauthorization provide additional flexibility that encourages these types of instructional changes. Although debate continues about appropriate methods of assessment, programmatic responses that go beyond discrete skill instruction are emerging. For example, many programs are changing from pull-out instruction to providing instructional assistance in students' classrooms. Full-day kindergartens, lowered class size, continuous monitoring of student progress, and thinking skills across the curriculum are a few initiatives that have occurred in response to the more flexible current guidelines (Clayton, 1991).

The U.S. Department of Education is encouraging the use of Chapter I funds to provide greater emphasis for preschool and kindergarten programs, regular classroom instruction, schoolwide projects that benefit all students, and increased time devoted to Chapter I instruction through extended-day programs, extended school years, Saturday programs, and home-based programs (LeTendre, 1991). One of the most important current themes is that Chapter I instruction should focus on prevention and early intervention rather than remediation, as traditionally has been the case (Slavin & Madden, 1991).

Multicultural Education

A response to an increasingly diverse U.S. population is the legitimation of the cultures of various ethnic and minority groups. Schools have attempted to accomplish this through programs of multicultural education.

The dual purposes of multicultural education are to promote equity among different cultures and ethnic and racial groups, and to prepare students to function productively and justly in a global society. More specifically, the goals of multicultural education have been stated as:

- transforming school so that students from both sexes, all cultures, and all social, ethnic, and racial groups will experience an equal opportunity to learn;
- helping all students develop positive attitudes toward different cultures, races, and ethnic and religious groups;
- empowering students from victimized groups by teaching them decision making and social action skills;
- helping students develop cross-cultural dependency and the ability to view themselves from perspectives of different groups;
- effecting an equitable distribution of power among members of all groups (Banks, 1989; Grant and Sleeter, 1989).

Hilliard (1991) has suggested that those who argue that the goals of multicultural education are to increase the self-esteem and academic achievement of minority group members miss the mark. Rather, the primary goal of multicultural education should be valid scholarship that presents a truthful and meaningful rendition of the whole human experience, not just that of one culture. Hilliard argued that the development of a multicultural curriculum should not be concerned with maintaining racial and ethnic quotas in terms of time and amount of instruction, but rather should be concerned with presenting an accurate account of history and culture that has been jointly constructed by scholars representing various groups.

One prominent multicultural scholar has argued that the ultimate goal of multicultural education is freedom. He noted that children are socialized into the values, beliefs, and stereotypes of their community cultures. When minority children enter school, they usually are forced to question their cultural beliefs since what is taught in school conflicts with what they have learned in their community culture. On the other hand, students from the dominant culture do not usually have this opportunity since what they are taught in school agrees with what they have learned at home. Consequently, they have little opportunity to become free of cultural assumptions that are monocultural, prejudicial, or otherwise narrowly parochial. Ultimately, education should affirm and help students understand their home cultures as well as helping free them from cultural boundaries (Banks, 1991).

The appropriateness of multicultural education, however, continues to be debated. Those in favor of multicultural education argue that traditional efforts to teach a common culture disparage the contributions of minority group members since only facts, knowledge, and language accepted by the dominant cultural group are taught. These individuals argue that the role of public schools is to teach and strengthen the separate identities of all ethnic, racial, and cultural groups (ethnocentrism). Ethnocentrists claim that common culture is a form of European domination.

Those opposing the ethnocentrist viewpoint argue that the historic mission of public schools is to help forge a common national identity and that schools should teach what we have in common. They see a multicultural approach as a threat to national unity. They claim that if we teach young people to identify only with members of their own group, we promote separatism and prejudice. Ravitch (1991) argues that the common culture is influenced by various separate cultures and in that sense includes them. She notes that "the common culture is multicultural" (p. 10) and was built over many generations by people from many different races, religions, ethnic groups, and cultural backgrounds. The latter view would be acceptable if it reflected the common culture that was actually taught. Unfortunately, in many cases it does not. What traditionally has been taught in schools as the common culture ignores the specific contributions made by underrepresented groups and fails to honestly discuss the historical warts of the dominant cultural group.

Advocates of multicultural education argue that they are merely asking for a more truthful, complex, and diverse curriculum that recognizes the contributions of African, African-American, and other cultural groups to European civilization. Banks (1991) has noted that we "need to deconstruct the myth that the West is homogeneous, that it owes few debts to other world civilizations, and that only privileged and upper-status Europeans and European-American males have been its key actors" (p. 34).

Bilingual Education

Another school response to increasing diversity is bilingual education. Bilingual education programs are designed to provide equal educational opportunity to students whose native language is not English. The language in which non-English-speaking students are instructed became a civil rights issue with the *Lau* v. *Nichols* case, which ruled that the civil rights of a student who did not understand the language of instruction were being violated. The court ruled that equality of educational opportunity did not simply mean providing the same facilities, textbooks, teachers, and curriculum, but rather the same opportunity to understand instruction in basic skills.

The increasing prominence that bilingual education programs are likely to have can be illustrated by looking at the growing number of students whose lack of knowledge of the English language affects their educational performance. These students are termed limited-English-proficiency students, and their number is currently estimated as being between 1.2 and 1.7 million. It is projected that they will number 6 million by the year 2020 (Nieto, 1992). Nearly two-thirds of current limited-English-proficient students do not receive any special educational services, and only about 15 percent are in federally funded bilingual programs (Nieto, 1992).

There are a number of different types of bilingual education programs. The most common type provides students with content instruction in their native language as well as English-language skill instruction. The objective of this type of program is to have students exit from the program when they are sufficiently proficient in the English language to shift content instruction from their native language to English.

This mode of instruction reflects the deficit, compensatory education mode of instruction. That is, the bilingual program student is viewed as having a deficit that knowledge of the English language fills. Conversely, the asset model of bilingual instruction views the native language and culture a student brings to school as an asset. Those advocating this mode of instruction argue that students should continue indefinitely in the bilingual program in order to preserve their original language and culture.

Successful bilingual programs have demonstrated that students can learn content in their native language while also learning English and achieving academically (Nieto, 1992). Studies have also shown that good bilingual programs motivate students to stay in school by making it a more meaningful and enjoyable experience (Nieto, 1992).

One of the problems with providing bilingual programs for students is that many schools and districts are extremely linguistically diverse but have few students representing any one language. This makes it difficult to dedicate personnel specifically for instruction in that language.

THE NEW AMERICAN SCHOOL

As can be evidenced by the wealth of demographics provided in this chapter, societal conditions affecting American youth have changed. Schools have responded with interventions such as compensatory education, bilingual, and multicultural education, and a plethora of locally initiated, at-risk programs, yet the deep structure of schools and the basic nature of instructional delivery have not changed radically. Certainly, current reforms that focus on raising academic standards and involving teachers in decision making are unlikely to solve the problems of the bottom third of our students who suffer from a variety of interrelated problems. In fact, if schools are to be faulted for what is becoming known as the "education problem," it is not because they are performing any less well than they ever have, but rather that they have not altered the basic paradigm of public schooling that has been in existence in this country since the days of the one-room schoolhouse.

The inability to change can be attributed to three possible reasons.

1. *Inadequate funding to rethink, let alone radically alter, existing policies, practices, and structures.* Although data from some sources have reported that the United States spends more money on education than other industrialized nations, the data are misleading. U.S. education expenditures include figures for higher education and the United States has 25 percent of the higher education students in the world. If instead of total expenditures we look at the percentage of the gross domestic product that is spent on education, the figures are radically different. Using this comparison, the United States ranks fourteenth out of sisteen nations in education expenditure (Hodgkinson, 1991a). As Reed and Sauter (1990) have noted, "All too often schools are given the burden of overcoming economic and social inequities, usually without adequate resources . . . . indeed, children who have been maimed by such new social epidemics as homelessness and crack use by pregnant women are already testing the resources and tolerance of the schools" (p. K8).

2. *A desire of those in power to maintain current social class relationships.* The United States has the knowledge and the funding to solve many of the societal problems that are at the root of the problems children bring to school. Child poverty can be almost entirely eliminated; appropriate prenatal care can be provided for all mothers; Head Start programs can be made accessible to all qualifying children; clinics can be established to provide basic health care for all children, and so on. Why then do we not develop a national child-care policy that provides such services? Hodgkinson (1991a) argued that we do not have the will to do so. Although the United States is second in the world in per capita income, we do not make it into the top ten on any significant indicator of child welfare (Hewlett, 1991). Yet we find the resources to increase defense spending 37 percent and spending on the elderly 52 percent during a period when spending on children has decreased 4 percent. Critical theorists would take Hodgkinson's contention a step further and suggest not only that we do not have the will to improve child policy, but that many consciously attempt to block such policy because it would be of greatest benefit to those from lower social classes and thus would jeopardize the favorable position of the dominant class in current social class differentiation.

3. *We are too rooted in our paradigm of schooling to be able to conceptualize other paradigms of schooling.* Barker (1985) referred to this as paradigm paralysis. He noted that significant change in a particular field

usually comes from outside the field. However, all of us have been socialized to the paradigm of schooling—at a minimum as students, and perhaps more extensively as professional educators. Thus, it is difficult to think of new ways of conceptualizing schooling and even more difficult to sell radical conceptions of schooling to those who must be involved in their implementation.

Nonetheless, changes in society and in the nature of childhood suggest several strategies schools should consider in being more responsive to children's needs.

Schools as Community Service Centers

The pervasive nature of many of the problems that confront children and their families—problems that affect the academic readiness and ability of children but extend well beyond it—has resulted in a recommendation from several quarters that schools serve as community service centers.

Levy and Copple (1989) have noted that schools alone cannot compensate for the disadvantage created by troubled homes and communities. Complex problems call for comprehensive services for the whole person. For example, families that are in poverty often face many problems simultaneously including substance abuse, inadequate health care, and lack of affordable housing. Under the community service center concept, schools would collaborate with a variety of social service agencies to provide educational, health, and other social services needed by children and families. The school would house the agencies and would serve as a broker of services.

In a sense, the increasing provision of various nonacademic services that youth need has been an ongoing response of schools. For example, a 1990 National School Boards Association survey found that 96 percent of school districts had drug and alcohol abuse programs, 83 percent taught pregnancy prevention, 77 percent offered parental and infant care classes for expectant mothers, 48 percent offered day care for students' children, and almost all provided AIDS education (Hall, 1991). Additionally, most schools provide a limited degree of health and counseling services. However, the current extent of services does not begin to meet the needs of children, nor does it address children's needs during their preschool years or while they are still in the womb. Additionally, current service levels are funded from school budgets that rightfully should fund educational services. The assumption is that under the school as community service center concept, other social service agencies would bring their budgets with them, with delivery of services being more efficient for both agency and recipient.

Currently, although many of the services required by children and families are available to some extent, there is great fragmentation and inefficiency in their delivery. For example, in California the 160 different programs that serve children and youth reside in thirty-five agencies and seven departments. The consequences of fragmentation are (1) an isolation and labeling of problems resulting in a patchwork of solutions (e.g., the interconnectedness between various problems such as poverty, poor health, and academic underachievement is not taken into account); (2) a discontinuity of care (e.g., various agencies that provide services to an individual do not communicate with each other); (3) conflicting service goals (e.g., some agencies view the purpose of services as acute care, and others view them as preventative or developmental); (4) an underutilization of available resources due to one service provider's being unfamiliar with services another provider has available; and (5) fragmented vision/purpose (i.e., each service provider looks at the child only in terms of the specific service he or she provides, with no one looking to see how all the pieces fit together) (Kirst & McLaughlin, 1990). The service center concept would help address the two main current problems with the delivery of services to children, underservice and service fragmentation, by integrating service delivery and thereby making it more efficient.

Schools are the logical choice for the structural center of coordination efforts since they are the only agency or institution through which all children pass, and they have more extensive contact with children than any other agency or institution. Schools also embrace the developmental perspective (as opposed to the acute-care perspective of many agencies) that is required to solve the problems of children.

As expected, there are several obstacles to coordination of services. These include few resources earmarked for coordination, finding mutuality (e.g., Who gets the money following a child if services are shared? Whose care philosophy predominates?), training segregation (i.e., no coordination/collaboration in professional training of various service providers), and turf protection (i.e., agency fear of losing stature or funding) (Kirst & McLaughlin, 1990).

There are a number of current existing models that work. Characteristics these positive exemplars have in common include:

- the reconstruction of children's services from clinical constricted notions of addressing individual pathologies to a view that recognizes continuous and evolutionary development;
- the identification of funding for purposes of coordination (frequently through foundations);
- cooperation among midlevel bureaucrats and commitment from top executives;
- adaptation to local contexts;
- employment of a case manager who coaches service seekers in identifying their problem and the appropriate course of action for solving it (Kirst & McLaughlin, 1990).

The last point is crucial. We must do more than simply contine to throw services at children. We must empower students and their families to examine and address the conditions that keep them in their place. Only in this way can the cyclical nature of poverty, child abuse, and other pathologies that plague endless generations of a family be broken.

Schools as Family

The community service center conception of schools can be thought of as creating schools for families. Although this is important, it may insufficiently meet the total needs of children unless we also begin thinking in terms of schools as families. Under this conception, in addition to serving as a center of community services for children and families, the school would also serve as a surrogate family for children, that is, a loving, nurturing environment that cares for the whole child—not just the academic child.

The deterioration of the family structure, the time deficit that characterizes many parent-child relationships, homelessness, and the influence of television in shaping values and behavior leave a void of traditional familial functions that must be filled. Widespread substance abuse, suicide, teenage pregnancy, and dropping out are all cries from students searching for love, humanity, and some sense of meaning in life—meaning that is difficult to sense without caring, human relationships.

The slack created by the fragmentation of the family and other social institutions must be picked up by schools. They and society must rethink the roles of schools if the "education problem" (which more realistically is the "society problem") is to be addressed in ways that are more productive for children and ultimately for society. Kirst and McLaughlin (1990) have noted that schools "must bridge the connection between the conditions of education and the total conditions of children" (p. 7). Narrow notions of the school as serving only educative functions must give way to more holistic, integrated notions of serving the total development of the child. Given the responsibility of schools to serve the educational needs of children and their current inability to do so due to the social realities of children's lives, the concept of school as family can be argued to be a moral responsiblity. If not the schools, then who else will accept responsibility for the child as a human being?

Schools must build on the notion of school as family, yet specific courses of action are less clear. Although a step in the right direction, simply involving families in the school is insufficient. Counselors, free breakfast and lunch programs, health services, and other functions of the expanded service school are also steps in this direction, but they do not go far enough. Schools must discover and develop ways of achieving significant relationships with children and adolescents. Current class sizes and teaching loads make this prohibitive. Simply lowering class size through hiring additional personnel or taking advantage of technological capabilities is also insufficient if teachers and other school personnel continue to fulfill their roles in traditional ways. Naisbitt (1984) argued that with the increasing use of technology, our society must not only become "high tech" but also "high touch." To become families, schools must think constantly in terms of high touch. Schools must decrease the size of the student body, but increase the overall service level. Small schools have been shown to increase student participation in school activities, increase attendance, and increase student satisfaction and identity with the school (Pittman & Haughwout, 1987).

IMPLICATIONS FOR PRACTICE

This chapter has outlined significant changes that have occurred and continue to occur in society. Although schools have responded with a variety of programs, the change has not been systemic. Students continue to occupy desks in classrooms and listen (sometimes) to what teachers say. Teachers continue to teach and fulfill their roles in much the same way they always have. Administrators continue to complete many of the same paperwork and management functions that they always have. (Only more so!) Basically, schools have not changed significantly.

The real challenge for school administrators in the 1990s and the twenty-first century will not be keeping the building clean, completing the paperwork, and making sure the buses are running on time, but rather the real challenge will be to rethink and re-create the school as an institution that is responsive to life in the twenty-first century.

FOR FURTHER DISCUSSION

1. What curricular changes should schools implement due to the change from a manufacturing to an information society?
2. Should the preparation of teachers and administrators be altered to respond to the changing needs of schools? If so, how?
3. This chapter has suggested several responses schools might make to the changes in society. What are some additional responses that might be considered?
4. How can schools become more "high tech" in order to allow them to become more "high touch"?
5. How might the role of the school administrator change in the community service center conception of schooling? How might it differ under the school as family concept?

OTHER SUGGESTED ACTIVITIES

1. Research existing conditions in schools in the 1950s and how schools responded to these conditions. List several significant conditions of schools in the 1990s and how schools are responding to these conditions. Develop alternative ways of responding.
2. There is disagreement between scholars advocating a multicultural curriculum and those in favor of a curriculum focused on the common culture. Hold a debate between the two sides.
3. This chapter has proposed that schools become community service centers. Others argue that today's schools have already lost sight of their basic educative mission by providing a variety of nonacademic services for students. Hold a debate between those advocating each viewpoint.
4. Expand the conception of the school as family. Begin by discussing traditional family life and listing all the functions traditionally served by families. Assess the extent to which today's families fulfill these functions. Identify and develop ways that schools can fulfill functions that are traditionally, but no longer adequately, served by many families.

5. Schools as community service centers and as families will require a degree of systemic change. Research and list alternative, more traditionally mainstream responses that have been found to be effective but are not widely implemented (e.g., implementation of Head Start programs for all).

REFERENCES

Alexander, K. L., & Pallas, A. M. (1984). Curriculum reform and school performance: An evaluation of the "new basics." *American Journal of Education,* 92, 391–420.

America's changing face (1990, September 10). *Newsweek,* pp. 46–50.

Banks, J. A. (1989). Multicultural education: Characteristics and goals. In J. A. Banks & C. A. McGee Banks (eds.), *Multicultural education: Issues and perspectives.* Boston: Allyn and Bacon.

————. (1991). Multicultural education: For freedom's sake. *Educational Leadership,* 49 (4), 32–36.

Barker, J. (1985). *Discovering the future: The business of paradigms.* St. Paul: ILI Press.

Bullard, S. (1991). Sorting through the multicultural rhetoric. *Educational Leadership,* 49 (4), 4–7.

Caissey, G. A. (1990, February). Skills for the information age. *Education Digest,* 55, 51–53.

Cetron, M., & Rocha, W. (1988). *Into the 21st century: Long term trends affecting the United States.* Bethesda, MD: World Future Society.

Clayton, C. E. (1991). Chapter I evaluation: Progress, problems, and possibilities. *Educational Evaluation and Policy Analysis,* 13 (4), 345–352.

Cohen, D. L. (1992, January 8). Conditions "bleak" for rural children, C.D.F. finds. *Education Week,* p. 7.

Coleman, J. S. (1966). *Equality of educational opportunity.* Washington, DC: U.S. Department of Health, Education, and Welfare, Office of Education.

Comstock, G., & Paik, H. (1987). *Television and children: A review of recent research.* (ERIC Document Reproduction Service No. ED 292 466)

Edmunds, P. (1990). *Demographics and cultural diversity in the 1990s: Implications for services to young children with special needs.* (ERIC Document Reproduction Service No. ED 325 565)

Education vital signs (1991), *Executive Educator,* 13 (12), A1–A27.

Elmer-Dewitt, P. (1990, Fall). The great experiment. *Time,* pp. 72–75.

Erickson, J. B. (1990). Poverty in Indiana. *F.Y.I.,* 2 (3), 1–2, 5.

Every day in America (1991). Community Education Star, 4 (2), 8.

Fetler, M. (1989). School dropout rates, academic performance, size, and poverty: Correlates of educational reform. *Educational Evaluation and Policy Analysis,* 11 (2), 109–116.

Frost, J. L. (1986). *Influences of television on children's behavior: Implications for war and peace.* (ERIC Document Reproduction Service No. ED 274 433)

Gibbs, N. (1990, October 8). Shameful bequests to the next generation. *Time,* pp. 42–46.

Grant, C. A., & Sleeter, C. E. (1989). Race, class, gender, exceptionality and educational reform. In J. A. Banks & C. A. McGee Banks (Eds.), *Multicultural education: Issues & perspectives.* Boston: Allyn and Bacon.

Groller, I. (1990, January). The future of the family. *Parents,* p. 31.

Hall, S. H. (1991). At the heart of the matter: Would a "hub" of needed services improve learning in your community's schools? *Network,* 17 (1), 1, 8–11.

Hewlett, S. A. (1991). *When the bough breaks: The cost of neglecting our children.* New York: Basic Books.

Hilliard, Asa G. III (1991). Why we must pluralize the curriculum. *Educational Leadership,* 49 (4), 12–16.

Hodgkinson, H. (1989). *The same client: The demographics of education and service delivery systems.* Washington, DC: Institute for Educational Leadership.

———. (1991a). Reform versus reality. *Phi Delta Kappan,* 73 (1), 8–16.

———. (1991b, October 30). Schools are awful—aren't they? *Education Week,* pp. 25, 32.

Kaufman, A. (1986). Trends in elementary and secondary education enrollment. In J. D. Stern & M. F. Williams (Eds.), *The condition of education* (pp. 140–157). Washington, DC: Office of Educational Research and Improvement.

Kimbrough, R., & Nunnery, M. (1988). *Educational administration: An introduction.* New York: Macmillan.

Kirst, M. W., & McLaughlin, M. (1990). *Rethinking children's policy: Implications for educational administration.* Bloomington: Consortium on Educational Policy Studies (Indiana University).

Krantz, P. (1990, February). Is your child hooked on drugs or alcohol? *Better Homes & Gardens,* pp. 41–43.

LeTendre, M. J. (1991). The continuing evolution of a federal role in compensatory education. *Educational Evaluation and Policy Analysis,* 3 (4), 328–334.

Levin, H. (1972). *The costs to the nation of inadequate education.* Report to the Select Committee on Equal Education Opportunity, U.S. Senate. Washington, DC: Government Printing Office.

Levy, J. E., & Copple, C. (1989). *Joining forces: A report of the first year.* (ERIC Document Reproduction Service No. ED 308 609)

McDill, E. L., Natriello, G., & Pallas, A. M. (1986). A population at risk: Potential consequences of tougher school standards for student dropouts. *American Journal of Education,* 94, 135–181.

McKay, E. (1986). *Hispanic demographics: Looking ahead.* (ERIC Document Reproduction Service No. ED 274 754)

Means, B., & Knapp, M. S. (1991). Cognitive approaches to teaching advanced skills to educationally disadvantaged students. *Phi Delta Kappan,* 73 (4), 282–289.

Naisbitt, J. (1984). *Megatrends: Ten new directions for transforming our lives.* New York: Warner Books.

Neill, S. B. (1979). *Keeping students in school: Problems and solutions.* Arlington, VA: AASA.

Nieto, S. (1992). *Affirming diversity: The sociopolitical context of multicultural education.* New York: Longman.

O'Hara, W. P. (1988). *The rise of poverty in rural America.* (ERIC Document Reproduction Service No. ED 302 350)

Orum, L. S. (1986). *The education of Hispanics: Status and implications.* (ERIC Document Reproduction Service No. ED 274 753)

Pallas, A. M. (1984). *The determinants of high school dropout.* Ph.D. diss., Johns Hopkins University, Department of Sociology.

Pittman, R. B., & Haughwout, P. (1987). Influence of high school size on dropout rate. *Educational Evaluation and Policy Analysis,* 9 (4), 337–343.

Postman, N. (1981, January 19). TV's disastrous impact on children. *U.S. News & World Report,* pp. 43–45.

Ravitch, D. (1991). A culture in common. *Educational Leadership,* 49 (4), 8–11.

Reed, S., & Sauter, R.C. (1990). Children of poverty: The status of twelve million Americans. *Phi Delta Kappan,* 71 (10), K1–K12.

Slavin, R. E., & Madden, N. A. (1991). Modifying Chapter I program improvement guidelines to reward appropriate practice. *Educational Evaluation and Policy Analysis,* 13 (4), 369–379.

Smolowe, J. (1990, Fall). Last call for motherhood. *Time,* p. 76.

Steinfield, J. (1973, April). TV violence is harmful. *Readers Digest,* 102 (612) 37.

Tanner, C.K. (1989). Positive educational policy with negative impacts on students. *The High School Journal,* 72 (2), 65–72.

The American teacher 1990 (1990). *New teachers: Expectations and Ideas.* New York: Metropolitan Life Insurance Company.

The fraying fabric: A portrait of America's poverty (1989). Mott Foundation, Flint, MI: Author.

The hunt for new Americans (1990, May 14). *U.S. News & World Report,* pp. 35–36.

Tregoning, J. (1986). *The effects of television on children.* (ERIC Document Reproduction Service No. ED 286 577)

U.S. Conference of Mayors (1989). *A status report on hunger and homelessness in America's cities, 1989.* (ERIC Document Reproduction Service No. ED 317 641)

U.S. General Accounting Office (1986). *School dropouts: The extent and nature of the problem.* (ERIC Document Reproduction Service No. ED 274 756)

Wright, K. (1990, March). The road to the global village. *Scientific American,* pp. 83–94.

CHAPTER 12

Demands for School Reform

Chapter Content

Public Perceptions of Education
1983–1987: Years of Criticism
The Second Wave
Failure and Hope
A Focus on Three Initiatives
Implications for Practice

*Professionalism is not a function of credentials or public status but rather a
state of mind that is sustained and enhanced by the way people are managed.*
—Shedd and Bacharach (1991, p. 3)

Educational reform has been advocated at numerous times since the founding
of the first public schools in the United States. The many frustrations produced
by these efforts have created an atmosphere of skepticism and gave rise to
questions as to whether lasting improvement would ever be achieved. What is
really wrong with our schools? Are they as bad as critics claim? Can meaningful
change be accomplished? Why do the demands for school reform keep surfacing?

To fully appreciate the importance of school reform, you should realize that
in the past one hundred years, public education repeatedly encountered the
menacing dilemma of choosing between two basic values—equity and excellence
(Cuban, 1988). At certain times, one became more weighty, but neither ever totally
disappeared. School reform efforts, including the most recent, continue to be
motivated by one or both of these conflicting forces. In this chapter, issues

surrounding the most recent quests for school reform, those that commenced in the early 1980s, are reviewed. Perhaps no other topic will have a greater effect on shaping the work life of school administrators in the next two to three decades. Today, we are witnessing serious and intense efforts to reshape schools and to redefine the roles of professionals who work in them.

PUBLIC PERCEPTIONS OF EDUCATION

Differences in public opinion regarding purposes of public education can be traced to the development of the earliest schools in this nation. During the common school era, circa 1830 to 1840, varying interpretations were already visible as to what public education was to achieve. Historical accounts of this period provide verification of these differing points of view. Spring (1990) wrote:

> On the one hand, there are those who see the common school period as a battle between liberals and conservatives for the establishment of a school system that would be of great benefit to all members of society. On the other hand, some historians argue that common schools were established to protect privileged economic and religious positions in society. These broad differences in historical interpretation contain elements of the debate that continues to this day about whose interests are served by public schools. (p. 75)

Values and beliefs that created individual perceptions of public education became increasingly diversified as the United States grew in population, welcoming immigrants with varying ethnic and cultural experiences. To this day, even local communities find it difficult to establish commonly accepted goals for schooling, let alone state-wide or national goals. A brief review of what has occurred just in the past three decades sheds light on reasons for this dilemma.

After the passage of the Civil Rights Act in 1962, the attention of the citizenry was drawn to human rights issues. Equity for minorities and the disadvantaged became critical education issues, especially in urban school districts. It was a time when the war on poverty was waged, ideas for desegregating the nation's schools were advanced, an unpopular war was fought in Vietnam, and curricula of elementary and secondary schools infused subject matter that related to multiculturism, human relations, and self-fulfillment. But in less than ten years, the social concerns that elevated issues of equity took a back seat to concerns about educational excellence. A good many political leaders, school board members, and even educators publicly declared that it was time to get "back to basics." And by the mid-1970s, such calls for redirection were influencing policy and practices. The confidence of the American public wavered, and schools found themselves immersed in yet another redirection effort (Finn, 1991).

Bacharach (1990) described equity as "the pressure to make each school responsive to the particular needs of its community constituency" and excellence as "the pressure to ensure that the general needs of the country are being met" (p. 3). Movement away from social issues that dominated the later 1960s to an emphasis on the "three Rs" and achievement testing in the mid to late 1970s gives meaning to these basic definitions. Experiences of this era exhibit how quickly and radically the focus of public education can be changed.

This meandering between equity and excellence has produced destabilizing consequences for schools. Courses change, laws change, and even teacher and administrator behaviors change—but only temporarily. The basic structure of schools remains intact, waiting for the next swing of the imaginary pendulum of public concern. Today, we still see vast differences in what the populace expects from its public schools. Some say the primary purpose is to prepare individuals for the workforce; some say it is to prepare problem solvers; some say it is to prepare well-adjusted human beings; some say it is to prepare good citizens; some say it is to prepare scholars; and still others say it is all of these. Schlecty (1990) warned that reform efforts will be attenuated if those leading the movement do not come to grips with the purpose of schooling in the twenty-first century. Contrary to public thought, the recent acceptance of America's education goals, six broadly stated objectives to be reached by the year 2000, does not resolve this concern. Many educators see these goals as unattainable generalizations designed to mollify public criticism.

Public schools were once considered highly effective. But this was at a time when only select portions of the population were served, and at a time when family, church, neighborhoods, and other social units provided those portions of a child's development and education not directly addressed in the context of formal schooling. The development of morals, ethics, and civic responsibility occurred more naturally in this environment (Finn, 1991). Our schools remain largely as they were in that era; yet, the communities in which they exist, and the needs of persons they serve, have changed radically. Problems created by this institutional inertia are central to understanding current reform efforts.

Public schools (and those who control them) deserve to be criticized. We should understand, though, that issues that give rise to contemporary dissatisfaction cannot be blamed solely on the schools. Finn (1991) correctly concluded that the task of school reform is made more difficult by a condition he labeled "schooling in a no-fault culture." Parents, communities, churches, the business community, and other agencies have not been willing to accept responsibility for their contributions to our present state of affairs. As a result, schools not only receive imputations they deserve for failing to remain relevant, they also are blamed for a whole host of societal and economic maladies.

1983–1987: YEARS OF CRITICISM

With the publishing of A Nation at Risk in 1983, the National Commission on Excellence in Education is credited with commencing the current round of educational reform efforts. Actually, the shift away from equity issues had begun nearly seven or eight years earlier. This report merely legitimatized quality and excellence as contemporary priorities (Finn, 1991). A Nation at Risk alarmed the American public by advancing the hypothesis that our schools had placed the national economy and security in a state of risk because too many students were failing to acquire basic skills. It characterized American public education as mediocre and declining.

Many who were influential in forming educational policy accepted the judgment that the effectiveness of our schools was at a new low even though there was little evidence to support this contention (Hawley, 1988). The timing of these shocking statements was most cogent. Many of the reform reports were developed and made public during the Reagan presidency. As noted in Chapter 5, President Reagan attempted to reduce the involvement of the federal government in public education, and he even tried to abolish the then newly created Department of Education (Marcus, 1990). In the context of this political climate, reformers often directed their urgings toward the leaders of state government.

In the period of 1983 to 1987, a number of reform reports were published, virtually all echoing the conclusions of the National Commission on Excellence. These continuing and mounting criticisms in concert with a shrinking federal interest in public education prompted many governors to pursue state-level reforms (Krotseng, 1990). These and related initiatives became known as the *first wave of educational reform.* Kirst (1988) outlined two key assumptions under-lying these efforts. First, he noted that there was a presumed linkage between international and interstate economic competition and education. That is, critics believed that America's lack of dominance in a global economy was partially attributable to shortcomings of public education. The second assumption was that education did not need to be fundamentally changed in order to achieve desired excellence. Reformers concluded that intensification mandates would produce higher educational outputs.

These assumptions were clearly visible in hundreds of bills pushed through state legislatures during this time period. Consider some of the more common recommendations for school improvement advanced during the period:

- Mandate longer school years.
- Mandate longer school days.
- Require students to complete more credits in order to graduate.
- Require students to do more homework.
- Require students to take more courses in mathematics, English, and science.
- Require more testing.
- Mandate remedial programs during the summer months.

Boyer (1985) warned that the increased role for state government in reform efforts may unwittingly produce a bureaucratic model that leaves teachers and principals more accountable and less empowered. Would we be able to create more effective schools by merely tinkering with structure or imposing additional requirements on students and teachers? Would we create even greater problems by further tying the hands of professional educators?

Although the cumulative benefits of first wave reforms remain unclear, it appears that the more direct and simple initiatives were able to meet their goals. For example, intensification efforts resulted in students' spending more time in school and taking more courses in mathematics and science at the high school level (Hawley, 1988). Expenditures for education and starting teacher salaries increased by approximately 25 percent during this five-year period (Kirst, 1988). Some states, however, quickly backed away from proposals that were either difficult to implement or too expensive. Political leaders discovered that programs such as merit pay, teacher testing, and recertification were ideas far more intricate than first imagined (Farrar, 1990).

From the perspective of organizational leadership, it is most noteworthy that reformers moved forward largely on the assumption that improvement could be accomplished without modifying the structure or culture of schools. That is, organizational dimensions of schools and school districts could remain intact and changes in rules and regulations would produce excellence. Additionally, virtually all of the recommendations during the first wave were legislated by state government, with the burden of implementation relegated to local school officials. These conditions produced major concerns for practitioners and theorists. On the one hand, the state imposed programs that largely ignored issues of equity. This alone generated criticisms from observers who knew all too well that such narrowly focused reforms eventually would cause problems. And on the other hand, the first wave resurrected an old and menacing concern—the centralization of policy development. Both directly and circuitously, the arena for formulating educational policy shifted from school boards to state legislatures, and this occurred at a time when there was increasing recognition that local decision making would be beneficial (Passow, 1988).

In the midst of the first wave, John Gardner in his book, *Excellence* (1984), again asked the troublesome and crucial question of whether our schools could be equal and excellent. His query appears to have had little effect on state government officials, who were preoccupied with competing among themselves to introduce bills calling for new intensification mandates that were drafted as if all schools were on equal footing. By the end of 1987, many experts were concluding that school improvement could not be achieved unless issues of equity were addressed. Metz (1990) summarized this concern:

> With one-fourth of our children growing up in poverty and one-third members of minority groups, we cannot afford to consider the education of such children a side issue. (p. 143)

Also, reformers started to change their beliefs that meaningful improvements could be accomplished by leaving the structure of public education intact.

THE SECOND WAVE

The second wave of educational reform constituted a major shift in thinking about school improvement. Following the publication of *A Nation at Risk,* schools faced two options. They could initiate cosmetic alterations that would create the illusion of change, or they could work toward substantive change (Rubin, 1984). For many political leaders, the former option seemed a necessity. Desiring reelection, many accurately perceived that the public wanted quick and painless improvements. But three or four years of legislative mandates clearly did not produce desired outcomes, and aggressive educators decided they should seize the opportunity to provide leadership for the reform movement.

Two primary commitments characterized second wave efforts: (1) an investment in children (a concern for addressing the needs of children at risk) and (2) an investment in teaching strategies (attracting and retaining competent teachers, and a restructuring of schools to give teachers the opportunity to define and administer school policy) (Hawley, 1988). The former was a reaction to concerns about equity, and the latter a response to growing concerns about centralized, bureaucratic-like policy development.

As previously mentioned, a number of educators criticized first wave reforms as being especially harmful to socially and academically disadvantaged students. Al Shanker (1988), president of the American Federation of Teachers, was among them:

> Undoubtedly, many able youngsters who have been too casual about their education will respond positively to greater demands, but we can also easily imagine how other kids, who cannot function in the current system, will react to even tougher standards. Tightening the current system probably will mean a better education for some students but increased frustration and failure for many others who, before reform, might have put in enough seat time to get a diploma. (p. 367)

There also was a political dimension to equity concerns. Reforms involve the allocation and reallocation of scarce resources, and there were continuing concerns that not all community constituents would equally benefit from the rash of laws generated by a quest for excellence (Scheurich & Imber, 1991). For instance, was it fair for states to give monetary awards to high-performing districts (as measured by achievement tests) when social and economic conditions are so uneven among local school districts? Did wealthy suburban districts benefit most from a reward system that was based exclusively on test scores?

Second wave efforts also addressed concerns of centralization and mandates, and did so largely by emphasizing the need to restructure schools. A realignment of authority, deregulation, and the development of school-driven reform agendas represent initiatives spawned by convictions that reform needed to include new roles for teachers and administrators. "Professionalism" and "empowerment" emerged as key words in speeches made by education leaders.

As noted several times, the American teacher has never possessed the autonomy and status accorded to practitioners in more established professions. They have had little control over the services they render (Sarason, 1990). Not only did first wave efforts fail to consider this problem, many initiatives actually had the net effect of further reducing the limited freedoms that existed for teachers. Newman (1990) described the net results of centralized policy development on the practices of classroom teachers:

Being able to work with relatively little direct supervision, escaping bureaucracy by closing the door, was one of the most attractive features of the occupation. The back-to-basics movement and minimum competency testing changed the situation drastically, ushering in an era of standardized teaching, testing, and grading. Teachers now feel pressure from their bosses, school board members and administrators, to teach by the cookbook. (p. 94)

Second wave reformers wanted to reverse this condition. More precisely, education leaders wanted to eradicate perceptions that teachers were merely technicians. To accomplish this, it would be necessary to create an image of teachers as professionals (Petrie, 1990). Professionalism would mean that teachers would be freed to make instructional decisions, to practice independently, and to share in the governance of their workplace. Correspondingly, such alterations would mandate new roles for administrators. In concert with this observation, Glickman (1991) urged that it was time to pay attention to research on successful schools and select principals who were instructional leaders capable of mobilizing and coordinating talent. But unlike the calls for instructional leadership that emerged in the 1960s, this one was molded around a professional relationship between principal and teacher. This new concept of educational leadership was less concerned with micromanaging teaching (Petrie, 1990).

A certain degree of teacher resentment toward administrative control and dicta is expected in American public education for two primary reasons: (1) most teachers see themselves as professionals, and (2) most work in bureaucratic-like settings (Goens & Clover, 1991). This discontent has been intensified in many communities by unionization and collective bargaining. The eradication of this resentment is most unlikely unless there are radical changes in the structure of schools initially, and the traditional relationships between administrators and teachers ultimately.

The second wave also includes recommendations for improving the preparation of teachers and administrators. If schools are to be restructured, we must not only change the local bureaucracies and existing mechanisms for state-level policy development, we must educate and socialize teachers to assume added responsibilities in areas such as evaluation, decision making, and organizational planning (Timar, 1989). Principals too must learn new skills if their role is to be restructured to concentrate on instructional leadership and facilitation (Johnson & Snyder, 1989–90). Already, there are signs that colleges of education are responding to these needs by placing greater emphasis on the acquisition of problem-solving skills through structured experiences with case studies, clinical practice, and internships (Kowalski, 1991).

First wave efforts were largely shaped by influential and politically powerful individuals outside the education profession. The second wave includes a greater diversity of key players. For substantive and procedural reasons, this fact is not insignificant. Finn (1991) noted the distinctive differences in educator-driven ideas:

If the reform tactics of the laity inclined toward the simple, uniform, universal, and abrupt, the kinds that sprang from the profession—and the decade saw lots of these, too—emphasized handcrafted, school-specific changes, the sort that are almost certain to be slow, gradual, and uneven. (p. 42)

Educators are more prone to favor reforms that are highly decentralized, geared to individual communities and schools, erected on shared power, and directed toward quality and equity rather than quality and efficiency.

FAILURE AND HOPE

As you consider the importance of school reform in relation to your plans to enter the practice of school administration, attention needs to be given to why reform efforts rarely result in lasting improvements. School administrators across the country are being asked why change has been so difficult. At Rotary Clubs and meetings of the Chamber of Commerce, they are repeatedly asked the same questions: Are our schools really as bad as everyone thinks? Have our schools really changed since 1983? Will we able to truly reconstruct our schools in the next ten to twenty years? If so, what must we do to accomplish this monumental task?

The Reasons for Failure

We know that educational reform efforts recur periodically; thus, we must conclude that solutions are either ineffective or short-lived. Cuban (1988) postulated that reform efforts often fail because they appear to address solvable problems when in reality they are engulfed in value-laden dilemmas. He made the following observation in this regard:

> . . . perhaps the problems were instead persistent dilemmas involving hard choices between conflicting values. Such choices seldom get resolved but rather get managed; that is, compromises are struck until the dilemmas reappear. (p. 329)

Mandates to increase school days or school years exemplify management solutions that provide assurances to the public that the schools are attempting to improve outputs. In this regard, they are compromises that defer problems until the next crisis is created by having to choose between equity and excellence. These myopic reactions to criticism are fostered by perceptions that administrators are largely management personnel and that schools can operate much like private businesses. Although politically expedient compromises may have provided brief relief from public criticism, there is little evidence that they produced lasting improvements. Mary Futrell (1989), former president of the National Education Association, lamented that history will view the 1980s not as the decade of educational reform, but rather as the decade of educational debate. Often we were able to induce temporary changes in behavior, but rarely did we modify basic values and beliefs that direct public schooling.

Some reform efforts fail because they are advanced with unacceptable strategies. Mandates, for example, have never really worked well in public education, especially when they are imposed from either the state or federal level. Reliance on laws, regulations, and mandates exemplifies one way in which reform efforts in the 1980s flew in the face of conventional wisdom (Finn, 1991). Given the wide range of differences in student needs and given the wide range of quality among this nation's public schools, reforms that treat schools, teachers, and students as if they were identical have very little chance of succeeding.

Some contend that reforms fail because they are not linked to appropriate rewards. Many initiatives developed in the 1980s focused on student outputs. Despite this emphasis, compensation systems for professionals were not reconfigured. Teachers and administrators in many schools continued to be rewarded for following routines and were not held accountable for student learning (Glickman, 1991; Shanker, 1990). But moving away from teacher salary schedules has proven to be a monumental task. In one sense, this inflexibility is further proof that school systems remain bureaucratic-like structures. There are, however, additional explanations for this resistance. Many teachers (and administrators) find comfort in the salary schedule because it is simple and dependable. The poor quality of performance evaluation is a reason often cited as to why time-honored methods of rewards should be maintained. Teachers observe that new reward concepts cannot simply be put in place without properly preparing those who will be affected.

Studies of existing conditions tend to support this contention. Concepts such as merit pay and career ladders require investments in staff development necessary to bring about improvements in the performance of both teachers and administrators (English, Clark, French, Rauth, & Schlecty, 1985–86). To date, there is little evidence of a wide-spread willingness to make this commitment. As Boyd (1988b) summarized, "In a quasimonopolistic, consumer-intensive setting of public schools, the reward structure is not oriented toward performance" (pp. 513–514).

Reforms also fail because they simply are rejected by those who operate the schools—administrators and teachers. Many educators believe that most reform reports were negative exaggerations. They feel that the authors of these documents had but limited insight into the "real world" of public education; as a result, they thought the reformers were were quick to criticize and reluctant to give credit. Such perceptions stem from the historical status of educators as essentially defenseless and powerless public servants. Throughout history there is evidence that educators periodically are blamed for society's problems (Callahan, 1962; Stinnett & Henson, 1982). Apple (1988) characterized the schools, and those who make them function, as scapegoats for failures in American business:

> . . . the political right in the United States has been very successful in mobilizing support against the educational system, often exporting the crisis in the economy to the schools. Thus one of its major victories has been to shift the blame for unemployment, underemployment, and the supposed breakdown of "traditional" values and standards in the family, education, and the paid workplace *from* the economic, cultural, and social policies of business and industry *to* the school and other public agencies. (p. 275)

One of the most noted scholars of the history of education, Lawrence Cremin (1989), postulated that education has always had its critics and that Americans have not been sufficiently appreciative of what public schools have accomplished. Skepticism and feelings of abuse are indeed major reasons why educators do not approach reform with greater enthusiasm.

Successful reform has been hindered by the lack of coordination of suggested improvements. Orlich (1989) noted that reforms often were contradictory in nature, poorly implemented, and eventually abandoned. A key issue since 1983 has been whether public education can reach excellence in incremental improvements. Soltis (1988) suggested that we cannot. He viewed many of the 1980s efforts as disjointed ideas that ignored the fundamental questions surrounding the purposes of schooling. Looking at the educational needs of urban children, Passow (1988) concluded that reform efforts since the 1960s have relied on fragmented and remedial approaches. Put simply, there were too many unconnected ideas, going in too many different directions, and advanced without any clear signs of public consensus relative to the primary functions of schools.

Failure also can be attributed to the rigidity of culture in many schools. Traditions of public education are so strong that even intense and prolonged criticism fails to bring about change. This issue is perhaps the most important with regard to school improvement, and it is discussed in detail in the next chapters.

Finally, reform failures need to be examined in an economic context. All during the 1980s, a number of government and business officials wanted the general public to believe that schools could be radically improved without additional funding. Although such notions have obvious political merit, they deserve to be challenged by leaders in the profession. Those who argue that money is not the problem (or part of it) are fond of citing statistics about the actual dollar increases in educational funding. Interestingly, they ignore facts and figures concerning poverty, cultural diversity, and the range of societal problems that have seriously complicated the missions of schools. Clearly, one of the greatest problems with reform efforts has been the notion that schools can be markedly improved without any additional funding (Boyd, 1988a).

Hope for the Future

Too often, when educators voice objection to reform ideas they are accused of being closed minded, obstinate, and inflexible. Critics sometimes compare educators to cancer patients. Initially, there is a denial that a problem exists. And eventually, when there is a reluctant acknowledgment of the problem, the tendency is to blame someone else for the condition. Hopefully, such characterizations are myopic. Many of the finest scholars in the education profession have put forward ideas, concepts, and paradigms that offer hope for the future. These recommendations are, however, often at odds with more expedient and politically acceptable initiatives, as exemplified by those advanced in the two or three years following the publishing of *A Nation at Risk*. Educator-driven recommendations have been predicated largely on the following query: If we cannot improve our schools with incremental mandates imposed from centralized authorities, what must we do?

First, we must begin to think of a total reformation and not of individual reform tasks (Soltis, 1988). Two observations are cogent in this regard: (1) improvement efforts must be coordinated, and (2) achieving real improvements within the current structure of schools is unlikely. Reavis (1990–91) noted that change by increment is a notion largely imbedded in a Cartesian-Newtonian driven paradigm that views nature as orderly, logical, and sequential. He observed that we need to accept our world and our schools as less orderly and sequential than commonly perceived. We are just beginning to explore new paradigms and theories to cope with the unexplained elements of schools as social systems. To accommodate a total revision of public elementary and secondary education, David (1991) argued that those who map and execute the change process must (1) receive a sincere invitation to restructure from those who hold real power, (2) be granted the authority and flexibility to institute change, (3) be given access to necessary knowledge, and (4) have adequate time to conduct their work.

Second, we need to build reforms that concentrate simultaneously on the values of equity and excellence (Futrell, 1989). In particular, special consideration needs to be given to revitalizing our poorest schools and to addressing the pressing needs of low-income and minority students. A number of theorists have noted that public schools are influenced by an inequitable distribution of knowledge, power, and resources and that schools perpetuate these inequities in policy and practice (Scheurich & Imber, 1991). It is politically expedient to talk about higher standards for education while ignoring social and economic problems that place literally millions of students at risk. Likewise, it is tempting to talk about "sink or swim" strategies without telling the public about the societal problems that are likely to be created by those who sink.

Third, the transformation of schools must be led by professionals. Goens and Clover (1991) contend that empowerment for practitioners must come in two forms: (1) structure, practices, and policies; and (2) personal choices professionals make in their own actions (p. 227). In essence, the organizational structure of schools must be transformed to allow professionalism, and educators must be properly prepared to assume the resulting responsibilities. Along these lines, Shanker (1988) suggested four basic principles for more meaningful reform:

1. Restructure the schools in order to give teachers maximum flexibility in making instructional decisions.
2. Increase teacher flexibility through the expanded use of technology.
3. Create professional-level salaries that will attract qualified persons to the teaching profession.
4. Create adequate support structures to augment the work of teachersl

Restructured schools need revamped curricula and improved accountability systems. These goals will more likely be accomplished if teachers and administrators are given added authority to make key decisions (O'Neil, 1990).

Fourth, there is a need to reconsider the relationship between schools and society. In particular, the American public ought to arrive at some reasonable consensus regarding the purposes of public education (Soltis, 1988). Signals society gives to its youth about what the culture deems most important, examples that are set for them, messages that are delivered, and values that are to be transmitted need to be included in the reform debate (Finn, 1991). All too often we approach the future wearing blinders, allowing present conditions to restrict our images of tomorrow. Trends, estimated problems, and alternative futures frequently are not injected into our projections. Reform efforts in the 1980s seldom were shaped by perceptive visions of the future (Kniep, 1989). As a result, random and disconnected ideas were allowed to dominate reform documents (Guskey, 1990).

School administrators are confronted with a massive challenge—and a massive opportunity. Orlich (1989) noted:

> The nation has wasted billions of dollars on poorly conceived but politically popular reform movements that have sapped the energies of school people. We need a national moratorium on reforms so that educators and local policy makers can analyze their own problems. This could lead to a new concept of *local system analysis*. (p. 517)

This effort will require imaginative and informed leadership at the school district and school levels.

A FOCUS ON THREE INITIATIVES

The attention given to public education during the 1980s produced a number of benefits. Among them was a refocusing on initiatives that could be instrumental in bringing about school restructuring. Three of these—parental choice programs, school-site management, and school partnerships—provide examples of ideas that are gaining popularity. Even though these initiatives differ, each is predicated on the belief that schools must be stimulated or cajoled to change structure and practices. Supporters believe these ideas could contribute significantly to improving student learning.

Choice Programs

The concept of parental choice must be addressed generally and specifically. Generally, one could argue that parents always have had choices with regard to their children's education. They could choose the school district in which they live; they could select a specific school within a given school district by residing within that school's boundaries; and if private schools were available, they had additional choices. Not all citizens had equal access to these options. Barriers usually existed for parents who could not economically control where they lived and for families living in remote areas. Recognizing such inequities, framers of the 1980s' choice agenda attempted to make their proposal a public policy initiative. That is, they wanted a law that would provide a reasonable degree of access for all families regardless of income or place of residence.

For decades, public education has been critically analyzed as a quasi-monopoly. Much like public utilities or television cable companies, public schools often are the exclusive provider of a service within a given geographic area. In the eyes of many critics, an institution that does not compete in an open market quickly becomes outdated and insensitive to real needs of the general public. Influenced by this judgment, those advocating educational choice contend that schools are mired in a state of inertia made possible by a lack of competition. More precisely, advocates suggest that the unwillingness of schools to change is explained by two conditions: (1) public managers lack property rights or profit motives in the successful performance of the organization, and (2) the organization receives a tax-supplied budget independent of satisfying consumers (Boyd, 1988b).

Choice is not a new idea; rather, it is yet another iteration of the belief that government should provide parents reasonable access to public school alternatives. During the 1970s, for instance, educational vouchers are championed for many of the same reasons that are used to support choice. Burrup, Brimley, and Garfield (1988) noted that the most popular version of educational vouchers was created by the economist Milton Friedman. They wrote:

> Reduced to its simplest terms, his plan recommended: (1) determination of a minimum level of education by each state, (2) the issuance to parents of vouchers that could be used in approved schools to purchase the education obtainable in that school, and (3) the payment by parents of the additional amount of money required by a particular school over and above the amount of the voucher. (p. 324)

The underlying justification put forward for both vouchers and choice is that the concepts will create competition, which will ultimately improve schooling. Voucher plans were attacked on several fronts including separation of church and state (e.g., allowing public funds to be used for partial payment of parochial education) and fiscal inequity (e.g., a flat payment to all families constituted an inequitable distribution of funds since family incomes and needs varied substantially).

The popularity of choice in the 1980s was enhanced by pervasive concerns that our public schools had put the nation at risk. In their book, *Politics, Markets, and America's Schools,* Chubb and Moe (1990) argued that public education is a massive bureaucracy requiring restructuring and competition to remain effective. They hypothesized that parental choice would force schools to change in positive ways. Faced with competition, they concluded, administrators and teachers who avoided change would be driven out of the market.

Confusion often surrounds the concept of choice because there are several versions of the idea. One variant, referred to as *choice within a school district,* allows parents to enroll their children in any public school within the school district in which they legally reside. Often districts offering such programs do so with "conditions attached." That is, exercising choice may be predicated on qualifications (e.g., there must be room at the school, racial balances cannot be affected negatively). Choice options within a school district typically are a matter of local district policy promulgated by the school board.

The second form of choice is *choice to attend any public school in a given state.* Here parents can elect to send their children to any public school in their state—even one located in a school district other than the one in which they reside. These programs too may be devised with qualifications. State-wide choice programs are promulgated by acts of the state legislature.

The final iteration, *public/private choice,* makes no distinction among school districts or between public and private schools. Put simply, parents can elect to send their children to any school. Financial support is given to those who elect private education in the form of tuition tax credits or vouchers. Tuition tax credits permit a deduction of all or part of tuition payments. Since public/private choice affects all children in a state, authorization for such public policy is framed in state law.

Contemporary efforts to provide with parents choice also are occurring outside the boundaries of public policy. For example, the Golden Rule Insurance Company in Indianapolis, Indiana recently provided vouchers of up to $800 each to 500 low-income families desiring to send their children to private schools. Such privately funded initiatives frequently pose serious concerns for public officials and educators. Criticisms suggest that these types of efforts serve to divert attention away from badly needed solutions for public education. The value of privately funded vouchers is often judged by public interest. In the case of Golden Rule, success was claimed on the basis of an overwhelming response from parents. But not all applauded the effort. Pipho (1991) wrote of Golden Rule chairman J. Patrick Rooney, "[he] thinks that business involvement in the reform of public education amounts to applying Band-Aids to a hemorrhaging school system" (p. 102).

By 1990, more than twenty states either passed choice legislation or were considering doing so (Association for Supervision and Curriculum Development, 1990). Beyond the more traditional arguments that center on the need for competition, some proponents also contend that choice is needed if we are to destroy the myth that there is "one best method" for educating children (Raywid, 1987). Choice, according to its advocates, would likely produce competing philosophies, curricula, and instructional methods. Supporters also suggest that being able to select schools will lead to strong bonds between schools and parents—a condition deemed to be lacking in many communities.

Clinchy (1989) detailed four conditions that should constitute a foundation for programs of choice if they are to succeed. First, there must be sufficient diversity to allow real choices to be made. Second, individual schools must be granted autonomy so they can be freed of regulations, permitting them to develop truly unique programs. Third, care must be taken that all parents and students have an equal opportunity to benefit from choice. And finally, there must be sufficient funding to permit program development to occur. Funding is an especially cogent consideration that often gets overlooked in political discussions. In fact, it is not uncommon for those advocating choice to suggest that sufficient funds are already available and that choice programs will simply bring about a needed reallocation of resources (i.e., good schools will drive bad schools from the market). In reality, educational improvement requires more than superficial changes in the appearance of schools. Offering a range of real choices requires adequate funding for functions such as staff development, curriculum revision, and appropriate assessment programs.

Choice has not been a popular concept among public educators. In part, this is due to a realization that countless considerations, ranging from transportation policies to assisting parents to make informed choices, must be made if the idea is to be successful (Glenn, 1989). Among educators, there are recurring concerns that are voiced in opposition to unrestricted choice programs (i.e., those that allow public-private choice). Consider the following examples:

- Choice ignores the importance of equity in public education. The idea is likely to accelerate the deterioration of inner-city schools rather than provide resources to improve these schools.

- Choice could create a two-tiered system of education. Urban schools, especially those in low-income areas, will find themselves serving students who are rejected by private or more prestigious public schools. Choice will benefit middle-class parents, but their gains will come at the expense of lower socioeconomic families.

- Not all parents are capable of making good choices. Students at risk are especially likely to come from homes where choice will be ignored or where parents are incapable of making informed choices.

- Parents are likely to select schools for the wrong reasons (e.g., convenience, athletics).

- Choice is politically popular because it is suggested to be a relatively inexpensive alternative to school improvement. In this regard, it constitutes a political and economic diversion.

- Students may be forced by their parents to change schools when they do not wish to do so. This will exacerbate problems with school adjustment.

- Choice could contribute to higher levels of racial segregation.

- When parents have a choice that includes private schools, public dollars could be provided to church-sponsored schools in the form of tuition transfers or tax credits.

- Choice will commercialize schools. More time will be spent on advertising and public relations than on curriculum development and evaluation.

- Choice obfuscates the real problems confronting public education; and as such, it will only further delay appropriate responses to societal ills such as poverty, teenage pregnancies, drug abuse, and an erosion of the family.

Choice provides an excellent example of an initiative that places administrators between opposing forces. Many high-status and politically powerful citizens (i.e., persons such as corporate presidents) view choice as a reasonable path to school improvement, and their views influence school board members, legislators, and governors. Analyses of the passage of a state-wide choice law in Minnesota, for instance, revealed that there was no public clamor or grassroots parent movement for the concept. Rather, the primary lobbyists were select coalitions consisting of upper-middle-class individuals who held socially valued positions (Mazzoni, 1991). Despite questions relative to actual taxpayer support, and despite widespread opposition among educators, concepts such as vouchers and choice continue to occupy a prominent position in the agenda for school reform.

Site-Based Management

One attribute that leads many critics to view schools as bureaucracies is the centralization of authority. During the 1960s and 1970s, centralization became even more pervasive because of school consolidation, union contracts, federal legislation (e.g., civil rights laws), the increased use of litigation to adjudicate education-related disputes, and increased federal and state regulations. Tyack (1990) noted that these changes created a compliance orientation for many school districts, a condition he labeled *fragmented centralization*. The massive increase of regulations made school board members and administrators apprehensive about allowing individual schools to stray from established district-wide policy.

Despite the trend toward increased centralization during this era, experimentation with prototypes of decentralization was evident during the 1960s and 1970s. Two of the more common approaches were known as "decentralized schools" and "site-based budgeting" (David, 1989). Philosophical components of decentralization (e.g., sharing authority), also permeated community education—a movement that gained popularity in the same era. As a reform initiative of the 1980s, however, the concept of site-based management (also called *school-site management*) emerged in a more formal and forceful way than did earlier versions of decentralization. Its supporters are found in all branches of the education community and society, ranging from governors to union leaders to superintendents. It is likely, however, that this support is largely attributable to discontent with standard practices rather than commitments to creating truly professional organizations. A recent study in Dade County, Florida, for example, found that principals, teachers, and union leaders supported shared management even though they were unclear about the precise aims of the process (Rungeling & Glover, 1991). Discontent with traditional practices is intensified by research outcomes that reveal the stifling effect of bureaucratic-like structures on the work of teachers (e.g., Frymier, 1987). Often it is difficult to separate dissatisfactions with traditional schools from ideological support for site-based management.

The professional literature suggests that organizations pursue decentralization paradigms in an effort to achieve one or more of the following goals: higher levels of flexibility, accountability, and productivity (Brown, 1990). All are cogent to reform. Flexibility is the least challenged of these goals, but there are many who remain skeptical as to whether site-based management will produce increased accountability and productivity.

Site-based management flows from several assumptions about school improvement: (1) meaningful change is most likely to occur at the school level rather than the school district or state level; (2) for change to occur, individual schools need flexibility with regard to regulations; and (3) broad representation of the school community in the decision-making process produces a level of commitment necessary to bring about lasting change. These premises are particularly relevant to concerns raised in the second wave of school reform efforts. The reconfiguration of lines of authority and deregulation arguably are prerequisites to substantive change. Often, schools must be freed of select policies, guidelines, and union contract provisions in order to permit creativity in program design. More precisely, two components are critical—autonomy and shared decision making (David, 1989). These attributes are visible in the following list of key characteristics of schools using site-based management assembled by Cawelti (1989):

- Decentralized budgeting procedures, permitting alternative uses of resources.
- Expanded basis of decision making through a team approach.
- Advisory committees providing a role for parents and high school students.
- Allowing personnel decisions to be more site based.
- Freedom to modify the school's curriculum.
- A clear process for seeking waivers from local and state regulations.
- Accountability in the form of an annual report detailing progress.

Because the concept involves a number of nontraditional practices, site-based management presents a degree of risk to school board members, administrators, and teachers.

As is the case with any innovation, site-based management generates a number of concerns relative to authority and responsibility. Consider the following:

- Critics are quick to note that involving larger numbers of persons in decisions does not necessarily lead to better decisions.
- Allowing schools to go in varying directions ultimately may lead to political and legal problems. Here the value of equity resurfaces as a troublesome issue, because the quality and quantity of programs among schools in the same district may vary markedly.
- Site-based management only will work if teachers truly become professionals. This means they need to sever ties with unions. To do less, concerned administrators note, may circuitously lead to union control of schools.
- Persons unprepared to make critical decisions will be given the authority to do so.
- Who will be held accountable for major decisions when they are made by committees? Critics of school-site management fear that the process will place school principals in an untenable position.

Beyond such concerns that focus on the procedural elements of decentralization, scholars also have pointed to organizational dynamics as an important consideration. English (1990), for example, observed that altering policy and rules for decision making may only give the appearance of meaningful change. In reality, bureaucracies are quite resistant to modifications in organizational culture. Hence, in many districts, site-based management may only prove to be another diversionary tactic—one that reduces public criticism but does little to change the actual operations and effectiveness of schools.

Without question, site-based management, if properly instituted, conceptually changes the practice of school administration. In schools where it is implemented, the roles of teachers and principals become less distinct (Hynes & Summers, 1990). Successful principals in these settings are able to share authority and work effectively with teachers by modeling the behaviors they value (Frase & Melton, 1992).

Many bright, energetic practitioners desire to work in challenging positions that require them to use their talents. For these individuals, the opportunity to engage in meaningful problem solving may outweigh concerns caused by role ambiguity. Schlecty and Cole (1991) wrote:

> Leaders of change in education must come to understand that most teachers and administrators need and want to think. But schools, as they are now organized, breed mindlessness. (p. 80)

Site-based management offers an opportunity to erect new professional relationships between principals and teachers—relationships that may invigorate both groups.

Like choice, site-based management comes in several versions. Brown (1990) identified five categories or themes for critical inquiry related to the process: structure, flexibility, accountability, productivity, and change. Each offers fertile ground for research as more and more schools move to adopt variants of decentralization. Indeed, much is yet to be learned about the potential and pitfalls of decentralization and its primary attraction, participatory decision making (Conway, 1984). What is the best organizational plan for collaborative decisions? How will change occur in schools where policy is developed by councils? Who will be held accountable for outcomes? Will the initial changes in structure and decision making become permanent or be just another passing fad? These are several of the many unanswered questions that surround site-based management.

School Partnerships

One of the buzz words of educational reform is *partnerships*. In 1983, only 17 percent of the schools were engaged in such ventures; by 1989, this figure rose to 40 percent (Marenda, 1989). The idea of linkages stems from observations that the problems schools face are multidimensional and that schools alone do not have the human and material resources necessary to eradicate them. It also is grounded in the realization that schools do not exist in a vacuum. The environment external to the organization frequently influences or even mandates the directions taken. Because of this dependence, reformers have called upon schools to build bridges with external constituents in an effort to monitor the environment and obtain additional resources. Partnerships, properly structured and instituted, constitute one form of bridge building—one that can be supportive of common goals in school restructuring (Pankake, 1991).

There are three popular forms of partnerships that involve schools: (1) schools and communities, (2) schools and businesses, and (3) schools and universities. Collaboration with communities is perhaps the most established, and these efforts produce a variety of programs. Historically, school-community programming has emphasized what the school can do for the community. Recreation programs and adult education are two of the oldest and best examples. More recent partnership ideas, those spawned by the reform movements of the 1980s, tend to focus more on what the community can contribute to school improvement. In this vein, parent-school partnerships have emerged as an especially popular idea. Parents are enlisted as volunteers for committees, for special projects, and even as teacher aides. A long-standing concept that advocates schools taking the initiative to create interagency coalitions to deal with needs that cannot be met by the schools alone is community education (Kowalski & Fallon, 1986).

The current problem of teenage pregnancies serves to explicate how community education can be an effective device to address simultaneously needs of schools and community. Schools often are unable to satisfy the social and economic needs of students who are directly affected by pregnancies. Likewise, community agencies find it difficult to address these needs fully because the individuals are students in the public schools. By working together, schools, hospitals, churches, mental health agencies, welfare agencies, and city government are more likely to produce necessary programs and resources.

Increasingly, school-community partnerships are relying on volunteerism. The public school system of Howard County, Maryland, designed a community-based model for evaluating its science program. Local scientists, administrators, teachers, parents, students, and graduates worked side by side in completing the task. Not only did this effort result in successfully written assessments, the school system saved approximately $60,000 by enlisting volunteers (Utterback & Kalin, 1989).

School-business partnerships have received tremendous attention since 1985. A survey by the American Association of School Administrators (1988) identified the following activities in school-business partnerships:

- Tutoring
- Field trips and special activities
- Donations of supplies and equipment
- Direct financial support
- Jobs for students
- Summer jobs for teachers
- Loaned executives
- Resource people for speaking to classes (p. 73).

The growing interest in educational reform among industrial leaders was motivated by several concerns, not the least of which included the preparation of an adequate workforce and the ability of American industry to compete in a global economy. McDonnell and Fuhrman (1986) concluded that a shrinking workforce (resulting from fewer births) coupled with an expanding technology caused industrial leaders to leave the sidelines and join the educational reform game. Because they saw the interests of schools and their own companies intertwined, many wanted to become actively involved with policy development generally, and the improvement of local schools specifically.

In pursuing their interests in public education, a number of corporate leaders remained dubious about the suggestion that more money was the answer to school improvement. They saw philosophical and structural problems. Schools were urged to become more goal-driven and demanding; and executives who actually became involved in school partnerships exhibited the greatest interest in projects that were highly focused, set within specific time parameters, and oriented toward outputs rather than process. Consider the following two examples:

- Often, school-business partnerships grow out of a need to revamp curriculum. When the Broward County school system in Florida wanted to update its electronics program, the program advisory committee assisted in enlisting several local businesses to become partners in the project (Dickenson, 1987).
- Partnerships with business have been enhanced by interests in technology. In Springfield, Massachusetts, the Monsanto Company created a partnership with local schools to do a seminar series on the technological revolution (Kinsley & Sweet, 1986).

Experience is proving that one key to building successful partnerships is mutual benefits; that is, both parties are able to gain from the association. For example, businesses can provide financial support for program development and student part-time jobs, and the school district can reciprocate by providing assistance with adult education, use of facilities, and formulation of staff development programs (Cameron, 1987). Emphasis on mutual benefits is a rather recent development, and it appears to be affecting policies and practices. In New York City, for instance, the term *adopt-a-school* has been avoided in an effort to establish that (1) schools are a public trust and not a public charity, and (2) partnerships are two-way ventures (Mann, 1986).

Even though many business partnership ventures prove to be fruitful, three concerns among school administrators have not been dispelled. First, there is a fear that corporate managers might use these joint ventures to impose their values on a public institution (i.e., treat public schools the way they do their own business). Educators often voice concerns that business leaders do not understand the ramifications of public administration. Second, private funding for public education occasionally produces cynical remarks that schools should be less dependent on public funds. A penny-pinching legislator or school board member may use private funding as an excuse to cut appropriations. Third, change in education does not occur rapidly. Some business partners may grow impatient and demand visible improvements long before they can realistically be achieved. Administrators fear that this tendency will lead to premature declarations of failure. Although these concerns persist, school leaders appear to be less apprehensive about business partnerships than they were one or two decades ago. Perhaps political reality is responsible.

Linkages between universities and school districts constitute another type of partnership that is growing in popularity. A book published by the American Association for Higher Education, *Linking America's Schools and Colleges: Guide to Partnerships & National Directory* (Wilbur & Lambert, 1991), lists approximately 1,300 school-college partnerships across the United States. To some degree, these associations grow out of a general service mission embraced by colleges and universities. However, many early partnerships were the result of individual firebrands who believed that higher education had an obligation to assist elementary and secondary schools (Pitsch, 1991). More recently, state universities have felt political pressures from governors and legislators to work more closely with schools in their respective states.

Collaborative projects between school districts and universities take four forms:

- Program assistance (e.g., programs for at-risk students, college courses for high school students)
- Programs and services for educators (e.g., staff development programs for teachers and administrators)
- Curriculum and assessment projects (e.g., helping with the development and evaluation of programs)
- Sharing educational resources (e.g., consultants, adopt-a-school programs) (Pitsch, 1991).

The sharing of resources is likely to become a critical issue in some states as an ever-growing demand for public services must be satisfied with shrinking resources. In some communities, duplicate facilities exist for a university, community college, and school system—all funded essentially by public dollars. Today, it is not uncommon for the leaders of these institutions to look more closely at how they can interface their services and resources.

Technology is playing a major role in fostering joint ventures between schools and universities. Several institutions such as Oklahoma State University and Ball State University already offer courses to high school students from their campuses via interactive television. Also, a number of institutions of higher education are moving to create electronic classrooms or state-of-the-art campuses with regard to integrating voice and video technology. These advancements are likely to spawn additional areas of mutual interest.

IMPLICATIONS FOR PRACTICE

Even though public scrutiny of elementary and secondary education has tended to be cyclical, the reform movement that commenced in the late 1970s and intensified through the 1980s is atypical. The force of criticisms, the persistence of government officials, and world conditions in which these efforts have occurred suggest that this era is not likely to pass without forcing changes in schools and the people who work in them.

Problems that confront public education are the product of decades of inflexibility. We have not appropriately balanced the values of equity and excellence; decentralization remains an elusive goal; and there continue to be widespread disagreements about the purposes of public education. These conditions persist even though our country and world have changed markedly in the last ten to fifteen years. We know that preparing students to live in the next century requires forethought about technology, worldwide economies, and changing social conditions; yet many schools continue to operate much as they did three or four decades ago.

Unfortunately, not all ideas for improving education are well conceived or properly structured. Many ignore the systemic nature of schools and society—an intricate context where even minor modifications can produce unanticipated by-products. Many of the major policy initiatives in the 1980s originated in the work of committees that consisted of socially elite persons. Few, if any, educators were included in these groups to help explain the real world of teaching and administration. In the aftermath of first wave efforts and failures, the education profession has a rare opportunity to lead the way to school improvement. Superintendents and principals who can develop proposals that join squarely the competing forces of equity and excellence, centralization and decentralization, and flexibility and accountability are likely to be in high demand in the next century.

What will our schools look like in the year 2005? What will be the roles of teachers, principals, and school superintendents? How will advancing technologies change the way we teach? What will be the role of the United States in the world, and how will this role affect the purposes of public schools? These monumental questions are likely to occupy center stage in the arena of educational policy for the next decade or so. As an educational leader, you will need to know more about coordinating human efforts, building coalitions, motivating others, resolving conflict, developing human resources, and capitalizing on the potentials of technology. You will need to be well versed in the latest teaching paradigms and curriculum packages. You will be expected to be a consumer of research. And your relationship with teachers may be far different from the norm of today.

In summary, the role of educational administrator is likely to be oriented less toward management and more toward the coordination of human resources in the future. Ideas such as parental choice and site-based management have the potential of bringing schools into a more appropriate and more productive balance with their environments (Raywid, 1987). In reviewing the reform efforts of the 1980s, Firestone, Fuhrman, and Kirst (1991) concluded, ''There is only one reform agenda: improving teaching and learning for all'' (p. 245). For this task, there always will be a high demand for creative, bold, and imaginative leaders.

FOR FURTHER DISCUSSION

1. What forces cause governors and state legislators to become activists for school reform?
2. Do you believe that most business leaders are sincere in their efforts to improve public education? Why or why not?

3. Why would the American Federation of Teachers look favorably on a concept such as site-based management?

4. In what ways are the roles of parents treated differently in the programs of parental choice and site-based management?

5. We often speak of teacher empowerment. Do you believe there is a need for administrator empowerment?

6. How would a superintendent's role be changed in a district that moved to site-based management?

7. In what ways does the existence of a global economy affect expectations for public schools?

8. Many educators respond to educational reform by saying, "This too shall pass." Do you agree?

9. What are some potential dangers of establishing partnerships with business?

10. In what ways do increased regulations and litigation contribute to higher levels of centralization in public school districts?

11. Do you believe most principals prefer to work in school systems that have high levels of centralization? Why or why not?

12. Do you believe that most principals view teachers as professionals?

OTHER SUGGESTED ACTIVITIES

1. Discuss the differences between "the application of technical skills" and "independence in professional practice."

2. Discuss the issue of social promotions from the perspective of excellence and equity.

3. Develop a list of the advantages and disadvantages of deregulation within a school district.

4. Visit a school that is employing site-based management. Determine if the school possesses the common features outlined in this chapter.

REFERENCES

American Association of School Administrators (1988). *Challenges for school leaders.* Arlington, VA: Author.

Apple, M. W. (1988). What reform talk does: Creating new inequalities in education. *Educational Administration Quarterly, 24* (3), 272–281.

Association for Supervision and Curriculum Development (1990). *Public schools of choice: ASCD issues analysis.* Alexandria, VA: Author.

Bacharach, S. B. (1990). Education reform: Making sense of it all. In S. Bacharach (Ed.), *Education reform: Making sense of it all* (pp. 1–6). Boston: Allyn and Bacon.

Boyd, W. L. (1988a). How to reform school without half trying: Secrets of the Reagan administration. *Educational Administration Quarterly, 24* (3), 299–309.

———. (1988b). Policy analysis, educational policy, and management: Through a glass darkly. In N. J. Boyan (Ed.), *Handbook of research on educational administration* (pp. 501–522). New York: Longman.

Boyer, E. L. (1985). In the aftermath of excellence. *Educational Leadership, 46* (6), 10–13.

Brown, D. J. (1990). *Decentralization and school-based management.* Philadelphia: The Falmer Press.

Burrup, P. E., Brimley, V., & Garfield, R. R. (1988). *Financing education in a climate of change* (4th ed.). Boston: Allyn and Bacon.

Callahan, R. E. (1962). *Education and the cult of efficiency: A study of the social forces that have shaped the administration of public schools.* Chicago: University of Chicago Press.

Cameron, S. L. (1987). School/business partnerships: We expanded the idea into a mutual-benefit plan. *American School Board Journal,* 174 (11), 42.

Cawelti, G. (1989). Key elements of site-based management. *Educational Leadership,* 46 (8), 46.

Chubb, J. E., & Moe, T. M. (1990). *Politics, markets, and America's schools.* Washington, DC: Brookings Institution.

Clinchy, E. (1989). Public school choice: Absolutely necessary but not wholly sufficient. *Phi Delta Kappan,* 71 (4), 289–294.

Conway, J. M. (1984). The myth, mystery, and mastery of participative decision making in education. *Educational Administration Quarterly,* 21 (1), 11–40.

Cremin, L. A. (1989). *Popular education and its discontents.* New York: Harper & Row.

Cuban, L. (1988). Why do some reforms persist? *Educational Administration Quarterly,* 24 (3), 329–335.

David, J. L. (1989). Synthesis of research on school-based management. *Educational Leadership,* 46 (8), 45–47, 53.

———. (1991). What it takes to restructure education. *Educational Leadership,* 48 (8), 11–15.

Dickenson, W. (1987). A committee as change agent. *Vocational Education Journal,* 62 (1), 31–33.

English, F. W. (1990). Can rational organizational models really reform anything? A case study of reform in Chicago. Unpublished paper presented at the annual meeting of the University Council for Educational Administration in Pittsburgh, Pennsylvania.

English, F. W., Clark, D., French, R., Rauth, M., & Schlecty, P. (1985–86). Incentives for excellence in America's schools. *National Forum of Educational Administration and Supervision Journal,* 2 (3), 1–17.

Farrar, E. (1990). Reflections on the first wave of reform: Reordering America's educational priorities. In S. Jacobson & J. Conway (Eds.), *Educational Leadership in an age of reform* (pp. 3–13). New York: Longman.

Finn, C. E. (1991). *We must take charge.* New York: The Free Press.

Firestone, W. A., Fuhrman, S. H., & Kirst, M. W. (1991). State educational reform since 1983: Appraisal of the future. *Educational Policy,* 5 (3), 233–250.

Frase, L. E., & Melton, G. R. (1992). Manager or participatory leader. *NASSP Bulletin,* 76 (540), 17–24.

Frymier, J. (1987). Bureaucracy and the neutering of teachers. *Phi Delta Kappan,* 69 (1), 9–14.

Futrell, M. H. (1989). Mission not accomplished: Education reform in retrospect. *Phi Delta Kappan,* 71 (1), 8–14.

Gardner, J. W. (1984). *Excellence.* New York: W. W. Norton.

Glenn, C. L. (1989). Putting school choice in place. *Phi Delta Kappan,* 71 (4), 295–300.

Glickman, C. (1991). Pretending not to know what we know. *Educational Leadership,* 48 (8), 4–10.

Goens, G. A., & Clover, S. I. (1991). *Mastering School Reform.* Boston: Allyn and Bacon.

Guskey, T. R. (1990). Integrating innovations. *Educational Leadership,* 47 (5), 11–15.

Hawley, W. D. (1988). Missing pieces in the educational reform agenda: Or, why the first and second waves may miss the boat. *Educational Administration Quarterly,* 24 (4), 416–437.

Hynes, J. L., & Summers, P. F. (1990). *The Southeastern Teacher Leadership Center: A program for the development of teacher leaders.* (ERIC Document Reproduction Service No. ED 326 535)

Johnson, W. L., & Snyder, K. J. (1989–90). Instructional leadership training needs of administrators. *National Forum of Educational Administration and Supervision Journal,* 6 (3), 80–95.

Kinsley, C. W., & Sweet, H. D. (1986). Inservice program for math/science teachers. *NASSP Bulletin,* 70 (490), 17–19.

Kirst, M. W. (1988). Recent state education reform in the United States: Looking backward and forward. *Educational Administration Quarterly,* 24 (3), 319–328.

Kniep, W. M. (1989). Global education as school reform. *Educational Leadership,* 47 (1), 43–45.

Kowalski, T. J. (1991). *Case studies on educational administration.* New York: Longman.

Kowalski, T. J., & Fallon, J. (1986). *Community education: Processes and programs.* Bloomington, IN: Phi Delta Kappa Foundation (Fastback Number 243).

Krotseng, M. V. (1990). Of state capitals and catalysts: The power of external prodding. In L. Marcus & B. Stickney (Eds.), *Politics and policy in the age of education* (pp. 243–262). Springfield, IL: Charles Thomas.

McDonnell, L., & Fuhrman, S. (1986). The political context of school reform. In V. Mueller & M. McKeown (Eds.), *The fiscal, legal, and political aspects of state reform of elementary and secondary education* (pp. 43–64). Cambridge, MA: Ballinger.

Mann, D. (1986). Building school-business coalitions. *NASSP Bulletin,* 70 (490), 1–5.

Marcus, L. R. (1990). Far from the banks of the Potomac: Educational politics and policy in the Reagan years. In L. Marcus & B. Stickney (Eds.), *Politics and policy in the age of education* (pp. 32–55). Springfield, IL: Charles Thomas.

Marenda, D. W. (1989). Partners in education: An old tradition renamed. *Educational Leadership,* 47 (2), 4–7.

Mazzoni, T. L. (1991). Analyzing state school policymaking: An arena model. *Educational Evaluation and Policy Analysis,* 13 (2), 115–138.

Metz, M. H. (1990). Hidden assumptions preventing real reform: Some missing elements in the educational reform movement. In S. Bacharach (Ed.), *Education reform: Making sense of it all* (pp. 141–154). Boston: Allyn and Bacon.

Newman, J. W. (1990). *America's teachers.* New York: Longman.

O'Neil, J. (1990). Piecing together the restructuring puzzle. *Educational Leadership,* 47 (7), 4–10.

Orlich, D. C. (1989). Education reforms: Mistakes, misconceptions, miscues. *Phi Delta Kappan,* 70 (7), 512–517.

Pankake, A. M. (1991). Learning the three Rs of restructuring through partnerships. *Educational Horizons,* 69 (2), 108–112.

Passow, A. H. (1988). Whither (or wither?) school reform? *Educational Administration Quarterly,* 24 (3), 246–256.

Petrie, H. G. (1990). Reflections on the second wave of reform: Restructuring the teaching profession. In S. Jacobson & J. Conway (Eds.), *Educational leadership in an age of reform* (pp. 14–29). New York: Longman.

Pipho, C. (1991). The vouchers are coming! *Phi Delta Kappan,* 73 (2), 102–103.

Pitsch, M. (1991, September 11). School-college links seen as fundamental to education reform. *Education Week,* 11 (2), 1, 12–13.

Raywid, M. A. (1987). Public choice, yes: Vouchers, no! *Phi Delta Kappan,* 70 (10).

Reavis, C. A. (1990-91). The science of chaos and school restructuring. *National Forum of Educational Administration and Supervision Journal,* 8 (1), 67–79.

Rubin, L. (1984). Formulating education policy in the aftermath of the reports. *Educational Leadership,* 42 (2), 7–10.

Rungeling, B., & Glover, R. W. (1991). Educational restructuring: The process for change? *Urban Evaluation,* 25 (4), 415–427.

Sarason, S. B. (1990). *The predictable failure of educational reform: Can we change course before it's too late?* San Francisco: Jossey-Bass.

Scheurich, J. J., & Imber, M. (1991). Educational reforms can reproduce societal inequities: A case study. *Educational Administration Quarterly,* 27 (3), 297–320.

Schlecty, P. C. (1990). *Schools for the twenty-first century: Leadership imperatives for educational reform.* San Francisco: Jossey-Bass.

Schlecty, P., & Cole, B. (1991). Creating a system that supports change. *Educational Horizons,* 69 (2), 78–82.

Shanker, A. (1988). Reforming the reform movement. *Educational Administration Quarterly,* 24 (4), 366–373.

———. (1990). A proposal for using incentives to restructure our public schools. *Phi Delta Kappan,* 71 (5), 344–357.

Shedd, J. B., & Bacharach, S. B. (1991). *Tangled hierarchies.* San Francisco: Jossey-Bass.

Soltis, J. F. (1988). Reform or reformation? *Educational Administration Quarterly,* 24 (3), 241–245.

Spring, J. (1990). *The American school: 1642–1990* (2nd ed.). New York: Longman.

Stinnett, T. M., & Henson, K. T. (1982). *America's public schools in transition.* New York: Teachers College Press.

Timar, T. (1989). The politics of school restructuring. *Phi Delta Kappan,* 71 (4), 264–276.

Tyack, D. (1990). Restructuring in historical perspective: Tinkering toward utopia. *Teachers College Record,* 92 (2), 170–191.

Utterback, P. H., & Kalin, M. (1989). A community-based model of curriculum evaluation. *Educational Leadership,* 47 (2), 49–50.

Wilbur, F. P., & Lambert, L. M. (1991). *Linking America's schools and colleges: Guide to partnerships & national directory.* Washington, DC: American Association for Higher Education.

CHAPTER **13**

Transforming the School

Chapter Content

Organizational Change
Why Schools Resist Change
The Importance of Culture and Climate
The Need for New Cultures
Leadership in Transformed Schools
Implications for Practice

In his enlightening book, *Teaching the Elephant to Dance: Empowering Change in Your Organization,* Belasco (1990) likens the evolution of organizational behavior to the training of elephants:

> Trainers shackle young elephants with heavy chains to deeply embedded stakes. In that way the elephant learns to stay in its place. Older elephants never try to leave even though they have the strength to pull the stake and move beyond. Their conditioning limits their movements with only a small metal bracelet around their foot—attached to nothing. (p. 2)

Many organizations too are bound by constraints that are more imagined than real, limitations that restrict creativity and change. A majority of public schools, unfortunately, are among them. These institutions often are hesitant to take risks, alter traditional roles, or adapt to the evolving needs of society. Ignoring repeated pleas to move forward, administrators and teachers stand motionless, conditioned by perceptions that schools ought not—and cannot—change.

The previous chapter detailed the intensity of society's demand for school improvement and the professional convictions that improvement cannot be achieved without fundamental changes in the structure of schools. If we accept reform as the critical issue for the next generation of school administrators, then it is logical for us to conclude that organizational change is the process necessary to achieve this goal. A number of critics (e.g., Cetron & Gayle, 1991) already have judged that school reform during the 1980s was a story of failure; and in large measure, they arrive at this conclusion because they see the structure and organization of elementary and secondary schools as fixed. Without question, the goal of reform and the process of change are intertwined (Fullan & Stiegelbauer, 1990). For this reason, a clear perspective of the former cannot be achieved without an understanding of how the latter does or does not occur. Your understandings of organizational change at the early stages of professional study are criticaliy important. Especially important is an awareness of how culture and climate are essential targets in the transformation of American schools.

ORGANIZATIONAL CHANGE

Each of us can readily think of experiences that we say "changed our lives." Some of these were occurrences over which we had virtually no control (e.g., a close encounter with death), whereas others were self-induced (e.g., changing our habits to sustain weight control). These experiences initially modify our behavior through instinctive responses, but if especially potent, they eventually revamp our values and beliefs (i.e., they have long-term effects on the way we conduct our lives). Organizations experience change in much the same way that we do. A refrigerator manufacturer, for instance, might respond to fiscal problems by laying off personnel. Yet, the conditions that led to the problem (e.g., poor budgeting practices) may be ignored. Thus, this fiscal crisis leads neither to changes in values and beliefs nor to improved fiscal practices. The problem is likely to recur because the organization does not allow experience to have a positive effect on the future.

Change is not something that is pursued solely for its own purposes. That is to say, it is not a product—it is a process (Belasco, 1990). Change is a medium for adaptation. It may be beneficial or harmful; it can be short-lived or permanent; it can be rapid or gradual; it can be planned or unexpected. But change, like conflict, is inevitable. The pantheist philosopher, Heraclitus, observed that "the only thing that is permanent is change."

Hanson (1985) defined organizational change as:

> . . . the altering of behavior, structures, procedures, purposes, or outputs of some unit within an organization. (p. 286)

Although all organizations continually encounter change, the ways in which they react to, encourage, and manage the process vary substantially—again, a condition not unlike the adaptive differences observed in people. Why did some automobile manufacturers in the 1970s cling to designs that were not economically practical for many consumers, whereas others quickly moved to design and build smaller cars? When the Catholic Church radically changed its liturgy in the 1960s, why did some church members readily adjust, yet others object to this very day? Everyday living provides repeated examples of differences in the adaptive behaviors of people and organizations. Inflexibility in both is a product of values, beliefs, needs, wants, and motivations.

There are several distinctions that are helpful with regard to understanding how change occurs. These distinctions are illustrated in Figure 13–1. In reality, change occurs along several continua. One change may be externally generated, unplanned, and spontaneous (e.g., a need to immediately cut budgets due to a problem with tax collections), whereas another may be internal, evolutionary, and planned (e.g., the incremental implementation of a set of instructional objectives). Change also varies with regard to importance (the impact on the organization), and duration (the length of time it is sustained by the organization). Therefore, discussions of organizational adaptations appropriately include some analysis of specific conditions associated with any attempted change. This is especially true of schools. Central to understanding organizational change are the following questions:

What is changed?

Why was it changed?

How was it changed?

How did the change affect people and groups in the organization?

Was the change supported and sustained?

Too often, we take for granted that those who are affected by change know the answers to these critical questions.

Much of the change experienced by public schools over the past thirty years flowed from external sources (Tyack, 1990). Take for instance the promulgation of laws protecting the rights of the handicapped during the 1970s. In the absence of such legislation, it is unlikely that schools would have adopted the practice of mainstreaming or insisted on the design of barrier-free school buildings. Legislative bodies and the courts frequently impose policies and practices on public institutions as a means of protecting individual or group interests and rights. Often these impositions are not popular among those who must implement them. Over time, they reinforce perceptions that change is inefficient and counterproductive.

Throughout much of the history of public schools in America, administrators were expected to preserve the status quo and to do so in an efficient manner (Knezevich, 1984). In the last half of the twentieth century, societal conditions coupled with a growing knowledge base about organizational behavior modified this expectation—at least in the literature. Well-informed policymakers warned that schools would quickly become ineffective if they failed to keep pace with

SOURCE

External_____**Internal**

{laws; court decisions;   {curriculum committees;
pressure groups   administrative initiatives}

TYPE

Unplanned_____**Planned**

{unexpected; not linked   {goals; strategic
to existing operations}   planning outcomes}

TIME   ORIENTATION

Spontaneous_____**Evolutionary**

{random occurrences;   {incremental occurrences;
occurs quickly}   implementation over time}

FIGURE 13-1   Conditions of Change

the needs of a dynamic society. Each time there was a national crisis, as was the case with the space race in the late 1950s or the concern for social justice in the 1960s, the literature in education focused on change and change agents. But these pressures to bring about more relevant programs do not entirely displace the expectations that public education transmit cherished values from one generation to another. As a result of these mixed intentions, administrators are left with a difficult, if not totally contradictory, task. They are expected to successfully integrate change and stability (Owens, 1991).

WHY SCHOOLS RESIST CHANGE

Zaltman and Duncan (1977) described resistance to change as "any attempt to maintain the status quo when there is pressure to change" (p. 63). If we examine the repeated attempts to transpose schools during the twentieth century and the outcomes of those attempts, a conclusion that public schools are immovable is logical. It is incorrect, however, to assume that all schools are equally inflexible. Schools differ in philosophy, resources, and leadership; and as a result adaptation efforts have been less than uniform. Accordingly, no simple, universally precise explanation can be given for the inertia that persists in a large number of elementary and secondary schools.

General Resistance

Most public schools share certain qualities that are suspected to inhibit change. Blumberg (1980), for example, observed that schools historically have been pre-occupied with maintaining peaceful environments (i.e., atmospheres that avoid turmoil); hence, these social institutions develop a character that generically moves them in the direction of resisting change. Resistance to change in schools also can be explained in part by attributes common to all social systems. Organizations, such as schools, exercise power over individuals and groups by providing a framework for values, beliefs, and practices that allow individuals to make sense of their lives. In schools, for example, policy, regulations, and curriculum help give structure and meaning to the work of teachers, students, and administrators. Change often is viewed as the threat to this framework and, in essence, a threat to the social system itself (Marris, 1975). Particularly when those affected by proposed change have little or no understanding of its purposes or potentialities, high levels of anxiety and resistance can be expected (Fullan & Stiegelbauer, 1990).

A major link in the shackle around the ankle of educators is the conviction that the organization and structure of schools are sacred. Pascarella and Frohman (1989) point out that purpose-driven organizations design structure to accommodate institutional goals, whereas other organizations are prone to determine function on the basis of form. And when form is viewed as immutable, meaningful change is nearly impossible. Over the past fifty years, schools have existed in a turbulent environment, but rather than restructure to meet changing needs, they have protected form and attempted to cope by establishing linkages with other agencies (Conners & Reed, 1983). Even though agency collaboration often is viewed as risky, traditional-minded managers prefer it over major organizational modification.

Specific Barriers

Because all organizations are social entities, all research conducted on the topic of institutional behavior has potential relevance for educators. This is especially true for organizations that must adapt to remain viable. In the business world, for instance, a company needs to do two primary things to remain competitive: (1) it must constantly monitor consumer needs and wants, and (2) it must use this information to adjust procedures, products, or services. This contention is exemplified in a study conducted by Beer, Eisenstat, and Spector (1988) of six major businesses desiring to increase their competitive edge. Among the most prevalent barriers to adaptation were the following:

- The organizations had far too many inflexible and unadaptive rules.
- The managers were not committed to change, and many did not possess the competence necessary to produce change.
- Managers and workers were out of touch with consumer needs.
- There was a low level of trust among employees, and this condition was exacerbated by a communication system that left many workers uninformed.
- The interaction among groups of employees was at a very low level.

These same conditions could well describe the operations of many public schools. They illustrate how a good bit of the resistance to change is associated with the social dimensions of organizational life.

In examining the difficulties of restructuring schools, Basom and Crandall (1991) created the following list of seven common barriers:

- A discontinuity of leadership deters change (e.g., many schools have frequent changes in personnel in key leadership positions).
- Many educators view change as unmanageable (e.g., administrators and teachers do not believe they can bring about purposeful change).
- Educators have not been properly prepared to deal with the complexity of restructuring schools (e.g., administrators and teachers know little about organizational behavior, conflict management, and other related topics).
- In following a "top-down" approach to making decisions, educators have not relied on research and craft knowledge to inform decisions (e.g., those making decisions find little need to provide professional justification).
- Educators are conditioned and socialized by the format of schooling they experienced and understand (e.g., a belief that school structure is not the problem).
- There are competing visions of what schools should become (e.g., teachers and administrators cannot agree on what changes are needed or what goals should be established).
- Time and resources have been insufficient (e.g., time and money are not available to conduct necessary staff development).

A critical barrier that can be added to this list is one of competing needs and wants. For example, change that benefits the school and students may not benefit teachers. Adding days to the school year without increasing the compensation of teachers is likely to produce political benefits for the organization and added learning opportunities for students—but more work and disenchantment for teachers.

To facilitate a better understanding of organizational inflexibility, Connor and Lake (1988) developed a three-category typology describing change barriers:

- barriers to understanding (not fully understanding what is proposed)
- barriers to acceptance (those affected will not accept the change)
- barriers to acting (factors inhibiting implementation).

The utility of this classification system becomes apparent when it is applied to contemporary reform efforts. During the first wave, approximately 1983 to 1987, the fact that classroom teachers and principals were not highly involved in developing proposals spawned all three types of barriers. First, educators often were confused by what was being proposed; second, they had little reason to be committed, politically or otherwise; and third, the proposals often ignored constraints such as fiscal resources or existing contracts that made implementation virtually impossible (e.g., intensification mandates to increase the length of the school day or school year would violate negotiated contracts with unions).

Barriers related to understanding, accepting, and acting also are visible in attempts to adopt site-based management. Some practitioners oppose the concept because they do not comprehend how it works, nor do they discern its purposes; others resist because it will change their work lives (e.g., a principal may not want to relinquish power and control to decision-making committees); and still others reject the idea because it will require human and material resources not available to the school (e.g., adequate funds to conduct staff development). Clearly, when persons affected by change are not allowed to provide input, or when they are poorly informed about the purposes and content of proposals, they are not likely to be supportive of change (Vogt & Murrell, 1990).

There are other specific circumstances, largely unique to public schools, that serve to block change. Status as a quasi-monopoly is one. Being assured students regardless of the quantity and quality of programming diminishes the demand to satisfy real consumer needs. Schools, unlike businesses, cannot motivate employees to change by dangling profit motives and bonuses before them. Teachers and principals, unlike their counterparts in business, fail to see a favorable cost-benefit ratio associated with major change. As noted earlier, change proposals create anxieties of uncertainty (e.g., being chastised for failure, getting fired), and these rarely are balanced by potential rewards.

The bureaucratic-like structures of many schools stifle teachers' ability to develop an internalized locus of control and leads ultimately to disenchantment and alienation (Frymier, 1987). Teachers in such schools often approach work with tunnel vision. They cannot see beyond their classrooms, largely because their work is compartmentalized. Consequently, a school's adaptability is reduced by the fact that many of the employees know relatively little about the total environment in which they work (Koberg, 1986). The division of responsibility and concentration of power common in bureaucracies creates an environment of isolation in which teachers neither feel a commitment to total school improvement nor believe that their views, needs, and concerns really matter to those who ultimately hold the power to make decisions. They see little relevance in organizational change unless it directly affects their classroom behavior.

Even though there are numerous change barriers existing in public education, none is more critical than climate. Some schools remain essentially as they were twenty-five years ago largely because the administrators and teachers perceive a societal expectation of institutional stability. Climate—the perceptions employees have of various aspects of the organization—can promote, retard, or totally discourage change. It is the imagined bracelet that prevents educators from moving forward.

THE IMPORTANCE OF CULTURE AND CLIMATE

There are three common perspectives of how change occurs in organizations. The first is a technical view erected on an assumption that increased knowledge and technical assistance produce change. This approach assumes rationality and focuses on the nature of the innovation (e.g., a new program). The second perspective accounts for power and influence that may be used by groups and individuals to support or ward off change. The focus is political behavior, and attention is given to both the innovation and the context of the organization. The third perspective looks at the shared values, beliefs, and norms of the organization. It is identified as the cultural perspective and emphasizes the importance of organizational context (Rossman, Corbett, & Firestone, 1988). After more than ten years of attempted reform, educators and the general public are recognizing the limitations of the first two approaches. Hence, more recent reform efforts have focused largely on the third category. More precisely, second wave change efforts are inquiring about the ways in which culture produces barriers that prevent change.

Imagine a situation in which a third-grade teacher is considering whether to administer corporal punishment to a disruptive student. What factors affect the decision? First, the teacher's behavior is influenced by personal values, experiences, and beliefs regarding the moral and practical dimensions of hitting a child. Additionally, the teacher hopefully considers whether corporal punishment is acceptable professionally and legally. The third, and often most influential, component is the teacher's perception of what the school expects from him or her. In other words, the teacher considers the school's norms. Do other teachers use corporal punishment? Does the principal advocate it? In some combination, the teacher weighs personal considerations (e.g., personal beliefs, motivations), legal and professional dimensions, and school-specific norms. Thus, even though the teacher may reject the use of corporal punishment, both personally and professionally, the act still may be carried out because of social pressures maintained by the school.

Defining Climate

The perceptions of what is expected in work-related behavior is a product of the atmosphere that exists within a school, and this internal condition, found in all organizations, is referred to as climate (Miskel & Ogawa, 1988). Climate is complex; it is not the product of any single person or condition. Several authors (e.g., Anderson, 1982; Owens, 1991) identify the work of Renato Tagiuri as providing the most comprehensive description of climate because it addresses the total environmental quality within a given school building. This is accomplished by grouping variables into four categories:

> *Ecology*—the physical and material features of an organization (e.g., school building, equipment, technology)
>
> *Milieu*—the people who comprise the organization (e.g., the needs, wants, motivations, dispositions, and so forth of teachers, administrators, clerical staff)
>
> *Social system*—the ways in which the school is structured (e.g., how teachers work with each other and administrators, the structure of the work tasks)
>
> *Culture*—the values, beliefs, norms that are characteristic of those who comprise the organization (e.g., the beliefs that the teachers in a school hold in common).

For purposes of clarity, the social system component can be separated into two parts: (1) patterns of behavior that exist between individuals and groups and (2) organizational characteristics such as calendars, schedules, and alignment of the curriculum. This latter component refers to nonhuman elements of the organizational structure. Figure 13–2 illustrates the perception of climate as consisting of five major components.

Even though each category is important, the five elements do not necessarily have the same potential for influencing climate. In recent times, the greatest emphasis has been placed on culture as the primary determinant of an organization's character and quality (Owens, 1991). Wilkens (1989), however, noted the importance of distinguishing between culture and character. He described organizational character as having the following components:

> *Shared Vision* (A common understanding of organizational purpose and identity; a sense of "who we are.")
>
> *Motivational Faith in Fairness* (of leaders and others).
>
> *Motivational Faith in Ability* (personal and organizational).
>
> *Distinctive Skills* (The tacit customs, the networks of experts, and the technology that add up to collective organizational competence.) (p. 3)

Culture (i.e., shared values, beliefs, and norms) shapes both the character and the climate of an organization.

Teachers and administrators hold perceptions of what is expected of them, and these perceptions are the collective product of a school's climate (Owens, 1991). Climate is, in essence, the commonly held interpretations of culture. It is climate that establishes parameters for such critical behaviors as risk taking and tolerance of error. Cues come from rewards, punishments, job descriptions, environmental factors, social interactions, and many other factors that serve to

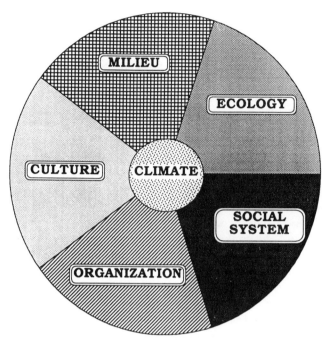

FIGURE 13–2 Elements of Climate

reinforce desired norms. Climate is pervasive and touches all functions of the school including personal interactions, student learning, and personal growth (Norton, 1984).

Importance of Climate and Culture

Even though climate is a primary factor in work-related decisions of educators, it is not the sole factor. Teachers and administrators also live in a world that extends beyond the school. In this respect, McKibben and Joyce (1980) noted:

> The general milieu of the school and the social movements of the times inter-act powerfully with the personalities of the teachers to create personal orien-tations which greatly influence how teachers view the world (and themselves in it). . . . (p. 254)

Socially driven issues such as poverty, civil rights, and child abuse as well as personal convictions that frame human needs and motivations interact with the norms of the school in the formulation of major decisions made by principals and teachers. These interactions among societal influences, personal values and beliefs, and a school's climate make the process of change a most complex task for educational leaders.

Some writers suggest that what occurs in organizations cannot be explained in the context of existing theories (e.g., Griffiths, Hart, & Blair, 1991). This void has led to a growing interest in studying the symbolic or cultural dimensions of schools to determine why certain behaviors are sustained and attempts at innovation are rejected. The design of school buildings offers a poignant example. In the late 1960s and early 1970s, literally hundreds of open-space facilities were built in the United States. The architectural designs for these structures were driven by ideas that were neither fully understood nor accepted by a majority of practitioners who eventually would work in these buildings. Superintendents (and school board members) assumed rationality; as such, they believed that curricula and teacher behaviors would, over time, adjust to the openness of these schools (e.g., teacher collaboration would increase, class units would become less structured). In many open-space schools, this simply did not occur. Instead, the resistance by faculty, and in some cases by principals, was so strong that the resulting political pressures forced a redesign to a traditional teaching environment (i.e., they put in walls to separate rooms).

What lessons can be learned from this experience? Changes in structure and environment do not guarantee corresponding changes in culture. School superintendents and school board members who elected to build open-space schools often did so either because experts advised them or because they believed at the time that this was the appropriate direction for facility design. And in reaching this critical decision, many superintendents failed to solicit input from principals, teachers, and parents. In the absence of a strong commitment to the philosophical underpinnings of open-space schools, parents and educators who worked in these environments tended to focus solely on the negative attributes of the concept (e.g., higher noise levels). Experiences with open-space schools exemplify the eventual problems created by structural changes to a school that are not supported by corresponding changes in culture and climate.

An organization can function when individuals and groups comprising it hold varying values and beliefs. This is an issue apart from the functional effects of individuals and groups' accepting and working toward common purposes (Wallace, 1970). Schools vary in the strength of their cultures. A strong culture is one in which there is nearly uniform acceptance of and adherence to shared values and beliefs—that is, nearly everyone knows, accepts, and works toward the achievement of the organization's goals. Deal and Kennedy (1982) contended that "a strong culture enables people to feel better about what they do, so they are more likely to work harder" (p. 16). But in the context of organizational change, is a strong culture an asset? Rossman, Corbett, and Firestone (1988) suggested that the answer to this query depends on the appropriateness of values and the established patterns of behavior. They believed that a school's norms define where change is legitimate. As such, a school could possess a strong culture that accepts the inevitableness of and need for change. Consequently, a strong culture can be an asset with regard to organizational change—or it can be a liability. The determinant is not the strength of culture; rather, it is the norms that are developed and protected by the culture.

Relationship of Climate, Culture, and Change

Can schools be restructured without changing culture and climate? Schools repeatedly have proven that they are capable of instituting structural changes, as evidenced by some of the first wave reforms in the 1980s. In the absence of normative modifications or legal requirements to sustain these changes, however, schools have exhibited a proclivity to return to traditional practices (Darling-Hammond, 1988). This organizational behavior is explained, in part, by the process of *organizational socialization,* which Boyan (1988) defined as "the communication of role expectations, reactions thereto, and the exercise of positive or negative sanctions in response to the actions" (p. 83).

Frequently, change is pursued by appointing new administrative staff. But forces in the school, school district, and community help to shape administrator behavior through socialization. If these forces are resistant to change, they present meaningful barriers to school improvement (Hart, 1991). The inertia is also explained by what Gold and Miles (1981) described as conflict between expertise and democracy. That is, change decisions imposed on public schools often are generated by planning procedures dominated by experts; and regardless of the value of these recommendations, those not included in the decision-making process often: (1) resent being excluded and (2) lack any political commitment to the innovations.

In the aftermath of the 1980s reform frenzy, researchers are looking more intensely at relationships between school culture and positive change. Firestone and Corbett (1988) pointed out that the literature on effective schools identifies distinctive characteristics leading to excellence, and these factors can be reinterpreted rather easily as cultural elements. That is to say, effective schools appear to possess cultures that set them apart from less effective schools. Yet, we know far too little about how these values and beliefs support effective performance and become a part of the school's normative structure. For instance, how do risk-taking teachers and principals affect student performance? Does risk taking become the expected behavior in a school through formal decisions, or does it occur through an evolutionary process? Despite the incompleteness of information, the knowledge base is sufficiently developed to conclude that culture and climate play critical roles in encouraging and sustaining change. Culture formalizes values and beliefs that give change a positive connotation, and climate encourages interpretations of culture that translate into desired action.

Although it is possible to change a school's culture, it is not always an easy or inviting challenge. Principals often find that the task is risky, expensive, and time-consuming (Deal & Kennedy, 1982). Additionally, some principals may not possess sufficient knowledge about organizational culture and the role that it plays in affecting behaviors. In part, these potential concerns explain the reluctance of many practitioners to engineer a new school culture.

THE NEED FOR NEW CULTURES

During the 1980s, principals, superintendents, and teachers contributed to reform largely by reacting to initiatives that were authored by others (e.g., legislatures). Cooper (1988) described the negative consequences:

> School people have surely not prospered, or even benefitted, from "received" culture and imposed wisdom. Yet school inhabitants have lived as though they

were unsophisticated natives ministered to by well-meaning missionaries who exude paternalism. Practitioners have had their shortcomings and inadequacies catalogued and classified and, sadly, have come to accept the blueprint of their deficiencies as though they had drawn it themselves. They have become passive and dependent in pursuit of their own voices. (pp. 45–46)

As the quest to create *empowered schools* (schools in which teachers and administrators function as professionals rather than semi-professionals) gains momentum, a number of questions emerge about the culture and climates of these institutions, about how they can be established, and the degree to which the general public will really be supportive. Despite this uncertainty, it appears likely that public education will continue to move toward professionalization; and although complete professionalization for educators may not be accomplished, the roles of teachers and administrators will be altered to some degree.

Change often is necessary for organizational survival. As public schools face increasing levels of competition, either through concepts such as choice or through state fiscal support that rewards student outputs, survival may well become a relevant issue in the next few years. Deal and Kennedy (1982) outlined several conditions that warrant cultural change in private companies, and two of them have particular relevance to public schools:

(1) When the environment is undergoing fundamental change, and the company has always been highly value-driven. (p. 159)

(2) When the company is mediocre, or worse. (p. 160)

Both of these reasons are found throughout the literature on school reform.

Experiences with reform efforts over the past few decades reinforce convictions that externally imposed intensification mandates provide only limited consequences for long-term educational improvement. As discussed in the previous chapter, the second wave of school reform is erected on a notion that schools and the roles of educators must change. But what needs to be changed, who must lead this change, and how much time do we have to change our schools? These have become monumental questions for school administrators.

Change Targets

Arguably, both culture and climate need to be change targets. The former establishes norms and the latter perceptions of norms that inhibit adaptations in schools. Yet, as Fullan and Stiegelbauer (1990) warned, the task will not be easy: "Cultural change requires strong, persistent efforts because much of current practice is embedded in structures and routines and internalized in individuals, including teachers" (p. 143).

Few dispute the contention that administrators need to play a primary role in bringing about new school environments in which teachers are treated as true professionals and students are provided programs that address individual needs. Contemporary practitioners face unprecedented criticism about the inflexibility of schools; they also are encountering professionally driven initiatives that attempt to create empowered schools where teachers are able to practice free of a quagmire of regulations. These two conditions converge to suggest (1) that there will be mounting expectations for schools to change to professional cultures, (2) that these changes will be implemented rather quickly, and (3) that administrators will be the primary change agents.

There are a multitude of values and beliefs that are critical to a school's culture. Do teachers believe that all students are capable of learning? Do the educators in a school believe that the school can really make a difference in the quality of life? Do they accept that schools ought to work side by side with communities? Joyce and Murphy (1990) reduced these many issues into four categories:

- norms of decision making
- ideas about research and scientific inquiry
- views of students and learning
- relationships.

Although there is general agreement regarding aspects of culture and climate that need to be reshaped, there is far less consensus regarding time parameters for completing the task.

The Issue of Time

A change in a school's culture can occur in one of three ways: evolution, staged changes, and radical transformation (Rossman et al., 1988). The first is best described as a "let nature take its course" approach. Alterations are essentially unplanned and occur as social, economic, and political needs dictate. The second approach is much like linear planning. Each phase constitutes a step toward the ultimate goal. The time element typically is lengthy, and there are no assurances that each stage will be successfully completed. Sizer (1991) pointed out that reform by incremental additions, a tactic that worked in the past, is no longer a valid option. The third approach, radical transformation, can be implemented in the shortest time span—but it involves the highest degree of risk. Radical transformation requires completely new ways of behaving, thinking, and perceiving by all those who are part of the organization (Kilman & Covin, 1988). This procedure is viewed as one of desperation, and it typically is spawned by high levels of dissatisfaction with the existing culture (i.e., situations where norms are severely challenged).

Massive and quick attempts to reshape an organization's culture are laden with potential problems. When attempted in educational settings, superintendents or principals usually feel compelled to condemn many past practices as a prerequisite to establishing new norms, values, and beliefs. Quick transformations rarely are successful, and they are likely to alienate most veteran employees. In observing business leaders who attempted to impose rapid and radical change, Wilkens (1989) observed that these initiatives often needlessly destroyed an organization's character. Because change was imposed so swiftly, key employees were demoralized and their opposition to change intensified.

Organizational transformation is an emerging field of study that has its roots in organizational development. Yet the two are distinctively different. Whereas organizational development concentrates on the unfolding, refining, and strengthening of behaviors, roles, attitudes, motives, beliefs, and values, organizational transformation focuses on totally re-creating these characteristics (Fletcher, 1990). In part, the materialization of organizational transformation is a reflection of the instability of our world and society. Change is occurring at an ever-accelerating pace, and organizations are literally forced to seek adaptations. Those that do not may actually face extinction. In these conditions of instability, leaders are more likely to take extreme risks.

A good many teachers, administrators, and staff employees in public schools resent criticisms of their work environment. Especially long-term employees are prone to defend existing culture and practices. For this reason, change in public school systems requires creative approaches that permit strengths of the old character to be applied to new problems. The transformation of culture is more likely to be accomplished in an evolutionary manner, and special care is taken to preserve those values, ideas, practices, one where beliefs that have proven to be successful. Radical transformation of long-standing social institutions, such as public schools, is extremely difficult.

Probability of Success

Recurring outcomes of research on effective schools provide evidence that restructured cultures can produce improved practices. The work of Purkey and Smith (1985), for example, identified characteristics commonly found in these schools. They included the following:

- a sense of community where teachers and administrators work toward common goals
- collaborative planning that permits teachers to have a collegial relationship with the principal
- the acceptance of common goals by those who work in the school
- a belief that the school is capable of identifying and solving problems
- a linkage to the community
- democratic decisions based on consensus
- a greater degree of responsibility placed on the professional staff.

Thus, creating new cultures is not simply a task of dreaming; it entails adapting the values and beliefs held in common by educators in a given school to coincide with practices that have been proven to be effective in other schools. It is myopic to judge that no long-term practices deserve to be preserved. Smith and Slesinski (1991) suggested that organizations use the simple and effective philosophy of Japanese leaders—get employees to commit to do old things better; do new things; build a flexible, adaptable, always-improving company.

Although the need to erect new cultures in our schools is evident, many remain dubious that the task can be completed. First, the goal cannot be reached by administrators and teachers alone. If teachers are to have more authority and power, they must be educated to perform a greater range of tasks. If teachers are to make decisions on critical issues, a degree of deregulation is required. Professional preparation and legislated acts are factors beyond the control of practitioners. Second, there are many unanswered questions related to the creation of new cultures. Judge (1988) identified several of the more cogent:

- What fate lies ahead for teacher unions if schools empower teachers to perform as professionals?
- How will we resolve potential conflicts between the interests of educators and the interests of the lay community (e.g., accountability and efficiency)?
- Are administrators willing to share power and authority by helping to create teacher leaders?
- Are teachers prepared and willing to assume all the added responsibility that accompanies empowerment?

Despite these informational voids, the quest for a new generation of American schools is already in motion. The New American Schools Development Corporation, an independent, nonprofit organization composed primarily of business leaders, intends to underwrite the design of new high-performance educational environments to jump-start learning in America. In its formal request for proposals, this organization makes the following statement:

> Think about every problem, every challenge we face. The solution to each starts with education. For the sake of the future—of our children and the nation—we must transform America's schools. The days of status quo are over. (New American Schools Development Corporation, 1991, p. 7).

The most relevant word in this statement is *transform*. Americans increasingly accept that change is necessary, but they still differ as to whether the remolding should be radical or evolutionary. While impatient politicians and business leaders demand quick and massive changes in public education, informed scholars caution that incremental modifications that build new cultures without destroying the character of American public education may be a more productive alternative.

LEADERSHIP IN TRANSFORMED SCHOOLS

Moving a school from its present state to a desired culture requires both vision and the ability to initiate and manage organizational adaptations. There are three primary sources of scholarly information that may assist educators to promote and manage change: research on change processes, research on leadership, and general studies about school administrators (e.g., behavior of principals). In examining all three, Hall and Hord (1987) concluded that formal organizational leaders keep emerging as the prime catalysts for action and change. Both the principal's support (Arends, 1982) and actual involvement (Lieberman & Miller, 1981) have been cited as recurring critical influences in research reviews. This information adds further support to the contention that the school administrator is a central figure in creating a climate that permits schools to adapt to changing needs.

Leaders versus Managers

Earlier in the book, it was noted that administrative behavior tends to fall on a continuum between management and leadership. As schools change to create professional environments, role expectations for administrators are likely to shift markedly. Whereas traditional schools have emphasized management, empowered schools emphasize leadership. This likelihood raises cogent questions about the behaviors of leaders and managers. In discussing such differences among executives in the private sector of the economy, Zaleznik (1989) observed that (1) managers tend to make decisions in a "zone of indifference," a reference to areas in which decisions are made where employees are neither affected nor interested; (2) they tend to focus on process and procedure and not on substance or individuals; and (3) they tend to communicate in signals rather than clearly stated messages. These same behaviors could well describe school administrators who devote virtually all of their time to managing facilities, supplies, lunch programs, and schedules.

Crowson and McPherson (1987), looking specifically at principals, observed that personal predilections and perceptions are influential in determining work behavior. For individuals who manifest managerial behaviors, adjustment to a new role—one predicated on risk, vision, and power sharing—requires not only additional knowledge and skills, but a reorientation of a personal view toward education, schools, teachers, and the role of administration. In essence, the successful transformation of public education will depend, in part, on a reorientation of school administration from a primary emphasis on management to a primary emphasis on leadership.

Sergiovanni (1991) viewed the challenge of contemporary leadership as one of making "peace between two conflicting imperatives: the managerial and the moral" (p. 329). Without question, schools need structure and management to protect the interests of the general public. But administrators also face issues that focus on the empowerment of teachers and the creation of schools where professionalism is the dominant consideration. Can principals empower teachers and maintain responsibility and control for the overall operations of schools? Can principals allow teachers wide latitude in making instructional decisions and yet not encounter problems with legislative bodies that protect the public from harm?

Transformational Leaders

Leaders in empowered schools must be able to diagnose complex organizational problems; they must understand how culture and climate affect worker behavior; they must be able to formulate and administer planned change; they must be capable of leading professionals to make collaborative decisions; they must understand and accept power-sharing strategies to school improvement; they must be capable of sustaining an open environment that allows the school to adapt to changing societal needs; and they must be able to sustain the strengths of the organization while simultaneously pursuing change. Erecting a new culture and climate in a school, for example, is not merely a technical process accomplished by reading a manual. A principal must work with staff in delicate ways to reduce expected anxieties of uncertainty. He or she assumes the responsibility of knowing which norms need to be challenged and how often they need to be challenged (Rossman, Corbett, and Firestone, 1988).

But the task of changing school climate and culture does not rest with the principal alone. Superintendents and other high-ranking central office administrators need to share the responsibility and work. Miller (1988) outlined contributions that central office staff can make:

- organizing projects on a district-wide basis that involve teachers as critical players (e.g., curriculum projects)
- directing staff development toward new roles for teachers and administrators
- allowing teachers to play a major role in determining the content and process of staff development
- engaging teachers in research as a process to solve problems.

These initiatives send messages to all professional employees in the school district. They help to establish new norms for behavior and expectations that teachers have greater authority and responsibility.

Given the perceived urgency of school improvement, the concept of transformational leadership is a cogent issue. What types of leaders are needed to execute a radical change in school cultures and climates? First and foremost, these will be administrators capable of empowering teachers. Goens and Clover (1991) proposed that administrators can help to prepare teachers to be true professionals by:

(1) creating clear visions, (2) connecting people to the purpose of the visions, (3) communicating effectively so that everyone understands and is working toward the same goals, (4) designing the plan for transformation, and (5) providing opportunities for followers to practice confidently and productively in the transformation process. (pp. 149–150)

Transformational leaders, according to Lewis (1987), are individuals who have a vision of the future, exhibit courage, believe in people, and possess the ability to encounter complexity, ambiguity, and uncertainty in performing the role of change agent.

IMPLICATIONS FOR PRACTICE

Sizer (1991) believes that meaningful reform in American education will be painful, because the job requires risk-taking leaders who are willing to change valued assumptions. He wrote:

> Challenging long-held assumptions, negotiating compromises, being decisive about what's truly important—these and other exacting processes are the seeds out of which can grow fundamental, lasting improvement of our schools. (p. 32)

The emerging role for school administration is far more complex and challenging than the traditional functions associated with managing people and things, and this role will be viewed in varying ways by those who contemplate a career as a principal or superintendent.

As second wave reforms succeed in transforming schools, the demand for capable leaders who can function in these environments should be quite high. These will be practitioners who possess advanced knowledge in the moral dimensions of leadership as well as the technical applications of management; they will accept teachers as colleagues rather than treating them as subordinates; they will view administration as a process of "pulling" rather than "pushing" people; and they will be leaders who truly believe that schools can make a critical difference in lives of individuals and the quality of society. They will be what Pascarella and Frohman (1989) described as "purpose-driven leaders," individuals who passionately embrace certain values that create a vision and who are capable of building mutual trust by demonstrating high levels of selflessness. Collectively, these qualities establish an image of a school leader that is far different from the bureaucratic manager.

At this point, you should understand why there is such a strong initiative to change the culture of American schools. Further, you should be able to visualize how radically different the practice of school administration is likely to become in these new empowered environments. In many respects, professionalization also empowers superintendents and principals. Imagine schools where decisions no longer are merely a series of political compromises. Imagine schools where instruction is extremely diversified to meet individual needs to ensure that all students are engaged in learning. Imagine schools where parents make appointments with teachers and principals to get advice about working with their children to enhance learning. And imagine schools where administrators, teachers, and students respect each other as members of a learning community committed to common goals. These are the positive images of the transformed schools—the ones that will entice the best and brightest to the challenges of careers in school administration.

FOR FURTHER DISCUSSION

1. Give examples of how schools have been expected to provide both change and stability. Why is it difficult for schools to do both?
2. What are some reasons why teachers might resist the creation of empowered schools?
3. What concerns is society likely to have with regard to empowered schools?
4. Do you believe that requiring principals to have experience as a classroom teacher will become more or less relevant if empowered schools become a reality?
5. In an empowered school, would the professional staff be more or less likely to address the needs of the "total child" (e.g., social, emotional, economic needs)?

6. Describe the differences between "risk taking" and "failure avoidance" as they relate to school administration.

7. Would empowered schools encourage or discourage programs designed to allow parents and students to choose the school they attend?

8. Describe the differences between evolutionary change and organizational transformation.

9. Identify the characteristics of effective schools. How is this information cogent to creating new cultures in schools?

10. What is the difference between culture and climate?

11. What is the difference between organizational structure and political activity?

12. Do you believe most schools have strong or weak cultures?

13. Do you believe most schools have a strong character?

OTHER SUGGESTED ACTIVITIES

1. Interview a principal who has at least five years of administrative experience and determine if he or she is supportive of the concept of empowered schools.

2. Develop a list of values and beliefs that are held in common in a school in which you work or have worked.

3. Assume you are hired to create an empowered school. Develop a list of qualifications for teachers you would employ.

REFERENCES

Anderson, C. S. (1982). The search for school climate: A review of the research. *Review of Educational Research, 52* (3), 368–420.

Arends, R. I. (1982). The meaning of administrative support. *Educational Administration Quarterly, 18* (4), 79–92.

Basom, R. E., & Crandall, D. P. (1991). Implementing a redesign strategy: Lessons from educational change. *Educational Horizons, 69* (2), 73–77.

Beer, M., Eisenstat, R., & Spector, B. (1988). *The critical path to change: Developing the competitive organization.* Boston: Harvard Business School Press.

Belasco, J. A. (1990). *Teaching the elephant to dance: Empowering change in your organization.* New York: Crown Publishers.

Blumberg, A. (1980). School organizations: A case of generic resistance to change. In M. Milstein (Ed.), *Schools, conflict, and change* (pp. 15–29). New York: Teachers College Press.

Boyan, N. J. (1988). Describing and explaining administrative behavior. In N. J. Boyan (Ed.), *Handbook of research on educational administration* (pp. 77–98). New York: Longman.

Cetron, M., & Gayle, M. (1991). *Educational renaissance: Our schools at the turn of the century.* New York: St. Martin's Press.

Conners, D. A., & Reed, D. B. (1983). *The turbulent field of public school administration.* (ERIC Document Reproduction Service No. ED 228 691)

Connor, P. E., & Lake, L. K. (1988). *Managing organizational change.* New York: Praeger.

Cooper, M. (1988). Whose culture is it, anyway? In A. Lieberman (Ed.), *Building a professional culture in schools* (pp. 45–54). New York: Teachers College Press.

Crowson, R. L., & McPherson, R. B. (1987). Sources of constraints and opportunities for discretion in the principalship. In J. Lane & H. Waldberg (Eds.), *Effective school leadership* (pp. 129–156). Berkeley, CA: McCutchan.

Darling-Hammond, L. (1988). Policy and professionalism. In A. Lieberman (Ed.), *Building a professional culture in schools* (pp. 55–77). New York: Teachers College Press.

Deal, T. E., & Kennedy, A. A. (1982). *Corporate cultures: The rites and rituals of corporate life.* Reading, MA: Addison-Wesley.

Firestone, W. A., & Corbett, H. D. (1988). Planned organizational change. In N. J. Boyan (Ed.), *Handbook of research on educational administration* (pp. 321–340). New York: Longman.

Fletcher, B. R. (1990). *Organization transformation theorists and practitioners.* New York: Praeger.

Frymier, J. (1987). Bureaucracy and the neutering of teachers. *Phi Delta Kappan,* 69 (1), 9–14.

Fullan, M. G., & Stiegelbauer, S. (1990). *The new meaning of educational change* (2nd ed.). New York: Teachers College Press.

Goens, G. A., & Clover, S. I. (1991). *Mastering school reform.* Boston: Allyn and Bacon.

Gold, B. A., & Miles, M. B. (1981). *Whose school is it, anyway? Parent-teacher conflict over an innovative school.* New York: Praeger.

Griffiths, D. E., Hart, A. W., & Blair, B. G. (1991). Still another approach to administration: Chaos theory. *Educational Administration Quarterly,* 27 (3), 430–451.

Hall, G. E., & Hord, S. M. (1987). *Change in schools: Facilitating the process.* Albany: State University of New York Press.

Hanson, E. M. (1985). *Educational administration and organizational behavior* (2nd ed.). Boston: Allyn and Bacon.

Hart, A. W. (1991). Leader succession and socialization: A synthesis. *Review of Educational Research,* 61 (4), 451–474.

Joyce, B., & Murphy, C. (1990). Epilogue: The curious complexities of cultural change. In B. Joyce (Ed.), *Changing school culture through staff development* (pp. 243–250). Alexandria, VA: Association for Supervision and Curriculum Development.

Judge, H. (1988). Afterword. In A. Lieberman (Ed.), *Building a professional culture in schools* (pp. 222–231). New York: Teachers College Press.

Kilman, R. H., & Covin, T. J. (1988). *Corporate transformation: Revitalizing organizations.* San Francisco: Jossey-Bass.

Knezevich, S. J. (1984). *Administration of public education* (4th ed.). New York: Harper & Row.

Koberg, C. S. (1986). Adaptive organizational behavior of school organizations: An exploratory study. *Educational Evaluation and Policy Analysis.* 8 (2), 139–146.

Lewis, J. (1987). *Re-creating our schools for the 21st century.* Westbury, NY: J. L. Wilkerson.

Lieberman, A., & Miller, L. (1981). Synthesis of research on improving schools. *Educational Leadership,* 38 (7), 583–586.

McKibben, M., & Joyce, B. (1980). Psychological states and staff development: Teacher development, personal and professional growth. *Theory into Practice,* 19, 248–255.

Marris, P. (1975). *Loss and change.* New York: Anchor Press.

Miller, L. (1988). Unlikely beginnings: The district office as a starting point for developing a professional culture for teaching. In A. Lieberman (Ed.), *Building a professional culture in schools,* pp. 167–184. New York: Teachers College Press.

Miskel, C., & Ogawa, R. (1988). Work motivation, job satisfaction, and climate. In N. J. Boyan (Ed.), *Handbook of research on educational administration* (pp. 279–304). New York: Longman.

New American Schools Development Corporation (1991). *Designs for a new generation of American schools.* Arlington, VA: Author.

Norton, M. S. (1984). What's so important about school climate? *Contemporary Education,* 56 (1), 43–45.

Owens, R. G. (1991). *Organizational behavior in education* (4th ed.). Englewood Cliffs, NJ: Prentice-Hall.

Pascarella, P., & Frohman, M. A. (1989). *The purpose-driven organization.* San Francisco: Jossey-Bass.

Purkey, S. C., & Smith, M. S. (1985). School reform: The district policy implications of the effective schools literature. *Elementary School Journal,* 85, 353–389.

Rossman, G. B., Corbett, H. D., & Firestone, W. A. (1988). *Change and effectiveness in schools: A cultural perspective.* Albany: State University of New York Press.

Sergiovanni, T. J. (1991). *The principalship: A reflective practice perspective* (2nd ed.). Boston: Allyn and Bacon.

Sizer, T. R. (1991). No pain, no gain. *Educational Leadership,* 48 (8), 32–34.

Smith, R. C., & Slesinski, R. A. (1991). Continuous innovation. *Executive Excellence,* 8 (5), 13–14.

Tyack, D. (1990). Restructuring in historical perspective: Tinkering toward utopia. *Teachers College Record,* 92 (2), 170–191.

Vogt, J. F., & Murrell, K. L. (1990). *Empowerment in organizations: How to spark exceptional performance.* San Diego: University Associates.

Wallace, A. F. (1970). *Culture and personality* (2nd ed.). New York: Random House.

Wilkens, A. L. (1989). *Developing corporate character: How to successfully change an organization without destroying it.* San Francisco: Jossey-Bass.

Zaleznik, A. (1989). *The managerial mystique.* New York: Harper & Row.

Zaltman, G., & Duncan, R. (1977). *Strategies for planned change.* New York: John Wiley and Sons.

CHAPTER 14

Women and Minorities in School Administration

Are women and minorities underrepresented in the practice of school administration? And if they are, why should this condition be a major concern for society? More precisely, why should it be a concern for those who are contemplating a career in school administration? This chapter addresses these and related questions.

Forty or fifty years ago, you would have had a difficult time finding material about women and minority school administrators in basic textbooks and leading journals. However, major court decisions and legislation in the 1950s and the 1960s helped to create an environment in which equity became a political, legal, and social agenda throughout American society. But despite such interventions, members of certain demographic groups remain grossly underrepresented in the practice of school administration. Policies, practices, beliefs, and values that contribute to this undesirable situation deservedly are under attack. This chapter helps you to understand that underrepresentation is a critical issue in school administration and provides insights regarding the potential effects of this condition.

WOMEN AND MINORITIES IN EDUCATION

Virtually all school administrators come from the ranks of teachers. As pointed out earlier in the book, a majority of states requires applicants for administrative licenses to have had experience as classroom teachers. For this reason, a historical perspective of women and minorities in teaching facilitates an understanding of present conditions.

In the earliest schools, teachers were predominantly men. Rury (1989) offered the following description of those times:

> . . . teachers as a group in colonial America were overwhelmingly white and male, largely middle-class and young, and often (though not always) well educated—at least by seventeenth—and eighteenth-century standards. (p.11)

The pattern of male dominance in teaching persisted until the latter part of the nineteenth century. As America grew in population, the emergence of urban areas brought with it novel challenges for public education. One was the requirement of providing schooling to a large number of students concentrated in relatively small geographic areas. In rural America, the model of the one-room schoolhouse was the standard because families were spread across large territories. Urbanization sparked larger enrollments, more sophisticated school buildings, and more complex and comprehensive curricula.

Underlying the entire program of urban public education was specialization (i.e., segmenting portions of education to increase productivity and efficiency). Beyond demographic realities, urban schools also were affected by the evolvement of state departments of education, agencies that gradually exerted control over decisions made in school districts, and the sheer expansion of knowledge (e.g., theories of industrial management, pedagogy). Combined, these diverse influences helped to mold both a public educational system and institutional roles for teachers and administrators.

Women in Teaching

One major innovation of the urban school system was the separation of students in elementary and secondary education. This was made possible by higher enrollments and encouraged by an ever-expanding curriculum. A product of that separation was the grammar school, a school that typically served students through grade 8. This newly created organizational format was to have a profound influence on the future of women in teaching. In fact, the separation of younger students into their own schools was probably the single most critical event that caused women to enter teaching. This was true for several reasons:

1. In general, those charged with the responsibility of employment avoided hiring women because of a perception that female teachers would be unable to control older students. The format of the one-room schoolhouse

required the teacher to be responsible for a relatively large group of students, including some in their teens. In this educational setting, there were no other teachers or a principal to assist with the control of pupil behavior. The creation of grammar schools reduced fears about controlling pupil conduct; as a result, school officials were less apprehensive about employing women in teaching positions (Clifford, 1989).

2. A major part of urbanization was industrial growth. The expansion of industry and commerce created a multitude of new jobs—many of which paid far more than teaching did. Men in teaching were relatively well educated for that time period, and that made them especially attractive to some employers. As a result, many left education to pursue more lucrative careers in the private sector of the economy (Rury, 1989).

These two influences, the emergence of grammar schools and the high demand for educated males in the private sector of the economy, combined to create conditions most favorable for women who wished to be schoolteachers.

In the past sixty years, there have been two significant trends with regard to women in the teaching force. First, the influx of women into teaching that commenced near the turn of the century proved to be more than a short-term phenomenon. Over the first three decades of the twentieth century, more and more women entered teaching. In large measure, this was made possible by the rapid growth of elementary schools across the country. Women entered the teaching ranks so rapidly that by 1940, only one in five teachers was male—a remarkable shift from the condition that existed prior to urbanization. This trend was diverted for a period of time following World War II and the Korean war. A number of men who were veterans of the armed services took advantage of the G.I. Bill—legislation that gave financial assistance to veterans to continue their education—and became teachers. Despite this increased entry of men into the profession during the 1950s and 1960s, teaching remained a predominantly female occupation (Ortiz & Marshall, 1988). In 1968, about 30 percent of the nation's teaching force was male—up about 5 percent from 1940. Data during the 1970s and 1980s indicate that the male presence in the teaching force is again declining—albeit slightly.

The second trend relates to the percentage of women teachers who marry and remain in the profession. In the first half of the twentieth century, women generally left teaching if they decided to marry and raise a family. In 1930, only 18 percent of the female teachers were married—by 1960, only 29 percent were unmarried (Clifford, 1989). Since 1950, women who marry tend to stay in the profession; and many take only brief absences to bear children (Rury, 1989). The retention of married females in the teaching profession is demographically significant. It has increased the pool of highly experienced female teachers (those with ten or more years of experience), and it has raised the average age of the teaching force.

In 1990, slightly over 70 percent of the nation's public school teachers were women—only a minor increase over 1968. More revealing, however, are data concerning new hires in the last half of the 1980s. Women constituted 78 percent of the teachers employed from 1985 to 1990 (Feistritzer, 1990). This statistic comes as a surprise to some given the effects of equity laws and court decisions in the previous decades. During the 1970s and 1980s, new career opportunities opened to women. Discrimination was less likely in gaining admission to professional study in areas such as law and medicine. Also, a relatively large number of women chose to major in business rather than in what had been the traditional majors for them—education and nursing. During the mid-1980s, however, a number of teacher education programs experienced a general increase in enrollments and a specific increase in female enrollments. Enrollment data and new hire-data from 1985 to 1990 provided indications that teaching was again becoming a popular career choice for women (Feistritzer, 1990).

Does a majority of women in teaching influence the ways teachers are treated and compensated? Several writers have speculated about political and economic consequences stemming from the workforce in education being dominated by women. Spencer (1986), for instance, saw a linkage between the majority of women in teaching and the public's perception of teachers as professionals: "The historical development of the structure of schools and the predominance of women in teaching has led to the quasi-professional status of teaching" (p. 13). Earlier in the book, it was noted that a quasi-profession is one in which practitioners have only limited control over their duties and responsibilities. Thus, the linkage of women to status as a quasi-profession is one embedded in societal prejudices that women require supervision in the workplace.

Women also have been blamed unjustly for the relative low salaries paid teachers. This attribution is embedded in the belief that taxpayers are unwilling to pay women higher salaries because historically many earned second incomes in their families. But more enlightened analysts argue that problems of status and compensation run deeper than gender-related prejudice. For example, Clifford (1989) aptly pointed out, "Teaching has been underpaid throughout history, regardless of the gender of the majority and the method of paying for teaching" (p. 317). In truth, women have been primary victims, not the causes, of society's unwillingness to compensate educators as true professionals.

Minorities in Teaching

Teaching has long been considered an attractive occupation for first-generation college graduates, especially those coming from lower and lower-middle economic groups. An example of this is seen in the experience of those of African heritage. Historically, African Americans in the United States who found the means to attend college frequently selected teaching as a realistic career goal. This was true even though job opportunities for many graduates was essentially restricted (e.g., throughout the first half of the twentieth century, African-American teachers worked predominantly in segregated schools located in rural areas) (Perkins, 1989).

Civil rights legislation and subsequent litigation altered the career aspirations of African-American college students in two very important ways—they lowered the demand for teachers and opened doors to new career choices. The demand for African-American teachers in many parts of the United States declined when racially segregated schools were forced out of existence. Even though the number of positions in public schools remained essentially the same, African Americans no longer had the job-related opportunities afforded by segregated schools. In locations where these schools previously existed, minority and white applicants now competed for the same positions. Laws and court orders that forced the closure of segregated schools did not change individuals who harbored racial prejudice. Especially in the South, teaching opportunities for African Americans in the 1960s and early 1970s declined. In addition, the civil rights movement opened doors to other professions for minority college graduates. Rather than become teachers, many African-American college students opted for majors in business, pre-professional studies for law and medicine, or areas related to government and social justice. Education employers could no longer depend on the best and brightest minority candidates' entering teaching (Perkins, 1989).

Through the 1970s, there was a steady increase in the enrollment of African Americans in higher education, and many still decided to pursue careers in teaching. Additionally, by the mid-1970s, many school board members and administrators increasingly realized that there was a growing need to employ minority teachers as role models. As a result of these two factors, the representation of African Americans in teaching increased. In 1980, they constituted nearly 10 percent of the nation's teaching force—the highest proportion in history (Rury, 1989). Despite this apparent gain, serious concerns persisted. Minority teachers were not distributed equally throughout the educational system—most were employed in schools with high minority student enrollments. In recent years, there has been growing evidence that the representation of African Americans in the teaching force is again declining even though their representation in the general population is increasing.

The National Center for Education Statistics computes concentration ratios for majors at the undergraduate and graduate levels. (The concentration ratio is calculated as the percentage of a minority group earning bachelor's degrees who majored in a selected field divided by the percentage of whites earning the same degree with the same major.) During the period of 1977–1989, the number of African-American undergraduate students choosing to major in education fell dramatically. In 1977, African Americans were more likely than white students to major in education, but by 1989 the reverse was true. In 1989, the highest concentration ratio of African-American undergraduate majors was found in business. The concentration ratio for Hispanic students who selected an education major has declined steadily since 1981. In 1989, education had the lowest concentration ratio for Americans of Latin ancestry (Hispanics) enrolled in undergraduate school—social/behavioral sciences, humanities, natural sciences, computer science/engineering, and business all had higher concentration ratios (National Center for Education Statistics, 1991). Data for new teacher hires between 1985 and 1990 show that only 5 percent were African Americans (Feistritzer, 1990).

Historically, the involvement of American Indians and Hispanics in the teaching profession too has been limited. In part, blame lies with public education itself for the ways it has treated both groups. The use of boarding schools, for example, essentially kept Indian students out of mainstream schools and created perceptions that public education was a ploy to train Indians to live in a white man's world. Many Hispanics also felt abused by public education. For example, Hispanic parents sometimes saw administrators looking the other way rather than enforcing compulsory attendance laws. Some saw their children being classified as "whites" so school districts could meet legal requirements related to desegregation (i.e., Hispanics students were pawns used to prevent Anglo-Saxon white children from being mixed with African-American children in desegregated schools) (Valverde & Brown, 1988). These experiences with public education did not foster perceptions that teaching would be a good career choice.

In 1975, only 1.7 percent of elementary teachers and 1.5 percent of secondary teachers in the United States were Hispanic. In that same year, only three-tenths of 1 percent of elementary teachers and two-tenths of one percent of secondary teachers were American Indians (Ortiz, 1982). Data for new hires in teaching between 1985 to 1990 reveal the following:

American Indians—less than 1 percent

Asian/Pacific Islanders—1 percent

African Americans—5 percent

Hispanics—2 percent (Feistritzer, 1990).

These figures reflect virtually no gains for these groups since the mid-1970s.

Data on recently employed teachers reveal an interesting pattern concerning minorities. In comparing two groups of new hires, those having traditional certification and those having alternative forms of certification, minorities were found to constitute a higher percentage of the latter group. Of the new hires with alternative certificates, 10 percent were African Americans, 16 percent Hispanic, and 1 percent American Indian (Feistritzer, 1990). In part, the higher figures in the alternative certification group reflect a negative balance between demand and supply created through traditional teacher education. Because many states link administrative certification to teacher certification, it is uncertain as to whether minorities who enter professional practice in nontraditional ways affect the number of minorities in school administration.

THE CONCERN IN ADMINISTRATION

To answer the question of whether women and minorities are underrepresented in school administration, two common points of comparisons have been made. The first is a comparison of teacher data to administrator data (percentage of teachers who belong to a given group as opposed to the percentage of administrators who belong to the same group), and the second is a comparison of student data to administrator data (percentage of students who belong to a given group as opposed to the percentage of administrators who belong to the same group). Most often, comparisons for women have been based on the former technique, whereas comparisons for minorities have concentrated on the latter.

Sheer numbers present only one dimension of underrepresentation—there also is a qualitative aspect to the concern. This is exemplified by the types of positions occupied by women and minorities in school administration. Ortiz and Marshall (1988) summarized the problem: "Women, especially minority women, but even minority men, continue to occupy the lowest positions in the administrative hierarchy, white males the higher and the more powerful positions" (p. 127). Women are found predominantly in the elementary school principalship or in central office positions that focus on instructional programs. A recent study found that 96 percent of superintendencies, 77 percent of deputy/assistant superintendencies, 88 percent of high school principalships, and 71 percent of elementary principalships are occupied by men. This same study found that only 3.4 percent of the nation's superintendencies were occupied by minorities (Jones & Montenegro, 1990).

The U.S. Department of Education's Office of Civil Rights projected that students who belong to minority groups totaled 38.7 percent of public school enrollment in 1989—and this figure is expected to reach 46 percent by the year 2020 (State of the states, 1991). In many urban school systems, there already exists a "minority majority" (i.e., the majority of the student population are officially classified as members of a minority group). Birth rates for Hispanics and African Americans suggest that these groups will continue to increase, whereas births among white females are declining (Hodgkinson, 1985). Reporting data for the 1990–91 school year, *The Executive Educator* (State of the states, 1991) magazine noted that between 1990 and 2010, the Hispanic school-age population alone should increase about 42 percent. These projections clearly indicate that problems that surround the underrepresentation of minorities in formal leadership positions will become increasingly severe.

Richards (1988) offered three reasons that educators and society should be concerned about the underrepresentation of women and minorities in school administration. First, establishing equity is a legal requirement. Title VII of the Equal Employment Opportunity Act and affirmative action require employers to seek equitable representation of women and minorities. Second, students learn much from what is called the "hidden curriculum" (i.e., things learned by students but not part of the formal curriculum of the school). Underrepresentation sends a number of messages to students about opportunity, prejudice, and other critical issues that influence student choices in life. Third, schools are a mirror of society. They provide symbolic messages to our own society and to the remainder of the world. Underrepresentation simply sends the wrong messages about equal opportunity and the equality of all citizens.

CHARACTERISTICS, PLACEMENTS, AND BARRIERS

There continues to be an imbalance between the number of women in professional preparation programs and the number actually holding administrative positions (Shakeshaft, 1988). Surveys reveal that women now constitute a majority of doctoral students pursuing educational administration as a major (e.g., Marshall,

1984b); yet, they occupy fewer than one-fourth of all administrative positions. Indicators of underrepresentation have encouraged a number of studies, especially doctoral dissertations authored by women, that examine the characteristics, job successes, and barriers facing females in school administration.

To a lesser degree, there also has been an increase in research activity examining the status of minorities in school administration. The percentage of practicing school administrators who are members of minority groups is substantially below the percentage of minorities in American society. For example, minorities constitute 15 percent of American society, but they occupy only about 3 percent of the public school superintendencies (Feistritzer, 1988). Therefore, the underrepresentation of minorities, like the underrepresentation of women, is a serious concern for society and the profession.

Often it is difficult to separate issues of women and minorities, because many women in school administration also are members of minority groups. Nevertheless, the two concerns are discussed separately here. Although empirical data verify that women and minorities are under-represented in the practice of school administration, far less is known about the specific causes of this condition (Motaref, 1987; Yeakey, Johnston, & Adkison, 1986). The following review illuminates issues of underrepresentation and questions that remain to be answered.

Women

Research on women in school administration can be divided into several categories. These include studies that (1) identify common characteristics (e.g., socioeconomic status, family life); (2) identify barriers to career development (e.g., mobility, school board member attitudes); (3) make comparisons (e.g., men to women, women administrators to women teachers); (4) quantify group representation (e.g., affirmative action); (5) identify career path and career decisions (e.g., entry-level positions, type of school district); (6) examine selection procedures (e.g., hiring practices); and (7) examine job performance (e.g., length of tenure, accomplishments). A comprehensive analysis of research and writings on this topic is found in Charol Shakeshaft's book, *Women in Educational Administration* (1989). Here, emphasis is given to three topics: characteristics, job placements, and barriers.

Characteristics. Because classroom teaching is almost always a prerequisite to entering school administration, several researchers have looked at differences between men and women with regard to experience before entering administration. In the mid-1970s, Gross and Trask (1976) found that whereas the average female had fifteen years of experience before assuming an administrative post, the average male had only five to seven years of experience. In looking specifically at superintendents, Schuster and Foote (1990) found that three-fourths of the women and only two-thirds of the men in their sample had more than five years of teaching experience. In a detailed study of seven female high school principals in the Washington, DC, area, all were found to have administrative experience prior to becoming a high school principal, and all taught at least six years before obtaining an entry-level administrative position (Featherson, 1988). These findings suggest that women may be required to produce more evidence of success to gain an administrative post. Also supportive of this hypothesis are findings that female superintendents tend to have higher IQs, attain higher levels of academic achievement, and are more likely to hold the doctorate than male superintendents (Schuster & Foote, 1990).

What motivates women to become administrators? Edson (1988) concluded that three factors were rather common: a need for change and challenge, a positive assessment of management potential, and an overriding concern for children's welfare. In a study of female administrators in the state of New York, Sulowski (1987) found two primary motives for entering administration: increased challenges and a feeling of being able to do better than persons occupying these positions. Although several researchers have associated underrepresentation of women in school administration with a lack of motivation, Shakeshaft (1989) takes exception with this linkage:

> Although it is true that women have traditionally applied less often than men for administrative positions and that women, more often than men, need to be encouraged to enter administration, there is little evidence that the reasons for this can be found in lower aspiration and motivation. (p. 86)

As to whether women are motivated differently than men, there are conflicting findings. Shakeshaft (1988) believes that women enter education initially because of a desire to be close to children and because they believe they can make a difference. As such, many do not desire positions that will remove them entirely from the instructional process. She concluded that research demonstrates that men and women administrators have differing motivations. Somewhat supportive of this conclusion is a finding by Wylie and Michael (1991) that women tend to place more emphasis on the importance of teaching experience for administrators than do men. But not all studies point to sharp motivational differences between men and women. A study of 153 administrators in Los Angeles, California, concluded that although minor differences existed, men and women essentially share the same basic motivations to become administrators (Brandes-Tyler, 1987).

One of the most cogent areas of inquiries entails comparisons of men and women with regard to leadership behaviors. This is especially true for characteristics that are congruent with practices in effective schools. Fauth (1984) examined a number of studies and found a pattern in which female administrators tended to associate more highly than male administrators with teachers and students. In comparing male and female superintendents, Pitner (1981) found that females were more likely to get involved in instructional programs, communicate in less formal ways, and exercise less control over meeting agendas and outcomes. (They also are less likely to dominate discussions and more apt to seek increased subordinate participation.)

Women in the principalship are more likely to require teacher conformity to the principal's standards and are more likely to monitor parent-teacher conferences and other contacts made between the school and home (Gross &

Trask, 1976). They also have been found to have a closer supervisory relationship with teachers (Charters & Jovick, 1981), and they are more likely to use democratic procedures than do male principals (Smith, 1978). Perhaps more importantly, women who use participative and democratic behaviors are judged more favorably by employees than males who employ the same behaviors (Astin & Leland, 1991). Overall, a review of research reveals a pattern where women administrators, both principals and superintendents, concentrate more heavily and directly on those responsibilities that are most closely aligned with instructional tasks (Ortiz & Marshall, 1988).

Placements.   Historically, women have tended to occupy two types of administrative positions: (1) the elementary school principalship and (2) central office staff positions that involve curriculum and instruction. In the mid-1980s, about 17 percent of all elementary school principals, but only 3.5 percent of secondary principals, were women (Shakeshaft, 1989). Since middle school and junior high school principals fall into the latter category, the figure for secondary schools is even more discouraging. Historically, relatively few women have been employed as assistant principals—the commom point of entry into school administration (Marshall, 1992).

Recent studies have produced varying figures for the number of women in school administration that may be attributable to sampling, job classification systems, and data-collection procedures. During the 1989–90 school year, Jones and Montenegro (1990) determined that 24 percent of all administrators were women; a study by Jacobson (1989) using a random sample of 1,508 administrators found that only 17 percent were women. Figures for the top administrative position, the superintendency, exhibit even higher levels of underrepresentation. In 1974–1975, a mere 1 percent of the nation's superintendents were female (Paddock, 1981); in 1989–1990, this figure rose to 6 percent (Jones & Montenegro, 1990). Comparing these two years, one could conclude that there is both good news and bad news. The good news is that the percentage of female superintendents increased substantially in the 1980s—but the bad news is that women are still grossly underrepresented in this key position.

Where do female administrators get employed? Jacobson (1989) reported that women are most likely to be found in large, urban districts. They are twice as likely to be in these settings than in rural and small-town districts; the frequency of placements in suburban districts falls between the extremes.

Barriers.   Barriers to women in school administration can be divided into two primary groups: internal and external. Shakeshaft (1981) developed a summary of dissertation research on this topic and offered the following distinctions:

> Internal barriers include aspects of socialization, personality, aspiration level; individual beliefs and attitudes; motivation; and self-image. External barriers researched were sex-role stereotyping, sex discrimination, lack of professional preparation, and family responsibilities. (p. 14)

In essence, internal barriers relate to aspects of personality, values, and attitudes of the individual; external barriers are environmental circumstances that mediate entrance into administrative positions (Leonard & Papalewis, 1987). Several examples of the more recognized barriers are discussed here.

Mobility is commonly identified as an intrinsic barrier, although there are circumstances where one could argue that it is both intrinsic and extrinsic. This factor has been identified repeatedly as a key issue in studying women in school administration. This is especially true for those who are married. Edson (1988), summarizing her research on 142 women administrators, noted both the importance of mobility and a changing attitude toward factors that made it a cogent issue. She wrote:

> Without doubt, the married women in this study feel an added burden in trying to assess the importance of their own career goals and personal needs with those of their husbands and children. They realize there is an element of risk involved in the broadened horizons they now have for themselves. But for these women, the past decision of automatically putting their careers on hold for their husbands' jobs is just that—a thing of the past. (p. 60)

Changing values and beliefs in society appear to have made mobility less of a barrier in recent years. Especially in situations involving higher-level, higher-paying positions, mobility often is less of barrier than it was thirty or forty years ago.

Negative attitudes toward career opportunities are another intrinsic barrier for many women (Marshall, 1984a). The fact that school administration has been, and continues to be, a white, male-dominated profession obviously affects career planning. In a review of research, Leonard and Papalewis (1987) also cited level of training, aspiration levels, a lack of confidence and initiative, and low self-image as internal constraints.

Sponsorship and mentoring—external barriers—have been studied on numerous occasions. These factors are associated with influential others who promote candidates for administrative positions. These influential persons, usually professors of educational administration or practitioners who are well connected politically, can provide tremendous assistance in the acquisition of jobs. Both primary groups of influential persons are dominated by white males, and these individuals have tended to offer the greatest support to other white males (Shakeshaft, 1989). This condition had led to what many have labeled as the "Good Ole Boys' Club." Ortiz and Marshall (1988) noted that even well-qualified women may suffer from being unable to attain sponsorship in a white male-dominated profession. Studies often reveal that women have difficulty gaining access to both the formal and informal male networks (e.g., Funk, 1986).

Closely related to the sponsorship issue is another external barrier—the separation of the work of educators by gender (sex-role stereotyping). Within administration itself, there is a tendency to see some positions as "male jobs" (e.g., high school principalship, business manager), and others as "female jobs" (e.g., staff positions in instruction) (Schmuck & Wyant, 1981). On a broader basis, administration often is viewed as work for men and teaching as work for women. Ortiz and Marshall (1988) described the ill effects:

> The effective separation of education into two professions, based considerably on gender, placed status and power in the hands of relatively few male administrators, who attended more to managing the enterprise than enhancing the technical core practiced by many. The separation is perpetuated in best-selling textbooks on school administration, in research that uses frameworks derived from theory on organizational control, and in long-standing reward systems and distributions of power that favor managers over the instructors. (p. 138)

Wheatley (1981), being more specific, noted that an emphasis of managerial skills, politicking, and control of students—tasks not viewed as work for women—often put female candidates at a disadvantage. Sex-role stereotyping can be intrinsic as well. This occurs when the individual's personal perceptions, beliefs, and values leads to a separation of jobs based on gender.

Discrimination continues to be an external barrier for some women. Overt discrimination—simply not hiring women because they are women—continues despite laws that prohibit such practices. Not all discrimination, however, is readily recognized. Life-related conditions that circuitously limit equal access often are not seen as sources of discrimination. These might include a lack of family support to pursue a career in administration, socializing women not to pursue careers in leadership, and facing gender bias in professional books and research while in graduate school. These are examples of life-related conditions that constitute covert discrimination (Shakeshaft, 1989).

Imagine a school district where virtually all administrators are males. They have informal contacts with each other through activities such as golf outings, playing poker, or going to athletic events. Male teachers who aspire to become administrators are much more likely to receive invitations to participate in these social activities than are aspiring females; thus, the males have an advantage of informal socialization. The administrators in these situations may be totally unaware that they are discriminating against women.

Minorities

Minority candidates seeking to enter school administration find that they encounter experiences different from those of whites (Valverde & Brown, 1988). It is extremely important to illuminate these differences if the problem of underrepresentation is to be understood and eradicated. The review of minority underrepresentation is divided into the same categories used to discuss women.

Characteristics. Compared to research on women, there is relatively little information available about characteristics of minorities entering school administration. Researchers, such as Ortiz (1982), suggest that minority teachers encounter several disadvantages not common to their white peers. One example is found in the types of positions commonly acquired. Many minority educators initially accept teaching positions in areas such as bilingual education, Spanish, physical education, and special programs for at-risk students. Not infrequently, these low-prestige assignments are located in remote areas of school buildings. One by-product is that the teachers in these assignments have below average contact with the principal and with other teachers. As a result, they may have fewer opportunities to exhibit leadership capabilities and receive less encouragement to become leaders.

The literature contains many indications that career paths of minorities and white males are different. Two factors appear especially cogent in this regard. As noted earlier, there are a growing number of schools, particularly inner-city schools, that have student enrollments classified as minority-majorities. (In 1991, four states—California, Hawaii, Mississippi, and New Mexico—already had minority enrollments that exceeded 50 percent of all public elementary and secondary school populations.) As might be expected, these demographic conditions have created a high demand for minority educators. Often minority candidates find employment benefits most attractive in school districts that have high minority populations (i.e., higher salaries, higher-level positions). Also, employers are prone to place minority administrators in schools where their services are in highest demand. Several studies have shown that at virtually all stages of their careers, minority administrators tend to be placed in minority schools (e.g., Ortiz, 1982; Wilkerson, 1985).

The second factor relating to differing career paths involves turmoil. When schools are experiencing serious problems, school boards and communities are willing to take risks. Academic degrees, experience, and even licensing may become less important employment criteria in times of crisis. Given a limited pool of minority candidates, school officials may elevate the importance of race or ethnicity. Such practices frequently are detected in research. Teaching experience is one factor where minorities and women, as groups, differ. Whereas women tend to have more teaching experience prior to entering administration than do males, the same does not hold true for minorities. Chance (1989), for instance, compared non-Indian and Indian administrators and found that the latter group possessed less time in the classroom.

Studies of African-American administrators have identified determination to be a key factor in career success. Spence (1990) found that African-American female administrators were able to overcome a number of serious obstacles by maintaining a high level of self-esteem and determination. Similarly, Cadman (1989) found that African-American male superintendents shared a career orientation that helped them focus on professional goals. Because barriers are so prevalant, minority administrators who succeed in reaching their career goals tend to be highly motivated individuals.

Since affirmative action plays an important role in creating access to jobs for minority candidates, opinions regarding the utility of equity laws is another area of inquiry. Edson (1988) found that minority women aspiring to administrative positions generally express confidence that they can overcome ill effects caused by quotas. She wrote:

Even though they know their minority status is useful in securing administrative employment, some believe—that once hired—their competencies will win over those who doubted their worth. (p. 175)

Many minority candidates make no apologies for their legal advantage in seeking employment. They see such laws as a necessary counteraction to race-related barriers such as discrimination.

Placements.   As noted, minority educators are most likely to be found in schools with high minority student enrollments. At both the level of the principalship and the superintendency, African-American administrators usually find themselves working in organizations that have high African-American enrollments. This pattern holds true for other minority groups as well. And since minority populations are heavily concentrated in large cities, minority administrators are overwhelmingly employed in urban school districts (Jacobson, 1989).

Ortiz (1982) discovered that minorities often enter administrative positions as directors of sponsored projects. She too noted that minority principals often are placed in minority schools, but added the observation that they are treated differently than their white counterparts by those in the highest-authority positions (i.e., by central office administrators and school board members). In studying differences in the ways minority and white administrators were treated, she found that none of the minority principals were part of the regular informal group in the school district (i.e., informal groups involved in social activities). Such findings suggest that minority males are likely to suffer the same disadvantages that are faced by females in male-dominated school systems.

In 1990, 12.5 percent of all administrators and 3.4 percent of the superintendents in the United States were members of minority groups (Jones & Montenegro, 1990). From 1985 to 1990, however, only 8 percent of the newly hired teachers in the United States was classified as minorities. Thus recent employment trends for teachers suggest that the pool for minority persons who may enter the study of school administrationis shrinking.

Two factors reduced the number of African Americans holding positions as school administrators. Both have been mentioned previously. First, the elimination of segregated schools during the 1950s and early 1960s meant that fewer African Americans found themselves in positions of power in public schools (Valverde & Brown, 1988). This was true because segregated schools almost always had African-American administrators. Second, affirmative action and other laws partially succeeded in opening all professions to minorities. These expanded opportunities, however, have not been offset by corresponding increases in minority college enrollments.

Representation of Hispanics and American Indians in school administration appears to be affected by cultural issues. Both groups historically have resented attempts by public schools to acculturate them to white Anglo-Saxon values and beliefs. Native Americans, for instance, are not adverse to Western education; they simply view it in a perfunctory manner because it is seen as an attempt to acculturate rather than educate (DeJong, 1990). Negative perceptions, deeply ingrained in culture, affect the career choices of many Hispanics and Native Americans.

Barriers.   Repeatedly, studies focusing on minority school administrators raise the issue of sponsorship. Minorities are far less likely to be sponsored than are whites. Ortiz (1982) noted that problems created by a lack of sponsorship were compounded by blockages to socialization. In this regard, minorities aspiring to be administrators typically do not have a mentor or sponsor assisting them and they find it difficult to gain entry to informal social situations. The importance of mentors and socialization has been established by a number of researchers (e.g., Polczynski, 1990).

Discrimination continues to be perceived as a major barrier by minorities seeking positions in school administration (Spence, 1990; Valverde & Brown, 1988). Persons most likely to face discrimination (i.e., women and minorities) appear to recognize that their careers can be affected negatively as long as society does not rid itself of this condition. Many also perceive that as they attempt to acquire higher-level positions in school districts, discrimination is apt to play an increasingly significant role (Edson, 1988). That is to say, the more successful a minority person is with regard to obtaining higher-level positions, the more likely he or she is to encounter discrimination.

SEEKING SOLUTIONS

Eradicating barriers to women and minorities has become a critical issue in school administration. Unfortunately, the task is complex and requires efforts on many fronts. Potential solutions exist in government, the workplace, and the profession, as well as in academic preparation.

Legal Interventions

The federal government often assumes an active role in attempting to resolve societal problems that involve constitutional issues. A prime example of this proclivity is civil rights legislation. As noted earlier in this chapter, laws and court decisions have addressed matters of job-related discrimination. These attempts to increase the number of women and minorities in school administration alter law and practices, but they frequently fall short with regard to changing individual values and beliefs. Judging by continuing debates over issues such as job quotas, federal intervention may even serve to harden opposition among those who reject forced remedies. American society remains very divided with regard to supporting such corrective measures.

Professional Preparation

Equity for women and minorities also can be advanced by social institutions and the profession of education (students, professors, and practitioners). Universities, to varying degrees, have taken steps to improve the presence of women and minorities in school administration. These efforts have included visible actions such as the following:

- scholarships
- special student recruitment efforts
- special faculty recruitment efforts
- vigorous enforcement of affirmative action
- seminars, lectures, and workshops highlighting opportunities for women and minorities in school administration.

Some equity advocates (e.g., Shakeshaft, 1989) advance academic revisions as a necessary action. Integrating the female experience into professional preparation courses and creating special seminars that examine the behaviors and roles of women in leadership positions are examples of how this initiative can occur. Blackmore (1989) has argued that leadership and organizational study have been cast in the male perspective by concentrating on factors such as power and control. To attract females to leadership roles, she contends that concepts central to the feminine experience need to be integrated into academic study. Other recommendations focusing on professional preparation include bringing women and minority administrators to speak to graduate classes, placing women interns with women administrators and minority interns with minority administrators, and requiring a course on equity and schooling (Shakeshaft, 1990). Leonard and Papalewis (1987) suggested other actions that could reduce barriers to women and minorities. These include (1) exposing the gatekeepers (those who control entry into the profession) to empirical data, (2) examining selection and promotion practices, and (3) providing support and counseling for career planning. Some universities are addressing the need for minority faculty by identifying promising undergraduate students and offering them counseling and financial assistance to pursue doctorates in school administration.

The Workplace

Public school systems that exhibit a concern for equity have concentrated largely on recruitment programs for underrepresented teachers and administrators—both external (attracting candidates from other school districts) and internal (identifying current employees with the potential and interest to enter administration). As might be expected, the sincerity of these efforts, and outcomes, varies markedly. A key question is whether the school board and superintendent are truly committed to equity or whether they are simply responding to political pressures and legal requirements. A few progressive school districts have established sponsorship programs in which administrators are assigned as mentors or sponsors for women and minority teachers who aspire to enter administration. Often school districts cannot muster enough resources to address adequately problems of underrepresentation. For this reason, collaborative efforts with universities and communities may be more effective (Klauke, 1990).

Professional Organizations

Professional organizations also have made efforts to address concerns related to the underrepresentation of women and minorities. The American Association of School Administrators, for example, has established designated offices (e.g., a deputy superintendent to oversee issues pertaining to women and minorities) and committees (e.g., AASA Women Administrators Committee) and has helped sponsor special projects (e.g., AWARE—Assisting Women to Advance through Resources and Encouragement). Professional organizations, especially at the state level, often assist with the establishment of networks—support groups that assist underrepresented practitioners to seek employment or deal with job-related problems.

Mentors and Sponsors

A number of authors (e.g., Edson, 1988; Richards, 1988) have underscored the advantage of securing a mentor or sponsor. Successful female and minority administrators frequently note that such persons were influential in their career development. These "significant others" are not necessarily the same gender, race, or ethnic group as those they guide. The role of mentor or sponsor often is assumed by a conscientious individual who views such guidance to be an extension of professional responsibilities. These experienced practitioners provide encouragement and help the aspiring educator to build confidence. More specifically, they demonstrate friendship, mutual respect, trust, and openness (Pence, 1989).

Society

The most difficult hurdles for equity are found in the societal context. As long as discrimination persists, the access of women and minorities to influential and powerful positions in school administration will be hindered by stereotypes and prejudices. Yeakey, Johnston, and Adkison (1986) summarized this concern:

> The larger body of organizational literature suggests, irrespective of attitudes and training programs, that no real change will occur until it is accompanied by broader societal change. That is, the basic problem of the exclusion of minorities and women from administrative positions is the subordinate role of women and minorities in all parts of society. (p. 137)

Shakeshaft (1989) also emphasized that discrimination continues in both society and schools:

> No matter how qualified, how competent, or how psychologically and emotionally ready women are to assume administrative positions in schools, they are still living and working within a society and school organization that is both sexist and racist. (p. 144)

Yet another reflection of this societal problem is visible in the increased incidents involving prejudice and racial animosity among students in our schools (Stover,

1991). Given the need to change society, social institutions, and the beliefs and values of individuals, problems of underrepresentation in school administration require a concerted effort combining the initiatives of the federal government, national and state organizations, universities, school districts, and individuals in the school administration profession.

IMPLICATIONS FOR PRACTICE

The underrepresentation of women and minorities remains a critical issue in school administration. As the population of the United States becomes increasingly heterogeneous, this concern will certainly intensify. What remains less certain is whether it will be remedied. All aspects of the profession are touched by this issue—ranging from recruitment to professional preparation to licensing, and ultimately to employment.

Within the profession itself, professors and practitioners face a myriad of unresolved issues pertaining to women and minorities. Should curricula be altered? To what extent should universities and school systems be committed to providing role models? In what ways can educators help to recruit talented women and minorities into school administration? Can research be used to produce solutions? These questions deserve your attention, because they are certain to remain relevant issues during your career as a school administrator.

The moral and ethical aspects of underrepresentation should be addressed by all who study and practice school administration. Especially challenging will be solutions that simultaneously address equity and school improvement. For example, does school restructuring offer opportunities for women and minorities to play a more prominent role in educational leadership? Will issues of equity and excellence be properly balanced if more minorities acquire formal leadership positions?

American public schools remain a primary force for creating opportunity in a diverse society. As such, those who lead these institutions should be committed to fairness and equal opportunity. The goal is to ensure that each student has an equal chance to learn and succeed. This worthy objective is made more difficult when existing conditions indirectly tell minorities and females that equality is merely a myth.

FOR FURTHER DISCUSSION

1. Identify the linkage between urbanization and the increase in the number of women in teaching.
2. In what ways does mentoring and sponsoring affect women and men attempting to enter school administration?
3. What is meant by "informal socialization"?
4. Do you see the underrepresentation of women and Hispanics in school administration to be equally important concerns? Why or why not?
5. What are some possible reasons why African Americans and Hispanics currently attending college are less likely to pursue a career in education than was the case in 1975?

6. Why do you believe research exhibits that women who enter administration are better educated and possess more teaching experience than men?

7. Do you agree with the observation that minority teachers often are isolated in schools (i.e., they teach in remote areas of the building)?

8. Identify the representation of women and minorities in public school administration in your state. Has this representation increased or decreased in the past ten years?

9. Do you agree with the contention that underrepresentation of women and minorities in school administration is largely attributable to sexism and racism?

10. Why are role models important for minority students?

OTHER SUGGESTED ACTIVITIES

1. Debate the issue of job quotas. Is this a reasonable approach to eradicating underrepresentation?

2. Determine what your state-level organizations for school administrators are doing to promote women and minorities for administrative positions.

3. Identify positive steps that school districts can take to encourage women and minorities to enter school administration.

4. Debate the advantages and disadvantages of allowing alternative certification for minority administrators in your state.

5. Invite a minority administrator and a female administrator to speak to your class. See if they agree or disagree with common assumptions about barriers to entering school administration.

REFERENCES

Astin, H. S., & Leland, C. (1991). *Women of influence, Women of vision*. San Francisco: Jossey-Bass.

Blackmore, J. (1989). Educational leadership: A feminist critique and reconstruction. In J. Smyth (Ed.), *Critical perspectives on educational leadership* (pp. 93–130). Philadelphia: Falmer.

Brandes-Tyler, K. (1987). A comparison of motivational differences between women and men to become educational administrators. Unpublished Ed.D. diss., University of LaVerne, California.

Cadman, R. O. (1989). Career patterns and successes of black superintendents in the Commonwealth of Virginia. Unpublished Ed.D. diss., University of Virginia.

Chance, E. W. (1989). *The BIA/contract school administrator: Implications for at-risk Native American students*. (ERIC Document Reproduction Service No. ED 331 682)

Charters, W. W., & Jovick, T. D. (1981). The gender of principals and principal-teacher relations. In P. Schmuck, W. Charters, & R. Carlson (Eds.), *Educational policy and management of sex differentials* (pp. 307–331). New York: Academic Press.

Clifford, G. J. (1989). Man/woman/teacher: Gender, family, and career in American Educational History. In D. Warren (Ed.), *American teachers: Histories of a profession at work* (pp. 293–343). New York: Macmillan.

DeJong, D. H. (1990). Friend or foe? Education and the American Indian. Unpublished M.A. thesis, University of Arizona.

Edson, S. K. (1988). *Pushing the limits: The female administrative aspirant.* Albany: State University of New York Press.

Fauth, G. C. (1984). Women in educational administration. A research profile. *Educational Forum,* 49 (1), 65–79.

Featherson, O. (1988). Case studies of female secondary school principals. Unpublished Ed.D. diss., George Washington University.

Feistritzer, C. E. (1988). A good ole boy mentality rules your schools. *Executive Educator,* 10 (5), 24–25, 37.

———. (1990). *Profile of teachers in the U.S.—1990.* Washington, DC: National Center for Education Information.

Funk, C. (1986). *The female executive in school administration: Profiles, pluses, and problems.* (ERIC Document Reproduction Service No. ED 285 282)

Gross, N., & Trask, A. E. (1976). *The sex factor and the management of schools.* New York: John Wiley & Sons.

Hodgkinson, H. (1985). *All one system: Demographics of education, kindergarten through graduate school.* Washington, DC: Institute for Educational Leadership.

Jacobson, S. L. (1989). School management: Still a white man's game. *Executive Educator,* 11 (11), 19.

Jones, E. H., & Montenegro, X. P. (1990). *Women and Minorities in School Administration.* (ERIC Document Reproduction Service No. ED 273 017)

Klauke, A. (1990). *Preparing school administrators.* (ERIC Document Reproduction Service No. ED 326 939)

Leonard, P. Y., & Papalewis, R. (1987). The underrepresentation of women and minorities in educational administration: Patterns, issues, and recommendations. *Journal of Educational Equity and Leadership,* 7 (3), 188–207.

Marshall, C. (1984a). The crisis in excellence and equity. *Educational Horizons,* 63, 24–30.

Marshall, C. (1984b). Men and women in public school administration programs. *Journal of the National Association of Women Deans, Administrators, and Counselors,* 48 (1), 3–12.

———. (1992). *The assistant principal: Leadership choices and challenges.* Newbury Park, CA: Corwin Press.

Motaref, S. (1987). Women in educational administration: An analytical synthesis and summing up of what we know and don't know. Unpublished Ph.D. diss., Florida State University.

National Center for Education Statistics (1991). *The condition of education 1991.* Vol. 2, *Postsecondary Education.* Washington, DC: U.S. Department of Education.

Ortiz, F. I. (1982). *Career patterns in education: Women, men and minorities in public school administration.* New York: Praeger.

Ortiz, F. I., & Marshall, C. (1988). Women in educational administration. In N. J. Boyan (Ed.), *Handbook of research on educational administration* (pp. 123–142). New York: Longman.

Paddock, S. C. (1981). Male and female career paths in school administration. In P. Schmuck, W. Charters, & R. Carlson (Eds.), *Educational policy and management of sex differentials* (pp. 187–198). New York: Academic Press.

Pence, L. J. (1989). Formal and informal mentorships for aspiring and practicing administrators. Unpublished Ph.D. diss., University of Oregon.

Perkins, L. M. (1989). The history of blacks in teaching: Growth and decline within the profession. In D. Warren (Ed.), *American teachers: Histories of a profession at work* (pp. 344–369). New York: Macmillan.

Pitner, N. J. (1981). Hormones and harems: Are the activities of superintending different for a woman? In P. Schmuck, W. Charters, & R. Carlson (Eds.), *Educational policy and management of sex differentials* (pp. 273–295). New York: Academic Press.

Polczynski, M. A. (1990). From barriers to challenges: The black and white female experience in educational administration. Unpublished Ph.D. diss., Marquette University.

Richards, C. (1988). The search for equity in educational administration. In N. J. Boyan (Ed.), *Handbook of research on educational administration* (pp. 159–168). New York: Longman.

Rury, J. L. (1989). Who became teachers? In D. Warren (Ed.), *American teachers: Histories of a profession at work* (pp. 9–48). New York: Macmillan.

Schmuck, P. A., & Wyant, S. H. (1981). Clues to sex bias in the selection of school administrators. In P. Schmuck, W. Charters, & R. Carlson (Eds.), *Educational policy and management of sex differentials* (pp. 73–97). New York: Academic Press.

Schuster, D. J., & Foote, T. H. (1990). Differences abound between male and female superintendents. *The School Administrator,* 2 (47), 14–16, 18.

Shakeshaft, C. (1981). Women in educational administration: A descriptive analysis of dissertation research and paradigm for future research. In P. Schmuck, W. Charters, & R. Carlson (Eds.), *Educational policy and management of sex differentials* (pp. 9–31). New York: Academic Press.

———. (1988). Women in educational administration: Implications for training. In D. Griffiths, R. Stout, & P. Forsyth (Eds.), *Leaders for America's schools* (pp. 403–416). Berkeley, CA: McCutchan.

———. (1989). *Women in educational administration* (updated edition). Newbury Park, CA: Sage.

———. (1990). Administrative preparation for equity. In H. Baptiste, H. Waxman, J. Walker de Felix, & J. Anderson (Eds.), *Leadership, equity, and school effectiveness* (pp. 213–223). Newbury Park, CA: Sage.

Smith, J. (1978). Encouraging women to enter administration. *NASSP Bulletin,* 62, 114–119.

Spence, B. A. (1990). Self-perceptions of African-American female administrators in New England public schools. Unpublished Ed.D. diss., University of Massachusetts.

Spencer, D. A. (1986). *Contemporary women teachers.* New York: Longman.

State of the states (1991). *The Executive Educator,* 13 (12), A20–A27.

Stover, D. (1991). Racism redux. *Executive Educator,* 13 (12), 35–36.

Sulowski, S. (1987). A descriptive profile of female line administrators in New York state. Unpublished Ed.D. diss., Teachers College, Columbia University.

Valverde, L. A., & Brown, F. (1988). Influences on leadership development among racial and ethnic minorities. In N. J. Boyan (Ed.), *Handbook of research on educational administration* (pp. 143–158). New York: Longman.

Wheatley, M. (1981). The impact of organizational structure on issues of sex equity. In P. Schmuck, W. Charters, & R. Carlson (Eds.), *Educational policy and management of sex differentials* (pp. 255–271). New York: Academic Press.

Wilkerson, G. J. (1985). Black school administrators in the Los Angeles Unified School District: Personal perspectives and current considerations. Unpublished Ed.D. diss., University of San Francisco.

Wylie, V. L., & Michael, R. O. (1991). Gender differences in career planning as a guide to improving preparation programs in educational administration. Paper presented at the annual meeting of the American Association of School Administrators, New Orleans.

Yeakey, C. C., Johnston, G. S., & Adkison, J. A. (1986). In pursuit of equity: A review of research on minorities and women in educational administration. *Educational Administration Quarterly,* 22 (3), 110–149.

PART V

A Career in School Administration

CHAPTER 15

Planning Your Career

Chapter Content

The Value of a Career Plan

Changing Attitudes and Assumptions

Building an Individual Plan

Implications for Practice

In an information society, the concept of career has received added attention; yet, many of us still have a difficult time separating work from career. Arthur, Hall, and Lawrence (1989) defined *career* as "the evolving sequence of a person's work experiences over time" (p. 8). Zunker (1990) defined career as, "the activities and positions involved in vocations, occupations, and jobs as well as related activities associated with an individual's lifetime of work" (p. 3). In both descriptions, career is much more encompassing than work, and the concept addresses evolving relationships among the individual, the employing organization, and society. Colantuono (1982) described a career as simply one's progress through a profession or occupation, and this brief definition is especially cogent for school administration.

Personal career planning is an individual activity that helps you determine goals and strategies for your working life. It is a continuous process that provides purpose and direction for occupational decisions that confront adults (Steele & Morgan, 1991). With specificity to school administration, personal career planning is defined as *the process of self-developing goals and strategies for entering, growing, and succeeding in the practice of school administration.* Growth and success are often misinterpreted objectives. They do not necessarily connote rising to the position of superintendent in a large school system. Many administrators develop professionally and attain myriad accomplishments by remaining at the same position level throughout their careers (e.g., the principalship, business manager).

In contemporary society, adults face a high probability of having to make critical career decisions until retirement. Unlike conditions that prevailed in an industrial society, contemporary decisions are more complex and are likely to be influenced by self-perceptions, personal needs, and experiences. No longer can one expect to spend adulthood in a single job or occupation. Economic and societal changes force many in the workforce to make difficult occupational decisions. Today, we are no longer surprised to hear about a forty-year-old corporate executive who decides to become an elementary school teacher, or a fifty-year-old dentist who decides to pursue a career as an artist. In an era when technology is playing such a critical role in our lives, many adults are weighing more heavily personal meaning and intrinsic motivators in making critical choices.

Educators who consider school administration as a career face two critical questions: (1) Why do I want to be an administrator? (2) To what type of position(s) do I aspire? Among the administrative staff in any school district, one is apt to receive differing responses to these queries. A desire for more responsibility, a quest for greater challenges, the need for a higher salary, and the desire for power exemplify the range of potential motivators. We know far more about the demographic characteristics of persons occupying administrative positions than we do about their work ethics, personal needs, and other traits or behaviors that constitute essential elements of career success.

THE VALUE OF A CAREER PLAN

Why develop a career plan? This question has been asked by countless graduate students who enter the study of school administration. Those who elect not to pursue a personal plan often are influenced by the notion that the cost-benefit ratio of the effort is negative. They see the task requiring a good bit of time, and they believe that career success is largely a product of "being in the right place at the right time." Other common excuses given by persons who fail to develop individual career plans include:

> "The process requires information I cannot obtain. It would be futile for me to try."
> "Your asking me to do something I know nothing about. I don't have enough information to do a plan."
> "In the end, a career plan has only limited value. You're better off devoting your time to nurturing political connections. That's what counts most."

These rationalizations make increasingly less sense in a world of practice where ambiguity and competition abound.

With regard to personal career planning, two major decisions must be made: (1) a commitment to career planning and (2) acceptance of personal responsibility to complete the task. As observed in the world of business, the assistance and guidance of others can be valuable; however, executives who want to succeed must take responsibility for their own career plans (Graen, 1989). Even our closest friends and colleagues may not have a clear understanding of the values, beliefs, wants, needs, and motivations that create satisfaction for us.

Buskirk (1976) offered three cogent reasons why a career plan is useful:

1. It helps you encounter uncertainty.
2. It provides emotional peace of mind.
3. It is a yardstick to measure how you are doing.

Over time, virtually every school administrator experiences peaks and valleys that spark opportunities or self-doubt. For example, a highly successful principal is offered a better-paying job in another school district; or conflict with teachers leads to thoughts about getting out of education. These stressful situations are made even more difficult by the absence of a personal plan that allows an individual to place specific situations in the context of lifelong goals. What are my objectives as a school administrator? How will my responses to the present situation affect what I want to accomplish? In the absence of such questions, impulsive behavior is probable.

In addition to the three broad reasons given for developing a career plan, there are more specific purposes:

- It provides a personal understanding of needs and wants related to work. That is, it causes us to look at ourselves—to seek linkages between ourselves and our work lives.

- It leads us to gain a better understanding of career opportunities. The mere act of planning requires information. By engaging in this process, you learn more about school administration, opportunities, rewards, and common employment practices.

- It enhances the likelihood of a mentor or sponsor relationship. The complexity of the task often encourages us to seek out an "influential other" to answer questions and provide guidance.

- It provides a framework that facilitates the identification of personal strengths and weaknesses. Many aspiring administrators fail to engage in introspection—a process of objective self-assessment. This observation is supported by difficulties many practitioners have in interview situations when they are asked to identify their strengths and weaknesses.

- In addition to aiding with the identification of personal strengths and weaknesses, the process encourages the planner to place career-related information into a meaningful context. That is, quality career plans promote a systemic relationship among bits of information (e.g., the person interfaces personal information with data pertinent to various positions in school administration).

- It prompts a comprehensive exploration of motivators. Why do you want to be a school administrators? Too often, practitioners focus solely on a narrow band of extrinsic inducements (e.g., salary). Although such factors are certainly relevant, they may be less potent considerations with regard to job satisfaction than intrinsic motivations (e.g., self-satisfaction gained from helping other people).

- It encourages an examination of potential barriers to goal attainment. Spokane (1991) observed that professions develop mechanisms that attempt to limit the number of recruits and aspirants. These may range from admission standards for professional education to licensing requirements to "ole boy networks" to outright discrimination. A comprehensive career plan integrates profession-related information.

- It provides a framework to be used in answering difficult career questions. For example, goals and objectives help to frame time parameters for seeking advancement or for enhancing professional skills. When is the best time to seek advancement? Should I return to school to work on a doctoral degree? These are questions that help illuminate the utility of a personal plan.

- It requires periodic assessments of performance and growth. You are able to determine if original goals and objectives were realistic and whether adjustments are required. In this regard, the plan is not a static document. Adjustments are necessary to compensate for unforeseen conditions.

- It helps to prevent complacency. That is, the targets (goals) serve as reminders of what is to be accomplished.

- It causes us to explore our individuality. How am I different from others who aspire to become school administrators? In what ways are my motivations, needs, wants, and expectations unique?

- It causes us to explore cogent needs and wants common to all humans. Developmental theories enhance an understanding of careers. For instance, the needs of individuals pass through distinct stages of their working lives. During the early part of a career, needs to develop job competency and initial professional identity are important; in the middle stage of a career, needs related to personal advancement replace exploration; and in career maturity, individuals seek to maintain their emergent status, gain affirmations of success, and pass knowledge and experience to others (Arthur & Kram, 1989).

Clearly, each of these purposes has potential merit, but perhaps the most cogent benefit is associated with introspection. This process helps us to understand why one principal may find great satisfaction in working toward and obtaining extrinsic rewards, whereas another achieves satisfaction from being able to assist teachers and students. In the final analysis, an understanding of school administration is of limited value if we do not have a valid understanding of ourselves.

Incomplete information increases the probability of poor career decisions. Orlosky, McCleary, Shapiro, and Webb (1984) illuminated this issue:

> Mismatches of individual abilities, needs, and aspirations on the one hand and job opportunities or requirements on the other, do occur in educational administration. When careers in education typically span periods of more than thirty years, it is tragic to discover how few give attention to or understand the rudiments of career planning. (p. 22)

As noted throughout this book, the practice of school administration has become both more demanding and complex. Changes in the structure and operation of schools continue to alter theoretical and actual roles for administrators. This instability strongly suggests that the future is not likely to be a mirror of the past. Demand for domineering, management-oriented principals and superintendents is being decreased by school reform initiatives. Schools that attempt to create professional work environments already exhibit a preference for persuasive, creative, and understanding leaders.

CHANGING ATTITUDES AND ASSUMPTIONS

Individual career planning is influenced by many things, not the least of which are attitudes and assumptions about employment, work, and career development. A willingness to devote the time and effort needed to create a personal plan will be predicated on views of how people get jobs, of what constitutes success, and the degree to which individual initiatives really matter. Unquestionably, beliefs help to determine behavior. Steele and Morgan (1991) summarized three common rationalizations concerning careers—each of which serves the purpose of deluding individuals into judging that planning is not necessary. The first defense mechanism is the declaration, "I've known what I wanted to be since I was in elementary school." Such a statement suggests that persons are predestined to do certain things in life. The second is summarized by the cliché, "let life decide." Here the individual remains uncommitted for as long as possible, believing that one day opportunity will be the deciding factor. The third is the "pick something that looks good" notion. Here the individual avoids a decision, believing that a career can be picked off the shelf at the right time. Each of these notions is little more than wishful thinking. They only serve the purpose of providing temporary comfort to one's ego.

Futurists frequently use trend analysis to make predictions. This is especially true when transformations are fairly evident (e.g., the shift from a manufacturing to an information society). In the area of career development, trends also help to establish the potential power of individual planning. What follows is a presentation of five such trends.

The Importance of Luck

Is the person, the organization, or blind luck the determinant of who fails and who reaches the top of the administrative ladder? This has long been a perplexing question for persons desiring to be organizational leaders. Research focusing on business executives suggests that each factor plays some part, but their influences are not fixed. That is to say, the actual weight of each is determined by situational variables (Bell & Staw, 1989). Research on the effects of career planning in school administration too is mixed. Some studies have found, for instance, that luck indeed plays a major role in acquiring desired positions. Yet, one must be careful not to assume that such conclusions are infallible—especially in a world where dynamic societal and professional conditions prevail. Many of the career development studies were conducted with constraints; and most are descriptive reports generating data from limited population samples (Miklos, 1988).

Too often, the debate of luck versus planning is cast as an either-or question. Clearly, chance plays some part in key events; however, this does not mean that the individual cannot exercise some control over success in life and career. In large measure, the desirability of individual control is driven by the uncertain and unstable environments in which contemporary practitioners work. It is also encouraged by realizations that truly great people prepare themselves for their careers (Buskirk, 1976). Accordingly, those who aspire to be school administrators, and those who help prepare them for their goals, are paying greater attention to literature and research in fields such as career counseling and planning. *The first trend is a change from relying on luck to one of relying on careful planning.*

Path to Success

Is there one best career path to becoming a principal or a superintendent? Career patterns are described as regularities in people's rise from position to position in a profession (Miklos, 1988). In school administration, for instance, it has been commonly held that you must first be an assistant principal before becoming a principal. Or, you must be a principal before you can be a superintendent. These beliefs have been fortified by observations and research that suggest that the vast majority of practitioners follow a common road to acquire certain positions. In today's world of practice, however, there is less uniformity and it is more feasible to pursue alternative career routes. The context of the community, needs of a given time, past experiences, or, as was illuminated in the last chapter, demographic considerations of applicants create unique conditions that affect employment decisions. Today, a school board may be more interested in applicants for the superintendency who have demonstrated an ability to work closely with teachers in instructional planning than they are in applicants who have decades of experience in varying types of management experiences. *The second trend is acceptance of the belief that there are multiple paths to career goals rather than one dominant path.*

Basis for Career Decisions

In many fields of endeavor, managers have been conditioned to put their careers above all else. This often is visible among large corporation executives who frequently endure the discomforts of relocating because transfers usually are associated with promotions. Similar decisions have been made by a good number of school administrators. Carlson (1972) in his study of school superintendents labeled administrators who were hired from outside an organization as "career-bound." He noted that these individuals accepted mobility as a means of advancing their careers. Take, for example, the principal of a large suburban high school who elects to take a superintendency in a small rural community even though he and his family have always lived in urban and suburban environments. Neither his spouse nor his children want to relocate; yet, he accepts the position because he believes that career advancement comes before all else.

The precept that career comes first is being challenged. Today, there is more of a tendency to integrate work-related decisions with other considerations such as family, leisure, and friends. Individuality makes it more difficult to predict the career decisions others will make (Borchard, Kelly, & Weaver, 1984). As a growing number of women enter the practice of school administration, the attitude of merging career with whole life is likely to become even more prevalent. Historically, women have been more likely to face conflicts between work and family or work and personal life choices (Vondracek, Lerner, & Schulenberg, 1986). *The third trend entails a movement from a belief that careers are most important to a belief that careers are integrated into one's entire life experiences.*

Measures of Success

Symbols mean much in our society. A person's clothes, house, and car are indicators of success. For many business executives, success is measured by extrinsic rewards such as salary, bonuses, and titles. In school administration as well, success has often been associated with position, salary, and size of school district (Carlson, 1972); the ultimate indices of success are, for example, to be a superintendent, to make a large salary, and to be employed in either a very large or a very prestigious school district. These impressions are being modified by a greater awareness of intrinsic rewards and the importance of career-related security. Manter and Benjamin (1989), conducting research among recent college graduates employed by twenty major corporations, found that these persons anticipated that they would be able to set the terms of their work life. They also expected their employers to be sensitive to their personal styles and values.

In school administration, there is growing evidence that success is defined differently by practitioners. For example, there are many educators who decide to devote their entire career to the principalship, or those who have no intention of leaving rural schools. For them, success does not mean working as a superintendent or being part of a large, affluent school district. In business and education, leaders today are more diverse in their expectations and values toward career success. *The fourth trend is a redefining of career success—moving from an emphasis on salary and position to multiple criteria that cover a range of extrinsic and intrinsic factors.*

Individual Control

One reason that many rely on chance to direct their lives is that they believe that self-management is either impossible or basically insignificant. For these persons, making decisions about life is a task to be addressed once a career has been established. Accordingly, where I live, the value of my house, the type of car I drive, and other aspects of my personal and social life are serendipitous products of career and job. In essence, these individuals accept the premise that quality-of-life decisions are shaped by employment-driven successes. An alternative to this traditional view of life and career is one in which the individual makes quality-of-life decisions first and pursues a career and specific positions subsequently (Borchard, Kelly, & Weaver, 1984). That is, a person develops lifestyle goals first, and a career second. This latter approach attempts to put the individual, not fate or others, in control.

A popular song of the 1980s, "Take This Job and Shove It," expressed the frustration of many blue-collar workers who found themselves locked into unfulfilling employment. Many corporate managers, presidents, and school administrators share the frustration of being trapped in jobs they dislike. Personal control over career is an initiative designed to avoid this pitfall. Two factors are especially cogent in this regard: (1) viewing career as a means to achieving life's goals, and (2) developing a career plan that interfaces career with quality of life goals. *The fifth trend entails a belief change from "career determines quality of life" to "desired quality of life helps determine career."*

BUILDING AN INDIVIDUAL PLAN

By now, it should be clear that the very nature of school administration will probably force you to make critical decisions about the type of job you pursue, the type of school or school district in which you will work, and even the type of community in which you will live. Additionally, experience will not necessarily diminish the number or difficulty of the decisions you must make. Seasoned principals and superintendents often find that deliberations regarding new jobs and advancement do not necessarily become easier with experience. A productive response to these conditions is an individual career plan—a personal guide to your professional life.

Required Knowledge

Creating an individual plan for your career requires more than a commitment; it requires knowledge and information. More specifically, the procedure necessitates four key ingredients: knowledge of self, knowledge of school administration, knowledge of contemporary conditions and trends, and knowledge of career planning. (See Figure 15–1.)

Knowledge of self, as already noted, entails the identification of personal strengths and weaknesses. But there is more. Steele and Morgan (1991) suggested

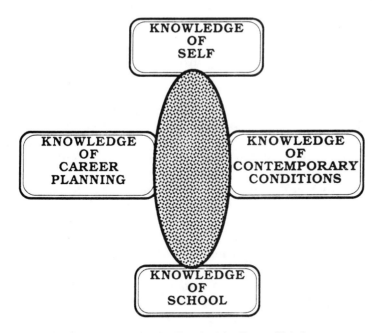

FIGURE 15-1   Knowledge Required for Career Planning

the following elements in a self-appraisal: education, work experience, interests, skills and abilities, personal traits, leadership interests and abilities, physical condition (including identification of handicapping conditions), the need for further development, achievements, and personal values. In professions, the factor of need for further development is particularly important.

Knowledge about school administration is largely related to information presented earlier in the book. First, it includes vocational data (types of jobs, job availability, roles, and responsibilities). Beyond this, it incorporates information regarding trends and changes affecting practice (e.g., collaborative decision making). And it also includes information about employment practices, laws, contracts, and any other facts that are specific to being a practitioner of school administration.

To plan your career successfully, you also need to know what is occurring in the world around you. What is society expecting from its public schools? How are changes in social values and family structure affecting schools—and the lives of school administrators? Does society provide rewards to school administrators that meet your career expectations and needs? Two considerations are especially important for education directly and school administrators indirectly: (1) movement to an information society and (2) movement to a global economy.

Finally, the creation of an individual plan requires some information about careers and career planning. One of the primary purposes of this chapter is to provide this knowledge. Additional assistance can be obtained either from self-help books in libraries or from faculty who specialize in career counseling.

Attributes of Effective Career Plans

Before reviewing the suggested components of career planning, a review of several desirable attributes is helpful. The first attribute of good planning is *perenniality*. No aspect of creating an individual plan for career development is more essential than the realization that the process is continuous. Planning is not something we do once and then put away in a drawer. Properly managed plans are perceived as documents that have the potential of becoming stronger, more realistic, and increasingly effective. Each year of experience helps one to fine-tune goals and objectives.

The second attribute of good planning is *flexibility*. Traditional planning models are built on assumptions of stability that suggest that the future will not be too different from the present. Hence, the planner believes that he or she knows precisely what goals are to be accomplished and the exact steps that are necessary to attain them. In the real world, these assumptions seldom are valid. A graduate student planning a career in school administration that may span two to three decades will encounter myriad changes—some personal, some environmental, and some professional. A quality plan considers multiple potentialities and provides for periodic assessments and adjustments to goals and objectives.

The third attribute is *veracity*—the person is honest with himself or herself. No plan can be very useful if it is erected on unrealistic dreams. Since it is an individual plan, the person needs to use the process of introspection to produce accurate self-assessments. This is not to suggest that one should avoid lofty goals. Rather, it implies that goals should have some relationship to reality; they should be reasonable career targets predicated on an individual's strengths and weaknesses and existing and anticipated conditions in the profession and society.

Finally, a plan is worthwhile if it actually affects behavior. For this to happen, the individual needs to believe that the process and the product will produce meaningful results. With these conditions present, the plan constitutes a framework that the author uses to make critical career decisions. Therefore, *influenceability*—the ability of the career plan to influence behavior—is the fourth attribute of good planning.

Individual Plan Components

Individual plans may vary in structure and specificity; however, there are several essential components that ought to be included in each effort. They are illustrated in Figure 15–2. Although these components are presented separately, this does not imply that they are independent. For example, determining what type of life we want to lead and an assessment of our capabilities obviously are interrelated tasks.

The first component of the individual career plan involves a *vision of life*. What kind of life do you want to have? To answer this question, you need to consider a number of issues such as income, status, family, personal satisfaction, self-actualization, and leisure. Buskirk (1976, pp. 16–20) developed a list of seven essential questions that are helpful to making quality-of-life decisions:

1. How much money do you really need to make to consider yourself successful?
2. What kind of work do you really want to do?

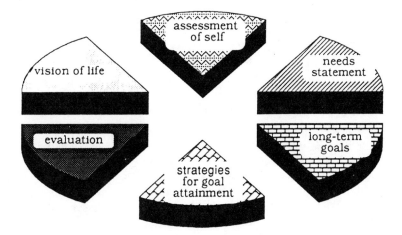

FIGURE 15-2   An Individual Career Plan

3. What type of environment do you want?
4. What are the social needs of both yourself and your family?
5. What kind of family life do you want to lead?
6. How much prestige does your ego require?
7. How much security must you have?

As noted already, far too many people do not even think about these issues until they have established themselves in a career. Perspectives toward the association of work, family, and leisure have changed markedly in the past four or five decades. This alteration has been caused by evolutionary forces occurring among individuals and within society. For example, the economy, personal values, and social conditions all contribute to a conclusion that career is not everything. Contemporary career planning focuses on quality of life, work motivation, and job satisfaction (Super, 1984).

Assessment of self is a process of bringing to the surface personal information that will facilitate career planning. It can range from very informal procedures such as self-evaluation to formal assessments conducted by others (e.g., career counselors). Among the areas that can be included in this component of the plan are aptitude, ability, achievements, interests, personality analysis, and the identification of personal philosophy. Aspiring school administrators also can turn to assessment centers for assistance with this phase of career planning. Several national organizations (e.g., the National Association of Secondary School Principals—NASSP) have created such centers in an effort to evaluate the administrative potential of persons seeking to enter the profession. Miklos (1988) described the activities of the NASSP Center as follows:

> Participants engage in simulation activities representative of the day-to-day administration of a school, including leaderless group activities, fact-finding and stress exercises, paper and pencil in-basket tasks, and a structured personal

interview. Typically, six trained assessors observe twelve participants over a 2-day period and prepare for each participant a comprehensive report on his or her strengths, weaknesses, and possible areas for development. The assessors then discuss the report with each participant. (p. 57)

Assessment centers generally serve two purposes: (1) a source of objective data on candidates, and (2) a source of objective data for making merit-based selection decisions from among a group of candidates (McCleary & Ogawa, 1985).

Once you have formulated a vision for your life and an assessment of yourself, you can create a *career needs statement.* This component identifies what you perceive to be your personal needs with regard to your work life. This might include statements about income, status, expected challenges, social interactions, opportunities for personal growth, and so forth. Needs are essentially statements of deficiencies between what is and what is desired.

A comprehensive career plan must include *long-term goals.* This component provides job-related targets that guide decisions. To be effective, goals should be precise, realistic, and measurable. Most importantly, they should be changeable. That is, they should be viewed as targets that may need fine-tuning over time. Unanticipated changes in one's personal life, one's work life, or in society may necessitate that goals be reshaped.

Once goals are in place, *strategies for goal attainment* need to be developed. These strategies outline alternative paths for each of the goals included in the plan. They are erected on information about job opportunities and the integration of your personal and work lives. For instance, a high school social studies teacher in a suburban high school aspires to become a high school principal in a school similar to where she now works. Her goal is to do so within seven years. She knows that she must complete the required academic studies and obtain a license. But she is uncertain about the route to her goal. Thus, she formulates two strategies for goal attainment. The first is to become an assistant principal in a suburban area within three years and to use this experience as a springboard for moving to the principalship. The second is to obtain a principalship in a small school within four years, and this experience then prepares her for her goal. In the second strategy, she expresses a willingness to relocate. Changes in her life, the job market, or in the economy may force her to eradicate or alter one or both strategies. But at the time they are formulated, they represent her best thinking on how she can achieve her goal. Planning for alternative futures permits one to deal with goals and strategies that may become inoperable (Hollis & Hollis, 1976).

The nucleus of a good career plan is *evaluation.* This component is the measuring stick for (1) overall progress; (2) determining whether our initial needs, goals, and strategies were realistic; and (3) determining whether components of the plan need to be adjusted. In other words, evaluation is the mechanism that helps to establish the adequacy of a plan. The process should occur at least every two years (preferably, every year). Each evaluation constitutes the end of a cycle. Data are used to reaffirm, eliminate, or alter needs, goals, and strategies. Once this is completed, a new cycle begins. This never-ending pattern exemplifies the attribute of perennialism.

Potential Pitfalls

The development of an individual career plan is not without potential problems. Hollis and Hollis (1976) identified five that are rather common:

1. Often, individuals focus solely on short-term goals. Given the overall purposes of the effort, goals should be projected to at least ten or fifteen years in the future.
2. The tendency to focus solely on one factor (e.g., career) results in "tunnel" planning. The planner fails to integrate other dimensions of life into the process.
3. Insufficient knowledge and information distort the quality of the plan. Not having sufficient insight of self or of job opportunities exemplifies this problem.
4. Plans can become too elaborate causing the author to lose sight of their true purpose. Individual career plans should be a guide for work-related decisions, not intricate documents that eventually cause confusion.
5. Individuals frequently set career goals too high or too low. More importantly, they fail to adjust original targets after several years of experience.

Other possible problems include failing to develop all key components in the plan, failing to engage in evaluation on a periodic basis, and expecting too much too soon. If you view your individual career plan as an evolving document, you are less apt to become frustrated.

IMPLICATIONS FOR PRACTICE

School administration is a diverse profession. Practitioners are faced with many important decisions ranging from the type of positions they will pursue to the type of schools in which they will work. Far too often, teachers start academic study in school administration simply to create the potential for moving to higher-paying positions. Have you heard students in school administration say, "I don't know if I want to be an administrator; but if opportunities come along, at least I'll be in a position where I can be considered"? For those who truly want to be leaders, this is an illogical strategy. Persons who rely on fate or luck to steer their lives tend to give little thought to their personal attributes, wants, motivations, and needs. Career planning is a mechanism for overcoming this common problem by giving meaning to one's professional studies and endeavors.

Career planning also encourages an integrative approach to controlling one's life. Traditionally, managers have tended to place career above all else. Promotions and salary increases were viewed as primary considerations in making major work-related decisions. This notion is being increasingly challenged in contemporary society by educated individuals who (1) attempt to balance their personal and professional lives and (2) desire to avoid being trapped in jobs they find unfulfilling. School administration is not only a demanding and challenging profession, it is one in which many practitioners intrinsically achieve satisfaction. Career planning is a means for you to fuse your professional and personal goals.

As you continue your studies in school administration, you should take time to consider what you want out of life. What role will career play in achieving these goals? You also should objectively assess your capabilities. Is school administration a realistic career given your strengths, weaknesses, abilities, needs, and interests? Once you have answered these weighty questions, you are in a position to develop more specific objectives that steer the decisions you will need to make.

Perhaps most importantly, you must accept responsibility for directing your own life. Pedler (1988) described self-development as a synthesis of previous ideas that involves a constant transfer from experience to reflection and back again. True professionals employ reflection as a method of growth. Each course, each clinical experience, and each day of work provide information that you should use in formulating, evaluating, and revising your professional career plan.

FOR FURTHER DISCUSSION

1. In what ways do the demands for school reform increase the relevance of career planning for school administrators?
2. Why do you think so many individuals fail to develop career plans?
3. What is meant by *career path*? Do you think that career paths are changing for school administrators?
4. Why is it important to conduct periodic evaluations of your career plans?
5. How can services available at the university you attend assist with career planning?
6. What is the purpose(s) of assessment centers? Are they used in your state? If so, what has been their impact?
7. Would it be a good idea to share your personal career plan with either an experienced administrator or a professor of school administration? Why or why not?
8. Why is it advantageous to develop alternative goals and alternative strategies for your career?
9. Given the changes that are occurring in education, it is more or less likely that an administrator can control his or her own destiny?

OTHER SUGGESTED ACTIVITIES

1. Invite a professor who specializes in career counseling to meet with you or your class to discuss the development of individual career plans.
2. Identify barriers that exist for persons who desire to enter school administration in your state.
3. Draft an outline of the components you would include in your career plan. Identify the information you possess and the information you would need to obtain to complete your plan.
4. Discuss common reasons why administrators encounter career failure. To what extent are these reasons related to career planning?

REFERENCES

Arthur, M. B., Hall, D. T., & Lawrence, B. S. (1989). Generating new directions in career theory: The case for a transdisciplinary approach. In M. Arthur, D. Hall, & B. Lawrence (Eds.), *Handbook of career theory* (pp. 7–25). Cambridge, Eng.: Cambridge University Press.

Arthur, M. B., & Kram, K. E. (1989). Reciprocity at work: The separate, yet inseparable possibilities for individual and organizational development. In M. Arthur, D. Hall, & B. Lawrence (Eds.), *Handbook of career theory* (pp. 292–312). Cambridge, Eng.: Cambridge University Press.

Bell, N. E., & Staw, B. M. (1989). People as sculptors versus sculpture: The roles of personality and personal control in organizations. In M. Arthur, D. Hall, & B. Lawrence (Eds.), *Handbook of career theory* (pp. 232–251). Cambridge, Eng.: Cambridge University Press.

Borchard, D. C., Kelly, J. J., & Weaver, N. P. (1984). *Your career* (3rd ed.). Dubuque, IA: Kendall/Hunt.

Buskirk, R. H. (1976). *Your career: How to plan it, manage it, change it.* Boston: Cahners Books.

Carlson, R. O. (1972). *School superintendents: Careers and performance.* Columbus, OH: Charles E. Merrill.

Colantuono, S. L. (1982). *Build your career.* Amherst, MA: Human Career Development Press.

Graen, G. B. (1989). *Unwritten rules for your career.* New York: John Wiley & Sons.

Hollis, J. W., & Hollis, L. U. (1976). *Career and life planning.* Muncie, IN: Accelerated Development.

McCleary, L. E., & Ogawa, R. T. (1985). Locating principals who are leaders: The assessment center concept. *Educational Horizons,* 12 (3), 7–11.

Manter, M. A., & Benjamin, J. V. (1989). How to hold on to first careerists. *Personnel Administrator,* 34 (9), 44–48.

Miklos, E. (1988). Administrator selection, career patterns, succession, and socialization. In N. J. Boyan (Ed.), *Handbook of research on educational administration* (pp. 53–76). New York: Longman.

Orlosky, D. E., McCleary, L. E., Shapiro, A., & Webb, L. D. (1984). *Educational administration today.* Columbus, OH: Charles E. Merrill.

Pedler, M. (1988). Applying self-development in organizations. *Industrial and Commercial Training,* 20 (2), 19–22.

Spokane, A. R. (1991). *Career intervention.* Englewood Cliffs, NJ: Prentice-Hall.

Steele, J. E., & Morgan, M. S. (1991). *Career planning and development for college students and recent graduates.* Lincolnwood, IL: VGM Career Horizons.

Super, D. E. (1984). Perspectives on the meaning and value of work. In N. Gysbers (Ed.), *Designing careers* (pp. 27–53). San Francisco: Jossey-Bass.

Vondracek, F. W., Lerner, R. M., & Schulenberg, J. E. (1986). *Career development: A lifespan development approach.* Hillsdale, NJ: Lawrence Erlbaum Associates.

Zunker, V. G. (1990). *Career counseling: Applied concepts of life planning* (3rd ed.). Pacific Grove, CA: Brooks/Cole.

CHAPTER 16

A Commitment to Excellence

Chapter Content

An Understanding of Success
Ethical Practice
Implications for Practice

By this point in the book, you should have developed a clear sense of the multiple influences, considerations, and complexity of administering and leading schools and school districts. This final chapter explores measures of success and failure in school administration with hopes that it will engender in you a personal commitment to successful practice as an educator.

AN UNDERSTANDING OF SUCCESS

Webster's dictionary (1971) defines *success* as (a) "a favorable result" and (b) "the gaining of wealth, fame, etc." (p. 741). Given the salary level of most educators, it is unlikely that individuals will become wealthy solely from their work in education. Nonetheless, some educators are motivated to pursue positions in school administration due to a perception that administrative positions provide an additional measure of wealth or fame.

Administrators generally have higher annual salaries than do teachers. However, in many entry-level administrative positions, the per diem pay is only slightly higher than that of teachers. The longer work year of administrators frequently makes it appear that their salaries are substantially higher than those of teachers.

Although entry-level administrative salaries may be comparable to those of teachers, the potential to earn substantially greater salaries than teachers does exist. For example, superintendents of large school districts may earn well over $100,000 per year. Even so, this is a paltry amount compared to the income of CEOs of business corporations such as Michael Eisner of the Disney Corporation, who recently earned more than $6 million in one year.

Just as school administrators are unlikely to become wealthy from their salaries, so also are they unlikely to achieve fame at a national level. Nonetheless, they frequently become "big fish in a small pond." For example, principals or superintendents may become well known and influential in their local communities.

Some individuals may be influenced to pursue administrative positions because of the greater opportunities for wealth and fame that administrative positions offer when compared to teaching positions, but defining success in terms of these criteria is a narrow and unacceptable perspective. The goal of "achieving favorable results" broadens this perspective somewhat, but it, too, must be carefully examined to obtain a fuller perspective of what is involved in success. The results that school administrators attempt to achieve are generally linked to the organization; that is, the success of the administrator is defined in terms of the effectiveness of the school or district.

Traditional Perceptions of Effectiveness

Imagine the following scenario:

The Washington Community School District contains three schools. In each school the principal plays an active role in the school. School A is located in an affluent section of the community. The school has the highest standardized achievement test scores in the district and a very low dropout rate. The principal is very task-oriented, resulting in a business-like but frequently tense environment. Teachers and students work hard, but there is a pattern of stress-related absences.

School B is located in a poorer section of the community than School A. School B does not receive as many resources as does School A. Students' achievement test scores are also not as high as those in School A, nor is their dropout rate as low. However, in view of the lesser resources and the lower socioeconomic status of students attending the school, they perform at a level comparable or slightly higher than School A. Although stress-related illnesses have not been evident, teachers and students are neither overly excited nor overly dismayed about coming to school each day. The principal in this school conducts himself in a professional, business-like manner.

School C does not have as high an achievement level as either School A or School B. The climate in the school is very laid back and relaxed. The principal's behavior reflects the climate. He spends the day wandering about the school, talking with teachers, students, and staff members. He always remains calm, even in crisis situations. Daily attendance in School C is higher than in the other two schools, and both teachers and students enjoy coming to school.

The three schools are examples of several common perceptions of effectiveness. Traditionally, organizational effectiveness has been measured in terms of productivity, efficiency, and employee satisfaction. School A provides an example of high productivity, School B an example of efficiency (that is, getting a high degree of output for the amount of input provided), and School C an example of employee satisfaction.

It is evident that each measure of effectiveness has a potential downside. In School A, productivity is achieved at the cost of excessive student and employee stress; in School B, efficiency is achieved but true student and employee commitment is not evident; and in School C, employee satisfaction is attained, but perhaps at the expense of productivity and efficiency.

Schools have also faced the problem of determining appropriate measures of productivity and efficiency. Businesses define their productivity in terms of units of output and their efficiency in terms of the company's profit. Obviously, neither of these measures is appropriate for schools.

The most extensively used indicator of school effectiveness has been student scores on standardized tests. Across-the-board conclusions about a school's effectiveness cannot be made, however, by simply comparing achievement test results across sites. Achievement test scores are an output measure that are affected by input variables that frequently are beyond the school's control. For example, achievement test scores are highly correlated with the socioeconomic status of a student's family.

An additional criticism of using standardized test scores to make judgments about school effectiveness is that traditionally developed standardized tests are able to measure only lower-level thinking skills. In effect, schools that emphasize higher-level thought processes in their curriculum and instruction may be indirectly punished since their students are unlikely to score as well on standardized tests as are students who have been subjected to an instructional emphasis that is similar to that tested by the exam.

Several years ago, the U.S. Department of Education began publishing a state-by-state comparison and ranking of educational indicators which has become commonly known as the "wall chart." During the development of the wall chart, extensive consideration was given to identifying appropriate indicators of school effectiveness (Ginsburg, Noell, & Plisko, 1988). The wall chart's developers determined that student test scores on the SAT and ACT college entrance examinations provided the best indicator. Test scores were supplemented by graduation rates to account for non-college-bound students.

In order to help make valid comparisons across states, the wall chart also provided background characteristics for each state's student population. Data were included for per capita income, percentage of five- to seventeen-year-olds who lived in poverty, percentage of minority enrollment, and percentage of handicapped individuals. Additionally, resource inputs of each state were included. For example, data for expenditures per pupil, pupil-teacher ratio, average teacher salary, and expenditures for teachers as a percentage of total expenditures were included. These latter data permitted the public to draw conclusions about the efficiency of a state's educational system as well as its commitment to education. Table 16–1 includes selected data for several states from one recent wall chart.

Using the measures provided by the wall chart, conclusions could be drawn regarding the productivity and efficiency of educational systems in each state. However, the question remained whether the measures of productivity used by the wall chart (SAT/ACT scores, graduation rates) were valid indicators of educational productivity. Those embracing a more wholistic perspective of education argued that additional considerations should include students' ability to use higher-level thinking and problem-solving skills, their degree of inquisitiveness, their love of learning, their concern for fellow human beings, their emotional stability, and their attitude toward school.

Similar considerations hold true for teachers. How well a teacher is teaching, the extent to which they become better teachers, how much effort they are willing to (and do) put into personal growth, and their concern for their students as learners and as human beings are all indicators of productivity. An additional consideration spawned by the recent emphasis on school restructuring efforts that advocate giving teachers a greater role in school decision making, is the scope and effectiveness of their contributions to school governance.

As the designated leader of a school, unit, or district, the school administrator's perceptions of effectiveness and success are tied to all these considerations. That is, administrators are likely to define their success in terms of the success of their organizations, which is the result of the composite success of students, teachers, and other constituents.

School administrators, however, should be cognizant of an additional consideration as they consider success or failure. This is the matter of ethical practice.

TABLE 16–1 Wall Chart Data for Selected States

State	SAT Score	Percent Taking SAT	Graduation Rate	Pupil/Teacher Ratio	Expenditure Per Pupil	Expenditure for Teachers as Percent of Total
California	906 (5)*	42.1 (22)*	65.9 (42)	22.7 (50)	3840 (31)	38.7 (42)
Florida	887 (15)	47.5 (19)	58.0 (51)**	17.1 (28)	4092 (25)	40.2 (34)
New Hampshire	932 (1)	56.4 (6)	74.1 (27)	16.2 (22)	4457 (17)	37.0 (46)
New York	890 (13)	65.6 (4)	62.3 (46)	14.9 (9)	7151 (2)	37.1 (45)
North Carolina	836 (22)	57.8 (13)	66.7 (41)	17.5 (31)	3368 (41)	45.0 (9)

Key: ( ) rank
  * rank out of 22 states taking SAT as primary college entrance examination
  ** 50 states and District of Columbia
SOURCE: U.S. Department of Education (1990). State Education Performance Chart: Student Performance, Resource Inputs, State Reforms, and Population Characteristics, 1982 and 1989.

ETHICAL PRACTICE

A Taxonomy of Ethical Issues

School administrators may achieve great productivity in an efficient manner, and may even have a high degree of employee and constituent satisfaction, but if their leadership is characterized by questionable ethical practices, it is debatable whether their administration can be considered successful.

Kimbrough and Nunnery (1988) noted that the conceptions of ethics that many individuals hold center around illegal acts such as embezzlement or gross faults of character such as dishonesty. In fact, many moral and well-intentioned administrators may dismiss the issue of ethics as unproblematic. They may reason that they have no intent of ever misusing public funds, committing sexual indiscretion, or engaging in other forms of illegal or immoral behavior; thus, the issue of ethics is not troublesome for them. In a sense, these administrators can be considered naive, for these issues are only one type of ethical dilemma that school administrators face. They are also more easily resolved than other types of ethical issues since legal and social guidelines prescribe appropriate courses of action.

Kimbrough and Nunnery (1988) noted that administrative ethics is much broader than this. Howlett (1991) echoed this sentiment, noting that "ethics begin where laws and doctrines of right and wrong leave off" (p. 19). These authors describe a variety of ethical situations that fit this broader perspective. Specifically, they cite problems dealing with bias, unfairness, discrimination, nepotism, disclosing confidential information, not doing one's best as an administrator, and yielding to influential constituents in order to avoid trouble.

Although Kimbrough and Nunnery's, and Howlett's categorizations expand mainstream notions of administrative ethics, their focus remains on the ethics of choices administrators make in critical situations (Starratt, 1991). A number of scholars have argued that ethics are rooted in the fundamentals of school administration and extend to establishing an ethical school environment (Starratt, 1991). Greenfield (1991) identified fundamental ethical issues of school administration as "the application of power, the shaping of people and organizations, the search for better values . . . and the unending . . . questioning of the justification of the administrator's power and choices" (p. 3). Indeed, Hodgkinson (1991) noted that "values, morals, and ethics are the very stuff of leadership and administrative life" (p. 11).

Administrative ethics can thus be divided into three categories:

1. **Nonroutine issues of morality and personal practice.** This category includes ethical choices administrators confront on an irregular basis, where one choice may result in personal pleasure or personal (as opposed to professional) gain. Examples falling into this category include misuse of funds, sexual indiscretion, and certain conflicts of interest.
2. **Nonroutine issues of professional practice.** This category includes ethical choices administrators confront on an irregular basis that deal with professional matters. Examples falling into this category include nepotism,

yielding to influential constituents in order to avoid trouble, and terminating teachers (e.g., those who need the salary provided by teaching and try hard, but are ineffective teachers).

3. Daily issues of administrative practice. This category includes the application of power (for example, the imposition of one person's will upon another), the shaping of people and organizations, the determination of "correct" values, the justification of power usage, and the justification of choices exercised.

As previously noted, the first category is the least troublesome in which to make ethical decisions since legal guidelines and social expectations exist to address these issues. Problems in the second category can have serious consequences for all parties involved and can be extremely problematic, intense, and focused during the time at which they are occurring. However, decisions in this category extend over a limited time period. That is, they may emerge, intensify over a period of time to the point where a choice must be made, and then lose intensity as the choice is implemented and gradually accepted.

Problems in the third category may not have the intensity or the immediate grave repercussions of problems in the second category; however, they are constant and are likely to have a more pervasive, long-term effect on the organization than problems from either of the other two categories. Essentially, these problems get at the essence of leadership.

Ethical Issues of Daily Practice

Leadership was described in the first chapter of this text as a social influence process in which a person steers members of a group or organization toward a specific goal or direction. Axiomatic in this definition is the concept of directionality, that is, the responsibility of leaders to move organizations in some direction. Embedded in directionality are ethical issues dealing with the determination of organizational direction and the influencing of organizational members to pursue this direction.

How should direction and purpose be developed in schools? Although in reality the manner in which organizational direction is determined varies on a continuum, it can be categorized into three basic variations. In one variation the designated leader determines the direction, autocratically dictates it to organizational members, and establishes accountability systems to ensure that followers pursue the direction. In a second variation, the leader allows great follower input into determining organizational direction, and much autonomy in implementing it. In a third variation, the leader may allow some input, but essentially decides what the organizational direction should be, and then places great effort into selling the direction to followers. The objective of this final variation is to attain follower commitment to the organization's direction and, thus, voluntary compliance in implementing it.

Each variation is rife with potential ethical dilemmas. In the case of autocracy, the issue is the extent to which followers have a right to their own opinion and to pursue courses of action suggested by it. To the extent that they do, is any opinion justifiable, no matter how poorly studied? Starratt (1991) has argued that an ethic of critique is one criterion for ethical practice. Thus, an opinion is not justifiable until it has been subjected to rigorous and systematic critique. However, once critique has occurred (albeit a continual process), the issue is the extent to which the administrator has an ethical responsibility to permit individuals to pursue personal conceptions of organizational direction. If administrators permit pursuit of individually critiqued courses of action, are they not begging for chaos and thus shirking their responsibility for positive organizational movement?

In cases where administrators allow extensive input into determining organizational direction, the ethical dilemma arises when the direction followers determine conflicts with the beliefs and values of the administrator. Roland Barth (1988), former director of the Harvard Principals Center, wrote, "As a principal, I used to think that I shared leadership . . . shared leadership for me was delegating to others, giving away to others, or sharing with others the making of decisions—as long as the curriculum, pupil achievement, staff development, and, of course, stability were not much altered" (p. 640). In instances of administrator-follower incongruency, the leader has several choices: (1) revert to autocratic means and dictate organizational direction (likely destroying credibility and organizational morale in the process); (2) honor the teachers' direction, but compromise personal values and beliefs in the process; (3) resign and seek an organization whose membership embraces values and beliefs more congruent with one's own; or (4) "sell" followers on one's own perception of organizational direction.

Scholars (e.g., Bates, 1987; Foster, 1986) have suggested that the last variation is manipulative and perhaps more intrusive of followers' rights than simple autocracy. Bates (1987) wrote that those advocating this strategy "are arguing for a shift from traditional forms of bureaucratic control, toward techniques of ideological control . . . . such a shift toward ideological control implies intervention of managers in the very consciousness of workers" (p. 83). The argument is that selling followers on purpose or direction is an underhanded way of accomplishing one's personal agenda. The implication is that if the leader is to be the one who determines organizational direction, then an autocratic approach is more desirable. The downside of this approach is that it mandates compliance; the upside is that it protects the sanctity of the personal beliefs of organizational members.

The ethical leadership question suggested by the previous discussion is the extent to which a leader has a responsibility to modify individual beliefs in order to move an organization forward. Sergiovanni (1991) addressed this issue noting:

> Leadership is not a right but a responsibility. Morally speaking, its purpose is not to enhance the leader's position or to make it easier for the leader to get what he or she wants. . . . The test of moral leadership under these conditions is whether the competence, well-being, and independence of the follower are enhanced. (p. 324)

Thus, the reason for involving followers in organizational direction setting and decision making is not simply to make them feel good about being part of a democratic organization, but to provide the opportunity for them to become more critically reflective about the purposes of education, schooling, and the role of their personal practice. Unfortunately, what frequently has happened is that focusing on "the right methods" has become a substitute for results (Sergiovanni, 1991, p. 329).

The popular notion of teacher empowerment is much more about improvement of personal practice than it is about teacher involvement in school decision making. Simply providing teachers with power is not empowering; providing opportunities for organizational members to become more reflective students of their practice is empowering. Chapter 10 provided one heuristic for facilitating this process. The objective is for all organizational members to more systematically study their practice and the practice of their schools as organizations in order to blend the two and improve each.

Essentially, ethical practice demands that individuals, schools, and districts continually ask themselves, "What serves as the warrant for our decision making and action?" Implied is a recognition that the professional values and beliefs that have developed and evolved from personal and professional experiences, as well as the more formal professional knowledge base that researchers and theorists have developed, play significant roles in informing practice. The reader will recognize that this goes well beyond the "seat of the pants" logic that informs the decision making and action of many education practitioners.

Having provided the opportunity and encouragement for organizational members to examine their professional practice, the responsibility of school administrators to honor individual beliefs is increased. It would be unethical to emphasize the importance of studying one's practice and then tell organizational members that what they had discovered about their personal practice had no significance beyond their classrooms—that is, that it was insignificant in the more expansive scope of school policy and practice.

The use of democratic processes, however, does not ensure ethical practice. Traditionally the issue debated has been whether the attainment of positive ends justified using means that were less than admirable. Quantz, Cambron-McCabe, and Dantly (1991) have broadened this perspective. They noted that democratic means do not justify undemocratic ends. For example, implementing a discipline policy that abuses the individual rights of students is not acceptable simply because the majority votes for it.

The example illustrates the interrelationship of critique, caring, and justice—three criteria Starratt (1991) proposed as integral to a model of ethical practice. (See Figure 16–1.) The concept of critique involves the study of practice with particular attention given to power relationships involved in policy and practice. Questions such as "Who benefits from these arrangements?" (Starratt, 1991) and "Whose interests are being served?" (Sirotnik, 1989) are addressed. A school staff could reach the conclusion that current practice in the school served the interests of students to the exclusion of faculty interests. The faculty response might be a discipline policy that overcompensates by serving faculty interests to the exclusion of student interests.

The ethic of caring acknowledges the right of individuals "to be who they are" and requires those who care for them to encounter them "in their authentic

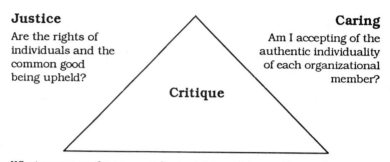

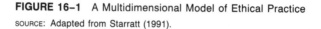

What serves as the warrant for decision making, policy, and practice?
Who benefits?

FIGURE 16-1   A Multidimensional Model of Ethical Practice
SOURCE: Adapted from Starratt (1991).

individuality'' (Starratt, 1991, p. 195). A discipline policy that honors the ethic of caring would avoid standardizing student behavior to fit preconceived notions of culturally appropriate behavior.

Acknowledgment of individuality, however, is not the same as acceptance of a morally relativistic, anything-goes philosophy. The ethic of justice demands that attention be given to both the rights of individuals and the common good (Starratt, 1991). The common good is not served by undisciplined chaos, nor is it served by totalitarian squelching of individuality. The challenge for the school staff in this instance is the development of a discipline policy that honors the rights of students to be who they are as individuals and as a group, but that recognizes that one individual's total freedom may restrict the freedom of others.

The development of school purpose encompasses one form of intentionality; the values that are communicated through routine and nonroutine actions, policies, and practices are generally less explicit and intentional, but may ultimately determine directionality more than formal school purpose. In other words, what leaders do speaks more loudly than what they say.

Seemingly, values indicated by daily actions would be congruent with the purpose of the school. However, values that individuals say they believe in are frequently incongruent with the values that are reflected in their daily practice (Argyris & Schon, 1974; Sergiovanni, 1991). For example, educators frequently espouse the value of meeting the individual needs of students. However, many of the practices in the daily organization of schools belie this practice. Two examples are the organization of high school classes into periods of approximately fifty minutes each, and the promotion of students to the next grade level every nine months. It is inconceivable that the content presented during a given class period is assimilated equally by all students in the class in fifty minutes, or that all students are ready to proceed to the next grade level after nine months. In order to achieve congruency between values and action we would need to make accommodations for students who assimilated content in more or less than fifty minutes and for those who were ready to proceed to the next grade level in increments other than nine months. Obviously, fifty-minute class periods and nine-month academic years are structures designed to manage large groups of students. The structures, however, serve the interests of teachers and administrators much more than they serve the needs of students. The responsibility of the ethical school that espouses the value of meeting the needs of individual students would be to discuss and develop accommodations within these structures or to replace them with structures more congruent with their espoused values.

IMPLICATIONS FOR PRACTICE

This chapter has argued that school administrators' perceptions of success are usually linked to the success of the schools, units, or districts for which they are responsible. Traditionally, organizational effectiveness has been defined in terms of productivity, efficiency, and employee satisfaction. An additional measure of administrative success is the extent to which administrative and school policy and practice are conducted in an ethical manner.

Whereas productivity, efficiency, and employee satisfaction are external measures, ethics is the internal component of the administrator's living with himself or herself. If success is achieved in the former external measures in an unethical manner, the administrator would be hard pressed to consider himself or herself a success. Thus, ethical behavior may be more significant in terms of perceptions of success or failure than efficiency, productivity, and employee satisfaction.

Ethics in administrative practice extends beyond making moral decisions in critical choice situations. The very essence of leadership is a moral and ethical act in that it involves influencing others to pursue specific courses of action.

Implied in the discussion in this chapter have been criteria that school administrators can apply to help ensure ethical practice. Table 16–2 provides a summation of these issues and criteria.

FOR FURTHER DISCUSSION

1. Discuss the advantages and disadvantages of using standardized test scores as an indicator of school effectiveness. Does heavy emphasis on these scores present any ethical dilemmas for administrators?
2. Discuss the wall chart data. Does the chart provide assistance in determining educational effectiveness?
3. To what extent should leaders involve followers in establishing organizational direction?
4. Discuss the following questions related to the ethical criteria provided in Table 16–2:
   (a) How should purpose and organizational direction be developed in schools?
   (b) How can organizational members be treated in empowering rather than manipulative ways?
   (c) What decision-making criteria can be used when there is conflict between the rights of individuals and the common good?
   (d) How can moral means of authority (i.e., shared ideas, ideals, values) be developed?
   (e) What is the distinction between right managerial methods and right results? Give some examples.

TABLE 16–2   Ethical Issues and Criteria for Ethical Practice

Ethical Issue	Criteria
• How is purpose developed in schools?	• Equal respect
• Toward what values and purposes is discretion exercised?	• Critique
• What values are communicated through routine daily actions, policies, and practices?	• Equal respect; espoused versus acted value congruence
• Are organizational members influenced in manipulative or empowering ways?	• Empowerment (enhancing followers' competence, well-being, and independence)
• Are the rights of individuals as well as of the common good served?	• Justice, equal respect, caring, common good, benefit maximization
• Are the opinions of others being honored?	• Caring
• Are the primary means of authority bureaucratic (rules, mandates, etc.), psychological (cleverness, guile, interpersonal style, political know-how), professional (expertness), or moral (shared ideas, ideals, values)?	• Shared ideas, ideals, values
• Is the focus on the right managerial methods or on the right results? On doing things right or on doing the right thing?	• Efficiency, effectiveness, justice, caring
• Does the leader opt for what is efficient and effective, or for what is just and caring? What is the leader's responsibility to each of these concepts?	• Efficiency, effectiveness justice, caring
• Are both means and ends democratic?	• Congruency in mean-ends, ends-means
• What serves as the warrant for decision-making and action?	• Critique of personal and professional beliefs, values, and knowledge
• Whose interests are being served?	• Critique of dominance relationships

SOURCES: Greenfield (1991); Sergiovanni (1991); Starratt (1991); and Strike, Haller, & Soltis (1988).

(f) What is the leader's responsibility for promoting efficiency, effectiveness, justice, and caring? When these concepts conflict, which should take precedence?

(g) What role should each of the following play in decision-making and action: personal values; professional beliefs; experiential knowledge; formally developed knowledge (e.g., research findings)?

OTHER SUGGESTED ACTIVITIES

1. Develop a personal conception of success as a school administrator. What implications for administrative action does your conception suggest?

2. Develop a personal conception of school effectiveness. What implications for administrative action does your conception suggest?

3. The movie *Lean on Me* is based on the life of Joe Clark, a New Jersey principal who used controversial techniques to bring about school change. View the movie and discuss (a) Joe Clark's perception of success and how this agrees or disagrees with yours and (b) the ethical dimensions of his practice based on principles discussed in this chapter.

4. Interview several principals about their perception of the ethical dilemmas they face in their positions. Do the dilemmas vary from principal to principal? If so, what can be learned from this? Into which of the three administrative ethics categories are the dilemmas most appropriately categorized? Do the ethical criteria included in Table 16–2 provide any assistance in resolving them?

5. Discuss the extent to which schools and other organizations in which you have been employed embodied the ethical criteria cited in Table 16–2.

6. Critique school or district policies and practices to determine who benefits from them (e.g., teachers, students, parents, administration, etc.). Discuss how they might be reconceptualized to serve the interests of those who do not benefit from them in their present form. Decide whether their current form or suggested alternatives are more appropriate.

REFERENCES

Argyris, C., & Schon, D. A. (1974). *Theory in practice: Increasing professional effectiveness.* San Francisco: Jossey-Bass.

Barth, R. S. (1988). Principals, teachers, and school leadership. *Phi Delta Kappan, 69,* 639–642.

Bates, R. J. (1987). Corporate culture, schooling, and educational administration. *Educational Administration Quarterly, 23* (4), 79–115.

Foster, W. (1986). *Paradigms and promises: New approaches to educational administration.* Buffalo: Prometheus Books.

Ginsburg, A. L., Noell, J., & Plisko, V. W. (1988). Lessons from the wall chart. *Educational Evaluation and Policy Analysis, 10* (1), 1–12.

Greenfield, T. B. (1991). *Foreword.* In C. Hodgkinson, *Educational leadership: The moral art* (pp. 3–9). Albany: State University of New York Press.

Hodgkinson, C. (1991). *Educational leadership: The moral art.* Albany: State University of New York Press.

Howlett, P. (1991). How you can stay on the straight and narrow. *Executive Educator, 13* (2) 19–21, 35.

Kimbrough, R. B., & Nunnery, M.Y. (1988). *Educational administration: An introduction.* New York: Macmillan.

Quantz, R. A., Cambron-McCabe, N., & Dantley, M. (1990). Preparing school administrators for democratic authority: A critical approach to graduate education. *The Urban Review, 23* (1), 3–19.

Sergiovanni, T. J. (1991). *The principalship: A reflective practice perspective* (2nd ed.). Boston: Allyn and Bacon.

Sirotnik, K. A. (1989). The school as the center of change. In T. J. Sergiovanni & J. H. Moore (Eds.), *Schooling for tomorrow: Directing reforms to issues that count* (pp. 89–113). Boston: Allyn and Bacon.

Starratt, R. J. (1991). Building an ethical school: A theory for practice in educational leadership. *Educational Administration Quarterly, 27* (2), 185–202.

Strike, K. A., Haller, E. J., & Soltis, J. F. (1988). *The ethics of school administration.* New York: Teachers College Press.

U.S. Department of Education (1990). *State education performance chart: Student performance, resource inputs, state reforms, and population characteristics, 1982 and 1989.* Washington, DC: U.S. Department of Education (Office of Planning, Budget, and Evaluation.)

Webster's new world dictionary (1971). New York: Meridian.

Author Index

Subject Index